INTEGRATING A VICTIM PERSPECTIVE WITHIN CRIMINAL JUSTICE

Advances in Criminology
Series Editor: David Nelken

Titles in the Series

Integrating a Victim Perspective within Criminal Justice

International debates

Edited by
ADAM CRAWFORD
and
JO GOODEY
Centre for Criminal Justice Studies
University of Leeds

DARTMOUTH

Aldershot • Burlington USA • Singapore • Sydney

Published by
Dartmouth Publishing Company Limited
Ashgate Publishing Ltd
Gower House
Croft Road
Aldershot
Hants GU11 3HR
England

Ashgate Publishing Company
131 Main Street
Burlington
Vermont 05401
USA

Ashgate website: http://www.ashgate.com

British Library Cataloguing in Publication Data
Integrating a victim perspective within criminal justice :
    international debates. – (Advances in criminology)
    1.Criminal justice, Administration of   2.Victims of crimes
    I.Crawford, Adam   II.Goodey, Jo
    341.7'7

Library of Congress Cataloging-in-Publication Data
Integrating a victim perspective within criminal justice : international debates / edited by
Adam Crawford and Jo Goodey.
        p.   cm.
    Includes index.
    ISBN 1-84014-486-6 (HB)
    1. Victims of crimes.   2. Criminal justice, Administration of.   I. Crawford, Adam.   II.
Goodey, Jo.

HV6250.25.I58   2000
362.88—dc21

99-053155

ISBN 1 84014 486 6

Typeset by Manton Typesetters, Louth, Lincolnshire, UK.
Printed and bound in Great Britain by Antony Rowe Ltd, Chippenham, Wiltshire.

Contents

Acknowledgements

We would like to thank all the delegates who participated in, and contributed to, the 'Integrating a Victim Perspective within Criminal Justice' conference, held in York in July 1998, out of which this book arose. We would also like to acknowledge our gratitude to the Nuffield Foundation which assisted in funding some delegates from voluntary sector organizations. We would particularly like to thank Jaishree Parmar for the enthusiasm with which she assisted in the preparation and realization of the original conference, without which this book would never have got off the ground. In addition, we are grateful to Jill Enterkin and Susan Flint for their editorial assistance and comments with regard to some of the chapters and to Suzanne Wellings for her close attention to detail. Our thanks also go to our colleagues Clive Walker and David Wall for their support and encouragement throughout.

Notes on Contributors

Andrew Ashworth is Vinerian Professor of English Law in the University of Oxford, and a Fellow of All Souls College. He was elected a Fellow of the British Academy in 1993 and was appointed an honorary Queen's Counsel in 1997. He was previously the Edmund-Davies Professor of Criminal Law and Criminal Justice at King's College London. He has written books on the criminal law, on sentencing and on the criminal process, including *The Criminal Process* (Clarendon, 1998, 2nd edn) and *Sentencing and Criminal Justice* (Butterworths, 1995, 2nd edn).

Adam Crawford is Senior Lecturer in Criminology and Deputy Director of the Centre for Criminal Justice Studies at the University of Leeds. He is author of *The Local Governance of Crime* (Clarendon, 1997) and *Crime Prevention and Community Safety* (Addison Wesley Longman, 1998) and has conducted research into victims and criminal justice in both France and England. He has worked for the New Zealand Ministry of Justice and the Northern Ireland Office in relation to matters of crime prevention and community safety.

Edna Erez is Professor and Chairperson of the Justice Studies Department at Kent State University. She has published extensively on victims and women in the justice system. She is currently involved in a federally funded research project on violence against immigrant women. Professor Erez has served as the editor of *Justice Quarterly* and has been a Visiting Professor in Australia, Poland and Israel.

Jo Goodey is Lecturer in Criminology at the University of Leeds and previously lectured in criminology at the University of Sheffield. In her current research which is examining the criminalization and victimization of non-EU citizens in the EU she is the coordinator of a six-country team. She is a member of the World Society of Victimology's research committee. Since gaining her PhD in 1995, she has published a number of journal articles and book chapters on children's fear of crime, masculinity theory and crime, and racism.

Gabrielle Maxwell is a Senior Research Fellow at the Institute of Criminology, Victoria University of Wellington. Her previous positions include working with the Office of the Commissioner for Children and as a senior lecturer in the Department of Psychology at the University of Otago. She has carried out research on a number of criminological topics notably related to youth and crime. She has been involved in the research evaluation of Family Group Conferences in New Zealand for a number of years and is co-editor (with J. Hudson, A. Morris and B. Galaway) of *Family Group Conferences: Perspectives on Policy and Practice* (Federation Press, 1997).

David Miers is Professor of Law at Cardiff Law School. He has written extensively about criminal victimization, with particular emphasis on compensating victims of violent crimes, his most recent book being *State Compensation for Criminal Injuries* (Blackstone Press, 1998). He has given many conference papers and advised both the Home Office and the parliamentary Home Affairs Select Committee on matters concerning victim compensation. In 1995 he was appointed Executive Editor of the *International Review of Victimology*.

Allison Morris is Professor and Director of the Institute of Criminology at Victoria University of Wellington. Previously she was a Reader in Criminal Justice at the Institute of Criminology at Cambridge University and, before that, a lecturer at the University of Edinburgh. She has carried out research on juvenile justice systems in Scotland, England and New Zealand and has published extensively on the subject of women and crime including *Feminist Perspectives in Criminology* co-edited with L. Gelsthorpe (Open University Press, 1990). She has been involved in the research evaluation of Family Group Conferences in New Zealand for a number of years and is co-editor (with J. Hudson, G. Maxwell and B. Galaway) of *Family Group Conferences: Perspectives on Policy and Practice* (Federation Press, 1997).

Kate Mulley has worked in the Victim Support's National Office since 1995. She is responsible for assisting the Chief Executive with policy development, promotion, membership liaison and the internal planning process. She was organiser of Victim Support London and, prior to that, a volunteer with the Southwark Victim Support Scheme.

Helen Reeves is Chief Executive of Victim Support, the national organization for crime victims in England and Wales, a position which she has held since 1980 when she was appointed the first Director of the newly created National Association of Victims Support Schemes (NAVSS, the predecessor of Victim Support). She is a member of the Home Office Victims' Steering Group, the Speaking Up for Justice Implementation Group and has also served on both the Home Office Working Party on the temporary release of prisoners and the National Board for Crime Prevention. She has written widely on the subject of victims of crime and the work of Victim Support. In 1986 she was awarded the OBE and in 1999 she was awarded the title of Dame for services to victims of crime.

Leslie Sebba is Associate Professor at the Institute of Criminology at the Faculty of Law of the Hebrew University of Jerusalem. He has published widely in the fields of victimology, penology, juvenile justice and the sociology of law. Recent publications include *Third Parties: Victims and the Criminal Justice System* (Ohio State University Press, 1996), *Social Control and Justice: Inside or Outside the Law?* (1996) and (co-edited with Gillian Douglas) *Children's Rights and Traditional Values* (1998). Professor Sebba is one of the editors of the *International Review of Victimology*.

Joanna Shapland is Professor of Criminal Justice and Director of the Institute for the Study of the Legal Profession in the Department of Law at the University of Sheffield. Trained in psychology and criminology before coming to rest in law departments, her research interests span civil and criminal justice. She was Chair of the JUSTICE Committee on the Role of the Victim in Criminal Justice and is co-editor of the *International Review of Victimology*. She is currently an independent assessor to the Review of Criminal Justice in Northern Ireland.

Jan van Dijk is currently Officer in Charge of the United Nations Centre for International Crime Prevention in Vienna and has been instrumental, with UNICRI, in the development and analysis of the International Crime Victims Survey. He was previously the Director of Strategic Policy Planning at the Ministry of Justice, in the Netherlands and Professor of Criminology at the University of Leiden. His other international activities include President of the World Society of Victimology and member of the Scientific Committee of the International Society of Criminology. In 1995 he received the Stephen Schafer Award, from the National Organization for Victims' Assistance in Washington, for outstanding contributions to the victims' movement in the field of research.

Lode Walgrave is Professor in Juvenile Criminology at the Catholic University of Leuven (Belgium) and Chair of the International Network for

Research on Restorative Justice for Juveniles. His main research topics are social exclusion and juvenile crime, crime prevention and restorative (juvenile) justice. Among his recent publications is a collection of essays (edited with G. Bazemore) entitled *Restorative Juvenile Justice: Repairing the Harm by Youth Crime* (Criminal Justice Press, 1999).

Richard Young is Assistant Director of the Centre for Criminological Research, Oxford University and a Fellow of Law at Pembroke College. His publications include *Criminal Justice* co-authored with Andrew Sanders (Butterworths, 1994), *Access to Criminal Justice* (Blackstone Press, 1996) and *Child Support in Action* (Hart, 1998). He was previously Senior Lecturer in Law at Birmingham University, and has been a Visiting Professor in the United States at the University of South Carolina and the University of Missouri at Kansas City.

Renée Zauberman is a CNRS (Centre National de la Recherche Scientifique) researcher at CESDIP (Centre de Recherches Sociologiques sur le Droit et les Institutions Pénales). She has been working on victims and victimization surveys in France since the beginning of the 1980s. Another of her fields of research is the policing activity of the *Gendarmerie Nationale*. Her publications include *Du Côté des Victimes un Autre Regard sur la Délinquance* (with Phillipe Robert) (L'Harmattan, 1995).

Series Preface

This new series is dedicated to publishing the best of new cutting-edge work in the areas of Criminology, Criminal Justice and Penology. Volumes published or in preparation include theoretically innovative treatments of the subjects of Foucault and governmentality; mediation; victimology; comparative criminal justice; post-modern policing; corporate crime; and women's prisons.

This volume by Crawford and Goodey offers a thorough and carefully organized assessment of international thinking about the possibilities for integrating victims' views and needs into the criminal process. It will represent a standard resource for those seeking to learn from its descriptions of current practice and critical thinking in this important and evolving area of criminal justice policy.

DAVID NELKEN
Series Editor

Introduction

Adam Crawford

The implications of introducing a victim's perspective into the delicate balance between state and offender raise fundamental issues for the future of criminal justice. As commentators have noted, the place of the victim within criminal justice raises wider questions about the role and purpose of criminal justice (Zedner, 1994: 1240). Victims' interests have become caught up in much larger political and philosophical debates about the meaning of criminal justice, its place within society, the role of the state in punishment, welfare and harm reduction, as well as the efficacy and effectiveness of the institutional apparatus erected to deliver justice. The 1980s and 1990s witnessed a proliferation of policy initiatives and practical developments across different countries which purport, in some way or other, to advance the cause of victims. In addition, recent years have seen the elaboration of concerns about victims of crime and their status within criminal justice at an international level.

This book outlines the contours of key debates concerning both how and whether victims' interests are served by, and through, their integration into criminal justice. It draws together contributions from leading international commentators from countries in which these issues are currently highly prominent. As such, it explores notable national, cross-national and international developments and debates. Given the contentious nature of many of the debates, the book does not seek to advance any particular perspective but rather draws together contributions from eminent proponents from different disciplines and representing divergent theoretical and philosophical positions. It brings together academics, researchers and practitioners to consider recent policy developments and contemporary empirical findings which relate to two questions. First, how *do* criminal justice systems and processes attempt to give victims greater agency and voice within and around the criminal justice process? Second, how *should* victims be given greater agency and voice in the resolution of their own criminal disputes? In so doing, the book outlines and considers both the present state and nature

1

of developments seeking to integrate a victim perspective within criminal justice and the appropriateness of such developments.

The book emerged from an international conference, of the same title, held in York at the College of Ripon and York St John in July 1998, and organized by the Centre for Criminal Justice Studies at the University of Leeds. In over two days some 140 academics, practitioners and policy-makers from over 20 different countries heard over 50 presentations and workshops.[1] All the contributors to this volume presented initial versions of their chapters at the conference and were stimulated by the debates and audience participation generated during the proceedings.

The book, like the conference before it, has three central aims: first, to consider the implications of introducing a victim perspective into the deli-cate balance between state and offender and the fundamental questions about the future of criminal justice to which they give rise; second, to examine recent legislative and policy developments in relation to victims, as well as practical experiences, research findings and theoretical debates from around the world; and, third, to explore the prospects and implications of a restorative justice approach. These three aims, to a greater or lesser extent, inform all the contributions to this book.

The Structure of the Book

Jo Goodey begins by offering an overview of a number of key themes which have informed international developments during the 1980s and 1990s in respect of integrating the victim within criminal justice. As such, she places some of the broad themes which transcend and inform the subsequent contributions in their wider context. The overview is linked around four strands. The first considers the historical and international growth of litera-ture concerning victims since the 1970s. The second explores a number of models offered by the literature in explaining or advocating the place of victims within criminal justice. The third strand examines the 'individuali-zation' of the victim – a theme directly taken up by Leslie Sebba in his subsequent chapter – and some of the implications to which this gives rise. The fourth and final strand problematizes criminal justice and whether services for victims can, or should, be delivered within, or outside, the orbit of traditional criminal justice – a theme which preoccupies Lode Walgrave in Chapter 12, albeit from a slightly different perspective.

The rest of the book is divided into three Parts relating to issues raised by the integration of victims within criminal justice. In turn, they examine: the status of victims in historical and contemporary perspectives; the role of victims within criminal justice and the debates consequent upon specific attempts to give victims a greater voice and role within criminal justice; and, finally, the prospects and pitfalls of a restorative justice approach and the place of victims within it.

Part I brings together a number of chapters which explore the status of victims by drawing on insights from history, legal philosophy and contemporary survey research. From a French perspective, Renée Zauberman combines a synthesis of history, legal theory and penal sociology in her analysis of relations between the state and victim and how we may make sense of them. Particular attention is paid to the contemporary context of increasing concerns about the place of victims within criminal justice and a growing discourse of victims' rights. She questions whether we can conceptualize victims who turn to the criminal justice system in the same ways as consumers of other public services. The essence of the relationship between victim and criminal justice, she argues, lies in the notion of the state. Through an historical analysis, Zauberman gives a very different inflection to an understanding of the victim–state nexus to that which is often assumed within the victimological literature and exemplified by Nils Christie's (1977) notion of the 'theft of conflicts' from victims by the modern state as a result of which the victim has become marginalised from dispute processing. She shows that the very exclusion of the victim from the criminal justice process was a precondition for the existence of modern criminal justice and an expression of state sovereignty. She suggests that, rather than providing a service of which victims are consumers, we need to understand criminal justice as a 'regulatory resource' to which victims may, or may not, turn. Victims, thus, need to be conceptualised as users, rather than consumers, of criminal justice.

In Chapter 3, Leslie Sebba relates the recent rise of concerns for the victims of crime with the demise, or eclipse, of the 'rehabilitational ideal' with regard to offenders. He suggests that the focus on victim attributes, and the victim orientation which has accompanied this, has coincided with a loss of interest in offender attributes. Consequently, we have witnessed a shift from 'the individualization of the offender to the individualization of the victim'. After developing Marvin Wolfgang's (1982) thesis that the presence of victim attributes might be appropriate given the absence of offender attributes, Sebba goes on to consider what some of the broader implications of the concept of victim individualization might be in the context of three different approaches: a victim rehabilitation model; a 'just deserts' model; and a victim's rights (or participation) model. He reviews recent policies and legislative changes in various countries in the light of these three models and the manner in which victim-related developments are homologous of, and echo, earlier offender-related policies. He also raises a number of questions concerning what the implications of the individualization of the victim might mean for criminal justice. For example, what extent does the personalization of the victim challenge traditional normative approaches? Do the greater demands for emotions and vengeance that accompany the individualization of the victim represent a shift to a *post*modern or *pre*modern condition? How does this individualization fit with an emphasis on group identities and the fact that much victimization is not an individual experience nor necessarily directed at an individual? And, consequently, does it provide a mechanism for empowering victims or merely stifling the voice of defendants? These are all questions which inform, and are echoed in, subsequent chapters.

In Chapter 4 David Miers squarely confronts a number of issues concerning the status of victims. Given the similar social and personal histories of victims and offenders and the observation that many victims have themselves been offenders, Miers examines issues concerning the status of victims, the distribution of blame for injuries, and, hence, of benefits to alleviate those injuries, which this implies. He does so with regard both to the response of victims themselves to their own, actual or perceived, victimization and to the response of the Criminal Injuries Compensation Authority (CICA) in Britain, as a pre-eminent social agency established in order to respond to specific forms of victimization. Yet, in order to explore the ascription of the status of 'victim' to individuals, Miers' central concern is the analysis of occasions in which the activities and response of victims are themselves perceived as 'offensive'. Thus, he begins by examining (perceived) victims who seek to assert either procedural or direct justice against (perceived) offenders in response to their victimization – who literally 'take the law into their own hands'. He then goes on to assess the CICA's response to victims who have applied for compensation but whom the CICA has deemed to be other than an 'innocent victim'. In exploring particular examples of both, Miers raises a number of vexed questions about the status of 'victim', the normative significance of its designation, some of the assumptions and expectations which it embodies and the powerful social processes through which the label of 'victim' is ascribed or denied. We should not forget, as Miers illustrates, that not all those who suffer are labelled victims when they take the law into their own hands, nor are they all deemed deserving of compensation for their suffering.

Part I concludes with an exploration of international research evidence regarding the integration of a victim perspective within the work of various criminal justice agencies. Jan van Dijk provides an examination of some of the key findings of the International Crime Victims Surveys (ICVS) and explores their implications with particular regard to repeat victimization. His analysis of the ICVS data demonstrates that a substantial proportion of victims in all countries are revictimized during the course of one year. He shows that this phenomenon is common for different types of crime across divergent world regions, broadly categorized as developing nations, nations in transition and developed countries. In addition, he explores the different expectations that repeat victims hold with regard to the responses of the police and victim support services as compared to those of 'one-time victims'. The data suggests that repeat victims across different world regions have distinctive and special needs which remain largely neglected due to the lack of an integrated approach by the police. Moreover, the data suggests a large gap between the demand and supply of specialized victim services and assistance for repeat victims. Van Dijk illustrates these issues through a detailed examination of the ICVS data with regard to two different groups of repeat victims: repeat victims of burglary and violence against women. Both groups, he suggests, are often in urgent need of protection against the activities of known offenders. In conclusion, he proposes that improved services targeting the specific needs of repeat victims are necessary and, moreover, constitute important opportunities for crime prevention and detection.

Part II considers the growing role of victims in criminal justice and procedures and the difficult questions and debates to which this gives rise. Helen Reeves and Kate Mulley (Chapter 6) bring the perspective of practitioners working within the 'victim movement' and seeking to advance the provision of services for victims of crime to bear on the subject of recent changes to the role and voice of victims within criminal justice in England and Wales. They review the recent growth of policies and provisions for victims and the influential role that Victim Support has played in the process. In light of this, they set out the philosophical position adopted by Victim Support with regard to debates surrounding the integration of victims within criminal justice and suggest a recent history which, on the one hand, shows significant activity and progress at policy level, but, on the other hand, highlights poor implementation and institutional, as well as cultural, resistance at practice level. They argue that, prior to the reintegration of the victim within criminal justice, the state must undertake to fulfil certain responsibilities which cluster under five main principles: compensation, protection, services, information and freedom from the burden of responsibility for decisions relating to the offender. They suggest that some of the more recent policy developments have failed to meet their desired aims often due to poor implementation as victim interests are subverted by traditional criminal justice concerns. Consequently, they call for a clarification of the aims and the clear communication of explicit intentions of given policy initiatives which purport to integrate a victim's perspective in order to prevent them being pulled in various competing directions and to temper falsely raising victims' expectations.

Drawing together related themes, Joanna Shapland, in Chapter 7, suggests that, over the last 20 years or so, remarkably little has changed in terms of victims' relation to criminal justice, which remains one of separateness. This is particularly striking given the fundamental transformations that have taken place with regard to other public services in England and Wales, which have been cajoled into measuring performance by results set against clear objectives – 'management by outputs' – and advocating a 'closeness to the customer' (Hood, 1991; 1995). Drawing on the JUSTICE Committee Report (1998), Shapland argues for integrity and accountability as key concepts around which victims' integration within criminal justice should be constructed. The relationship between victims and criminal justice which she articulates is a reciprocal one, in which each has rights and responsibilities with regard to the other. In this formulation, the responsibilities of criminal justice agencies are the rights or expectations of victims whilst the responsibilities of victims are the expectations which criminal justice agencies can have of victims. However, she is clear that the already existing responsibilities of victims should not extend to that of taking decisions with regard to the prosecution, conviction and sentencing of offenders. She advocates a shift in thinking towards 'responsible agencies' which have a duty to meet the legitimate expectations of victims (and offenders) and that this duty of responsibility should largely be driven by financial and informational accountability. Shapland welcomes the contribution that recent public service reforms have made towards fracturing a traditional image of criminal justice agencies as fiefdoms jealously guarding their own conflict-processing 'patch', but suggests that these reforms have their own limitations. She seeks to move the debate about criminal justice beyond the confines of the managerialist reforms of recent years which, in focusing on value for money, performance measurement for individual agencies and individual services to customers/users, have neglected the coordination of the overall performance of the criminal justice system as a *public* service. Such a new conception, she argues, should acknowledge the multiple nature of accountabilities and responsibilities of criminal justice agencies, as well as victims, offenders and witnesses. A responsible, coordinated criminal justice system, she argues, would place victims and offenders in the centre of criminal justice, rather than in a series of disconnected agencies around which victims, offenders and witnesses are required to revolve.

In Chapter 8, Edna Erez traces and assesses probably the most contentious recent development to be advanced, in a number of countries, under the auspices of 'integrating a victim perspective within criminal justice' – namely, victim impact statements. She sets out and clarifies the contours of the controversial debates, identifying the viewpoints held by proponents and critics of victim impact statements and draws on research findings to consider the effects and consequences of such statements on court practices where they have been introduced. She examines the research in relation to three key tensions around which debates about the implementation of victim input rights have coalesced. These relate to the effects of victim input: first, on court processes and outcomes; second, on the conceptions of justice in an adversarial system and defendant's rights; and, third, on victims' welfare and satisfaction with justice. The empirical evidence, she argues, demonstrates that the introduction of victim impact statements, notably in the USA and Australia, has lived up to neither the high hopes of victims' rights advocates nor the misgivings of critics. Moreover, it has had little effect on both criminal justice processes and victims' satisfaction with them. Nevertheless, she suggests the research shows that, with proper safeguards, victim impact statements do provide victims with a limited voice which can be both empowering to victims and can enhance justice in adversarial court proceedings. In contrast to Ashworth's view in Chapter 9, and to a certain degree that of Reeves and Mulley in Chapter 6, she advocates providing victims with what she terms a 'meaningful voice' through the use of victim impact statements.

From a somewhat more sceptical perspective, Andrew Ashworth, in the following chapter, reviews the often confused and problematic place that victims increasingly occupy within criminal justice. Within the context of a confluence of a growing 'victim perspective' and a political climate of 'popular punitiveness' (Bottoms, 1995), he warns of two particular dangers – namely, 'victims in the service of severity' and 'victims in the service of offenders'. Against these dangers he considers a number of normative debates concerning: first, the procedural protections for victims, witnesses and offenders within the court; second, the extent to which initiatives in restorative justice attain appropriate standards of procedural and substantive fairness; and, third, whether victims should be granted procedural rights. In assessing these debates, Ashworth attempts to chart a map in which questions of principles and ethical standards in the delivery of criminal justice are given prominence. In so doing, he draws on, and reviews, the European Convention on Human Rights and criticizes the current protection granted to victims and other witnesses in the adversarial court process. He goes on to reiterate the need to distinguish between, on the one hand, procedural rights for victims and, on the other, systems of restorative justice. Consequently, he advocates the recognition of the reasoned limits of 'restorative justice' regarding the extent to which state power can be exercised over offenders. He argues for a system that does not grant substantial rights to victims in matters which do not legitimately concern them and for which there is a wider 'public interest'. In this regard, he is critical of victim impact statements relating to matters beyond compensation or reparation to victims in contrast to the position advanced by Erez in the preceding chapter. Ashworth's contribution begins to raise some of the issues which surround the growing interest in what is generically referred to as 'restorative justice', the subject of the final set of contributions.

Part III draws together a number of chapters which explore the relationship between a victim perspective and restorative justice, as well as the implications and prospects of the latter for the former. In Chapter 10 Allison Morris and Gabrielle Maxwell examine these issues through the practice of family group conferences in New Zealand and draw on the research conducted to date. In many senses, this example is particularly apposite, not only because family group conferencing in New Zealand has acted as a catalyst for, and beacon to, the international restorative justice 'movement' informing both theory (Braithwaite and Mugford, 1994) and practice (Hudson *et al.*, 1996), but also because, as a reform strategy, the New Zealand developments (institutionalized by the 1989 Children, Young Persons and Their Families Act) were not originally conceived of in explicitly restorative justice terms. Morris and Maxwell use the case study of family group conferences in New Zealand as a basis for a much wider series of discussions about the place, potential and pitfalls of restorative justice. They identify the importance of offender and victim participation – choice and control – in the process of conferences, notably decision-making, suggesting that the deficiencies identified in the New Zealand experience, particularly with regard to insufficient victim involvement, have been a product of poor practice rather than any fundamental objections to, or flaws in, conferencing itself. While they highlight the importance of returning offences to the parties involved in the dispute and reconnecting them with their communities, they define community in a specific and narrow sense with regard to a victim's and offender's direct 'communities of interest' or 'communities of care' which can play a supportive role at conferences and can reinforce the offender's acceptance of the wrongfulness of his or her offending. They also raise concerns about the operationalization of shame in restorative justice, preferring the notions of making amends and remorse.

In Chapter 11, Richard Young interrogates the concept of 'the victim' – often seen as unproblematic in much of the restorative justice literature – in terms of how this might be understood in refiguring criminal justice away from 'an offence against society' model to one which accords an appropriate role to victims. In this he reflects some of the arguments touched upon in Part I of the book (by Sebba in particular). Young argues that crimes typically involve a range of harms to multiple victims, affecting individuals, groups, communities and society as a whole. In line with some of the arguments in Part I about the status of victims, he asserts that it is essential to move beyond an individualized victim perspective towards a multi-victim perspective in order to ground a restorative approach. Furthermore, he holds that, through such an approach, the stereotyped images of offender and victim can be confronted and the complexities of crime and victimization become more lucid and intelligible. Consequently, he examines some of the implications and insights gained from the practices and theoretical development of a model of family group conferencing or 'restorative cautioning' in England. He draws on the case study of a well publicized initiative by the Thames Valley Police to argue that it is only through the adoption of a multi-victim perspective embracing those indirectly harmed by an offence that a process such as cautioning can become genuinely restorative.

From a continental European perspective, Lode Walgrave offers a compelling argument, in Chapter 12, for incorporating a victim perspective within a much broader and systemic understanding of restorative justice. He highlights some of the risks, alluded to by other contributors to this volume, associated with isolating a victim perspective – as an end in itself – from a broader goal of improving criminal justice in interpersonal, social and legal ways for victims of crime and their offenders. He then outlines a programme for restorative justice, which has at its heart a concern for giving victims greater agency and voice within a broader systemic reform of criminal justice but which recognizes the inherent coercive framework within which criminal justice operates. Walgrave suggests that advocates of restorative justice need to come to grips with the complex, and yet central, challenge of conceiving and delineating an appropriate role for the state in such a way that it does not impede the restorative process, while performing its norm-affirming and enforcing role. He argues for a 'maximalist option on restorative justice' and against a diversionist approach which seeks to locate itself outside the orbit of the criminal justice system. Such a maximalist approach, which seeks to confront the dominance of retributive and rehabilitational justice whilst attracting significant serious cases, must be at the heart of criminal justice rather than its periphery. As such, Walgrave outlines the defining normative role and social function of the third party within conflict processing and resolution – a function which is all too often ignored as the focus of enquiry and concern has shifted from the offender to the victim (as well as between them). Walgrave problematizes this third party and how it is defined, notably within the restorative justice literature, particularly the appeal to community which such definitions often embody. But, in the face of impossibilist arguments, he asserts a defining role for the state as the pre-eminent power-container and social force; since restorative justice constitutes more than a series of bipartisan accords, it must be bounded by the limitations of legal rights which contain excesses of power, safeguard individuals and guarantee dominion. As a consequence, he argues that restorative actions can (and must) include coercive elements. Coercive restorative sanctions have a role to play as part of a maximalist and systemic alternative which is premised on a normative theory, has a social voice – whilst simultaneously guaranteeing agency and voice to the offender and victim – and which can confront, and hold back, the advances of the dominant retributive and rehabilitative paradigms.

In the concluding chapter, Adam Crawford summarizes some of the salient issues raised by the various commentators, as well as their points of convergence and departure. To the two dangers noted by Ashworth of victims being used to service the 'interests of severity' and the 'interests of offenders', he warns of a third danger – namely, 'victims in the service of system efficiency', whereby victims are 'consumed by' rather than the 'consumers of' criminal justice. Expanding on some of Shapland's insights in Chapter 7, he identifies the manner in which criminal justice has produced and proliferated its own new *system criteria* against which the 'success' of public services are to be measured and which may have little to do with meeting victims' needs. He goes on to ask whether the shifts and developments outlined in the various contributions to the book represent and reflect a growing 'civilianization', 'humanization' or 'privatization' of criminal justice, drawing out issues concerning legitimacy, obligation and the (re)distribution of responsibilities that are implied by shifts in criminal justice policy and practice in the name of integrating a victim perspective. Echoing a number of points raised by Walgrave he suggests that careful consideration be given to the limitations of restorative justice and the feasibility of restoration. The danger for the restorative justice movement and for victims of crime may lie in proponents of restorative justice promising and claiming too much, which may only serve to disappoint in the face of falsely raised expectations. Criminal justice, after all, is intrinsically bound up with state coercion and is not necessarily the appropriate cradle of redistributive justice.

Note

1   Some of the other papers presented at the conference are published as a special edition of the *International Review of Victimology*, **7**(3), 2000.

References

Bottoms, A.E. (1995), 'The Philosophy and Politics of Punishment and Sentencing', in C. Clarkson and R. Morgan (eds), *The Politics of Sentencing Reform*, Oxford: Clarendon Press, 17–49.

Braithwaite, J. and Mugford, S. (1994), 'Conditions of Successful Reintegration Ceremonies: Dealing with Juvenile Offenders', *British Journal of Criminology*, **34**(2), 139–71.
Christie, N. (1977), 'Conflicts as Property', *British Journal of Criminology*, **17**(1), 1–15.
Hood, C. (1991), 'A Public Management for all Seasons?', *Public Administration*, **69**, 3–19.
Hood, C. (1995), 'The "New Public Management" in the 1980s: Variations on a Theme', *Accounting, Organisations and Society*, **20**(2/3), 93–110.
Hudson, J., Morris, A., Maxwell, G. and Galaway, B. (1996) (eds), *Family Group Conferences: Perspectives on Policy and Practice*, Annandale, NSW: The Federation Press.
JUSTICE (1998), *Victims in Criminal Justice*, Report of the Committee on the Role of the Victim in Criminal Justice, London: JUSTICE.
Wolfgang, M.E. (1982), 'Basic Concepts in Victimology Theory: Individualisation of the Victim', in H-J. Schneider (ed.), *The Victim in International Perspective*, Berlin: de Gruyter, 47–58.
Zedner, L. (1994), 'Victims', in M. Maguire, R. Morgan and R. Reiner (eds), *The Oxford Handbook of Criminology*, Oxford: Clarendon Press, 1207–46.

1 An Overview of Key Themes[1]

Jo Goodey

Introducing Four Themes for Discussion

In the opening pages to the 1974 edited collection of papers from the First International Symposium on Victimology, the editors make the following observation:

> Students and professionals in the criminal justice system have become increasingly aware that a victim of a criminal becomes – more often than not – also the victim of the criminal justice system. (Drapkin and Viano, 1974: x)

Criminal justice has come a long way since 1974, in its efforts to improve the position and treatment of victims. This book, with its focus on victims in criminal justice, is testimony to the continuing and growing recognition of 'victims' from the policy and practitioner fields as well as from academia. However, at the same time the persisting focus on victims in criminal justice can be praised, ongoing debates highlight dilemmas which remain. This chapter presents a brief overview of key themes, at an international level, which provide an insight into recent developments that 'place' the victim in criminal justice as we enter the twenty-first century.

The title of the conference from which this book stems, 'Integrating a Victim Perspective Within Criminal Justice: International Debates', forms the basis of this chapter with regard to four central themes that attempt to contextualize and critically examine some of the ideas and questions that are addressed and also remain unanswered in the book. First, the historical and international growth of victim literature since the 1970s provides a brief introduction to the state of victim-centred research in the late twentieth century whilst helping, at the same time, put this book in context. From here, an overview of international criminal justice developments for victims is presented as a series of dichotomies which are reflected in the prioritization of various criminal justice 'models'. The chapter then turns to an examination of the individualization of 'the' victim which, while providing a level of service provision and due process to individual cases, can be accused of neglecting marginalized group experiences of victimization and criminal justice. Finally, the chapter engages with recent developments for victims that are on the fringes of traditional criminal justice – namely, restorative justice initiatives which help challenge the primacy of existing criminal justice practices.

Taking each theme in turn, the chapter provides an introduction to selected debates concerning the victim's place in criminal justice. The intention is to raise questions for consideration rather than answer them – questions which serve to critique victim-centred criminal justice developments through the lens of academic discourse and international policy developments.

The Internationalization of the Victim

The Historical and International Context of Victim Literature

Since the 1970s there has been a steady growth in victim-centred literature throughout the developed world. This book, focusing as it does on how victim's interests are served by and through their integration into criminal justice, reflects and engages with some of the key debates that have emerged since that time. Of course, each victim-centred publication is a product of its time, reflecting academic debates, research interests and the policies of the period. While academic victimology, victim policy initiatives, practitioners and, in particular, victim lobby groups have often made uneasy bedfellows over the last quarter of the twentieth century, their various inputs and disagreements have ensured that the victim field has not remained a stagnant area for intellectual debate and policy development at an international level.

After the founding work of the earliest scholars in victimology (von Hentig, 1948; Mendelsohn, 1956; Wolfgang, 1959), the study of the victim and victim aetiology surfaced as areas of renewed research interest during the 1970s (Amir, 1971; Ash, 1972; Christie, 1977). Much like the rebirth of feminism from its beginnings at the turn of the twentieth century, so victimology, as the academic subdiscipline of criminology, was reborn and politicized during the 1970s. Victim-centred projects, with diverse political origins, emerged. In the same period, the UK witnessed the setting up of both the politically 'neutral' Victim Support and feminist-inspired women's refuges mirroring developments in other parts of the world. While the 1970s can be characterized as a period of intellectual development and grassroots activism, the 1980s, also a period of radical research and activism (Dobash and Dobash, 1980; Hanmer *et al.*, 1989), was the pivotal decade for the mainstreaming of victim-centred policy and, in turn, a burgeoning literature on the subject of 'victims' (Joutsen, 1987; Maguire and Pointing, 1988; Shapland *et al.*, 1985).

One of the most significant developments for victims in the 1980s was the broad application of the victim survey by national governments and local administrations. However, the 1980's adoption of the victim by criminal justice administrations has been attributed to governments' failure to halt the rising crime rates which afflicted North America and Western Europe during the latter half of the twentieth century (Boutellier, 1996). While the victim survey was a tool of 1980's 'administrative criminology', it should not be forgotten that, as a tool, the survey method was also very useful to political and grassroots movements which set out to highlight the experiences of some of the most vulnerable victims (Young, 1986). Victim surveys have variously documented people's 'hidden' experiences of crime and 'fear of crime' through the application of general, large-scale questionnaires or small targeted surveys which attempt to uncover specific instances of victimization, such as domestic violence and marital rape (Hanmer and Saunders, 1984; Painter and Farrington, 1998). In the case of the UK, the Islington Crime Survey revealed experiences of victimization particular to local populations in a community (MacLean *et al.*, 1986; Crawford *et al.*, 1990) and, in so doing, married policy with academic insights in the guise of new left realism, concerning crime, victimization and victim satisfaction with local policing.

In recent years many victim surveys have extended their remit to include questions about victim satisfaction with police services and their experiences of other criminal justice personnel and processes (van der Vijver, 1993). Likewise, victim surveys have traversed national borders to compare international experiences of victimization and criminal justice responses to victims. The United Nation's International Crime Victims Survey (ICVS) has had three sweeps to date (1988, 1992 and 1996) and is reported in depth in Chapter 5 by Jan van Dijk. The ICVS presents international research with the largest bank of cross-national information on victims and criminal justice systems. While the problems of trying to compare the results of the ICVS are legion (Mayhew, 1993) this should not detract from its contribution to international research and policy concerning victims.

The extent to which victim-centred research in the 1980s and 1990s reacted to policy developments and practical initiatives, rather than setting its own agenda, is a question that emerges when documenting the historical and international context of victim-centred literature. A number of meetings, which have resulted in publications, have testified to the parallel importance of policy and practitioner debates alongside the intellectual development of victim-centred discourse, two examples being: first, Jan van Dijk's 1985 report on the Sixteenth Criminological Research Conference of the European Committee on Crime Problems, the focus of which was research on victimization; and, second, Viano's 1989 account of the proceedings of the Fourth International Institute on Victimology gathering, which met as a NATO Advanced Research Workshop and convened task forces to develop a broad response to selected themes which questioned a narrow focus on 'victims', as victims and witnesses of *crime* per se (Viano, 1989: xvii). Likewise, Lurigio *et al*.'s edited book *Victims of Crime: Problems, Policies and Programs* (1990)[2] which, according to its introduction, attempts to take stock of 'recent' research, legislation and services directed at victims, reaffirms the centrality of policy and practitioner developments for academic research. Having said this, one can note Marshall's comments concerning the relationship between theory and practice with regard to mediation and, latterly, restorative justice, since the 1980s:

> The *theory* of all this has been built on as an afterthought, and has not been, in my experience, a cause of innovation at all … . Indeed, in some respects, the theory has done more damage than good. (Marshall, 1996: 35)

Marshall's critique, focused as it is on the UK, is contestable given the extent of international academic input into restorative justice as intellectual theorizing and practice (Braithwaite, 1989). However, he usefully highlights the point that much victim-centred policy and practice since the 1980s has been a pragmatic response to the perceived needs of victims and the increasing pressures placed on criminal justice to be victim-centred. The extent to which academic debate concerning victims informs, or is informed by, practice is beyond the scope of this chapter; suffice to say that the literature reflects a close association between the two. Similarly, the influence of international debates and practice on national developments for victims is reflected in the literature (Hudson *et al*., 1996).

Throughout the 1990s a number of publications, such as Lurigio *et al*. (1990), have attempted to take stock of international policy, practitioner and academic developments for victims; for example, 1991 saw the publication of an extensive three-volume collection, *Victims and Criminal Justice* (Kaiser *et al*., 1991) on the occasion of the Seventh International Symposium on Victimology. International edited collections have also taken the form of retrospective overviews of significant developments in victimology and criminal justice practice; for example, Rock's 1994 collection highlights pioneering work in the field, with contributions including Margery Fry's short, but important, 1959 article on victim compensation. Around the same time as

Rock's publication, Singh Makkar and Friday (1995) published a collection of previously unpublished and published material – some symposia papers and some written specifically for the collection – under the title *Global Perspectives in Victimology*, Part III of which focused on 'The victim and the criminal justice system'. Looking at this 'list' of prominent collections, and trying to comment on the place of victims in late twentieth-century criminal justice, as a reflection of the literature, it is notable how far academic and practitioner developments have been 'internationalized'. The degree to which victim-centred debates and practice is imported from one country, from one context, to another, demands a critique of the comparative at an international level.

Turning to more focused international collections, such as Wright and Galaway's edited book *Mediation and Criminal Justice* (1989) and the *European Journal on Criminal Policy and Research*'s 1996 volume on 'Restorative Justice and Mediation', it can be seen how, from the late 1980s onwards, selective debates and practices have successfully transcended continents and bridged the traditional divide between adversarial and inquisitorial justice systems (Joutsen, 1987; see also Declaration of Leuven, 1997). What can be discerned from any reading of research developments in the 1980s and 1990s is not, perhaps, the policy or academic nature of these developments or their European, North American or Australian/New Zealand origin but, rather, the marrying of diverse standpoints in a shift towards victim-centred criminal justice initiatives worldwide.

Whether single authored or edited collections, whether focused on national or international developments and whether an academic narrative or political directive, publications are often heralded as marking a 'watershed' or 'turning point' in victim-centred discourse and policy initiatives. To an extent, the above introduction to some of the important victim-centred literature since the 1970s does point to phases in research interest and practice: for example, victimology's rebirth and the burgeoning influence of feminist research in the 1970s; administrative criminology's focus on the victim survey and the growing recognition of victim service provision in the 1980s; international reflections on the victim's place in criminal justice in the 1990s; and the introduction of a, possible, new criminal justice paradigm for victims in the form of the restorative justice debate during the same period. While publications *do* reflect shifts in victim-centred criminal justice developments, the point at which one can refer to '*a*' shift in victim debates and policy developments becomes problematic, particularly when attempting to make comparisons between countries. Debates resurface and are renewed when taken from one country, or continent, to the next. What any international overview of theoretical and policy development, like this book, should acknowledge is the Anglo-American, Euro-centric and English language-dominated nature of much of the literature and discourse. Having noted this, the following paragraphs introduce some of the key developments for victims which have emerged from countries where victim provisions are high on the criminal justice agenda.

International Developments for Victims

International developments for victims can be interpreted through a series of dichotomies which, like an overview of the literature, help highlight the various academic and policy debates focusing on victims since the 1970s. Briefly, these include international developments, alongside national movements, in terms of the following, selective, dichotomies: research-led developments versus victim advocacy; legal provisions versus service standards or rights versus needs; and retribution versus reconciliation.

With regard to, 'Research-led developments versus victim advocacy', one can refer to Fattah's comments which usefully encapsulate the much bemoaned split between academic victimology and victim advocacy:

> The ideological transformation of victimology from the study of the victim into the art of helping victims, the over-identification with crime victims, and the missionary zeal with which the 'interests' of those victims are defended and pursued were quite manifest in victimology conferences held in recent years (Zagreb, 1985; Jerusalem, 1988; Rio de Janeiro, 1991). (Fattah, 1992: 12)

Fattah's reference to 'missionary zeal' accuses victim lobby groups of effectively hijacking the academic study of victimology during the mid-1980s and early 1990s. During this period, criminal justice policies in most developed countries did become increasingly retributive, with certain victim lobby groups calling for harsher penalties against offenders (Elias, 1990). Victims' rights were heavily promoted in the United States, often, as has been vigorously argued (Ashworth, 1993), at the expense of defendants' rights. However, to characterize this period as brimming with developments for victims which were, apparently, at the offender's expense and at the expense of liberal rehabilitative policies and research led developments, is to neglect the wider picture.

As noted earlier, since the 1970s, North America, Western Europe and Australia/New Zealand have witnessed the growing demands of grassroot feminist groups and academic feminists to take violence against women seriously. These demands were not necessarily embedded in a culture of vengeance against victims but, rather, determined to highlight the shared experiences of certain women as victims, and, in so doing, managed to transcend the divide between victim advocacy and academic insight with a thoughtful analysis of the causes of violence against women which also challenged the provision of services for vulnerable victims by criminal justice agencies.

While feminist-led victim movements and campaigns against racist discrimination, harassment and violence can be characterized as grounded in concerns about social inequality, political marginalization and equality of treatment, later 'single-issue' victim lobby groups were based on a more limited remit. Organizations such as SAMM ('Support After Murder and Manslaughter') in the UK (Rock, 1998) or, for example, early advocates of legislation demanding the registration and community notification of sex offenders did not set out to explain the aetiology of violence and victimization against certain groups. The concerns of single-issue groups tended to centre on treatment of *the* victim or the victim's family and, also, on the need to punish the offender and keep 'him' out of society (Sarat, 1997). While this paints a crude picture of many victim lobby groups, a distinction has to be made between the origin and orientation of organizations with wide political agendas that are concerned to connect victim, offender and 'society' (or 'community'), and those organizations which focus on particular instances of victimization that often seem targeted on the act and outcome of individual cases.

The split between what has generally been referred to as the 'scientific' interest of academic victimology and the practitioner and lobby group response to victims' needs has been variously commented on since the 1980s (Cressey, 1988; Fattah, 1989), a decade which also saw the height of the victims' needs versus victims' rights debate which, in practice, emerged as the division between service standards and formal legal provisions (Mawby, 1988; Maguire. 1991).

The United States, reflecting its political precedence for rights and the strength of its victim lobby groups, was at the forefront of victims' rights initiatives which were made concrete as formal legal provisions such as Congress's enactment of the Victims of Crime Act in 1984 and the adoption of a victim bill of rights in over half the states of the Union by the mid-1980s (see Bowers Andrews, 1992). In comparison, the Council of Europe, in 1985, typically deferring to non-enforceable directives (see Mawby and Walklate, 1994), adopted recommendation R(85)11 on the 'Position of the Victim in the Framework of Criminal Law and Procedure'. In the same year, the United Nations adopted the Declaration of Basic Principles of Justice for Victims of Crime and Abuse of Power. These recommendations or declarations, along with similar developments at the level of individual countries (such as the UK's 1990 and 1996 Victim's Charter), have been accused of providing little more than a 'band-aid' for victims because they are not legally binding (Fenwick, 1995; Brienen and Hoegen, 1998). However, while recommendations, declarations and charters have their limitations with regard to their impact on actual victims' treatment and needs, they do act as standard-bearers for change. Whether these various developments can be said to be *for* victims' ultimate benefit or the benefit of those making the declarations who are seen to be 'doing something' for victims, remains to be seen; suffice to say that, as national and international developments, they indicate the willingness of governments to take victims seriously. In turn, each political development has to be viewed on its own merits: for example, the UK's Victim's Charter was concerned to construct the victim as a 'consumer' of criminal justice services (Nettleton *et al.*, 1997) and the United Nations' Declaration gave wider consideration to the status of victimization beyond the narrow confines of the criminal law.

While, in the 1980s, it was relatively straightforward to distinguish the rights-based agenda of victim-centred developments in the United States from the largely needs-based approach of victim developments in Europe, this polarized characterization of victim-centred initiatives is progressively less tenable when the actual impact of victim provision in different countries is examined. Formal legislation or good practice guidelines are no guarantee of provision *for* victims which, in practice, can depend on victim compliance with criminal justice authorities – that is, the victim playing their part in the process as a 'victim citizen'. To examine criminal justice provision for victims as dichotomous and oppositional – 'rights versus needs' or 'retribution versus reconciliation' – is usually to present victims and criminal justice with a false choice. As Sebba's (1982) early work on the victim's role in the penal process illustrates, to place the victim with either the 'adversary–retribution model' or the 'social defence–welfare model', and their derivatives, is most usefully interpreted as providing a framework for evaluating the victim's role at successive stages of the criminal justice system – in other words, both models can be variously applied at different stages of criminal justice. Similarly, van Dijk's 1985 report on the European Committee on Crime Problems refers to four main currents in the victims' movement at the time: the care ideology; the instrumental ideology; the retributive ideology; and the abolitionist ideology. He concludes:

> On reflection, none of the four different pro-victim ideologies seems to square fully with the victim's real needs … . The models, however, complement each other. The ideal package of victim services seems to be a mixture of community-based care provision and a less bureaucratic criminal justice system. (van Dijk, 1985: 20)

It would appear from the evidence of these commentaries on victim 'models' from the 1980s that politically polarized victim provision did not, and does not, offer victims a full and comprehensive service. International developments for victims, from retributive to reconciliatory, can be identified between countries and criminal justice systems over time. However, the application of these models is not, in reality, a clear-cut process (Dignan and Cavadino, 1996). The UK can be characterized as having a retributive criminal justice system under its last period of Conservative rule, but this period also saw victim provision under the traditional victim-centred welfare model in the form of government funding of the politically 'neutral' organization of Victim Support, and the government-backed Victim's Charter which, although different on paper than in practice, set out standards of criminal justice service provision for victims. Showing concern for improving criminal justice services for victims can, somewhat confusingly, seem to marry right-wing demands of 'justice' for victims, through retributive policies against offenders, with liberal calls for victim-centred initiatives that do not set out unduly to 'punish' the offender but, rather, strive for restoration/reintegration of both offender and victim.

Restorative justice, as a new development for criminal justice, provides a key point of reference in the book, as it encompasses a wide range of established and more recent worldwide victim-centred initiatives which also take on board concerns for the offender and, ultimately, the community. The question whether restorative justice presents a new model, or even a new paradigm, for criminal justice, with its potential to reframe criminal justice as social or communitarian justice, will be discussed in more detail in the last section of this chapter and Part III of this book. Looking to the recent Crime and Disorder Act (1998) for England and Wales,[3] one can see a number of provisions that mesh traditional criminal justice with restorative justice initiatives and, in so doing, appear to merge victims' interests with offenders' interests, as well as those of the community and State (see Chapter 11 in this volume). Here, the victim is reconceptualized as a 'citizen' with incumbent 'rights' (or more accurately 'standards of service provision') as well as responsibilities to both community and state. This example serves to illustrate the problem of continuing to focus on dichotomous depictions of criminal justice that can be characterized as 'pro-victim' and, often in the same breath, as 'anti-offender', or as 'rights'- rather than 'needs'-based, or even as 'retributive' or 'restorative'. Nevertheless, this chapter and, hopefully, the book, do not set out to establish the ascendancy of one model of criminal justice, the 'victim model', over another model of criminal justice. The connections between developments for *victims* in criminal justice, which also encompass developments for offenders, communities and state, are there to be made at an international level.

Reassessing 'the' Victim and 'Criminal Justice'

Beyond 'a' Victim Perspective

The title of the conference and this book, *Integrating a Victim Perspective within Criminal Justice*, is somewhat misleading as there is no single victim perspective that can be encompassed by criminal justice. Yet, as a title, it reflects the individualization of the victim to which many contributors return. Reference to *a* victim perspective has echoes in earlier periods of victimology and criminal justice practice and can be interpreted with respect to the construction of 'the' deserving victim and the neglect of collective harm.

Theories on victim aetiology and appropriate criminal justice responses were originally developed with an image of the 'ideal' victim in mind (Christie, 1986). In other words, *a* victim perspective demanded a set of shared victim values. These essentialist constructions of 'the' victim variously resulted in ideas of victim precipitation or victim 'blaming' as it came to be known (Amir, 1971). Any victim who was other than 'blameless' did not come under the umbrella of criminal justice's paternalism. So, the ex-criminal, or the individual whose lifestyle was regarded as putting him/her 'at risk', did not warrant criminal justice provision to the extent of the 'ideal' victim – that is, the ostensibly 'innocent' and 'vulnerable' victim. Certain women – for example, those in stable relationships – came under the description of the deserving victim. In comparison, women with independent lifestyles and who were regarded as sexually liberated (for example, prostitutes or even the sexually promiscuous) were not, and continue not to be, given the degree of due process and service provision as victims who comply or fit criminal justice constructions of the deserving victim (Kennedy, 1992; Lees, 1997).

In recent years adversarial criminal justice has seen one of the most significant and controversial developments 'for' victims in the form of the 'victim impact statement'. In this book, Erez's chapter on victim impact statements (Chapter 8) and Ashworth's chapter, 'Victims' Rights, Defendants' Rights and Criminal Procedure' (Chapter 9), present a complementary introduction to ongoing debates concerning the desirability of victim impact statements in the trial process. While the victim impact statement is frequently interpreted as a conflict between victim and offender rights, there are other considerations that are aired in debates with respect to its function – namely, the 'individualization' of the victim not only assigns or, rather, reassigns the victim a 'voice' at the trial, but also serves to make the victim experience apolitical (see Chapters 3 and 8 by Sebba and Erez respectively; also Zauberman's account of the historical place of the victim in the criminal justice systems of England and France in Chapter 2). This is achieved through the victim's presentation of the impact of their experience of victimization in isolation – that is, recounting one experience of victimization reinforces the victim experience as an individual harm. Young, in Chapter 11, extends this critique to restorative justice which, he suggests, succeeds in individualizing victimization by means of its emphasis to let *the* victim or victims speak about a particular incident. Thus, criminal justice initiatives for victims, such as victim impact statements, in serving some victims' needs to have a voice, do no more than provide a space for the victim to have their say about one event that fails to bring in the process, context and aetiology of victimizing events that are shared between victims. The victim impact statement can be viewed as a mute political gesture to appease certain victims and victim lobby groups whose focus is on the role and treatment of victims in the criminal justice process. However, if the aim of victim impact statements is simply to provide victims with a voice at trial, then questions of victim aetiology become largely irrelevant.

At another level of victim-centred service provision, many victim organizations, such as the UK's Victim Support (see Chapter 6 by Reeves and Mulley) and INAVEM (Institut National d'Aide aux Victimes et de Médiation) in France, have limited their role to one of service provider for victims and, in so doing, have distanced themselves from the victim advocacy of their US counterparts. Yet this role has its limitations and difficulties – such as the tendency to concentrate on the uniform provision of a standardized service to established categories of victims. This level of service provision can be criticized for its interpretation of victims' needs as founded on established ideas of vulnerability and vulnerable groups. The ex-offender and, more notably, most young men continue to remain outside the remit of *focused* victim service provision. This is not to deny the vulnerable status that results from particular experiences of victimization, such as a sexual assault (which tends to be gendered), or the vulnerable status of certain groups of victims, such as children. Similarly, noting the limited resources which are assigned to victim support services, it is not only understandable but also practical that attention should be focused on victims who are regarded, and indicate themselves to be, most vulnerable in the event and aftermath of victimization. However, with the recognition of the needs of hitherto neglected victim groups, such as young men, may come a degree of new insight into experiences of victimization and criminal justice responses. Any suggestion for a fresh look at those other groups of victims, such as young men, may set alarm bells ringing among victim campaigners who have sought to highlight victimization against vulnerable groups, typically, by men. To counter people's legitimate fears, research must target the need to understand and respond to the cycle of victimization and offending that exists for significant subgroups in society.

Dichotomized depictions of the deserving victim and the undeserving offender do not reflect the continuum of the 'crime' experience, as potentially victimization *and* offending, for many people and, as noted, certain young men. Fattah's (1994) monograph, *The Interchangeable Roles of Victim and Victimizer* and Miers' chapter in this book, on victims as offenders, begin to point to fields of victimological and criminal justice research on 'victims' which remain largely untapped; such as the subject of dichotomized interpretations of victim and offender subgroups with respect to the contentious subject of racism (Goodey, 1998). However, this is not to promote a particular research interest but to open debates in consideration of a number of factors that might serve to challenge a focus on 'victims' in isolation to offenders.

While the UK's Victim Support, by its very name, is legitimated in its declared focus on 'victims', this is not to deny the need for academics and practitioners to become more fully engaged with shared victim/offender subgroups. The most marginalized groups in society often share some of the highest rates of known victim and offender populations – for example, intrafamilial violence and child abuse. Likewise, the most marginalized social groups (such as young, unemployed men) contain individuals who have experienced both victimization and offending throughout their lives. The message that victimology and criminal justice practitioners should take from feminist (Kelly, 1987) and anti-racism research (Bowling, 1998) is this: the continuum of lifetime experiences, relating to violence against women and ethnic minorities, is also shared by other significant subgroups in the population who experience victimization as an ongoing process throughout their lives. In other words, the interpretation of one incident of victimization in isolation from a lifetime's experiences of victimization – or, more critically, an understanding of a lifetime's experiences of victimization as separate from that lifetime's experiences of offending – may yield only a limited understanding of the victimization process. The individual victim, or certain groups of victims, may have particular needs from, and reactions to, criminal justice intervention because of their experiences of victimization or both victimization *and* offending over a lifetime.

With the recognition of lifetime experiences of victimization has come a belated recognition of 'repeat victimization'. Ken Pease's work (1998; see also Genn, 1988; Farrell, 1995) in this area presents academic victimology, criminal justice and crime prevention practitioners with a wealth of new insights into the extent, nature of and appropriate responses to repeat victimization. Victims' issues, particularly with regard to repeat victimization, have played an important role in crime prevention theory and practice (Crawford, 1998) and illustrate the far-reaching integration of 'the' victim perspective beyond the confines of formal social control, such as the criminal justice system, to include informal social control. The example of crime prevention shows how the state can target the needs of, and allocate resources to, some of the most vulnerable groups in society who are prone to victimization.

Chapter 5 of this book, by van Dijk, refers to the ICVS's findings on repeat victimization across the world and, in so doing, highlights the extent of this problem for significant victim subgroups, such as female victims of domestic violence. Recognition of repeat victimization and a multi-victim perspective (see Chapter 11 by Young), alongside the critique of this book's title for its reference to *a* victim perspective, returns us to a consideration of victim vulnerability as a phenomenon of marginalized social groups. Repeat victimization is usually experienced by the most socially, economically and politically marginalized people in any group (for example, the intraclass victimization of working-class women by working-class men) or between groups (for example, the interclass victimization of ethnic minorities by members of a majority population). An understanding of repeat victimization can serve to inform criminal justice practitioners, such as the police, of the need to respond to certain instances of victimization as part of a continuum, or process, of victimization–abuse against marginalized groups.

Repeat victimization's recognition of collective harm, as repeat victimization against vulnerable groups, brings the discussion round to the increasingly important role played, at an international level, by restorative justice with respect to ideas of victim and community harm.

Beyond Traditional Criminal Justice

Restorative justice has progressively emerged as a strong contender for victims in the face of traditional adversarial criminal justice systems and also with respect to inquisitorial systems of criminal justice which provide more legal scope for the application of mediation initiatives (Dünkel and Rössner, 1989; Dünkel, 1996; Walgrave and Aertsen, 1996). Christie's much quoted 1977 article, on the 'theft' of victim/offender conflicts by the state, reflects the beginnings of the academic and practitioner sea change towards alternative methods for resolving conflicts which, it has been argued, place a greater emphasis on victims and allow victims to have a greater voice.

Restorative justice has many guises from victim–offender mediation through to restorative cautioning initiatives and family group conferencing (see Chapter 10 by Morris and Maxwell). As Christie noted, and as Zauberman describes in Chapter 2, restorative initiatives have an ancient history in common law and civil justice. It is only relatively recently, in the twentieth century, that restorative justice ideals have re-emerged to pose an alternative to long established systems of both adversarial and inquisitorial justice which take the professional abstraction of conflicts as their basis. Dittenhoffer and Ericson's (1983) report on Canada's victim–offender reconciliation work, which emerged as an alternative to incarceration of offenders during the 1970s, is one of the earliest critiques of restorative justice for its net-widening potential with regard to minor misdemeanours which would not, normally, result in imprisonment. While Dittenhoffer and Ericson's concerns are legitimate and repeated in the late 1990s (see Chapter 12 by Walgrave), restorative schemes have been variously adopted both as a means for reducing recidivism, particularly among young offenders, and for involving victims and, latterly, communities in the resolution of conflicts and the restoration of well-being for the parties involved. Generally speaking, early academic, practitioner and government reports on victim–offender reconciliation initiatives were enthusiastic about their potential (Marshall, 1984; Wright, 1991). However, particularly in the case of Britain's mediation schemes, enthusiasm has not always been translated into the political and, hence, financial support needed to keep projects going (Warner, 1992). Family group conferencing and community conferencing are emerging in countries with adversarial systems of criminal justice as the latest derivatives of the restorative justice model in preference to mediation schemes. The academic milestones on 'reintegrative shaming' (Braithwaite, 1989) and 'communitarianism' (Etzioni, 1995) have informed politics in countries with traditional adversarial systems of justice such as the UK, Australia and the United States, such that conferencing initiatives appear to be in ascendancy over earlier mediation schemes as a result of their involvement of 'community' and ideas of active 'citizenship' in the resolution of conflicts.

Whether restorative justice can be heralded as the new 'model' or 'paradigm' for criminal justice, as Lode Walgrave's chapter in this volume calls for, is, however, debatable. Likewise, just as the sensibilities of pitching 'victim' rights against 'offender' rights needs to be questioned, so the desirability of presenting restorative justice as an alternative to traditional criminal justice has to be critiqued. As concluded by van Dijk (1985: 20) perhaps 'a mixture of community-based care provision and a less bureaucratic criminal justice system' is the most practical and effective route to be adopted when considering criminal justice developments for victims. Moreover, it is the extent to which restorative justice is for victims that must not be forgotten when examining restorative justice's claims to be holistic in its restorative approach. With the focus here on 'integrating a victim perspective', one has to consider the immediate and long-term impact of restorative initiatives on victims. If victims are adequately informed about the nature and goal of restorative initiatives to include victim, offender and 'community' in the resolution of conflicts, then victims' voices should be listened to not only at, but in the aftermath of, restorative meetings to establish the extent to which their needs have been met.

It would seem that, rather than providing a wholesale challenge to traditional criminal justice, restorative justice is applied selectively alongside existing criminal justice provisions (see Chapter 12 by Walgrave). Family and community conferencing is largely used as a means for resolving conflicts involving young offenders and their victims and as a means for dealing with less serious offences like sexual assault and murder. This is not to deny the possibility of these initiatives being extended to a wider range of offender groups, offence categories and, therefore, victim groups. To what extent the extrapolation of restorative justice will be to victims' benefit is, as yet, speculative. There needs to be a critical and honest review of initiatives by those who proclaim restorative justice as victim-centred. If restorative justice is ultimately to divert young offenders from the traditional criminal justice system then, surely, this is not a problem if, as a result of this, some victims feel more involved in the management of their own conflicts while others do not go on to be victimized again.

Criminal justice has come some way towards integrating victims' perspectives into the various stages of the system; this is evident in the implementation of victim statements in various jurisdictions throughout the world in combination with the more sensitive treatment of victims (particularly *some* women and children) by criminal justice personnel from the police through to the courtroom. These developments are taking place within existing criminal justice systems and cannot be claimed to directly reflect the influence of restorative justice which, to date, is operating alongside traditional justice. This apparent shift in both established and 'newer' forms of justice to consider the needs of the victim could be said to reflect wider concerns for accountability and service provision which can be seen with respect to victims, offenders and the public who, in interacting with justice, are its main source of information with regard to instances of victimization. The culture of criminal justice has had to change since the 1980s when the question of victims' needs and rights, and the culture of consumerism and service provision, encroached on the criminal justice establishment.

We might ask whether criminal justice has been rebottled as a service provider to the public and victims, under the various labels of 'accountability', 'citizenship rights' and 'restorative justice'. The culture of managerialism, with its demands that each criminal justice agency be accountable and audited, does not, as Shapland argues in Chapter 7, present criminal justice as a *system* with parts (police, judiciary, probation) that interact for 'clients' (offender, victims, or public). The 'revolution' in the criminal justice system called for by the JUSTICE report (1998), and restated in Shapland's chapter, is the reality of criminal justice as 'public service' with an incumbent provision for victims, offenders and community at the local level. The laudable recommendations of the JUSTICE report seem to echo earlier calls for a less bureaucratically enthralled justice system and a more people- or community-based approach to justice. In this respect, suggestions forwarded in the report appear to marry with the principles of restorative justice if, that is, restorative justice is a true challenge to the current limitations of criminal justice rather than an alternative means for processing offenders.

Concluding Comments

Having presented a brief overview of recent literature and developments that help to frame the integration of a victim perspective into criminal justice, there are a series of overarching themes or questions which recur throughout the book.

First, in whose interest is it to integrate a victim perspective into criminal justice? In other words, is it in the interest of victim, offender, criminal justice agency or community/public? Ample evidence (from those whose remit lies with victims, offenders or any one of the criminal justice agencies) can be provided on the extent to which the integration of victims into the various stages of criminal justice is, or is not, beneficial. For example, supporters of victim impact statements might point to evidence revealing victims' satisfaction with being heard in court, while opponents might counter with the warning that victim impact statements erode defendants' rights. Many similar examples can be cited, the point being that all measures to integrate victims into criminal justice impact on victims, offenders and the criminal justice system. In focusing, as this book does, on victims, one has to question the extent to which developments are primarily *for* victims or aimed at reducing recidivism and promoting the reintegration of offenders back into the community; or, whether victim-centred initiatives are a means by which criminal justice agencies can develop public support.

The reconstruction of criminal justice as 'service provider' to victims' needs to be more frequently interpreted as a four-way process that can benefit victims, offenders, the public and the state. When the state actively pursues victim-centred criminal justice initiatives they should be cautiously welcomed as 'victim-friendly' – for their remit, though not directly stated, might not be with victims. Criminal justice agencies need to establish a good relationship with victims so that information will pass between the state and victim; after all, it is victims and the public who are the main source of information for criminal justice agencies with regard to instances of victimization. As Wemmers comments towards the end of her book examining the Dutch experience of victim–criminal justice interaction:

Besides enhancing victims' suffering, negative experiences with legal authorities are associated with diminished victim co-operation with authorities, decreased support for authorities and reduced respect for the law. This realisation has triggered governments to introduce policy changes in order to improve the treatment of victims of crime. (Wemmers, 1996: 215)

In other words, the integration of a victim perspective into criminal justice is not undertaken by criminal justice agencies for purely selfless reasons. Criminal justice needs victims' cooperation just as much as victims need to feel that they are needed and are respected by the agencies they turn to in the quest for 'justice' – be that a compensation claim or a desire to see an offender caught. However, to construct victims' needs as different from those of offenders, as some victim lobby groups are apt to do, or as different from criminal justice's needs, is not to the long-term benefit of victims if one considers recidivism, repeat victimization and the state's role as arbitrator between victim and offender. The question 'In whose interest is it to integrate a victim perspective into criminal justice?' should be rewritten as 'Why do "we" (as victims, offenders, public and state) need to integrate a victim perspective into criminal justice?'.

This leads us to a second, related question: what is the cost of not integrating victim, offender and community into criminal justice? The acknowledgement of restorative justice's current inroads into traditional criminal justice arenas indicates, to some extent, the increased emphasis on the non-separation of victim–offender and community needs; however, restorative justice is in its infancy and would appear, as yet, to be a branch of criminal justice rather than a wholesale challenge to the system's traditional separation of victim from offender and its negation of 'community'. While the offender and the state have been the central focus of criminal justice over the last few centuries, the costs to society of failing to consider the victim and community is increasingly apparent in terms of secondary victimization of the victim by the criminal justice system, increased reluctance of victims and the public/community to cooperate with the system, and the sense in which victims and communities feel they have no control over their experiences of 'crime' as part of a continuum from fear through to victimization. In turn, the alienation of the victim and community from criminal justice, particularly with regard to non-cooperation, can incur a cost to the system if offenders are not caught and restored to the community. Nevertheless, 'community', like 'cost', is a loose term which can encompass a wide range of contexts and peoples. 'Community', as a term, is easy to throw into the equation that considers victims, offenders and criminal justice, yet it is meaningless if inadequately defined and if it plays no useful role in the resolution of conflicts. Much research has yet to be conducted into the resolution of conflicts that attempt to reintegrate victim and offender into the 'community' in contexts which are not obviously conducive to this process. The 'cost' of not attempting this process, in or alongside traditional criminal justice, can, one may argue, already be witnessed among the most marginalized and crime-ridden communities; in such contexts, victims, offenders and communities share the experience of crime.

Finally, academics, practitioners and policy-makers need to ask: are we witnessing a level of consensus between academics, practitioners and policy-makers with regard to the integration of victims into the criminal justice system? As this book illustrates, the answer, as ever, depends on when you ask the question and to whom you direct it. Over the last few decades there has been a shift towards the integration of the victim into criminal justice which is variously supported, actioned and legislated for by academics, practitioners and policy-makers. How, and to what extent, this integration should occur is, however, open to debate. Just as victims have no single 'voice' but a series of 'voices', so those who speak on their behalf are prone to disagreement. If anything, continued disagreement between academics, policy-makers, practitioners and victims themselves is not a bad thing. The ongoing debates on the desirability of, and how to, integrate victims into various stages of the criminal justice system indicates, if anything, that theory, practice and politics are not stagnant in this area. The threatened prospect that criminal justice might finally swing too far in favour of victims still remains a threat that is grounded in a polarized vision of competing models. The consensus, such that it is, seems to be that those from inside and outside the criminal justice system are increasingly having to recognize the interplay of victim, offender, community and state in the resolution of crime.

The prospect of integrating *a* victim perspective into *criminal justice* might now, at the end of this chapter, appear limited to bounded constructions of victim and, hence, offender, and also to narrow interpretations of criminal justice that negate community. If there is any consensus among the various parties working for or researching victims it must be this – change is afoot for victims and for the criminal justice system as we currently know it, albeit the precise outcomes and implications of this change remain uncertain.

Notes

1   I would like to thank Adam Crawford for his helpful comments on an earlier draft of this chapter.
2   Now in its second edition.

3   See, http://www.homeoffice.gov.uk, under Crime and Disorder Act; also Dignan (1999).

References

Amir, M. (1971), *Patterns of Forcible Rape*, Chicago: University of Chicago Press.
Ash, M. (1972), 'On Witnesses: A Radical Critique of Criminal Court Procedures', *Notre Dame Lawyer*, **48**, 386–425.
Ashworth, A. (1993), 'Victim Impact Statements and Sentencing', *Criminal Law Review*, 498–509.
Boutellier, H. (1996), 'Beyond the Criminal Justice Paradox: Alternatives Between Law and Morality', *European Journal on Criminal Policy and Research*, **4**(4), 7–20.
Bowers Andrews, A. (1992), *Victimization and Survivor Services*, New York: Springer Publishing Company.
Bowling, B. (1998), *Violent Racism: Victimisation, Policing and Social Context*, Oxford: Clarendon Press.
Braithwaite, J. (1989), *Crime, Shame and Reintegration*, Cambridge: Cambridge University Press.
Brienen, M. and Hoegen, E. (1998), 'Information Systems for Victims of Crime: Results of Comparative Research', *International Review of Victimology*, **5**, 163–88.
Christie, N. (1977), 'Conflicts as Property', *British Journal of Criminology*, **17**(1), 1–15.
Christie, N. (1986), 'The Ideal Victim', in E. Fattah (ed.), *From Crime Policy to Victim Policy*, London: Macmillan, 1–17.
Crawford, A. (1998), *Crime Prevention and Community Safety*, Harlow: Addison Wesley Longman.
Crawford, A., Jones, T., Woodhouse, T. and Young, J. (1990), *Second Islington Crime Survey*, Middlesex: Middlesex Polytechnic.
Cressey, D.R. (1988), 'Research Implications of Conflicting Conceptions of Victimology', in P. Zvonimir Separovic (ed.), *Victimology: International Action and Study of Victims*, Vol.1, Zagreb: Papers given at Fifth International Symposium on Victimology, 1985.
Declaration of Leuven (1997), 'On the Advisability of Promoting the Restorative Justice Approach to Juvenile Crime', *European Journal on Criminal Policy and Research*, **5**(4), 118–22.
Dignan, J. (1999), 'The Crime and Disorder Act and the Prospects for Restorative Justice', *Criminal Law Review*, 48–60.
Dignan, J. and Cavadino, M. (1996), 'Towards a Framework for Conceptualising and Evaluating Models of Criminal Justice From a Victim's Perspective', *International Review of Victimology*, **4**, 153–82.
Dittenhoffer. T. amd Ericson, R.V. (1983), 'The Victim/Offender Reconciliation Programme: A Message to Correctional Reformers', *University of Toronto Law Journal*, **33**, 315–47.

Dobash, R.E. and Dobash, R.P. (1980), *Violence Against Wives*, Shepton Mallet: Open Books.

Drapkin, I. and Viano, E. (1974) (eds), *Victimology: A New Focus*, Toronto and Lexington MA: Lexington Books.

Dünkel, F. (1996), 'Täter-Opfer Ausgleich: German Experiences with Mediation in a European Perspective', *European Journal on Criminal Policy and Research*, **4**(4), 44–66.

Dünkel, F. and Rössner, D. (1989), 'Law and Practice of Victim/Offender Agreements', in M. Wright and B. Galaway (eds), *Mediation and Criminal Justice*, London: Sage, 152–77.

Elias, R. (1990), 'Which Victim Movement? The Politics of Victim Policy', in A.J. Lurigo, W.G. Skogan and R.C. Davies (eds), *Victims of Crime: Problems, Policies and Programs*, New York: Sage Publications.

Etzioni, A. (1995), *New Communitarian Thinking*, Charlottesville, VA: University of Virginia Press.

Farrell, G. (1995), 'Preventing Repeat Victimisation', in M. Tonry and D. Farrington (eds), *Crime and Justice: A Review of Research*, **19**, 469–534.

Fattah, E. (1989), *The Plight of Crime Victims in Modern Society*, London: Macmillan.

Fattah, E. (1992), 'The Need for a Critical Victimology', in E. Fattah (ed.), *Towards a Critical Victimology*, London: Macmillan Press, 3–26.

Fattah, E. (1994), *The Interchangeable Roles of Victim and Victimizer*, Helsinki: The European Institute for Crime Prevention and Control.

Fenwick, H. (1995), 'Rights of Victims in the Criminal Justice System: Rhetoric or Reality?', *Criminal Law Review*, 843–53.

Fry, M. (1959), 'Justice for Victims', *Journal of Public Law*, **8**, 191–4.

Genn, H. (1988), 'Multiple Victimisation', in M. Maguire and J. Pointing (eds), *Victims of Crime: A New Deal?*, Milton Keynes: Open University Press, 90–100.

Goodey, J. (1998), 'Examining the "White Racist/Black Victim" Stereotype', *International Review of Victimology*, **5**, 235–56.

Hanmer, J., Radford, J. and Stanko, E. (1989) (eds), *Women, Policing and Male Violence*, London: Routledge.

Hanmer, J. and Saunders, S. (1984), *Well-Founded Fear*, London: Hutchinson.

Hudson, J., Morris, A., Maxwell, G. and Galaway, B. (1996) (eds), *Family Group Conferences: Perspectives on Policy and Practice*, Annadale, NSW: The Federation Press/Criminal Justice Press.

Joutsen, M. (1987), *The Role of the Victim of Crime in European Criminal Justice Systems: A Cross-National Study of the Role of the Victim*, Helsinki: HEUNI.

JUSTICE (1998), *Victims in Criminal Justice*, Report of the Committee on the Role of the Victim in Criminal Justice, London: JUSTICE.

Kaiser, G., Kury, H. and Albrecht, H.J. (1991) (eds), *Victims and Criminal Justice*, Volumes 50–53, Freiburg: Max-Planck-Institut.

Kelly, L. (1987), 'The Continuum of Sexual Violence', in J. Hanmer and M. Maynard (eds), *Women, Violence and Social Control*, London: Macmillan, 46–60.

Kennedy, H. (1992), *Eve Was Framed: Women and British Justice*, London: Vintage.

Lees, S. (1997), *Ruling Passions: Sexual Violence, Reputation and the Law*, Buckingham: Open University Press.

Lurigio, A.J., Skogan, W.G. and Davies, R.C. (1990) (eds), *Victims of Crime: Problems, Policies and Programs*, New York: Sage.

MacLean, B., Jones, T. and Young, J. (1986), *Preliminary Report of the Islington Crime Survey*, Middlesex Polytechnic: Centre for Criminology and Police Studies.

Maguire, M. (1991), 'The Needs and Rights of Victims of Crime', in M. Tonry (ed.), *Crime and Justice: A Review of Research*, Chicago: Chicago University Press, 363–433.

Maguire, M. and Pointing, J. (1988), *Victims of Crime: A New Deal?*, Milton Keynes: Open University Press.

Marshall, T. (1984), *Reparation, Conciliation and Mediation*, Paper No. 27, London: Home Office Research and Planning Unit.

Marshall, T. (1996), 'The Evolution of Restorative Justice in Britain', *European Journal on Criminal Policy and Research*, **4**(4), 21–43.

Mawby, R. (1988), 'Victims' Needs or Victims' Rights? Alternative Approaches to Policy Making', in M. Maguire and J. Pointing (eds), *Victims of Crime: A New Deal?*, Milton Keynes: Open University Press, 127–37.

Mawby, R. and Walklate, S. (1994), *Critical Victimology*, London: Sage.

Mayhew, P. (1993), 'Research Issues', in A.A. del Frate, U. Zvekic and J.J.M. van Dijk (eds), *Understanding Crime: Experiences of Crime and Crime Control*, Rome: United Nations Publications, 381–4.

Mendelsohn, B. (1956), 'Une Nouvelle Branche de la Science Bio-psycho-sociale: Victimologie', *Revue Internationale de Criminologie et de Police Technique*, 10–31.

Nettleton, H., Walklate, S. and Williams, B. (1997), *The Politicisation of Work with Victims by the Probation Service in England and Wales, and the Marginalisation of Feminist and Self-Help Victims' Groups*, paper presented at the Ninth International Symposium on Victimology, Amsterdam.

Painter, K. and Farrington, D. (1998), 'Marital Violence in Great Britain and its Relationship to Marital and Non-Marital Rape', *International Review of Victimology*, **5**, 257–76.

Pease, K. (1998), *Repeat Victimisation: Taking Stock*, Police Research Group Crime Detection and Prevention Series, Paper 90, London: Home Office.

Rock, P. (1994) (ed.), *Victimology*, Aldershot: Dartmouth.

Rock, P. (1998), *After Homicide*, Oxford: Clarendon Press.

Sarat, A. (1997), 'Vengeance, Victims and the Identities of Law', *Social and Legal Studies*, **6**(2), 163–89.

Sebba, L. (1982), 'The Victim's Role in the Penal Process: A Theoretical Orientation', *American Journal of Comparative Law*, **30**(2), 217–40.

Shapland, J., Willmore, J. and Duff. P. (1985), *Victims in the Criminal Justice System*, Aldershot: Gower.

Singh Makkar, S.P. and Friday, P.C. (1995) (eds), *Global Perspectives in Victimology*, Jalandhar, India: ABS Publications (export edition).

Van der Vijver, K. (1993), 'Policy Development in the Police Organisation: The Role of the Citizen Surveys', in A. del Frate, U. Zvekic and J.J.M. van Dijk (eds), *Understanding Crime: Experiences of Crime and Crime Control*, Rome: United Nations Publications, 227–40.

van Dijk, J.J.M. (1985), *Regaining a Sense of Community and Order*, General Report of the Sixteenth Criminological Research Conference of the European Committee on Crime Problems, The Hague: Dutch Ministry of Justice.

Viano, E. (1989) (ed.), *Crime and its Victims*, New York: Hemisphere Publishing Corporation.

von Hentig, H. (1948), *The Criminal and His Victim*, New Haven, CT.: Yale University Press.

Walgrave, L. and Aertsen, I. (1996), 'Reintegrative Shaming and Restorative Justice', *European Journal on Criminal Policy and Research*, **4**(4), 67–85.

Warner, S. (1992), *Making Amends: Justice for Victims and Offenders*, Aldershot: Avebury.

Wemmers, J.A. (1996), *Victims in the Criminal Justice System: A Study into the Treatment of Victims and its Effects in their Attitudes and Behaviour*, Amsterdam: Kugler Publications.

Wolfgang, M.E. (1959), *Patterns in Criminal Homicide*, Philadelphia: University of Pennsylvania Press.

Wright, M. (1991), *Justice for Victims and Offenders*, Milton Keynes: Open University Press.

Wright, M. and Galaway, B. (1989) (eds), *Mediation and Criminal Justice*, London: Sage.

Young, J. (1986), 'The Failure of Criminology: The Need for a Radical Realism', in R. Matthews and J. Young (eds), *Confronting Crime*, London: Sage, 4–30.

PART I
THE STATUS OF VICTIMS

2   Victims as Consumers of the Criminal Justice System?

Renée Zauberman

When I was told the title of this book[1] (and the conference from which it arose) – *Integrating a Victim Perspective within Criminal Justice* – it immediately brought to mind the way the issue has been addressed in France in recent years: can citizens who turn to the criminal justice system to have their victimization problem solved be viewed as consumers in the same sense as the consumers of any other public service offered by the administration? A number of intellectual and practical developments during the 1980s and 1990s seem to indicate an affirmative response. First, two actors are definitely involved: there is a victim – an ordinary citizen who has been swindled, robbed, assaulted – with a right to demand of a public actor – the criminal justice system – that justice be dispensed.

From a less theoretical standpoint and basing its viewpoint on the principles of the welfare state, according to which it is intolerable that a victim of violence receive worse treatment than a victim of an accident at work, and on the notion of victims' rights, the far-ranging international 'pro-victim'[2] movement has been deploring the second-rate status attributed to victims in the criminal justice process and has tried to put victims at the forefront. This has been achieved by providing them with a full range of instruments through which they may defend their rights: the right to compensation, through public insurance schemes; the right to participate fully in the penal process; the right to be listened to; and the right to receive help and support, thanks to various assistance schemes set up to care for their needs and suffering.

The purpose of this chapter is not to describe these new or revitalized schemes: there exists a vast literature promoting, describing and, in some cases, evaluating this aid to victims.[3] Rather, in the face of this apparently necessary progress, my aim is to make some brief remarks on this evolution and to consider whether the concept of victims as 'consumers of a public service' is truly adequate to account for their relations with the criminal justice system.

Elements of a response to this question may be sought in a number of directions. For example, law, history and penal sociology may all be useful in comprehending the distance that separates victims from criminal justice in the different systems that have developed in the European sphere (and possibly also in its colonialist offshoots) since the end of the Middle Ages. I will refer essentially to the French system in as much as it exemplifies the centralizing state project that provokes the wrath of contemporary champions of the cause of victims because – in the henceforth classic words of Christie (1977) – it has taken away from them the conflict to which they were a party. We will discover, however, that although this French model was unique in Europe, it retains considerable heuristic value for the comprehension of many of our criminal justice systems, from the oldest ones to those still under construction (Fisher, 1975).

Victims in Legal Theory

In France, the conventional legal view has traditionally been suspicious of victims as party to the criminal justice process. Throughout the nineteenth century (Hélie, 1846–66) and well into the twentieth century (Granier, 1956; Vidal, 1963), legal doctrine considered their presence within procedure as some kind of surviving relic of a still barbarian state of law, close to a system of vengeance. The concept of vengeance, believed to be primitive and endless, therefore tending towards the death of society, was perceived to lie in direct opposition to regular, institutionalized justice whose exclusion of the victim seemed to be a major victory of civilization in a society pacified at long last.

In the history of criminal law as produced by jurists, *Wehrgeld* – the rate set to pay the price of the harm inflicted – was portrayed as only a timid, not very successful, attempt to escape from barbarism. Only with the gradual, although not smooth, emergence of the abstract concept of the state as the embodiment of the general interest as opposed to the private interest of the victim, was barbarism supposed to have been left behind. England offers an interesting point of comparison. In the mid-1830s, when Chadwick, a reformer charged by the Royal Commission on a Constabulary Force for England and Wales with counting the number of Associations for the Prosecution of Felons, arrived at a low estimate of about 500. He used this figure as the basis of a claim that 'the community in which they arose was relapsing in a state of barbarism' (Philips, 1989: 120). Yet, what he designated by this violently disparaging term was simply the action of honourable landowners who had grouped together, since at least the mid-eighteenth century, to ensure their collective defence, particularly by sharing expenses, because the constables were quite ineffectual and the court action which every freeborn Englishman was entitled to take against any offender had become too complex and costly.

This doctrinal use of barbarism as a mythical foil was accepted unconditionally for a long time, despite important anthropological studies showing that vengeance is by no means anarchic and uncontrolled, but rather an infinitely regulated, precise mechanism. It is based on exchange, aims at redress and includes procedures for appeasement and reconciliation: it 'weaves the subtle thread of generalised interdependency, thus thwarting generalised paroxystic violence' (Claverie and Lamaison, 1982: 254). If this is the case, the jurists' 'evolutionist' narrative of a mythical changeover from immediate, excessive, blind personal vengeance to mediated, measured, personalized public justice can no longer be seen as a historical view of law, but rather as an ideology of law within the context of the construction of a state intent on appropriating a monopoly on force and punishment (Verdier, 1980, 1984; Emsley, 1997). In our present society, as we will see, it is impossible to observe victims without finding the state on our path – they form a sociological and historical couple, so to speak.

Criminal Justice in the Legal Theory of Public Service

In France, the notion of public service was constructed principally by jurists specialized in public law, although initially the dogma did not link this concept with what we now view as its natural corollaries – namely, the benefits and services provided and the consumers of them. The underlying idea of a general, or collective, interest to be satisfied does exist, but the field of application of the latter has varied, or rather been extended, over time. Those corollaries were not essential as long as the state's tasks were conceived as exclusively political – based on a theory of the public authority (Chevallier, 1987) that consisted mostly of 'organising and running the war-making, police and justice agencies' (Laubadère, 1984). They began to become meaningful when the economic and social transformations of the second half of the nineteenth century developed public agencies of a more technical character, aimed at providing services to the people (education, transportation, energy, etc.). What was involved here was public service whose 'purpose was to satisfy private individuals *directly* and *individually*' (Rivero, 1983: 458, emphasis added). The latter must contact the agencies to obtain the service and are their consumers, or even customers, in the case of industrial or business-type services.

Clearly, these various notions bring us to the marketplace categories, in which supply, demand, service, satisfaction, goods and clients are the relevant terms. Some writers then contend that the ultimate justification of public service is 'the service provided to the public' or, formulated in market terms, 'consumer satisfaction'. This formulation also began to be used for victim–criminal justice relations in England in the 1980s. In the context of shrinking public investment, it was easier for an institution such as the police, for instance, to justify its budget by measuring satisfaction of victims–consumers rather than by the clear-up rates (Burrows and Tarling, 1987).[4] However, this assimilation should not be exaggerated. While consumers have some freedom of movement within the market and the ability to leave it, the consumer of the justice system as a public service is usually captive. The existence of a private security sector cannot, by any means, provide the entire supply of justice that the members of a community generally expect of their sovereign. At most, this assimilation has the perverse effect of emphasizing the unequal purchasing power with respect to this service, thus seriously damaging the legitimacy of the provider, the state, which in a democracy is based precisely on the equality of citizens.

The legal tradition, in actuality, regards justice as one of those public functions whose legitimacy resides more in the fact that it is consubstantial with the exercise of power than in the services rendered to the people, although – however commonplace the reminder – it is grounded in a 'demand' of the entire social body. If the ancient notion of the public authority, that some reject as the basis of state action, has found refuge anywhere, it is definitely in the criminal justice system. Despite all the case law and doctrinal evolutions, the latter has continued to be one of the 'regalian' state functions, intrinsically tied to its sovereignty and not coming under the category of public services provided to individuals.

In short, a look, however brief, at legal theory clearly shows that the crux of the victims–criminal justice relationship resides in the concept of the state. History probably has more to teach us about this than legal discourse, which has often been no more than a rationalization reflecting political practices.

Criminal Justice, State Business

In Europe, it is France that has exemplified a project of centralization, beginning with the entourage of the medieval suzerain and extended by modern princes and their administration (Rousseaux and Lévy, 1997). The establishment of a criminal justice system, along with control of the army and of finance, was one of the principal – if not the principal – contribution to the construction of the modern state as a centralized political entity with a high degree of autonomy with respect to the citizenry. Criminal justice – in definite contrast to civil justice – was not created in order to 'provide the benefit' of justice to wronged citizens but to personify the public authority; its matrix resides in the crime of lese-majesty (Sbriccoli, 1974), and it has always functioned as a political instrument for asserting sovereignty over a territory. Its implantation varied in form and pace, covering territories ranging from the town (Zorzi, 1997) or the county (Rousseaux, 1993) to an entire monarchy (Sharpe, 1997). At the end of the Middle Ages, all of Europe was developing forms of *ex-officio* prosecution conducted by representatives of the prince in areas – fire, sex and bloodshed, all combined, in the end, in witchcraft – perceived as true threats to the political, religious and social order, and thus justifying the intervention of the authorities (Gauvard, 1997: 92). Let us take a look at England and France. The former, with meagre resources, had its citizens play the role of private entrepreneurs taking charge of prosecution in the name of the Crown, so to speak, and relied on the power of local gentry within their community for law enforcement. The latter was richer, and indulged in the luxury of circumventing the local powers, with the establishment of a network, covering the entire land, of public officers directly tied to the royal authority (Langbein, 1974; Strayer, 1970; Kaeuper, 1988; Bourdieu, 1997), and made extensive use of the King's grace to draw all of the social classes into the penal nexus (Gauvard, 1991, 1997).

Thus, through totally different strategies, these two great monarchies both succeeded in drawing the criminal justice function into the arena of state power, and by the end of the nineteenth century, criminal prosecution was definitely in the hands of public institutions – the police in England (Hay and Snyder, 1989)[5] and the Public Prosecutor's Office in France (Aubusson de Cavarlay, 1993).

Consequently, while 'pro-victim' militants may well view the exclusion of the victim from the criminal justice process as an unfair aberration, the historian sees it as the very precondition for the existence of the criminal justice system. Historically speaking, the criminal trial exists when the action is taken in the name of the sovereign rather than in the name of the direct victim. At that point, redress of the particular wrong becomes secondary, the main point being punishment of the attack on the supreme power. Similarly, the history of the police shows (Williams, 1979) that the police force was not created to provide its services to subjects, but in order that the sovereign's order might reign over public space, thus creating public order in the modern sense of the terms. There are few things that naturally belong to the state, according to Sorman (1984), a staunchly anti-state French neoliberal: the criminal justice system at least belongs to it by 'culture', and this makes the tie no less solid.

The congenital link between justice and power – between the criminal justice system and the state in the present case – is in fact the source of the difficulty in defining the nature of the service provided, and even of the 'consumers' or beneficiaries. There is the concrete service that consists of putting an end to the disorder caused by the offence, of making sure the offender can do no further harm, of restoring the proper state of affairs, redressing the wrong experienced by the victim, and, more generally, ensuring a degree of public peace. But symbolic benefits are just as important in the production of criminal justice. If we still accept the idea of the latter as the institutionalization, however historically dated, of a 'need for justice' inherent in every human group, it may be said to play an essential role of defining right and wrong, marking the boundaries of the group and thus reasserting social bonds.

First, it is most important to acknowledge that victims are not the only beneficiaries of those broader benefits. Second, their content is not contained in their designation: there is no general agreement on what justice, the boundaries of the group or the nature of social bonds should be. Conceptions of these depend on the values and representations of the various social groups, which have different definitions of the goals to be attributed to justice and, consequently, of all the types of service and benefit expected of it. For some people criminal justice derives its power from the religious sphere and should punish every misdemeanour and all deviant behaviour. For others, it has a minimal regulatory function and should promote the humanist values of freedom and equality. Still others contend that it should shield the weak, their property and their person (Ocqueteau and Pérez-Diaz, 1989). Conceptions of justice are also linked to individual social positions and to what those positions entail, very concretely, in terms of relations with the institutions embodying criminal justice. Historians, and the English in particular, have clearly shown the social conflicts that have developed around criminal law (Hay *et al.*, 1975; Thompson, 1977), which could not be viewed in the same way by, say, the aristocracy defending its hunting rights and the ploughman who poached to make a living. Later, much further into the nineteenth century – which was nonetheless to end with a broad consensus of opinion favourable to the police – the violent attacks of the lower classes against the police show how deeply they disagreed about the type of behaviour they wished to have controlled – betting, fighting, drinking, striking and so on – which were integral parts of their lifestyle and social culture (Storch, 1975; 1976; Weinberger, 1981; Davis, 1989). Nowadays, when social distinctions sometimes correspond to ethnic distinctions, as is the case in many industrialized countries of the Northern hemisphere which attract immigrants from the South, conflicts with the police, especially in immigrant neighbourhoods (Scarman, 1986; Cappelle, 1989; Cashmore and

McLaughlin, 1991; Lapeyronnie, 1993), as well as differential treatment by the courts (Tonry, 1997), indicate that criminal justice, far from necessarily producing a consensus, may be at the heart of the most deep-seated splits. Thus, the difficulty in determining who the consumers are harks back to the difficulty in defining what services it should provide.

In the final analysis, the description of victims' relations with criminal justice in terms of consumers of a public service seems to be sufficiently controversial to justify the search for another conceptual framework. I would suggest that, rather than providing a service, criminal justice, owing to its ties with the authority of the state, is a regulatory resource used in conflicts between social actors: depending on their own particular strategies, victims do or do not resort to it, and it is as users of criminal justice, then, that we should study them.

However, the fact that control through criminal justice was one element of the emergence of the regalian state in the late Middle Ages and that it has continued until modern times tells us nothing about the weight of criminal justice in the social arena throughout the centuries during which the state was being constructed in Europe. So, once again, we must turn to history.

Criminal Justice at the Heart and on the Outskirts of Society

In France, under the *Ancien Régime*, state justice with no true infrastructure, no financing and no police had nothing to do with the ordinary regulation of behaviour. The economy of this system, with its minimal forces, required that it be used with great moderation and, in fact, the King's justice apparently made every attempt to dissuade people from lodging complaints, and 'the costs, arbitrary decisions and uncertainty as to the outcome' led them to concoct compromise solutions within their own community (Lévy, 1987).

The King's justice was not popular, and people preferred to take their conflicts to 'less formidable and less formal' agencies. As late as the eighteenth century, and occasionally even well into the nineteenth (Castan, 1980; Claverie and Lamaison, 1982), arrangements were negotiated locally under the auspices of the locally influential or, possibly, before the mediocre seigniorial courts (Ditte, 1990), in the 'realistic framework of social relations' (Castan, 1980; Castan and Castan, 1982). But, then, how many litigants there were! In France, during that period, the court played a considerable role in social affairs (Lebigre, 1988): the lawsuit was one of a number of weapons in local conflicts, used to speed up an informal settlement or to cast lasting shame on an adversary; and relationships between individuals and the relative strength of groups were not necessarily upset by being played out in the courtroom (Billacois, 1990). As for the King's justice, it served as a threat, to be used cautiously, with discernment, to support one's bargaining position, and only as a last resort, once all the usual attempts at mediation had failed. At the end of the eighteenth century, the very time when the crisis in the autonomous regulatory processes led people to resort to it, we find it used by groups – well-to-do craftspeople, country gentlemen – who viewed it as a way to climb the local social ladder when the interplay of influence left them with no hope of winning through an arrangement.

Use of criminal justice as a strategy has also been clearly documented in England, where the system, which turned every Englishman into a prosecutor, offered enormous possibilities for bringing suit: a farmer who wished to avoid paying years of back wages to a servant would accuse him of theft; the same servant would defend himself against the master's abuse by accusing him of poaching on the land of the local lord; in business conflicts, the accusation of forgery or counterfeiting was often enough to ruin a reputation; in the industrial towns, employers prosecuted their workers when there was too much pilferage, to make an example; workers, whose disorderly living conditions were extremely trying, brought suit against their quarrelsome housemates for common assault. In many instances, the case was not pushed very far, the idea being to intimidate or cause trouble, without carrying through (Hay, 1989; Davis, 1989).

In short, recourse to criminal justice was just one of a number of alternatives used to gain satisfaction in a conflict; simply, it was played on a different scene, with the victim commanding the rise of the curtain in accordance with his or her own interests.

Victims and Criminal Justice Today

Private Parties

What remains today of that strategic use of criminal justice? Traditional local networks of solidarity, in which the economy of the previous system was grounded, have gradually dissolved and, with them, community pressure to find an arrangement. And in fact, with whom would one seek an agreement? Private individuals are primarily victims of property offences – property being more abundant than ever, under little surveillance and easy to sell on the black market (Cohen and Felson, 1979; Cohen *et al.*, 1980; Sutton, 1995) – committed by unknown offenders. The vast majority of these cases are never cleared and therefore end their short judiciary career in closets marked as 'dismissals' (Robert *et al.*, 1994). What, then, is the sense, for a victim, of resorting to the criminal justice system? Since the context of a strategy within social relations is non-existent, there is nothing left but the automatism: between two-thirds and the quasi-totality of victims of thefts and burglary file complaints (Robert *et al.*, 1994; Mayhew and Van Dijk, 1997), and their decision is determined first and foremost by the insurance companies which demand this as a prerequisite for compensation or in order to clear the victim's responsibility, when the object has been registered.

But this instrumentalization does not completely account for the automatism, which is also a repetition of the lesson that one should turn to the state. This lesson has been gradually inculcated since the nineteenth century in a society in which the earlier conflict-solving processes still prevailed: in France, victims still expect a great deal of the state; they explain their recourse to the police in terms of 'penal' motivations – the need to punish or to prevent crimes being repated on others – and above all by a civic attitude – one brings suit because 'you should', a response that is also encountered in the UK more frequently than elsewhere (Zauberman and Robert, 1995: 60; Mayhew and van Dijk, 1997: 43).

There are, nonetheless, 'residual' instances in which recourse to criminal justice by an individual victim seems to correspond to the traditional logic: in interpersonal violence, there is nothing automatic about lodging a complaint. These instances of victimization are treated in more varied ways than are property offences: whereas the latter usually produce complaints as a pure formality, as we have seen, the former more rarely lead to a complaint – between three and four of every ten victims (Robert *et al.*, 1995). Conversely, such violence is frequently registered in a more informal way, at the request of the victim, on a record that has no legal consequences (Lévy, 1987). In private quarrels, then, recourse to the criminal justice system is used as a means of pressure, a threat, an attempt to use the authorities to one's own advantage (Zauberman, 1982; Bonnemain, 1978; Shapland *et al.*, 1985). Variations in degree of recourse to criminal justice and bargaining with the offender are thus seen as real alternatives, among which victims make choices or develop combinations in accordance with their personal strategy, independently of any logic of punishment (Zauberman, 1991).

Organizations

Strategic recourse to criminal justice is also observed in situations in which the victim is not an individual actor but one possessing some degree of organization.

Businesses such as department stores or banks, affected by offences such as theft and fraud, may resort to the criminal justice system in accordance with their commercial strategies. Their bureaucratic nature makes them much better adapted to the bureaucratic functioning of this system (Hagan, 1983) than individual victims: their own permanent instruments for offence-detecting, such as private security services in the case of large department stores (Ocqueteau and Pottier, 1995) and their routine procedures for transmitting cases to the official institutions, as with legal departments in banks, enable them to deal with offences and offenders according to their own needs: for example, to minimize losses: to intimidate without dissuading customers: to only resort to the justice system in well chosen cases where the outcome is calculated to make an example of, or obtain repentance from, an unmanageable offender (Zauberman, 1982; Hagan, 1983). The minority of cases that receive this treatment then reach the criminal justice system in much better condition than those coming from private parties, since they are already elucidated – offences and offenders are delivered in a single package, ready for 'consumption'.

Let us take a few examples: studies of labour conflicts show how the collective actors involved – trade unions and company managers – may attempt to 'instrumentalize' (Robert, 1988a) the penal system in the pursuit of their own goals. In the 1978–79 Renault–Flins dispute, for instance, the management, intent on maintaining or restoring production levels to honour their contracts, lodged a complaint against the strikers for impeding the liberty to work. Furthermore, this 'productive logic' of recourse to criminal justice went hand-in-hand with a definite conflict-management strategy: by transferring the conflict to the courts it concealed the actual industrial dimension, and avoided the bargaining process demanded by the workers. The recourse to criminal action also had a symbolic aspect – as a way of disqualifying striking. In an equally symbolic action, its opponent, the CFDT trade union, lodged a complaint against the head of Renault for impediment of freedom of strike, in an attempt to tarnish the management's image (Soubiran, 1988).

Other studies have looked at the criminal justice strategies of organizations defending the collective interests of various 'unstructured publics' – occasional victims in fields such as consumer's rights and environmental issues (Robert, 1988b). They, too, reserve their meagre resources, and especially the heavy artillery represented by legal prosecution, for exemplary cases (Pinto, 1989; Secondi-Nix, 1994). The logic of their action is to put an end to the disorder, possibly by negotiating a settlement: the criminal suit, for which, they prefer to support a prosecution initiated by an individual victim is always viewed as a last resort, never as a matter of principle, and is in fact impossible to carry through due to lack of means (of the type available to trade unions, with their specialized legal departments).

These examples of the use to which victims put the criminal justice system show that, while the latter is a resource for the regulation of conflicts, it conforms to the principle governing resources – that is, unequal distribution among the social actors, in this case to the detriment of individuals, and especially of the victims of property offences.

The question then arises: if the victim must, at the very least, be 'organized' for recourse to criminal justice to be meaningful and socially effective, is there a future for individual victims, and in their wake, for consumers of criminal justice? Shapland (1988) puts the question of whether, in the face of the 'fiefs' developed by the criminal justice institutions including the police and justice system, the 'peasants' – that is, the victims – have any choice other than to constitute 'fiefs' of their own – that is, to unite, in order to ward off the predations of the former and perhaps even conquer a territory of their own. But although organized victims are more effective than isolated victims, their collective strength is not necessarily a panacea: when faced with these organizations, private individuals may well find themselves in the same position as when they face the police as claimants – that is, at a loss, faced with professionals who sort out those complaints that correspond to their own priorities. Here, we are reminded of the Associations for the Prosecution of Felons, in the eighteenth and nineteenth centuries: they were typically organizations aimed at overcoming the difficulties – in terms of the high costs and complicated procedures – encountered by isolated victims, but took no more charge of all complaints than do their modern counterparts. With their limited resources, they attempted to maximize their efficiency by selecting the best cases; that is, those that were exemplary, or had a good chance of succeeding.

The question of the right of the individual victim to conduct prosecution was the very emblem of political freedom, which the English inclined to oppose. But even in France, the classical jurists who defended that state system hardly feared the private individual whose right to set the prosecutorial machinery in motion was never really questioned, neither by the doctrine nor in case law, since, with few exceptions, it was considered reasonable. What was feared was the power ascribed to interest groups. To the jurists fed, for generations, on the political ideology of the French Revolution, the monsters looming on the social horizon were the organized intermediaries. The integrity of the state was threatened by the power of organized groups; the state alone was able to represent a truly general – 'absolutely' general (Larguier, 1958; Patin, 1957) – interest, whereas groups of victims would necessarily represent only relatively general interests at best, or simply specific, even private, interests at worst (Granier, 1956).

Now that the state has a firm grip on criminal justice, these fears have subsided, and a pragmatic position prevails. Given the proliferation of many types of repressive provision tied to the intervention of the state in every area of social life, victims – in fact the organizations defending real or potential victims – are accepted as auxiliaries of the public prosecutor for the prosecution of offences. There are some instances, such as the fight against racism, in which prosecutorial policy is the fruit of real cooperation between the Public Prosecutor's Office and citizens' groups whose familiarity with the scene enables them to suggest when to take public action (Secondi-Nix, 1998).

What, then, will be the ultimate refuge of individual victims? In theory, it is true that French criminal law is now resolutely engaged in the protection of individual interests; the new 1994 Criminal Code represented a turning point in this respect. Until then, symbolic priority was given to protecting the interests of the political structure: it was important that any threat to the democratic forms of government – any act that weakened the foundations of the republic – be punished. Criminalization of offences against individuals, their property and their honour was only secondary, in terms both of its place in the Code and of the severity of the sentences; as of 1994, public order, as defined by the Criminal Code, constructs the common weal essentially through individuals, their interests and the values attached to these. The chapters dealing with them were the only ones to have been thoroughly detailed by the committees in charge of the reform, and now head the document (Lascoumes *et al.*, 1989; Lascoumes and Depaigne, 1997).

It is a fact that the development of the welfare state has weakened the conventional view of the state as transcendental, vehicled by legal doctrine and case law throughout the nineteenth century and well into the twentieth. To the purely sovereign state, based on the general *will*, it adds another aspect: the state as a conglomeration of public services, based on the public *interest*. Whereas citizens were initially simply passive beneficiaries, the subsequent trend toward a consumerist view has tended, despite its ambiguities, to turn them into evaluators of public provision of services. Although criminal justice definitely remains solidly attached to the regalian side of the state, it has not been completely spared by the transformation of the relations between public services and consumers of them (Chauvière and Godbout, 1992).

Its ability to resist has probably been undermined by the ambiguity of its relations with victims in that the punitive logic tends to marginalize them. On the other hand, the penal process is largely fed by the propensity to lodge complaints, and a criminal justice system to which citizens ceased to turn would lose its legitimacy; since it would only judge offences against the public order it would be seen as simply the praetorian guard of the state. What makes criminal law legitimate is the punishment of murder and theft, not of assaults on state security; it is the security of citizens, not the tranquillity of the power structure. This means that justice must, to some extent, cease to pose as the defender of the city walls and don the uniform of provider of services for what is now in fact a quite 'disenchanted' public – one for whom the justice system is no longer sacred, but is simply in charge of dealing with some worldly problems.

Notes

1 This chapter is a revised version of 'La Victime, Usager de la Justice Pénale' in Chauvière and Godbout (1992: 77–92) and has been translated into English by Helen Arnold.
2 Van Dijk (1988) calls it 'victimagogic'.
3 See, for example, *inter alia*, Drapkin and Viano (1974); Elias (1983); Rock (1986); Fattah (1986); Mawby and Gill (1987); Maguire and Pointing (1988); Lurigio *et al.* (1990); Roberts (1990); Sebba (1996). The French literature is less extensive, but see Dulong and Ackermann (1984); d'Hauteville (1988); Faget (1992).
4 On this point see also Jefferson and Shapland (1995) and Mawby and Walklate (1994).
5 The fact that legal ideology makes it possible to view a police officer who undertakes prosecution as no more than a simple citizen does not affect the crux of the issue: from its origins in the first third of the nineteenth century, the police has definitely always been an institution proceeding from the public authority.

References

Aubusson de Cavarlay, B. (1993), 'La mise en place du ministère public en France et son évolution d'après les statisiques pénales, 1831–1932', *IAHCCJ Bulletin*, **18**, 114–42.
Billacois, F. (1990), 'Clio chez Thémis', *Droit et Cultures*, **19**, 7–10.
Bonnemain, C. (1978), *Le contrôle social de la déviance; recherche au niveau d'un service de police*, Paris-Poitiers: CES, Institut de Sciences Criminelles de la Faculté de Droit et de Sciences Sociales de Poitiers.
Bourdieu, P. (1997), 'De la maison du roi à la raison d'État. Un modèle de la genèse du champ bureaucratique', *Actes de la Recherche en Sciences Sociales*, **118**, 55–68.
Burrows, G. and Tarling R. (1987), 'The Investigation of Crime in England and Wales', *British Journal of Criminology*, **27**(3), 229–51.
Cappelle, J. (1989), 'La police et la contestation publique en Grande-Bretagne, 1980–1987', *Déviance et Société*, **13**(1), 35–80.
Cashmore, E. and McLaughlin, E. (1991) (eds), *Out of Order? Policing Black People*, London: Routledge.
Castan, N. (1980), *Justice et répression en Languedoc à l'époque des lumières*, Paris: Flammarion.
Castan, Y. and Castan, N. (1982), 'Une économie de justice à l'âge moderne: composition et dissuasion', *Histoire, Economie, Société*, **3**, 361–67.
Chauvière, M. and Godbout, J.T. (1992) (eds), *Les usagers entre marché et citoyenneté*, trans. Helen Arnold, Paris: L'Harmattan.
Chevallier, J. (1987), *Le Service Public*, Que Sais-Je?, Paris: Presses Universitaires de France.
Christie, N. (1977), 'Conflict as Property', *British Journal of Criminology*, **17**(1), 1–15.
Claverie, E. and Lamaison, P. (1982), *L'impossible mariage. Violence et parenté au Gévaudan, XVIIe, XVIIIe et XIXe siècles*, Paris: Hachette.

Cohen, L.E. and Felson, M. (1979), 'Social Change and Crime Rate Trends: A Routine Activity Approach', *American Sociological Review*, **44**, 588–608.

Cohen, L.E., Felson, M. and Land, K.C. (1980), 'Property Crime Rates in the USA. A Microdynamic Analysis', *American Journal of Sociology*, **86**(1), 90–118.

Davis, J.S. (1989), 'Prosecutions and their Context: The Use of the Criminal Law in Later Nineteenth-Century London', in D. Hay and F. Snyder (eds), *Policing and Prosecution in Britain: 1750–1850*, Oxford: Clarendon Press, 397–426.

d'Hauteville, A. (1988), 'Victimes mieux aidées, mieux indemnisées, des perspectives nouvelles', *Revue de Science Criminelle et de Droit Pénal Comparé*, **1**, 172–75.

Ditte, C. (1990), 'La mise en scène dans la plainte: sa stratégie sociale: l'exemple de l'honneur populaire', *Droit et Cultures*, **19**, 23–48.

Drapkin, I. and Viano, E. (1974) (eds), *Victimology: A New Focus – Society's Reaction to Victimisation* (vol. II), Toronto and Lexington, MA: Lexington Books.

Dulong, R. and Ackerman, W. (1984), *L'aide aux victimes, premières initiatives, premières évaluations*, Paris: MSH.

Elias, R. (1983), *Victims of the System. Crime Victims and Compensation in American Politics and Criminal Justice*, New Brunswick, NJ and London: Transaction Books.

Emsley, C. (1997), 'The Nation-State, the Law and the Peasant in Nineteenth-century Europe', in X. Rousseaux and R. Lévy (eds), *Le pénal dans tous ses États. Justice et sociétés en Europe (XIIème–XXème siècles)*, Brussels: FUSL, 153–78.

Faget, J. (1992), *Justice et travail social: le rizhome pénal*, Toulouse: Erès.

Fattah, E.A. (1986) (ed.), *From Crime Policy to Victim Policy – Reorienting the Justice System*, London: Macmillan.

Fisher, S.Z. (1975), 'The Victim's Role in Criminal Prosecution in Ethiopia', in I. Drapkin and E. Viano (eds), *Victimology: A New Focus*, Lexington, MA: Lexington Books, 73–93.

Gauvard, C. (1991), *De grace especial crime: État et société en France à la fin du Moyen-Âge*, Paris: Presse de la Sorbone.

Gauvard, C. (1997), 'La justice pénale du roi de France à la Fin du Moyen-Âge', in X. Rousseaux and R. Lévy (1997) (eds), *Le pénal dans tous ses États. Justice et Sociétés en Europe (XIIème–XXème siècles)*, Brussels: FUSL, 81–112.

Granier, J. (1956), 'Quelques réflexions sur l'action civile', *JCP*, **I**, 1386.

Hagan, J. (1983), *Victims Before the Law. The Organizational Domination of Criminal Law*, Toronto: Butterworths.

Hay, D. (1989), 'Prosecution and Power: Malicious Prosecution in the English Courts, 1750–1850', in D. Hay and F. Snyder (eds), *Policing and Prosecution in Britain: 1750–1850*, Oxford: Clarendon Press, 343–95.

Hay, D., Linebaugh, P., Rule, J.G., Thompson, E.P. and Winslow, C. (1975), *Albion's Fatal Tree – Crime and Society in Eighteenth-Century England*, Harmondsworth: Penguin.

Hay, D. and Snyder, F. (1989) (eds), *Policing and Prosecution in Britain: 1750–1850*, Oxford: Clarendon Press.

Hélie, F. (1846–66), *Traité de l'instruction criminelle*, Paris: Plon.

Jefferson, T. and Shapland, J. (1995), 'Criminal Justice, Criminology and the Production of Order and Control: Trends in Research and Policy since 1980 in the UK', in P. Robert, L. Van Outrive, T. Jefferson and J. Shapland (eds), *Research, Crime and Justice in Europe: An Assessment and Some Recommendations*, Sheffield: Centre for Criminological and Legal Research, The University of Sheffield, 109–39.

Kaeuper, R.W. (1988), *War, Justice and Public Order: England and France in the Later Middle Ages*, Oxford: Oxford University Press.

Langbein, J.H. (1974), *Prosecuting Crime in the Renaissance: England, Germany, France*, Cambridge, MA: Harvard University Press.

Lapeyronnie, D. (1993), *L'individu et les minorités. La France et la Grande-Bretagne face à leurs minorités*, Paris: PUF.

Larguier, J. (1958), 'L'action publique menacée' (À propos de l'action civile des associations devant les juridictions répressives), *Dalloz*, 29.

Lascoumes, P. and Depaigne, A. (1997), 'Catégoriser l'ordre public: La réforme du Code Pénal français', *Genèse*, **27**, 5–29.

Lascoumes, P., Poncela, P. and Lenoël, P. (1989), *Au nom de l'ordre: Une histoire politique du Code Pénal*, Paris: Hachette.

Laubadère, A. de (1984), *Traité de Droit Administratif*, Vol. 1, 9th edn by J.C. Venezia and Y. Gaudemet, Paris: LGDJ.

Lebigre, A. (1988), *La justice du roi. La vie judiciaire dans l'ancienne France*, Paris: Albin Michel.

Lévy, R. (1987), *Du suspect au coupable. Le travail de police judiciaire*, Geneva: Medecine et Hygiène.

Lurigio, A.J., Skogan, W.G. and Davis R.C. (1990) (eds), *Victims of Crime: Problems, Policies and Programs*, London: Sage.

Maguire, M. and Pointing, J. (1988) (eds), *Victims of Crime: A New Deal?*, Milton Keynes: Open University Press.

Mawby, R.I. and Gill, M.L. (1987), *Crime Victims: Needs, Services and the Voluntary Sector*, London: Tavistock.

Mawby, R.I. and Walklate, S. (1994), *Critical Victimology*, London: Sage.

Mayhew, P. and van Dijk, J.J.M. (1997), *Criminal Victimisation in Eleven Industrialised Countries: Key Findings from the 1996 International Crime Victims Survey*, Den Haag: WODC.

Ocqueteau, F. and Pérez-Diaz, Cl. (1989), 'Le regard des français sur la justice pénale', *Bulletin CLCJ*, **19**, 41–47.

Ocqueteau, F. and Pottier, M.-L. (1995), *Vigilance et sécurité dans les grandes surfaces*, Paris: L'Harmattan, IHESI.

Patin, M. (1957), 'L'action civile des tribunaux répressifs', *Recueil Général des Lois et de la Jurisprudence*, 8–12.

Philips, D. (1989), 'Good Men to Associate and Bad Men to Conspire: Associations for The Prosecution of Felons in England 1760–1860', in D. Hay and F. Snyder (eds), *Policing and Prosecution in Britain: 1750–1850*, Oxford: Clarendon Press, 113–70.

Pinto, L. (1989), 'Du 'pépin' au litige de consommation', *Actes de la Recherche en Sciences Sociales*, **76–77**, 65–81.

Pradel, J. (1980), *Droit Pénal, Tome 2: Procédure Pénale*, Paris: Cujas.

Rangeon, F. (1987), 'Ils ont encore…', *Informations Sociales*, **4**, 82–6.

Rivero, J. (1983), *Droit Administratif*, Paris: Dalloz.

Robert, P. (1988a), 'Le sociologue et le droit', *Sciences Sociales et Santé*, **6**(1), 69–76.

Robert, P. (1988b), 'L'action des groupements: Des stratégies évolutives', *Archives de Politiques Criminelles*, **10**, 59–78.

Robert, P., Aubusson de Cavarlay, B., Pottier, M.-L. and Tournier, P. (1994), *Les comptes du crime*, Paris: L'Harmattan.

Robert, P. and Lévy, R. (1985), 'Histoire et question pénale', *Revue d'Histoire Moderne et Contemporaine*, **XXXII**, juillet–septembre, 481–526.

Robert, P., Zauberman, R., Pottier, M.-L. and Lagrange, H. (1995), 'Mesurer le crime: entre statistiques de police et enquêtes de victimation (1985–1995)', *Revue Française de Sociologie*, **40**(2), 255–94.

Roberts, A.R. (1990), *Helping Crime Victims: Research Policy and Practice*, London: Sage.

Rock, P. (1986), *A View from the Shadows*, Oxford: Clarendon Press.

Rousseaux, X. (1993), 'Initiative particulière et poursuite d'office. L'action pénale en Europe (XIIème–XVIIIème siècles)', *Bulletin de l'IAHCCJ*, **18**, 58–92.

Rousseaux, X. and Lévy, R. (1997) (eds), *Le pénal dans tous ses états. Justice et sociétés en Europe (XIIème–XX^{ème}siècles)*, Brussels: FUSL.

Sbriccoli, M. (1974), *Crimen Laesae Majestatis*, Milan: Giuffre.

Scarman, L. (1986), *The Scarman Report: The Brixton Disorders, 10–12 April, 1981*, Harmondsworth: Penguin.

Sebba, L. (1996), *Third Parties: Victims and the Criminal Justice System*, Columbus: Ohio State University Press.

Secondi-Nix, M. (1994), *Bilan des actions civiles, 1976–1994*, Paris: Union Fédérales des Consommateurs.

Secondi-Nix, M. (1998), 'Criminal Justice and the Fight against Racism', *Penal Issues*, **9**, 3–5.

Shapland, J. (1988), 'Fiefs and Peasants: Accomplishing Change for Victims in the Criminal Justice System', in M. Maguire and J. Pointing (eds), *Victims of Crime: A New Deal?*, Milton Keynes: Open University Press, 187–94.

Shapland, J., Willmore, J. and Duff, P. (1985), *Victims in the Criminal Justice System*, Aldershot: Gower.

Sharpe, J. (1997), 'The Law, Law Enforcement, State Formation and National Integration in Late Medieval and Early Modern England', in X. Rousseaux and R. Lévy (eds), *Le pénal dans tous ses États. Justice et sociétés en Europe (XIIème–XX^{ème}siècles)*, Brussels: FUSL, 65–80.

Sorman, G. (1984), *La solution libérale*, Paris: Fayard.

Soubiran, F., (1988) 'Grève et guerre judiciaire: Le recours au juge pénal dans un conflit du travail', *Déviance et Société*, **12**(1), 57–74.

Storch, R.D. (1975), 'The Plague of the Blue Locusts: Police Reform and Popular Resistance in Northern England, 1840–1857', *International Review of Social History*, **20**, 61–90.

Storch, R.D. (1976), 'The Policeman as Domestic Missionary: Urban Discipline and Popular Culture in Northern England, 1850–1880', *Journal of Social History*, **9**(4), 481–509.

Strayer, J.R. (1970), *The Medieval Origins of the Modern State*, Princeton, NJ: Princeton University Press.

Sutton, M. (1995), 'Supply by Theft. Does the Market for Second-hand Goods Play a Role in Keeping Crime Figures High?', *British Journal of Criminology*, **35**(3), 400–16.

Thompson, E.P. (1977), *Whigs and Hunters. The Origin of the Black Act*, Harmondsworth: Penguin.

Tonry, M. (1997) (ed.), *Ethnicity, Crime, and Immigration: Comparative and Cross-National Perspectives*, Chicago: Chicago University Press.

van Dijk, J.J.M. (1988), 'Ideological Trends within the Victim Movement: An International Perspective', in M. Maguire and J. Pointing (eds), *Victims of Crime: A New Deal?*, Milton Keynes: Open University Press, 116–26.

Verdier, R. (1980), *La vengeance, études d'ethnologie, d'histoire et de philosophie*, Vol 1: *Vengeance et pouvoir dans quelques sociétés extra-occidentales*, Paris: Cujas.

Verdier, R. (1984), 'Le désir, le devoir et l'interdit: Masques et usages de la vengeance', *Déviance et Société*, **8**(2), 181–93.

Vidal, J. (1963), 'Observations sur la nature juridique de l'action civile', *Revue de Science Criminelle et de Droit Pénal Comparé*, 481–528.

Weinberger, B. (1981), 'The Police and the Public in Mid-Nineteenth-Century Warwickshire', in V. Bailey (ed.), *Policing and Punishment in Nineteenth Century England*, London: Croom Helm, 65–93.

Williams, A. (1979), *The Police of Paris 1718–1789*, Baton-Rouge: Louisiana State University Press.

Zauberman, R. (1982), 'Renvoyants et renvoyés', *Déviance et Société*, **6**(1), 23–52.

Zauberman, R. (1991), 'Victimes en France: Des positions, intérêts et stratégies diverses', *Déviance et Société*, **15**(1), 27–49.

Zauberman, R. and Robert, P. (1995), *Du côté des victimes: Un autre regard sur la délinquance*, Paris: L'Harmattan.

Zorzi, A. (1997), 'La justice pénale dans les états Italiens (communes et principautés Territoriales) du XIIIème au XVIème siècle', in X. Rousseaux and R. Lévy (eds), *Le pénal dans tous ses États. Justice et sociétés en Europe (XIIème–XX[ème]siècles)*, Brussels: FUSL, 47–63.

3　The Individualization of the Victim: From Positivism to Postmodernism

Leslie Sebba

To describe the transformations in penal philosophy and penological practice in the second half of the twentieth century as a move 'from the individualization of the offender to the individualization of the victim' – a theme elaborated by the late Marvin Wolfgang in a lecture, considered below – certainly captures the spirit of much that has occurred during this period.

During the 1950s the rehabilitation of the offender was still the dominant declared objective of correctional philosophy, as evidenced by the perusal of any textbook of the period (for example, Barnes and Teeters, 1959). While the developments which occurred during the following decades were complex and multifaceted (cf. Cohen, 1985) the decline of the rehabilitational ideal (if not its total disappearance)[1] has been widely acknowledged. This development appears to have reached its peak in the 1970s with the publication of trenchant critiques of the rehabilitation ideology (American Friends Service Committee, 1971) and of its achievements (Lipton *et al.*, 1975), accompanied by suggested alternative policies (Fogel, 1975; von Hirsch, 1976). This same decade also witnessed the emergence of victimology and the victim movement, with the development of victim compensation boards and victim support programmes, as well as the organization of the First International Symposia on Victimology.[2]

While there appears to be no *direct* connection between these two sets of developments, their related chronology was surely no mere coincidence. On the ideological level rehabilitation was replaced by 'just deserts' as the dominant objective in the penological discourse. This model, as advocated by Andrew von Hirsch (1976; 1985), argued that the sentence imposed upon the offender should be determined by the seriousness of the offence, which in turn was to be measured primarily, albeit not exclusively, by *the amount of harm inflicted on the victim*. While this development by no means gave full expression to the demands of the victims' rights movement, the conceptual link between the 'justice model' and the victim is nevertheless clear (a theme to which I return later). On a more practical level, victim advocates often drew attention to their frustration at the emphasis, in the then prevailing criminal justice process, on the offender's needs – a process in which the victim played no part. Finally, on a systemic level, it is arguable that the retreat from the concern with the treatment of offenders – and the resources invested therein – freed energies for a new target, namely victims.

In this context it is interesting to note that while from a present-day perspective these two developments – the de-emphasis on the concern for the offender and the rise of a concern for the victim – appear to have occurred simultaneously (with the 1970s as the critical period for both), at the time it seemed otherwise. Attention was first drawn to this theme in the victimological literature by Wolfgang in a seminal lecture (published in 1982 but delivered in 1979), in which he stated that 'although the absence of attributes about the offender is *now* considered appropriate in a sanctioning system, the presence of victim attributes *might be* considered acceptable…' (Wolfgang, 1982: 49, emphasis added). At that time, the principle of offender individualization had already been abandoned, while victim individualization was merely being mooted.[3]

The precise sequence of events, however, is not the main focus of this chapter. Its purpose is, rather, to consider some of the broader implications of the concept of victim individualization. In an earlier article co-authored with Edna Erez – by way of tribute to Professor Wolfgang[4] – we noted that two distinct meanings were attributed to this expression. In considering the possibility of a sanctioning system with a greater victim orientation, Wolfgang cited examples from historical codes wherein sanctions were differentiated according to whether the victim was a slave or a master, while he noted that certain modern penal provisions made reference to the age and gender of the victim. In the spirit of the old–new just deserts' philosophy, such variables could be incorporated into a sentencing tariff, which might be based on the techniques he himself had developed with Thorsten Sellin for the measurement of offence seriousness.[5]

The concept of victim individualization envisaged here by Wolfgang, despite its purported symmetry with the *offender* individualization that it was supposed to be replacing, was actually very different from the latter. Wolfgang's sanctioning scheme did not seem to be premised on the courts having any specific knowledge about the *personality* of the victim, in the way that a probation officer's report would enlighten the court in respect of the offender under the old system. A few basic sociodemographic (or political) variables relating to the victim would seem sufficient for the court to locate the appropriate directive in the tariff for the case in question. Thus, although the term he invoked was 'individualization', Wolfgang was really focusing on *categories* of victims, rather than the personalities and/or circumstances of *individual* victims. The article by Erez and Sebba (1999) referred to earlier shows how officially formulated contemporary penal policy has, at least in some areas, opted for the more literal meaning of individualization (as reflected, for example, in victim impact statements), but the article also refers to empirical findings by one of the authors which indicate that, in the course of the implementation of the policy, criminal justice personnel generally resort to categorization or typification of the cases[6] – thereby in effect adopting a policy of individualization in Wolfgang's sense.

Further reflection on this dichotomy between individualization in the narrow sense and categorization suggests that the tension between these two concepts may serve as a point of departure for an analysis of the relationship between contemporary victim orientation and the offender orientation that preceded it, and for a consideration of a number of current issues pertaining to the victim's role in the criminal justice system. It may also stimulate some wider concerns relating to the locus of the victim in the community and the survival of 'modernism' in a victim-oriented system. In the discussion which follows I will consider the varying nature and significance of victim individualization in the context of three models:

1 a victim rehabilitation model;
2 a just deserts model; and
3 a victim's rights or participation model.

I will conclude with a brief consideration of the wider issues referred to.

A Victim Rehabilitation Model

The expression 'from the individualization of the offender to the individualization of the victim' suggests that the policies hitherto applicable to the offender would now be applicable to the victim. Individualization of the offender was the watchword of the rehabilitation model[7] which was adopted in the late nineteenth century and held sway until the 1970s. As noted above, the decline of this ideology was coincidental in time with the rise of the victim movement. In ideological terms, however, the development of a victim rehabilitation model would have been in no way incompatible with a *continuation* of the offender rehabilitation model, subject only to the availability of resources. Both policies are consistent with the premises of positivism and social defence, and the state's assumption of responsibility for the provision of remedies for social problems.[8] It may be observed in this connection that early critics of victimology did indeed note certain similarities in the approaches and the methodologies of victimology and criminology – in particular their common weaknesses (see Bruinsma and Fiselier, 1982). These writers focused mainly on the characteristics of *aetiological research* in criminology and victimology. However, the similarities may be even stronger in the area of *societal responses* to the respective phenomena (that is, to criminality on the one hand and to victimization on the other).

Thus, for example, one of the key concepts in the development of the penal system in the late nineteenth century was the term 'classification', which was seen as a *sine qua non* for the application of scientific methods to the rehabilitation of offenders.[9] Rather than being punished exclusively on the basis of their offences, offenders were to be placed in a prison regime or treatment programme in accordance with their characteristics, as deemed appropriate by professional experts (the concepts of classification and individualization are interwoven here: see below).

Two distinct types of classification developed in Victorian penal policy. These came to be labelled 'horizontal' and 'vertical' classification. The former refers to the allocation of offenders *ab initio* to their appropriate sanctioning framework. The latter designates the need to re-evaluate the appropriateness of the mode and duration of the punishment/treatment as the offender progresses through the system (Grunhut, 1972: 179 ff.). While this last process seems inevitably to have incorporated a strong component of individualization in the literal sense, the initial (horizontal) classification would have been based mainly on general characteristics such as the age, sex, and criminal record of the offender (ibid.: 180). In the words of Max Grunhut:

> *Individualisation... is a relative concept.* In its extreme, it would imply an almost unlimited discretion, incompatible with the general rules and standards of any legal system at all. In the light of practical experience, a reasonable and sufficiently flexible Progressive Stage system facilitates that degree of individualisation which is possible and desirable for the treatment of some 500 prisoners in an average penal institution. (Ibid.: 88, emphasis added)

This usage of the term 'individualization' bears some resemblance to the meaning attributed to it by Wolfgang, that is, a sophisticated form of categorization.[10]

In some respects, the classification and categorization of offenders were intensified during the first half of the twentieth century. The 'social defence' school proposed that correctional resources should be targeted on the 'dangerous' (Ancel, 1965: 51, 110–11), while most legal systems created new categories of offender – recidivists, habitual offenders, sexual or dangerous psychopaths – for whom longer and more intensive penal regimes were provided, such as so-called 'preventive detention' in the UK and the 'Baumes Law' in the United States (cf. Grunhut, 1972: ch. 14; Rennie, 1978).

Beyond such classification, a more 'extreme' form of individualization (to use Grunhut's expression) was envisaged by Grunhut himself in some instances – notably in the context of probation. A 'prognostic orientation' and a casework approach were to be adopted in the pre-sentence investigation (Grunhut, 1972: 305), while the supervisory function of the probation officer involved a total involvement in the offender's life – 'a highly individualised treatment ... as multiple in its features as human affairs usually are' (ibid.: 308).

A number of parallels with contemporary approaches to the victim can be observed here. While the public in general is perceived as being in need of protection and as requiring assistance on being victimized, certain categories of the population are seen to be particularly vulnerable to victimization and therefore in need of special protection. There is surely an analogy here with the special provisions directed at dangerous offenders referred to above.

Thus, for example, recent legislation in Israel (Sebba, forthcoming) specifies higher penalties for offences committed against 'vulnerable persons' and mandates their reporting to the police or social services. Children involved in sex offences or domestic violence for whom a courtroom ordeal might prove to be traumatic testify via social workers rather than in court, unless the social worker certifies that no harm will be caused to the child by testifying in court. Adult victims of sex offences may also be relieved from facing their (alleged) attackers in the courtroom by a statutory provision for a video link or its equivalent. Victim impact statements, too, are restricted to sex offences. Such provisions, many of which are also prevalent in other jurisdictions, may be compared with the 'horizontal classification' of offenders. The next stage may well be to make special provision for repeat victims in view of their aggravated trauma, in symmetry with earlier policies relating to recidivist offenders.[11]

Further, many victim-related provisions in the area of evidence and procedure (including most of those referred to above) are not applicable automatically but are invoked at the discretion of the court (cf. ibid.). The policy reflected therein is thus even more unequivocally one of individualization (that is, in its literal meaning), since the relevant provisions are only implemented insofar as they are perceived to meet the needs of the particular victim in the instant case.

The individual victim rehabilitation model is today applied most explicitly *outside* the narrow framework of the criminal justice system by the community agencies engaged in victim assistance and support, including the specialized centres for rape victims, hostels for battered women and so on – even though these agencies may have additional agenda, such as victim, or female, empowerment (see Mawby and Gill, 1987). While such programmes are, by definition, restricted to certain categories of victim, they all inevitably emphasize meeting the specific needs of the individual victim. Thus, we have here a combination of 'horizontal classification' and personalized individualization which would seem to correspond to the apogee of the erstwhile treatment model.

Another form of community, or state, assistance takes the form of compensation for the victim from a public authority. Since this is paid from the public exchequer it may be viewed as a form of victim rehabilitation rather than mere restitution, which should in principle be payable by the offender. Here, too, there is tension between the two meanings of individualization. The UK Criminal Injuries Compensation Board has recently moved from a scheme of open-ended benefits, where the amount was based on a calculation of the extent of the injury and its consequences (akin to tort law), to a standardized tariff system (cf. Miers, 1997: ch. 8; Duff, 1998).

A more specific parallel between offender and victim rehabilitation may be noted in the explicit invocation of the 'medical model' in the diagnosis of some victims who are perceived as suffering from certain pathological conditions, such as battered women syndrome or post-traumatic stress disorder (cf. Weed, 1995: ch. 2). By the same token, research suggests that while many – indeed, apparently most – victimizations are overcome within a relatively short period (cf. Sebba, 1996a: ch. 4), others may endure for years, even decades. These findings raise the question as to whether, on the analogy of prison terms, victim assistance should be offered for a determinate or indeterminate period.

Another link of great symbolic significance between these two rehabilitational orientations – addressing the needs of the offender and the victim respectively – is found in the role of the probation officer. Probation has represented, even more than imprisonment, the hope and belief that a method had been developed whereby offenders could indeed be rehabilitated on an individual basis (cf. Grunhut, 1972: ch. 12; Rothman, 1980: chs 2 and 3), the probation service providing both the chief diagnostic tool (the pre-sentence investigation or 'social enquiry' report) and the main treatment agency for this purpose (probation supervision). In recent years the probation officer has been required to apply these skills to a new object – the victim.[12] Thus, probation officers may be involved both in determining the impact of the offence on the victim and in attending to the victim's welfare – akin to their diagnostic and treatment functions with offenders (Williams, 1996).

The final point which links individualized offender and victim rehabilitation arises in the context of selecting the optimal treatment. Much of the research conducted on victim-oriented programmes – like the early research on offender treatment – may be criticized on methodological grounds, and the findings as to the relative effectiveness of the various programmes must be considered inconclusive (cf. Sebba, 1996a; Fattah, 1999). For victim rehabilitation, then, the 'What works?' debate is still in its infancy.

Just Deserts and Victim Individualization

As noted earlier, according to Wolfgang, the concept of the individualization of the victim could play a key role in developing the just deserts model of sentencing – a model reflected in the US legislative reform which was being adopted when he presented his views (Wolfgang, 1982: 48). Wolfgang noted the de-emphasis of the individualization of the offender under this model:

> None of the attributes of the offender – his personality needs, his mental status, his prior record, his emotional state – is important when the moment of sentencing disposition arrives. Only the seriousness of the crime should be considered. (ibid.)[13]

Wolfgang then considered what was meant by 'seriousness'. While in the conclusion to his article he declared that 'the seriousness of the crime can be defined not only in terms of the culpability of the offender but (and perhaps principally) by the degree of harm inflicted on specified victims' (ibid.: 57), in the earlier part he placed greater emphasis on the victim's *characteristics and attributes* (ibid.: 48). Indeed, after citing examples of victim attributes incorporated in contemporary and earlier legislation, he presented a taxonomy of the potentially relevant variables (some relating to the victimization, others to the victim), many of which could be assigned weightings on the basis of the national survey conducted by him and his colleagues on the perceived seriousness of crime. The variables he considered were grouped as follows: age, sex and time (that is, duration of the victimization); injury severity; emotional trauma and economic loss; and the victim–offender relationship.

As noted earlier in this chapter, Wolfgang's 'individualization' here seems essentially to envisage a carefully calibrated scale, linking penalties with the seriousness of harms – which in turn would take account of certain victim characteristics. He doubted how far emotional trauma could be incorporated in a sentencing scale: 'Perhaps so varied in degree and complex in content are these psychological harms that no formal rules can be established to satisfy the principles of equity' (ibid.: 55), although he leaves open the possibility that 'the most glaring and obvious psychological effects' might be taken into account (ibid.).

It is indeed in this limited sense that structured sentencing, in the spirit of the 'just deserts' ideology, has incorporated individualization of the victim. Thus, for example, the US federal sentencing guidelines specify certain variations in the severity of the sentence in accordance with the age or vulnerability of the victim, whether in the context of particular offences or general 'victim-related adjustments'. Unusual cases of physical or psychological injury might give rise to departures from the guidelines (for a more detailed discussion, see Erez and Sebba, 1999). It should be observed, however, that while such a structured sentencing system may provide for victim impact statements to enable the court to make an accurate assessment of the extent and gravity of the harm inflicted, it does not in principle accommodate substantial deviations in the sentence in the light of highly personalized accounts of harm or unusual attributes on the part of the victim. These would be inconsistent with the ideology of just deserts, which focuses on the 'objective' harm inflicted – or even, according to von Hirsch (1985), on the amount of harm *typically* inflicted in that category of case. Moreover, substantial deviations in particular cases are in principle *precluded* by a proportionate sentencing scale (such as the federal guidelines), which fix predetermined ranges of sentence according to the parameters specified, subject only to departures in exceptional cases. The same structuring which was designed to prevent individualization of the sentence in respect of the offender, also, *pace* Wolfgang, prevents extreme forms of individualization in respect of the victim.

These issues have come to the fore in recent years in the light of trends on the part of both legislatures and courts to support sanctioning policies which would take account of both victim-specific accounts of harm (including, in particular, emotional harm) and references to the attributes of the victim, particularly, in homicide cases, of deceased victims). Notable cases in the US Supreme Court which focused on these issues were *Booth* v. *Maryland* (1987 55 LW 4836) and *S. Carolina* v. *Gathers* (1989 490 US 805) – both murder cases in which juries sentenced the defendants to death after hearing victim-related testimony. In *Booth* a victim impact statement was read to the jury, describing in some detail the emotional strain suffered by the bereaved children of the victims, as well as the upstanding character of the victims themselves. The survivors' views of the defendants and their sense of justice were also referred to. In the second case reference was made by the prosecutor to the attributes of the victim, who was a lay preacher. In these cases a majority of the Supreme Court was not prepared to recognize the relevance of such victim differentiation[14] and disapproved of the idea of 'a mini-trial on the victim's character'. Apart from the perceived inflammatory nature of some of the evidence in these cases, the question of the defendant's awareness of the victim's characteristics, and the foreseeability of the precise consequences of the criminal act, raised questions as to the culpability of the defendants with respect to these factors – seemingly important considerations in desert sentencing.

Shortly after these cases were decided, however, the Court (the composition of which had meanwhile been altered in a conservative direction, see Sebba, 1994: 161, fn. 7) changed its policy. A majority in *Payne* v. *Tennessee* (1991 115 L Ed 2d 720) in effect overruled *Booth*, and held that the emotional impact on the victims was a legitimate consideration in capital sentencing, while descriptions of the victim's attributes were permissible in order to indicate each victim's 'uniqueness as a human being' (in the words of Chief Justice Rhenquist) and his or her individuality (according to Souter J). The degree of victim individualization implicit in this decision appears to derogate from the just deserts philosophy with its implicit standardization of sentencing tariffs.

Such deviation from this philosophy will be further aggravated insofar as recognition be given to a third form of victim individualization which has become institutionalized at the sentencing stage – namely, the victim's *expression of views regarding the appropriate sentence*. While such evidence was held in *Booth* to be inadmissible (at least in capital cases), and this ruling was not reversed in *Payne* (on the ground that the point had not been argued), it is nevertheless sanctioned by many of the victim-oriented legislative and constitutional reforms, whether in the form of the victim statement of opinion, victim allocution or otherwise. Since the just deserts model cannot satisfactorily accommodate these developments, an alternative analysis must be considered.

A 'Victim's Rights' or Participatory Model

From the preceding discussion it emerges that, as noted by Wolfgang, the just deserts model indeed promotes the significance of the victim but, in the context of individualization, the victim's role is subject to a number of limitations:

1   In the first instance, the victim is not perceived here as being significant in his or her own right, but merely as part of a new orientation in sentencing in which victim harm is the primary measure of the seriousness of the offence. Information relating to the extent of the victimiza-

tion will thus be critical in determining offence seriousness, and the victim is likely to be an important source of such information. However, there is no interest in the victim as a person, and consequently no rights, whether procedural or substantive, are accorded to the victim within the framework of this model.

2   Since the nature of the victimization is relevant for the purpose of developing a sophisticated, but as nearly as possible standardized, sentencing tariff, highly personal expressions of emotional suffering will not be relevant.

3   Similarly, the personal attributes of the victim – beyond those relevant to the offence description – will also not generally be relevant. The irrelevance of the last two factors will also follow from the principles of culpability, inasmuch as they would not in many cases have been anticipated by the offender.

4   The other limitation is that if any victim attributes, or the more subjective aspects of the victimization, are nevertheless considered relevant under the just deserts model, their effects will be limited by the structure of tariff sentencing.

The above limitations are largely absent in the context of the *rehabilitation model*, in which the focus is on the victim as a person, and the scope of the enquiry as to the victim's needs is not, as a matter of principle, limited, but will vary only according to the dictates of policy and budget. This model, however, has limitations of a different character. Under the rehabilitation model, the victim (as previously was the case with the offender) is an object of policies implemented by professionals or bureaucrats who make determinations as to his or her best interests. This was the connotation of individualization when positivist criminology held sway. However, the second half of the twentieth century saw an increasing sensitivity to human rights, with the autonomy of the individual as one of its key concepts.[15] This, indeed, was one of the reasons for the decline of the rehabilitative ideal. Today, it is almost inconceivable to hold to a concept of individualization which does not incorporate personal autonomy. This in turn implies a much more active role than that possessed by the victim (or the offender) under the rehabilitation model; autonomy imports such rights as participation, self-expression and representation.

As is well known, recent years have witnessed a flood of victim-related legislation.[16] Many states in the USA have enacted 'victims' bills of rights', by way of analogy with the early amendments to the federal constitution, generally known as the (suspect/defendant's) bill of rights. Furthermore, a number of states have amended their constitutions in order to guarantee recognition of victims' rights, and an amendment to the federal constitution is currently under consideration (see National Victim Center, 1996; Beloof, 1999a). Not all this legislation concerns what I have referred to here as autonomy rights; much of it is more concerned with victim rehabilitation – for example, provision for victim services and compensation. Some provisions are designed to ensure that the victim is kept informed of the progress of the investigation and trial, while others are somewhat vague, such as those guaranteeing victims the 'right to dignity'.

The expression 'victims' rights' may be applied to all such provisions where the provisions are non-discretionary.[17] Since the present discussion is only concerned with provisions which grant the victim an active role in the system, the term *victim-participatory model* may be more appropriate here (cf. Beloof, 1999b). Provisions which fall firmly within this paradigm include those which guarantee the victim the right to be heard at all relevant (or 'critical') stages of the criminal justice system. Such a provision is found in the Florida constitution, and is the basis of the proposed amendment to the federal constitution. The right would apply, *inter alia*, to the decisions on the part of criminal justice agencies to release on bail, to charge, to negotiate a plea-bargain, to convict, to sentence and to grant parole.

Provisions of this nature render the victim not merely a source of information as to the dimensions of his or her victimization, but rather an active party in the criminal process, even if not fully recognized as such. This enhanced role for the victim has given rise to much controversy (see Henderson, 1985; Hall, 1991; Sebba, 1996a), and to a number of evaluations as to its effects (see Hillenbrand and Smith, 1989; Erez, 1994; Sebba, 1996; Kelly and Erez, 1997; Beatty *et al.*, 1997). In the context of this chapter, however, the interesting question relates to the implications of such provisions for the 'individualization of the victim'.

On one level, the very participation of the victim in the proceedings (other than as a mere witness) gives a tangible meaning to this expression beyond that possible under the just deserts model considered above, which in principle is only concerned with an account of the harm inflicted upon the victim, not with the victim as a person. Moreover, active participation on the part of the victim inevitably obviates the restrictions referred to earlier in the context of the just deserts model: the full extent of victim harm will be in evidence, as will victim attributes.[18]

Thus, while the courts may try to reconcile these more encompassing expressions of victim participation with the more conservative objectives of victim impact statements,[19] it seems that, underlying these developments, there are, in principle, two distinct styles of victim involvement. The more passive style is designed primarily to ensure that the decision-making authorities are fully apprised of the victim's situation, and in particular the full extent of the victimization. This style is thus largely consistent with a just deserts philosophy. Moreover, insofar as it may also take into account various needs of the victim, such as the prevention of trauma in the courtroom, this style of victim involvement in the process is also in keeping with a rehabilitation philosophy. It will allow for a victim impact statement, but will fall short of permitting such active participation as might directly influence the outcome of the proceedings[20] – including even an indirect presentation before the court of the victim's views as to the appropriate sentence by means of a victim impact statement or otherwise. This has been the policy generally advocated in the UK, as reflected in the recent report issued by JUSTICE (1998: ch. 4), and is consistent with the policy of the Court of Appeal (ibid.: 88) to the effect that the mercifulness or vengefulness of the victim should not be considered a relevant factor.

However, even this differentiation – between victim impact and victim views – may not always be clear-cut. In a recent Court of Appeal case (*R.* v. *Mills* [1988] 2 Cr. App. R. (S) 252) the defendant was convicted of assaulting the mother of his child who was endeavouring to end their relationship. Her subsequent forgiving attitude was taken into consideration by the court on the grounds that it was relevant to the *impact of the offence*. Similarly, in a capital murder case in the state of Nevada it was held that 'in asking the jury to show no mercy' K (a survivor) was not expressing her opinion as to what sentence W (the defendant) should receive, but was 'only asking the jury to return the most severe verdict that it deemed appropriate under the facts and circumstances'.[21]

As noted, however, a more explicit contribution by victims to the process has been expressly incorporated in many recent enactments in the United States. The constitutionality of the presentation of testimony as to victims' views on the sentence was left open in the *Payne* case, but has been assumed by many courts to be permissible, at least in non-capital cases. Thus in another Nevada case, in which the defendant was sentenced for murder to life imprisonment without parole, the US Supreme Court found no objection to the testimony of the murdered woman's son to the effect that the defendant and the co-defendant 'would spend the rest of their lives in jail and that they would die there. And have every torment possible that a jail can give them.'[22]

Granting victims active participation rights, on the other hand, may itself be a relativist policy that is not necessarily calculated to have a radical effect on the criminal justice system. For an individual victim to have a significant influence on the outcome of the case would require that:

1 the victim elects to exercise his or her participation rights;
2 the participation is active; such that

3   some variance is apparent with the respect to the input of different victims (even where subjected to similar harm) and/or victims' views differ from those of the relevant criminal justice personnel whose policies would otherwise prevail; and

4   victims' views are, at least to some extent, heeded by the decision-making authorities.[23]

As to the third point, attitude surveys of the general public and of victims are often cited to indicate certain trends – for example, that levels of punitiveness are reduced when respondents are presented with specific cases, or that the gap between the public's views and court practices is less wide than generally believed.[24] But even in surveys indicating a high degree of overall consensus within samples there remains substantial variance among individuals (in respect of 'outliers'). On the first two points, however, studies show that victims do not necessarily avail themselves of the opportunity to participate (Kelly and Erez, 1997: 240–41), while some early experiments indicated that even participating victims (in a plea negotiation proceeding) appeared to have been intimidated by the experienced law enforcement personnel and added relatively little to the proceeding (Kerstetter and Heinz, 1979; Buchner *et al.*, 1984). As to the effects of victim interventions or opinions when expressed (the fourth point above), empirical evidence on this is as yet sparse, but some studies suggest that the effect of victim-related testimony may be modest (cf. Walsh, 1986; Kelly and Erez, 1997: 238–39; Erez and Roger, 1999).[25] Based, *inter alia*, on this type of finding, some writers have argued that victims' rights legislation has a purely symbolic function and is not really intended to change the existing system. A more charitable view would emphasize the value to victims of participation for its own sake (Wemmers, 1996; Sebba, 1996a; Kelly and Erez, 1997: 239–40). Whichever evaluation is correct, the individualization of the victim as a tenet of criminal justice policy is, on this analysis, of modest dimensions.

The legislative formulations referring to victims' statements of opinion and the victims' right to be heard, together with the surrounding rhetoric, suggest a far more significant impact on the part of individual victims (or in the name of deceased victims) than indicated by most of the empirical studies referred to above. Its importance should not entirely be discounted in the light of the empirical evidence, since this rhetoric may influence – as well as reflect – the public agenda and thereby longer-term policies. Moreover, the empirical evidence is not uniform.

Furthermore, even the US Supreme Court cases referred to above, in which the admissibility of victim's *views* was not explicitly acknowledged, are perceived in the literature as opening the door to a revolutionized criminal justice system based on vengeance and personalized justice (Boudreaux,

1989; Sarat, 1997). The rhetoric of the Supreme Court in these cases and its analysis of the traumatic nature of the criminal acts and their emotional effects upon the victims (or survivors), as well as their allusions to the lifestyle and morals of the victims, suggest a new dynamic of the personalization of the victim which may be difficult to identify with traditional normative approaches. According to one view: 'Such an assertion of individuality and of the sanctity of the individual represents *the victims' rights movement's response to the challenge of postmodernism*' (Sarat, 1997: 175, emphasis added).

Some Contemporary Perspectives: Postmodernism and 'Community'

Sarat's designation of the victim-oriented assertiveness of the US Supreme Court in the cases referred to as a reflection of 'the victims' rights movement's response to the challenge of postmodernism' may indeed be of assistance in understanding this trend towards a more personalized, even volatile, orientation in the criminal justice system – at least at the sanctioning end. While the term 'postmodernism' conveys a wide variety of meanings (Wicke, 1994), it is generally understood as standing for an antagonism to universals or 'monolithic truths', to the perception of knowledge as objective, and to rationality and bureaucratic order (Best and Kellner, 1991; Ferrell, 1998).

In the present context, clearly von Hirsch's desert model of justice represents modernism, with its purported Kantian universalism, and its advocacy of pseudo(?)-scientific mechanisms (such as sentencing guidelines) for its implementation.[26] It will be recalled that this model, with its emphasis on victim harm as a measure of offence seriousness and therefore as the basis for determining the severity of the sanction, was the point of departure for the concept of victim individualization. Even the notion of victim *categories* may be problematical for postmodern approaches based upon 'fragmentation and differences, rather than unity and diversity' (Freeman, 1994: 1149). Thus a retreat from modernism would result in the replacement of (purportedly) measured and predictable sanctioning responses by less predictable responses. Insofar as postmodernism also comports the erosion of judgmental authority (Ferrell, 1998), the sanctioning response may rather reflect the wishes of the individual victim[27] – including vengeance. Such an approach would be reminiscent of traditional systems of justice such as encountered in the recent Saudi case of the Australian nurses where, following Islamic law, commutation of the death penalty was dependent upon the consent of the family of the victim. The anti-modernist character of this approach thus becomes clear: it is a return to *pre*-modernism.[28]

Attention should also be drawn here to the emphasis in the Supreme Court judgments and the related literature on *hearing the victim's voice*. This may be consistent with two distinct trends in contemporary legal analysis. On the one hand, hearing the victim may enable a greater focus to be placed on the *emotional aspects* of the harm inflicted. The call for a greater emphasis in the context of legal claims (both in the civil and criminal spheres) on emotional suffering is forcefully argued by feminist writers (see, e.g., Laster and O'Malley, 1996) – a call which may be consistent with postmodern analysis (cf. Barnett, 1998).[29] Secondly, postmodern approaches lay emphasis on the importance of interpretive activity (see, e.g., Munger, 1998), and of how the 'subject' understands the system (Freeman, 1994: 1149, citing J.M. Balkin) – a minimum condition of which is surely to grant the subject 'voice'.

This, in turn, leads to the focus on narrative and 'storytelling' which is the concern of much contemporary legal writing (see, e.g., Brooks and Gewirtz, 1996). There has been some discussion as to whether the emphasis on storytelling in the legal system is calculated to empower weaker parties or to bolster up the powerful.[30] Thus Minow (1993) lays emphasis on the importance of heeding the stories of 'outsider' populations. Gewirtz (1996), identifying the victim as such an outsider, adopts this argument to justify the granting of victims a greater voice in the system. Bandes (1996), on the other hand, sees such measures not as a mechanism for the empowerment of oppressed victims, but rather as a means of overriding the voice of oppressed defendants. This view is consistent with those critiques of the victim movement who perceive it as having furthered the 'law and order' agenda (Elias, 1993; Scheingold et al., 1994).

Another issue of particular interest in the present context is to what extent the 'victim's voice' should in fact be identified with the *individual* victim, or whether s/he should be perceived as representing 'the community' – or a sector thereof.[31] It is sometimes argued that the justification for victim participation in sentencing is that victims' views reflect those of the community (Beloof, 1999b).[32] Indeed, postmodernist approaches, which, as noted, tend to see society as fragmented, base their analysis on its division into myriad cultural units. The 'subjectivities' are thus primarily not individual subjectivities, but *group* subjectivities.[33]

This individual-group tension is in fact more complex in the context of victimization, and raises definitional issues with regard to the question: 'Who is the victim?' Underlying the foregoing analysis of the individualization of the victim was an implicit assumption that victimization was indeed an individual experience. This assumption is of course invalid for at least two reasons. In the first place many acts of victimization are directed at groups – whether households, businesses, religious, ethnic or community institutions – and persons belonging to the same social/ethnic/religious group as the immediate victim may feel threatened even if not directly victimized. Secondly, most victim experiences, even if directed at individuals, are shared by a number of family members and other support persons who are directly (or at least indirectly) affected by the victimization.[34] This group of indirect victims corresponds roughly to the concept of the victim's 'personal community' (Weed, 1995: 35, citing Jules Henry). These empirical arguments for extending the concept of victimization beyond the individual to a wider community definition may dovetail with the cultural claims referred to above regarding 'group subjectivities'. The criminal justice system, it is argued, should take into account the 'emotional property rights' of the family and friends of the victim, such that 'the harm done to an individual's personal community can become a moral claim against society...' (ibid.: 34–5).

This line of argument need not inevitably lead to a vengeance-wreaking criminal justice system. If the objective is to empower the individual victim and to facilitate his/her self-expression, this can surely be better achieved by alternative and more humane forms of destructuring, such as restorative justice or conferencing.[35]

In conclusion: Marvin Wolfgang's new sentencing paradigm whereby individualization of the offender would be replaced by individualization of the victim seemed to indicate a new but rational sentencing structure, essentially consistent with von Hirsch's desert model. However, the pressures in favour of a more *participatory* victim-oriented criminal justice system, encouraged by some contemporary post-modern and communitarian orientations may be leading to a more open-ended and uncertain system, in which empathy, emotions and subjectivities play a significant role. These pressures have the potential for being directed by political forces either in the direction of vengeance and law-and-order repressiveness or towards more conciliatory models of informal justice.

Notes

1 Recently there seems to have been something of a revival of this ideal, whether in the form of empirical evaluations of 'What works?' (Goldblatt and Lewis, 1998; Sherman *et al.*, 1998), or in the context of neo-rehabilitational theories such as restorative justice.

2 For accounts of the development of the victim movement, see Doerner and Lab (1995), Weed (1995), and Sebba (1996a).

3 Wolfgang accordingly formulated his proposal as follows: 'The *de*-individualisation of the offender may be replaced by the individualisation of the victim' (1982: 49, emphasis added). From today's perspective, the 'de' seems inappropriate.

4 See Erez and Sebba (1999). The article appears in a special issue of *Advances in Criminological Theory* which was intended to honour Professor Wolfgang in his lifetime, but regrettably will be in his memory.

5 See Sellin and Wolfgang (1978). See also the application of this methodology to sentencing policy envisaged in Wolfgang (1976).

6 See also Erez and Rogers (1999). There is a parallel here with Sudnow's concept of 'normal crimes', based on his finding that negotiations between prosecutors and defence counsel were determined by the typification of the cases rather than their actual content (see Sudnow, 1965).

7 See Saleilles' (1911) monumental analysis.

8 I have considered a comparison between this approach to the victim and its main alternative – namely, the involvement of the victim in adversary proceedings – in earlier publications (see Sebba, 1982; 1996a; and 1999). For other analyses of this type see van Dijk (1988), Ziegenhagen and Benyi (1981), Dignan and Cavadino (1996) and Beloof (1999b).

9 See Grunhut (1972: 178 ff.) and also Cohen (1985: 191 ff.) who refers to 'the obsession with classification' (ibid.: 192).

10 Cf. also Saleilles (1911) who identified three types of individualisation of punishment: (a) 'legal' (i.e. statutory); (b) 'judicial'; and (c) 'administrative'. According to this differentiation, the categorization becomes more personalized from stage to stage.

11 The phenomenon of repeat victims is discussed in Chapter 5 of this volume by Jan van Dijk.

12 These developments naturally give rise to a problem as to the 'allegiance' of the probation service and how it is perceived by offenders and victims respectively. The recent Israeli law providing for victim impact statements specifies that the same probation officer should not fulfil both functions, but this may not resolve the issue of how the agency as a whole is perceived.

13 This de-emphasis of the offender's personality has indeed been perceived by later commentators to constitute an integral part of the Supreme Court's victim-oriented analysis in recent cases: see Sarat, (1997: 178–79).

14 Wolfgang also was conscious of the undemocratic nature of a sentencing policy which took account of 'a hierarchy of differences' in respect of victims: see Wolfgang (1982: 48).

15 This was not necessarily true at the earlier stages of the development of human rights concepts. For example, under the UN Declaration of the Rights of the Child of 1959, 'children's rights' were to be guaranteed by ensuring that children receive education, adequate food, etc. However, by the time the UN Convention on the Rights of the Child was adopted 30 years later the child had became the holder of autonomy rights such as those referred to here. *A fortiori*, such rights must be attributed to adults.

16 The National Victim Center in the USA recently assessed their legislative database as including 28 000 victim-related statutes!

17 For a discussion of victims' service rights in an English context, see Fenwick (1995).

18 This is literally true only of *live* victims. In practice, however, under this approach provision is generally made for survivors of murder victims to convey such testimony in relation to these victims.

19 See the Court of Appeal case (*R* v. *Mills*) considered below.

20 For an analysis of the different models of victim impact statement, see Ashworth (1993).

21 *Witter* v. *Nevada* 921 P 2nd 886, Lexis 113. In *Payne* v. *Tennessee* (referred to above) the prosecutor, in the course of his argument before the jury in favour of the death

penalty, claimed that the surviving son (then an infant) would, when grown up, 'want to know what type of justice was done,' adding: 'With your verdict, you will provide the answer.' This, too, was not considered to be an expression of opinion on the part of the victim – presumably because it was attributed to the victim by the prosecutor.

22   *Randell* v. *State* 846 P.2d 278 (Nev. 1993). See also *State* v. *Matteson* 851 P. 2d 336 (Idaho, 1993).

23   This further condition would, of course, be unnecessary if the victim were to have some actual control over the decisions reached, as has sometimes been advocated (cf. Wainstein, 1988). This would also apply in informal proceedings (see below).

24   See, especially, Blumstein and Cohen (1980); Roberts (1992: 149 ff.). A German study found, on the contrary, that the public was very receptive to the idea of restitution as a sanction, even for serious offences: see Boers and Sessar (1991).

25   A study of parole decisions in Pennsylvania, however, found that victim impact statements, which frequently incorporated views expressed against early release of the prisoner, had a significant effect on the outcome (Bernat *et al.*, 1994: 124–25).

26   Wayne Morrison, however, takes a different view. In his opinion just deserts is merely 'a formula of regulation' and 'a mechanism divorced from the sets of narratives which gave a totality to classicism' (Morrison, 1994: 109).

27   It should be noted, however, that one of the central concerns of postmodern analysis is the complexity of the individual, who comprises a multiplicity of subjectivities and identities: see Barnett (1998:179), Freeman (1994: 1148-9).

28   It is arguably a return to 'pre-law', inasmuch as vengeance is often held to have been *replaced* by the earliest legal systems.

29   In the context of the 'loss of certainties and limits' characterizing postmodernity 'the victim offers a certainty, that of the experience of pain or fear or frustration, the certainty of the passionate body' (Young and Rush, 1994: 168).

30   For the same debate within the wider context of law and postmodernism, see Freeman (1994: 1153-4).

31   This point is not independent of the previous one. One purpose of focusing on disadvantaged victims is to empower that category. This approach conflicts with the view which sees litigation as disempowering per se, since it atomises the conflict among individual members of the group, rather than enabling them to act in combination; cf. Sebba (1996b: 298-9).

32   Beloof cites empirical support for this thesis. Moreover: 'Some judges have permitted community members to make oral or written presentations, implicitly relying on the assumption that the represented community itself is a "victim of the crime"' (Beloof, 1999a: 641 – extract from an article by K. Long).

33   De Sousa Santos (1993), in his essay 'The Postmodern Transition: Law and Politics', identifies four main subjectivities - the individual, family, class and nation. The outcome of this is that 'modern men and women are configurations or networks of different subjectivities' (ibid.: 106). On the complexity of the role of the individual in postmodern writings, see n. 27.

34   A study conducted several years ago by New York's Victims' Services Agency (Friedman et al., 1982) found that on average five persons were affected by each victimization.

35   I do not enter here into the question as to whether informal dispute resolution can also be a vehicle for the furtherance of *collective* interests; cf. n. 31.

References

American Friends' Service Committee (1971), *Struggle for Justice*, New York: Hill and Wang.

Ancel, M. (1965), *Social Defence*, London: Routledge and Kegan Paul.

Ashworth, A. (1993), 'Victim Impact Statements and Sentencing', *Criminal Law Review*, 498–509.

Bandes, S. (1996), 'Empathy, Narrative and Victim Impact Statements', *University of Chicago Law Review*, **63**, 361–412.

Barnes, H.E. and Teeters, N.K. (1959), *New Horizons in Criminology*, (3rd edn), Englewood Cliffs, NJ: Prentice Hall.

Barnett, H. (1998), *Introduction to Feminist Jurisprudence*, Cavendish: London.

Beatty, D., Howley, S.S. and Kilpatrick, D.G. (1997), *Crime Victim Responses Regarding Victims' Rights*, Arlington, VA: National Victim Center.

Beloof, D.E. (1999a), *Victims in Criminal Procedure*, Durham: Carolina Academic Press.

Beloof, D.E. (1999b), 'The Third Model of Criminal Process: The Victim Participation Model', *Utah Law Review*, 289–330.

Bernat, F.P., Parsonage, W.H. and Helfgott, J. (1994), 'Victim Impact Laws and the Parole Process in the United States: Balancing Victim and Inmate Rights and Interests', *International Review of Victimology*, **3**, 121–40.

Best, S. and Kellner, D. (1991), *Postmodern Theory: Critical Interrogations*, Basingstoke: Macmillan.

Blumstein, A. and Cohen, J. (1980), 'Sentencing of Convicted Offenders: An Analysis of the Public's View', *Law and Society Review*, **14**, 223–61.

Boers, K. and Sessar, K. (1991), 'Do People Really Want Punishment? On the Relationship between Acceptance of Restitution, Need for Punishment, and Fear of Crime', in K. Sessar and H-J. Kerner (eds), *Developments in Crime and Crime Control Research*, New York: Springer-Verlag, ch. 7.

Boudreaux, P. (1989), '*Booth v. Maryland* and the Individual Vengeance Rationale for Criminal Punishment', *Journal of Criminal Law and Criminology*, **80**, 177–96.

Brooks, P. and Gewirtz, P. (1996) (eds), *Law's Stories: Narrative and Rhetoric in the Law*, New Haven: Yale University Press.

Bruinsma, G.J.N. and Fiselier, J.P.S. (1982), 'The Poverty of Victimology', in H-J. Schneider (ed.), *The Victim in International Perspective*, Berlin: de Gruyter, 87–95.

Buchner, D., Clark. T.F., Hausner, J., Hernon, J.C., Wish, E.D. and Zielinski, C.M. (1984), *Evaluation of the Structured Plea Negotiation Project, Executive Summary*, Washington, DC: INSLAW.

Cohen, S. (1985), *Visions of Social Control*, Cambridge: Polity Press.

de Sousa Santos, B. (1993), 'The Postmodern Tradition: Law and Politics', in A. Sarat and T.R. Kearns (eds), *The Fate of Law*, Ann Arbor: University of Michigan Press, 79–118.

Dignan, J. and Cavadino, M. (1996), 'Towards a Framework for Conceptualising and Evaluating Models of Criminal Justice from a Victim's Perspective', *International Review of Victimology*, **4**, 153–82.

Doerner, W.G. and Lab, S. (1995), *Victimology*, Cincinnati: Anderson.

Duff, P. (1998), 'The Measure of Criminal Injuries Compensation: Political Pragmatism or a Dog's Dinner?', *Oxford Journal of Legal Studies*, **18**, 105–42.

Elias, R. (1993), *Victims Still: The Political Manipulation of Crime Victims*, Newbury Park: Sage.

Erez, E. (1994), 'Victim Participation in Sentencing: And the Debate Goes On', *International Review of Victimology*, **3**(1–2), 17–32.

Erez E. and Rogers, L. (1999), 'Victim Impact Statements and Sentencing Outcomes and Processes: The Perspectives of Legal Professionals', *British Journal of Criminology*, **39**(2), 216–39.

Erez, E., and Sebba, L. (1999), 'From Individualization of the Offender to Individualization of the Victim', in W. Laufer and F. Adler (eds), *Advances in Criminological Theory*, New Brunswick, NJ: Transaction, 171–98.

Fattah, E. (1999), 'From a Handful of Dollars to Tea and Sympathy – The Sad History of Victim Assistance', in J.J.M. van Dijk, R.G.H. van Kaam and J-A. Wemmers (eds), *Caring for Crime Victims*, Monsey: Criminal Justice Press.

Fenwick, H. (1995), 'Rights of Victims in the Criminal Justice System: Rhetoric or Reality?', *Criminal Law Review*, 843–53.

Ferrell, J. (1998), 'Stumbling toward a Critical Criminology (and into the Anarchy Imagery of Postmodernism)', in J.I. Ross (ed.), *Cutting the Edge: Current Perspectives in Radical/Critical Criminology and Criminal Justice*, Westport: Praeger, 187–206.

Fogel, D. (1975), *'We Are the Living Proof …': The Justice Model For Corrections*, Cincinnati: W.H. Anderson.

Freeman, M.D.A. (1994), *Lloyd's Introduction to Jurisprudence*, 6th ed, London: Sweet and Maxwell.

Friedman, K., Bischoff, H., Davis, R. and Person, A. (1982), *Victims and Helpers: Reactions to Crime*, Washington, DC: US Department of Justice.

Gewirtz, P. (1996), 'Victims and Voyeurs at The Criminal Trial', *Northwestern University Law Review*, **90**, 863–97.

Goldblatt, P. and Lewis, C. (1998), *Reducing Offending: An Assessment of Research Evidence on Ways of Dealing with Offending Behaviour*, London: Home Office.

Grunhut, M. (1972), *Penal Reform* (first published 1948), Montclair, NJ: Patterson Smith.

Hall, D.J. (1991), 'Victims' Voices in Criminal Court: The Need for Restraint', *American Criminal Law Review*, **28**(2), 233–66.

Henderson, L.N. (1985), 'The Wrongs of Victim Rights', *Stanford Law Review*, **37**, 937–1021.

Hillenbrand, S.W. and Smith, B.E. (1989), *Victims' Rights Legislation: An Assessment of its Impact on Criminal Justice Practitioners and Victims*, Report of the American Bar Association to the National Institute of Justice, Washington, DC: American Bar Association.

JUSTICE (1998), *Victims in Criminal Justice*, Report of the Committee on the Role of the Victim in Criminal Justice, London: JUSTICE.

Kelly, D.P. and Erez, E. (1997) 'Victim Participation in the Criminal Justice System,' in R.C. Davis, A.J. Lurigio and W.G. Skogan (eds), *Victims of Crime* (2nd edn), Thousand Oaks, CA: Sage, 231–44.

Kennard, K.L. (1989), 'The Victim's Veto: A Way to Increase Victim Impact on Criminal Case Dispositions', *California Law Review*, **77**, 417–53.

Kerstetter, W.A. and Heinz, A.M. (1979), *Pretrial Settlement Conference: An Evaluation*, Washington, DC: US Department of Justice.

Laster, K. and O'Malley, P. (1996), 'Sensitive New Age Laws: The Reassertion of Emotionality in Law', *International Journal of the Sociology of Law*, **24**, 21–40.

Lipton, D., Martinson, R. and Wilks, J. (1975), *The Effectiveness of Correctional Treatment: A Survey of Treatment Evaluation Studies*, New York: Praeger.

Mawby, R.I. and Gill, M.L. (1987), *Crime Victims: Needs, Services and the Voluntary Sector*, London: Tavistock.

Miers, D. (1997), *State Compensation for Criminal Injuries*, London: Blackstone.

Minow M. (1993), 'Partial Justice: Law and Minorities', in A. Sarat and T.R. Kearns (eds), *The Fate of Law*, Ann Arbor: University of Michigan Press, 15–77.

Morrison, W. (1994), 'Criminology, Modernity, and the "Truth" of the Human Condition: Reflections on the Melacholy of Postmodernism', in D. Nelken (ed.), *The Futures of Criminology*, London: Sage, 134–53.

Munger, F. (1998), 'Mapping Law and Society', in A. Sarat, M. Constable, D. Engel, V. Hans and S. Lawrence (eds), *Crossing Boundaries: Traditions and Transformations in Law and Society Research*, Evanston: Northwestern University Press, 21–80.

National Victim Center (1996), *The Victims' Rights Sourcebook*, Arlington, VA: National Victim Center.

Rennie Y.F. (1978), *The Search for Criminal Man: A Conceptual History of the Dangerous Offender*, Lexington, MA.: Heath.

Roberts, J.V. (1992), 'Public Opinion, Crime and Criminal Justice', *Crime and Justice*, **16**, 99–180.

Rothman, D.J. (1980), *Conscience and Convenience: The Asylum and its Alternatives in Progressive America*, Boston: Little Brown.

Saleilles, R. (1911), *The Individualisation of Punishment* (2nd edn, first published 1908), London: Heinemann.

Sarat, A. (1997), 'Vengeance, Victims and the Identities of Law', *Social and Legal Studies*, **6**(2), 163–89.

Scheingold, S.A., Olsen, T. and Pershing, J. (1994), 'Sexual Violence, Victim Advocacy, and Republican Criminology: Washington State's Community Protection Act', *Law and Society Review*, **28**, 729–63.

Sebba, L. (1982), 'The Victim's Role in the Penal Process: A Theoretical Orientation', *American Journal of Comparative Law*, **30**(2), 217–40.

Sebba, L. (1994), 'Sentencing and the Victim: The Aftermath of Payne', *International Review of Victimology*, **3**, 141–65.

Sebba, L. (1996a), *Third Parties: Victims and the Criminal Justice System*, Columbus: Ohio State University Press.

Sebba, L. (1996b), 'Informal Modes of Dispute Resolution – The Debate Continues', in L. Sebba (ed.), *Social Control and Justice: Inside or Outside the Law?*, Jerusalem: Magnes Press, 278–311.

Sebba, L. (1999), 'Victims' Rights – Whose Duties?', in J.J.M. van Dijk, R.G.H. van Kaam and J-A. Wemmers (eds), *Caring for Crime Victims*, Monsey: Criminal Justice Press, 141–58.

Sebba, L. (forthcoming), 'Victims' Rights and Legal Strategies: Israel as a Case Study', *Criminal Law Forum*.

Sellin, T. and Wolfgang, M.E. (1978), *The Measurement of Delinquency* (first published 1964), Montclair, NJ: Patterson Smith.

Sherman, L.W., Gottfredson, D.C., MacKenzie, D.L., Eck, J., Reuter, P. and Bushway, S.D. (1998), *Preventing Crime: What Works, What Doesn't, What's Promising*, Washington, DC: National Institute of Justice.

Sudnow, D. (1965), 'Normal Crimes: Sociological Features of the Penal Code in a Public Defender Office', *Social Problems*, **12**, 255–76.

van Dijk, J.J.M. (1988), 'Ideological Trends within the Victim Movement: An International Perspective', in M. Maguire and J. Ponting (eds), *Victims of Crime: A New Deal?*, Milton Keynes: Open University Press, 115–26.

von Hirsch, A. (1976), *Doing Justice: The Choice of Punishments*, New York: Hill and Wang.

von Hirsch, A. (1985), *Past or Future Crimes*, New Brunswick: Rutgers University Press.

Wainstein, K.L. (1988), 'Judicially Initiated Prosecution: A Means of Preventing Continuing Victimization in the Event of Prosecutorial Inaction', *California Law Review*, **76**, 727–67.

Walsh, A. (1986), 'Placebo Justice: Victim Recommendations and Offender Sentences in Sexual Assault Cases', *Journal of Criminal Law and Criminology*, **77**, 1126–41.

Weed, F.W. (1995), *Certainty of Justice: Reform in the Crime Victim Movement*, New York: Aldine de Gruyter.

Wemmers, J.A. (1996), *Victims in the Criminal Justice System: A Study into the Treatment of Victims and its Effects on Attitudes and Behaviours*, Amsterdam: Kugler.

Wicke, J. (1994), 'Postmodern Identity and the Legal Subject', in M.D.A. Freeman (ed.), *Lloyd's Introduction to Jurisprudence*, 6th ed, London: Sweet and Maxwell, 1166–78.

Williams, B. (1996), 'The Probation Service and Victims of Crime: Paradigm Shift or Cop-out?', *Journal of Social Welfare and Family Law*, **18**(4), 461–74.

Wolfgang, M.E. (1976), 'Seriousness of Crime and a Policy of Juvenile Justice', in J.F. Short (ed.), *Delinquency, Crime and Society*, Chicago: University of Chicago Press, 267–86.

Wolfgang, M.E. (1982), 'Basic Concepts in Victimology Theory: Individualisation of the Victim', in H-J. Schneider (ed.), *The Victim in International Perspective*, Berlin: de Gruyter, 47–58.

Young, A. and Rush, P. (1994), 'The Law of Victimage in Urbane Realism: Thinking Through Inscriptions of Violence', in D. Nelken (ed.), *The Futures of Criminology*, London: Sage, 154–72.

Ziegenhagen, E.A. and Benyi, J. (1981), 'Victim Interests, Victim Services and Social Control', in B. Galaway, and J. Hudson (eds), *Perspectives on Crime Victims*, St Louis: Mosby, 373–83.

4   Taking the Law into their Own Hands: Victims as Offenders

David Miers

Introduction

It is a common observation that many victims have themselves been offenders. Such a personal history creates difficulties where victims seek the beneficial allocation of goods or services; of particular significance are decisions of the Criminal Injuries Compensation Authority (CICA, formerly the Criminal Injuries Compensation Board). Nor are such decisions just a matter of distributing blame as between a victim (on this occasion) and his or her offender: a central feature of societal responses to victimization is the perception of, and the ascription to, the individual of the status 'victim' (Miers, 1989; Walklate, 1989; Mawby and Walklate, 1994). This chapter seeks to examine the notion of victim status through two connected responses to victimization:

- the response of victims (or potential victims) to actual or perceived offending;
- the response of one social agency (the CICA) to the actions of such victims, where these result not in the prevention or neutralization of offending behaviour, but in these actions being perceived as 'offensive' and in their own personal victimization by others.

The first section analyses victims' (or potential victims') responses in terms of their efforts to assert either procedural or direct justice against offenders (or potential offenders), direct justice taking one of three forms: passive, reactive, and proactive. The second section describes and comments on the CICA's response to victims who have applied for compensation whom it perceives as other than innocent. This response may usefully be compared to that of the civil courts where the victim/plaintiff sues the offender/defendant for damages. The chapter begins with a brief exploration of the normative significance of the designation 'victim'.

The Social Functions of Victimization

Victims perform an important role in social life. Consider the role of the victim as a justification for the distribution of blame for injuries caused by another and of benefits to alleviate those injuries. Where a person acts offensively, the presence of a victim helps to identify and confirm losses, identify proscriptions and validate official responses against the offender. Conversely, where there is no victim, blaming an 'offender' is often controversial. A traditional argument concerning the limits of the criminal sanction has been that, if there is no victim, the case for blame is weakened; but this is itself clearly a controversial position (Wertheimer, 1977; Skolnick and Dombrink, 1978). Amongst other objections, it begs the question whether there is a victim, when the answer is clearly a matter of choice among competing values (Quinney, 1972). So it is that those who wish to argue that some behaviour is offensive will typically find it politically useful to create a victim where none apparently existed before. A primary strategy of groups opposed to experimenting on animals or hunting elicits public sympathy by presenting them as victims of human greed or callousness, sacrificed in the pursuit of commercial or purely hedonistic values. In other contexts, it is 'society' that is the victim, although quite what groups or individuals are implied by that label often (deliberately) remains obscure. Nor, indeed, is the word confined to sentient beings: recently the environment has often been described as the victim of industrial pollution. In a criminal context, the slogan, 'What about the victim?' is a useful reminder of the strength of emotive appeals and moral panics to clarify or reaffirm a certain set of values about crime, offenders and victims (Downes and Rock, 1998; Mawby and Brown, 1984; Ziegenhagen, 1978).

The point about the power of the label 'victim' can equally well be illustrated by considering the distribution of benefits or of praise to individuals. Where a person is injured in circumstances which are regarded as victimizing, it is typically easy to justify the extension of sympathy to that person and to allow the person to suspend his or her normal social obligations. When recognized as such, victims may enjoy access to those financial, organizational and material benefits which have been set aside to alleviate the particular instance of suffering, but this access will only be permitted so long as the claimant can maintain his or her inclusion within the class 'victim'. Deviant victims will be excluded from such benefits.

Labelling People as Victims

Indeterminacy and Convention

In his analysis of the social construction of homicide, Rock observes that situated descriptions of crime have elided issues of harm and suffering. What is required is

> ... an appreciation of how crime is experienced by those it injures and by those who observe that injury; that is, of how victims and witnesses construct and are constructed by the processes in which they are anchored. (Rock, 1998: 186)

Clearly, both as individuals and as groups, we do not respond uniformly to suffering – that is, we do not all respond in the same way to a particular instance of suffering, nor do those who share a response to one instance of suffering necessarily agree on others. Whether a person responds sympathetically depends on his or her notions of what constitutes a victimizing event. It follows from this that if a person does sustain an injury or loss and wishes to have it recognized by others as such, it is usually necessary to present that suffering in terms that comply with those others' definitions of victimizing events.

From the observer's standpoint, a major problem in deciding whether to ascribe victim status to an instance of suffering lies in the fact that social cues and signs may be vague or ambiguous. One response to this pervasive social phenomenon has been the development of conventions which stereotype certain instances of suffering as victimizing events. Paradigm instances are elderly victims of robberies, burglaries, assaults and the like; children who are sexually abused; people killed or injured by terrorist activity; and the victims of medical negligence. These Nils Christie (1986) memorably named 'ideal victims'. Some of these 'bounded categories' (Watson, 1976; Sudnow, 1965) are institutionalized as legal, medical or psychiatric norms; others, such as those held within family or peer groups, may be less formalized. Whether formalized or not, these conventions may also vary considerably in the precision of their definition.

Legal norms tend to be more precisely formulated than those applicable in less formalized settings, but indeterminacy as to what elements of the suffering are to be regarded as significant in the consideration of an appropriate response is endemic to these conventions. Thus, there may be profound disagreement between individuals and groups as to the appropriateness of a sympathetic response in given cases. Such factors as the sufferer's personal characteristics and circumstances – age, class, economic status and education, gender, ethnicity (McCahill *et al.*, 1979; Kerstetter and van Winkle, 1990; Vrij and Fischer, 1997; Goodey, 1998) – and the nature of his or her suffering – its duration, intensity, impact and extent – are all central to the way in which the individual sufferer, or those acting on his or her behalf, must manage and present that suffering (Winkel and Renssen, 1998). An important dimension of this process is the negotiation of the suffering with professional observers and participants in formal settings such as courtrooms and compensation tribunals, so that it conforms with the stereotype projected by their available conventional responses (Walster and Berscheid, 1967; Kooppelaar *et al.*, 1997).

Claiming, Ascribing and Denying the Label

Put at its simplest, this process comprises the negotiation of a claim by, or on behalf of, a sufferer to be accepted as a victim and the willingness of those having the power to do so to ascribe the label in any case. How that power is exercised is central to any critical evaluation of victimology (Elias, 1984, 1993; Walklate, 1989; Mawby and Walklate, 1994). A necessary ingredient for victim status is the presence of harm, suffering or injury (Burt, 1983). The experience of harm is a precondition to being accorded victim status, but not all such experiences will be so treated. As has already been noted, to be a victim means to suffer in a way that particularly conforms to a social definition of a victimizing event: 'the determination of victim status is a social process which may conform or conflict with self-identification' (Zeigenhagen, 1978: 17).

Typically, such events entail the individual suffering as the result of some act or omission on another's part, and the suffering needs to be caused by some agency other than the victim. Self-inflicted suffering does not usually qualify for victim status (and in some institutions, such as the military, may indeed result in the punishment of the 'victim'). A person who contracts cancer as the result of the active inhalation of cigarette smoke is less likely to be regarded as a victim than one who contracts the same disease as the result of passive smoking, but the matter is often more complex and subtle than this. What may first appear to be self-inflicted suffering, such as drug, alcohol or video game (Nintendo wrist) dependence, may come to be perceived as an illness or condition in which the dependent individual is a 'victim', and thus partly excusable for his or her dependence and its consequences. Such shifts in perception may themselves depend on the individual publicly accepting this diagnosis of his or her circumstances and agreeing to comply with a treatment regime.

On the other hand, it by no means follows that, because a person has experienced harm, he or she will either regard this as a victimizing event, or indeed make any claim that others should so regard it. Those who do wish to claim the status will have to present themselves as victims, and this may firstly involve a cognitive process of self-labelling. Different interactions are perceived differently in different communities, and what constitutes a victimizing event for one group need not do so for another. One of the difficulties which the first organizers of victim survey research encountered in trying to provide an alternative method of assessing the incidence of crime was that many of their respondents did not share their notion of victimization; as Biderman noted, they did not rate victimization as having a significant impact in their lives (1967: 31). The difficulty persists (see van Dijk, Chapter 5 in this volume). Salience is a function of what is culturally acceptable by a particular group: what constitutes an assault for some may simply be part of the vicissitudes of life for others.

Furthermore, it may well be that while those who have the power to apply the label are prepared to do so in a particular case, the individual sufferer rejects it. The application of the label 'victim' results in the individual being accorded a status which carries with it a set of expectations which he or she will have of others and which others will have of her or him. Social learning likewise enables us to develop a concept of being a victim (Scott, 1969; Boyce, 1982; McBarnett, 1983; Downes and Rock, 1998: 197–201), and, inasmuch as this contemplates attributes of dependence or acceptance of the situation, it may well be objectionable to some. Prime among this group are those women 'survivors' of domestic violence or of rape who have rejected the label precisely because of its overtones of passivity and helplessness in the face of adversity.

Conversely, those with the power to label people as victims may refuse to do so because the individual presents some characteristics – whether biographical or circumstantial – which conflict with the values they hold. But the matter may well be more complicated than simple rejection for all purposes. Within the criminal justice system, for example, a person may be a victim for the purpose of bringing a prosecution, yet be denied that status for the purpose of compensation payments – a matter to which we will return.

Victim Status: Being a Victim

Being a 'victim' results in the individual being accorded a status that carries with it a set of expectations which he or she will have of others,[1] and which others will have of her or him (Erez, Chapter 8 in this volume). For example, victims may be expected to express gratitude for sympathy or other compensating behaviour, and should not be perceived as exaggerating the extent of the harm suffered or of the excusing opportunities presented for suspending the expectations others normally have of them. Conversely, a victim should not appear to enjoy her or his suffering, and should try to avoid, in the future, the circumstances that occasioned it. A victim may also be expected to express anger, and possibly vindictiveness against those who caused the harm, but here again, such sentiments have traditionally been expected to be constrained within tolerated limits – for example, victims of burglaries may not cause grievous bodily harm to their offenders. Likewise, victims of assaults, or even of rape, will themselves commit offences if they carry weapons for the purpose of self-protection. But these limits remain tendentious. In recent years the popular reaction to victims, whether in real life or in fiction, taking up arms on their own, or on behalf of others against real or supposed offenders, has struck a deep and responsive chord. Officialdom, on the other hand, takes a sterner view of vigilantism and of those who take the law into their own hands.

Empowering Victims

Introduction

Greater involvement of victims is widely held to be desirable and beneficial, both to the criminal justice system and to the victims themselves (Shapland *et al.*, 1976; Fletcher, 1995; JUSTICE,1998). Equally, the lack of clarity as to exactly what those benefits are, the elision of the public and the private interest in the determination of criminal and penal justice decisions, the potential for the subjectivization of criminal justice, and the adoption of more punitive arrangements against offenders, are matters that trouble a number of commentators (see Ashworth, 1986; Fenwick, 1995; Miers, 1992; Sebba, 1996).

Viewed historically, the empowerment of the victim is seen by some to be no more than a long overdue return to criminal justice values that were improperly subordinated to those of the state (the 'golden age of the victim' thesis). But against the background of successive British Crime Survey reports, all of which show substantial unreported victimization (a picture confirmed by the International Crime Victims Surveys (van Dijk, Chapter 5 in this volume), victims' frustration with the criminal justice system has led to a kind of self-empowerment which, in some instances, threatens rather than supports its values. Critical assessments argue that victim self-empowerment was both reinforced and manipulated by the Conservative governments of the 1980s as part of a wider political agenda to bring its market ideology to the matter of policing crime (Reiner and Cross, 1991). Do-it-yourself justice takes a number of forms, two of which, touched on here, are the initiation of legal proceedings by the victim against the offender (procedural justice) and the adoption of direct justice by victims against actual or reputed offenders.

Procedural Justice

With a few exceptions, there is, of course, no legal obstacle to the victim of an offence initiating either civil or criminal proceedings against the offender, assuming identification. Where there is a reasonable prospect of conviction the state will prosecute, but where it does not there are serious obstacles to a private prosecution.[2] Over the past few years there have been a small number of successful civil actions,[3] but these are rare. In the case of offences against property, insured victims have no incentive to pursue the offender and, in the case of the uninsured, the offender is typically likely to be without substantial means. In the case of personal victimization, civil actions are rare primarily because of the standard combination of factors inhibiting any plaintiff (uncertainty of outcome, delay and the high cost of civil proceedings). In addition, unlike road traffic accidents, medical negligence and other actions in tort, there is no insurance company (or the Motor Insurance Bureau (MIB)) standing behind a potentially impecunious defendant.[4]

Direct Justice

More prevalent, it seems – although the evidence is selective and anecdotal – has been an increase in the number of actual and potential victims taking direct action against actual or reputed offenders, reflecting perhaps the New Right agenda encouraging private responsibility for crime prevention (Crawford, 1997). Broadly speaking, this action falls into three categories:

1 passive justice;
2 reactive justice; and
3 proactive justice.

The key point here is that the excessive or misplaced exercise of direct justice threatens, rather than supports, the claimed values implicit in the criminal justice system, as well as the values implicit in claiming the status of, or being labelled, a victim (Miers, 1980). But as Black (1993) observed, much of the everyday violence that flourishes in modern society involves ordinary citizens who seemingly view their conduct as a perfectly legitimate exercise in social control. Such conduct supplements or provides an alternative to a value system that constrains the exercise of self-help. For the powerless victim, for those who suffer multiple and repeat victimization (Farrell, 1992; Brown, 1998; Maung, 1995), or for those victims who do not share the prevailing criminal justice values, direct justice re-establishes the moral balance between them and their offenders (Garland, 1996).

Passive Direct Justice

A key crime preventive strategy of the 1980s and 1990s has been 'target hardening' – of cars, shops and homes (see Crawford, 1997; 1998). In addition to standard home security devices, this may include planting fake landmines that explode with a loud bang (*The Times*, 2 June 1995), but some home-owners go further. Designing out crime by electrifying the front gate or other conductive features of the entrance to a house, including window frames, constitutes an offence under s. 31 of the Offences against the Person Act 1861 (setting traps). In *Pownall* (*The Times*, 19 February 1994), the householder (who had been burgled many times and whose electrified security gate inside his front garden could deliver a fatal shock) was convicted of this offence. In passing sentence in this case the judge observed,

> In the wretched society we live in it is not unusual for people to fortify their homes because they fear violence. What cannot be tolerated is people who set in place devices that cause serious harm. We do not want to reach the stage where people can be killed making innocent calls to homes. (Ibid.)

It was such an innocent victim who sustained an electric shock when he touched some wires protruding from a car parked in the car park for which he was responsible. These were part of a device installed by its owner as a response to repeated attempts to steal his car. Nevertheless, the jury acquitted the owner of assault, of possessing a prohibited weapon or causing a noxious thing to be administered.

Target-hardening can also take the form of carrying weapons for self-defence. Where the weapon is, for instance, a flick-knife or swordstick, the 'victim' may well be committing an offence, typically under s. 1 of the Prevention of Crime Act 1953 or s. 139 of the Criminal Justice Act 1988, depending on whether or not the court is prepared to accept such conduct as constituting a lawful excuse.[5]

Reactive Direct Justice

The typical instance of reactive direct justice is the use of strong self-defence measures in response to an actual or threatened assault on one's self or another, or in defence of one's property. In English law a victim who honestly believes that unlawful force is imminently to be used against him, or where such force has already been used, may himself use reasonable force in response. The law permits pre-emptive strikes in circumstances in which the victim could not reasonably be expected to wait for the threat to become more fully realized and also views the proportionality of the violence used by the victim in the light of the prevailing circumstances.[6] There are cases in which victims have exceeded what the law would normally permit, with the result that some have themselves been prosecuted or, in some cases, sued for damages by their offenders. This second group of cases, in particular, have been productive of considerable media hysteria about the unfairness of a system that penalizes those who are only seeking to uphold law and order.

Victims as defendants in criminal cases   As already noted, excessive use of force in self-defence may have the result that 'the victim becomes the offender and vice-versa' (Black, 1993: 36). Sometimes the result is the conviction of the 'victim';[7] on other occasions, although he has *prima facie* committed an offence, other outcomes are possible. These typically include the decision by the Crown Prosecution Service not to prosecute because it would not be in the public interest to do so,[8] a directed acquittal,[9] or jury acquittal. A significant example of the latter is *Revill* v. *Newbery* ([1996] 1 All ER 291). The facts were that Newbery, a 76-year-old man, was sleeping in the brick shed on his allotment in order to protect his gardening equipment because his shed had been burgled on previous occasions. He was awoken in the night by the sound of someone attempting to break in. He loaded his shotgun, and without being able to see whether there was anybody directly in front of the door, fired a shot through a small hole in the door, wounding Revill in the arm and chest. Revill was subsequently prosecuted for other offences he had committed that night, pleading guilty. Newbery, too, was prosecuted for an offence against the person but was acquitted by a 'plainly sympathetic jury'.[10]

Victims as defendants in civil cases   Such events can also result in the victim figuring as a defendant in civil proceedings. This was one outcome of the shooting in *Revill* v. *Newbery*. Although there was clearly an element of contributory negligence on the plaintiff/offender's part, the victim/defendant was ordered to pay him £4000 damages.[11] Another possible 'damages' award may take the form of a compensation order on conviction of the victim. For example, in a case in which a shopkeeper shot the person who had caused criminal damage to his shop on a previous occasion, the 'victim' was also ordered to pay the 'offender' £10 compensation.[12]

Proactive Direct Justice

'Autonomous civil activity', to use Johnston's term (Johnston, 1991: 29), may constitute both making threats or the use of force against those suspected of having committed offences, as well as the use of force against those 'known' to have committed an offence but who have escaped prosecution or conviction or, if convicted, regarded by their victim (or another) as having been insufficiently punished. Sometimes, although not always, it is possible to distinguish proactive justice where exercised, first, by the victim (or by extension, the victim's immediate family) and, second, by others acting on behalf of the victim (with or without his knowledge or consent).

Action by the victims or their families   Where prosecuted, direct action by victims (or by members of their immediate families) may result in conviction,[13] but a jury may well perceive such action as entirely justified, resulting in an acquittal in the face of strong evidence of guilt. This is illustrated by a case in which the defendant fatally stabbed a man accused of offences of indecency against her daughter (*The Times*, 29 January 1994). Despite evidence of earlier threats to cause him grievous bodily harm ('if he walks he will be walking with a knife between his legs. I am not going to kill him. I will get him where it hurts') and of witnesses to the attack who saw her aim three or four stabs at his groin, the defendant was acquitted both of murder and of manslaughter (the former verdict is consistent with what was reported, the latter only with difficulty). Noting that the deceased had not been prosecuted (due to lack of evidence), his killer was, in the prosecution's words, 'judge, jury and executioner'.[14]

Vicarious action: collective self-help   Vigilantism has a long and dishonourable history. Seeking out and victimizing potential and actual offenders may take a variety of forms: punishment beatings (*The Times*, 15 October 1994), physical ostracism,[15] humiliation rituals,[16] kidnapping and threats of violence. A particularly contentious example of the latter which attracted a great deal of publicity was *R v. Chapman and Bond* (*The Times*, 29 June 1993). Two men kidnapped a 16-year-old boy whom they suspected of stealing some work tools, bundled him into a van, tied his hands and told him that they would douse him with petrol if he did not own up. The men were convicted of assault and were sentenced to five years' imprisonment. Given their clean backgrounds, this was certainly an excessive sentence, and the incident sparked widespread support for the two men, popularly known as 'The Norfolk Two', who were portrayed as honest citizens trying to stem the rising tide of crime to which the police were either unwilling or unable to respond effectively. A fighting fund was organized by a national tabloid newspaper and a cabinet minister (the local MP) wrote to the Lord Chancellor asking for action. On appeal, the sentences were reduced to six months, the Lord Chief Justice observing that to regard as mitigation the fact that the two men were frustrated by the police's inability to take action and thus that their decision to take the law into their own hands was justified, 'would be to validate the very conduct that it was the business of their Lordships to deter' (*The Times*, 29 June 1993).

Values and Extremism

In many of the instances mentioned, the victim (whether or not subsequently a defendant in a civil or criminal proceedings) has sought to justify the action taken by reference to such values as individual self-determination (the police can't or won't do anything); 'the good old days'; respect for persons, particularly for adults (or, the 'yoof' problem);[17] values implicit in the conception of a recent past in which there were clear and unproblematic understandings of right and wrong; and in the importance of retributive and exemplary punishments, in contrast to the 'holidays and pats on the back for the kids who make people's lives a misery' (*The Times*, 21 July 1995). As Brake and Hale (1992: 27) observe of the ideological context of conservative criminology, such appeals nostalgically romanticize a cultural history which never existed.

A final, and for our purposes revealing, theme is the attempt to articulate the importance of a clear differentiation between 'innocent' victims who are doing no more than trying to stem, or respond to, the rising tide of crime and offenders, typically young, male, and unemployed, who have nothing better to do than to prey on the law-abiding and hardworking citizen. This theme is powerfully articulated by groups representing the survivors of homicide – the victim's family – or its secondary victims. Rock comments:

> There is little room for greyness in the moral world of many survivors ... . Recounted in meetings of support groups, transformed into strong narratives, embedded in the here-and-now, familiar world of survivors, a firm line is traced between the victim and the offender, innocence and guilt, the good and the bad, us and them, the feeling and the unfeeling ...'. (Rock 1998: 195)

We have also seen how some of these instances of victim empowerment potentially or actually endanger the lives of others, some of whom are themselves entirely innocent victims (the security guard, for example, electrocuted by the car owner who had wired his car to deter thieves). Three recent cases well illustrate the dangers of an uncritical acceptance of the victim's standpoint. The headlines in *The Times* say it all:

- 'Lynch mob of teenage girls kills theft suspect in street': the man killed by some 13 girls in Manchester had a criminal record and was apparently suspected by them of committing a number of local burglaries (no police action had been taken) (*The Times*, 23 May 1998).
- 'Killer of suspected paedophile gets life': a man tortured and killed the victim in trying to force him to confess to sexually assaulting a young girl (*The Times*, 23 May 1998).
- 'Vigilantes' innocent victim tells how he feared for his life': relatives of a burglary victim concluded that a man known to them, but wholly innocent of that offence, had committed it; they kidnapped, stripped and doused him in petrol, threatening to set fire to him (*The Times*, 8 November 1998).

It may be objected that these are no more than instances of personal victimization in which, in each case, there is an innocent victim of the vigilantes' actions. What is argued here is that there is more to them than that. 'Much of this conflict', according to Black, 'is a punishment or other expression of disapproval, whether applied reflectively or impulsively, with coolness or in the heat of passion. Some is an effort to achieve compensation, or restitution, for a harm that has been done' (Black, 1993: 31). As instances of – admittedly extreme – victim empowerment they distort the values normally associated with victim integration in criminal justice: engagement, cooperation, information exchange, greater satisfaction with the system and its personnel.[18] They also underline the point made earlier, that not all who suffer are labelled victims when they take the law into their own hands; nor, to turn to the second illustrative context, are they all deserving of compensation for their suffering.

Compensation and Undeserving Victims

We turn now to consider the response of one social agency (the Criminal Injuries Compensation Authority) to the action of such victims, where this results not in the prevention or neutralization of offending behaviour, but in their own action being perceived as 'offensive' and in their own personal victimization by others. This response may usefully be compared to that of the civil courts where the victim/plaintiff sues the offender/defendant for damages.

The Criminal Injuries Compensation Authority

The Criminal Injuries Compensation Authority (CICA) is a statutory body established by Criminal Injuries Compensation Act 1995 for the purpose of compensating innocent victims of personal crime. It replaces, but is very similar to, the earlier non-statutory scheme administered since 1964 by the Criminal Injuries Compensation Board. While its remit extends to injuries received in acts of law enforcement and arising from the offence of trespass on a railway, over 90 per cent of applicants are victims of ss. 18, 20 or 47 of the Offences against the Person Act 1861. The offender does not need to be prosecuted, nor even identified, but there are stringent reporting require-ments with which the injured victim must comply. Compensation is payable to eligible victims according to a tariff, £1000 being the minimum loss. A condition of eligibility is that the victim is free from immediate blame for the injury and, indeed, in other respects is a blameless person (see, gener-ally, Miers, 1997: 156–85).

The Policy of Only Compensating the Innocent Victim

The original criminal injuries compensation scheme proceeded from the view that it would be inappropriate for those with significant criminal records, or whose own conduct led to their being injured, to receive compensation from public funds (Home Office, 1961: para. 31). Paragraph 6(c) of that scheme permitted the Board to withhold or reduce compensation if it con-sidered, having regard to the conduct of the applicant (or, in cases of unlawful killing, the deceased) before, during or after the events giving rise to the claim or to his character as shown by his criminal convictions or unlawful conduct, that it would be 'inappropriate to make a full award, or any award at all'. Its implementation occasioned frequent criticism: many of the applications for judicial review of the Board's decisions concerned the exercise of its discretion under this paragraph. The central issue turned on the varying conceptions of the relevance of the victim's conduct and charac-ter that were held by the Board, its supporters and its critics, in particular concerning what the Board should be able to take into account when consid-ering the relevance of the applicant's biography to his application.

This wide power continues to play a significant role in the new scheme which came into force in April 1996. The CICA's first report reiterates that the scheme exists to benefit 'blameless' victims (CICA, 1998a: para 1.8). Though quantitatively small (of the 57 814 applications resolved in the second year of the new scheme (1997–98), 5467 were rejected on this basis (CICA, 1998b: para. 3.11), this issue is qualitatively of prime importance. It is the one facet of a compensation scheme which most strikingly brings into focus the assumptions which lie behind the notion of the 'innocent' and hence 'deserving' victim (Miers, 1990).

The first problem is that because delinquent victims resemble offenders too closely and may indeed have been formally so defined in the past, the possibility of their receiving compensation threatens the stereotype of the 'innocent' victim for whom such schemes are created. Second, the possibility that 'offenders' might, as victims, be eligible for compensation, subverts a prime objective of criminal injury schemes, which is to distinguish victims of crime from offenders. The politicization of the victim of crime requires that the taxpayer be asked to compensate only those victims who present 'deserving' characteristics. It becomes necessary therefore to exclude the delinquent victim (however defined) from the scheme's beneficial provisions (Home Office, 1986: para. 6.2).

The Criminal Injuries Compensation Scheme: Para. 13(d)

Suppose a victim takes the law into his or her own hands in the ways described earlier and, as a result, suffers personal injury caused by her/his targeted 'offender'. How will the CICA respond to an application for compensation? The victim's behaviour falls under one of two disentitling conditions: either he or she has engaged in 'conduct before, during or after the incident' which, in the terms of para. 13(d) makes it 'inappropriate that a full award or any award at all be made', or under para. 13(e), which permits the claims officer to reach the same decision by taking account of the available evidence. Following the equivalent paragraph in the old scheme (para. 6(c)), which permitted the Board to refuse or reduce compensation whether the unlawful conduct was connected with the injury or not), it may be expected that such a victim to be disqualified under para. 13(d) of the new.

In *Revill* v. *Newbery* we saw that, while he was engaged in unlawful behaviour (attempted burglary), Revill was able to recover damages in a civil action against Newbery because Newbery's response was itself unreasonable (and *prima facie* unlawful). Millett, LJ said:

> For centuries the common law has permitted reasonable force to be used in defence of the person or property. Violence may be returned with necessary violence. But the force used must not exceed the limits of what is reasonable in the circumstances. Changes in society and in social perceptions may have meant that what might have been considered reasonable at one time would no longer be so regarded; but the principle remains the same. The assailant or intruder may be met with reasonable force but no more; the use of excessive violence against him is an actionable wrong. ([1996] 1 All ER 291: 301–2)

However, this is not a basis for compensation under the scheme. In an early decision the Board rejected an application from a burglar who had been peppered with shot by the irate householder (CICB, 1970, para. 5(4)). More recently the CIC Appeal Panel reached the same decision on essentially the same facts: CICAP 1998 (para 5.5). If a plaintiff, such as in *Revill* v. *Newbery*, were to make an application under the new scheme, it would surely be rejected. The fundamental justification for the continuation of this approach is that the taxpayer should not be called upon to compensate offenders who happen to become victims at the time of their offending. Such cases are distinguishable from the criminal liability of the victim's assailant because the state properly has a general interest in punishing offences against the person where these cannot be justified as instances of the reasonable use of force in the prevention of crime or in self-defence. They are also distinguishable from the civil liability of the assailant, since this will amount to a charge on private, and not public, funds. There is also, no doubt, an element of just deserts in the rejection of such applications.

Conclusion

In welcoming initiatives such as those evident in the recent JUSTICE report and in this volume, we should also reflect on the danger of thinking that there is a single victim perspective to be integrated within criminal justice and that, so far as there is a multiplicity of perspectives, they are all equally welcome.

I have sought to argue that, in seeking the integration of the victim, care needs to be taken at both the conceptual and empirical level that we are clear both as to what we mean when we say that a person is a victim of crime, and as to the values that we associate with that attribution.

Notes

1 For example, that where individuals have been injured in terrorist activity and been 'officially' recognized as its victims, the government should not accord any similar status to the 'victims' of army action against such terrorists ('IRA Victims Attack Plan to Meet Relatives', *The Times*, 22 January 1999)

2 In 1995 two women successfully prosecuted Christopher Davies for rape – according to *The Times* (20 September 1995), this was the first such 'private' conviction. The difficulties are substantial, as the Stephen Lawrence killing demonstrates, and not only for reasons associated with the obtaining of evidence: see [1995] *Criminal Law Review* 658.

3 *Halford* v. *Brooks* [1991] 3 All ER 559 (damages awarded for an unlawful killing notwithstanding the defendant's acquittal on a charge of murder); *Calascione* v. *Dixon*

(damages awarded to a mother whose son was killed by the defendant's driving; defendant convicted of an offence: *The Times*, 20 and 22 February 1992); *Griffiths* v. *Williams* (plaintiff awarded £50 000 in a county court jury action for trespass to the person arising from an alleged rape, the defendant being acquitted at trial, upheld by CA; *The Times*, 13 April and 22 November 1995); Lorraine Miles who, in 1989, was awarded £20 000 damages against her assailant, the CPS having decided not to prosecute (*The Times*, 20 September 1995); and *Francisco* v. *Diedrick* (£50 000 for assault and battery arising from the defendant's unlawful killing of Joan Francisco, Diedrick never having been charged with an offence: *The Times*, 25 May 1998).

4   The court may order a person convicted of an offence against property or the person to pay the compensation to the victim. In terms of their proportion of offenders convicted and of their equivalence to civil damages, the number and the value of compensation orders is low: see Home Office (1996: Table 7.21).

5   On 'good reason' under s. 139 see *Emmanuel* [1998] *Criminal Law Review*, 347. For examples of convictions see *The Times*, 12 August 1983: a rape victim carrying a flick-knife for self-defence was fined £150 under the Prevention of Crime Act 1953; *The Independent*, 11 September 1987: a man carrying and using a swordstick in self-defence was sentenced to 28 days' imprisonment, suspended for nine months under the 1953 Act.

6   See *also Chamberlain* v. *Lindon* [1998] 2 All ER 538 in which the defendant was held to have a lawful excuse in destroying a wall which he believed obstructed his right of way, notwithstanding that it had been in place for some time, and was not guilty of criminal damage.

7   For example, the shopkeeper given a conditional discharge following a conviction for maliciously wounding an offender who had committed criminal damage against his shop (*The Independent*, 27 October 1987). See also *The Times*, 7 December 1995: the chairman of the local Neighbourhood Watch prosecuted under ss. 20 and 18 of the Offences against the Person Act 1861 after shooting two men who broke into his bonded warehouse with a shotgun.

8   See *The Times*, 16 July 1996: the case involved a householder who disturbed two burglars at his home and, having been attacked by them, seized a kitchen knife and killed one of them. The burglars were convicted, the judge observing, 'thugs like you who attack householders in this country and subject them to the violence that you did cannot be surprised if the householder fights back in self defence'. The householder was not prosecuted.

9   See *The Independent*, 1 October 1987: reporting that a rape victim was acquitted of murder on a direction by the trial judge.

10   H.H. Judge Woods, who tried the case, *The Times*, 7 December 1994, letters. These facts are similar to a number of other instances during the mid-1990s in which victims of burglary and personal violence took retaliatory action, injuring their offenders, and which attracted widespread publicity; see, for example, *The Times*, 25 and 26 January 1995 and 23 July 1998.

11   Rougier J's decision prompted considerable criticism, including hate mail (*The Times*, 2, 6 and 3 December 1994). The judge took the unusual step of writing a letter to *The Times* (6 December 1994) defending his decision, which was upheld by the Court of Appeal. In a similar case in 1997, a burglar successfully sued a farmer (Wiles) who had kicked him in the head while he was lying on the ground semi-conscious from an earlier blow. That blow was lawful, the second was not, being unreasonable (*The Times*, 9 May 1997). See also *The Times*, 30 September 1983: where a burglar was awarded £512 damages in a civil action against the householder who shot him with a revolver.

12 *The Independent*, 27 October 1987. See also *The Times*, 15 October 1994: a case in which a former PC was fined £10 following his conviction for common assault on two girls who had tipped rubbish over his car and ordered to pay £15 by way of compensation.

13 *The Times*, 21 July 1995: in this case the victim was fined £100 following conviction for beating the offender who had caused damage to his garden; *The Times*, 4 August 1995: here, the victim was convicted but given a conditional discharge after beating a boy who was stealing his apples.

14 See also *The Times*, 16 June 1993: the victim was acquitted by the jury of firearms offences after he had shot and wounded a lorry driver who had killed his 12-year-old son in a hit-and-run accident; and *The Times*, 7 January 1995: parents and a brother-in-law were convicted of kidnapping a school bully who had victimized their son. The judge remarked, 'when public opinion is so movingly articulated as it is in this case it is something which any judge would ignore at his peril'.

15 *The Times*, 16 June 1993: this case involved running offenders out of town.

16 *The Times*, 22 June 1993: this case involved stripping the offender, tying him to a lamp post and taking photographs.

17 'The message this sends out to the yob culture is "go out and have a really good drunken time, cause devastation to a village and damage cars"' (*The Times*, 15 October 1994); 'the yobs and vandals always seem to get away with it but it seems that justice is only for adults' (*The Times*, 21 July 1995); or the country is 'going to the dogs' (*The Times*, 26 January 1995).

18 See, for example, the public response to the release of Sidney Cooke, a convicted paedophile: *The Times*, 25 April 1998.

References

Ashworth, A. (1986), 'Punishment and Compensation: Victims, Offenders and the State', *Oxford Journal of Legal Studies*, **6**, 86–122.

Biderman A. (1967), *Report of a Pilot Study in the District of Columbia on Victimisation and Attitudes Towards Law Enforcement*, President's Commission on Law Enforcement and Administration of Justice, Field Survey I, Washington, DC: Government Printing Office.

Black, D. (1993), 'Crime as Social Control', in D. Black (ed.), *The Social Structure of Right and Wrong*, London: Academic Press, 27–46.

Boyce, M. (1982), 'How to Be a Victim', *Transactional Analysis Journal*, **12**, 249–51.

Brake, M. and Hale, C. (1992), *Public Order and Private Lives*, London: Routledge.

Brown, S. (1998), *Understanding Youth and Crime: Listening to Youth?*, Milton Keynes: Open University Press.

Burt, M. (1983), 'A Conceptual Framework for Victimological Research', *Victimology*, **8**, 261–69.

Christie, N. (1986), 'The Ideal Victim', in E. Fattah (ed.), *From Crime Policy to Victim Policy*, London: Macmillan, 1–17.

Crawford, A. (1997), *Local Governance of Crime: Appeals to Community and Partnerships*, Oxford: Clarendon Press.

Crawford, A. (1998), *Crime Prevention and Community Safety*, Harlow: Addison Wesley Longman.

Criminal Injuries Compensation Appeals Panel (CICAP) (1998), *Annual Report 1996–97*, Cm. 3840, London: HMSO.

Criminal Injuries Compensation Authority (CICA) (1998a), *Annual Report 1996–97*, HC 631, London: HMSO.

Criminal Injuries Compensation Authority (CICA) (1998b), *Annual Report 1997–98*, HC 131, London: HMSO.

Downes, D. and Rock, P. (1998), *Understanding Deviance*, (3rd edn), Oxford: Oxford University Press.

Elias, R. (1984), *Victims of the System. Crime Victims and Compensation in American Politics and Criminal Justice*, New Brunswick, NJ: Transaction Press.

Elias, R. (1993), *Victims Still*, London: Sage.

Farrell, G. (1992), 'Multiple Victimisation: Its Extent and Significance', *International Review of Victimology*, **2**, 85–102.

Fenwick, H. (1995), 'Rights of Victims in the Criminal Justice System: Rhetoric or Reality?', *Criminal Law Review*, 843–53.

Fletcher, G. (1995), *With Justice for Some: Victims' Rights in Criminal Trials*, New York: Addison Wesley.

Garland, D. (1996), 'The Limits of the Sovereign State: Strategies of Crime Control in Contemporary Society', *British Journal of Criminology*, **36**(4), 445–71.

Goodey, J. (1998), 'Examining the "White Racist/Black Victim" Stereotype', *International Review of Victimology*, **5**, 235–56.

Home Office (1961), *Compensation for Victims of Crimes of Violence*, Cmnd 1406, London: HMSO.

Home Office (1986), *Criminal Injuries Compensation: A Statutory Scheme*, London: HMSO.

Home Office (1996), *Criminal Statistics England and Wales 1995*, Cmnd 3421, London: HMSO.

Johnston, L. (1991), 'Privatisation and the Police Function: From New Police to New Policing', in R. Reiner and M. Cross (eds), *Beyond Law and Order*, London: Macmillan, 18–40.

JUSTICE (1998), *Victims in Criminal Justice*, Report of the Committee on the Role of the Victim in Criminal Justice, London: JUSTICE.

Kerstetter, W. and van Winkle, B. (1990), 'Who Decides? A Study of the Complainant's Decision to Prosecute in Rape Cases', *Criminal Justice and Behaviour*, **17**, 268–83.

Kooppelaar, L., Lange, A. and Van de Velde, J-W. (1997), 'The Influence of Positive and Negative Credibility on the Assessment of Rape Victims: An Experimental Study of Expectancy–Confirmation Bias', *International Review of Victimology*, **5**, 61–85.

McBarnett, D. (1983), 'Victims in the Witness Box: Confronting Victimology's Stereotype', *Contemporary Crises*, **7**, 293–303.

McCahill, T., Meyer, L. and Fischman, A. (1979), *The Aftermath of Rape*, Lexington, MA: Lexington Books.

Maung, N. (1995), *Young People, Victimisation and the Police*, Home Office Research Study 140, London: HMSO.

Mawby, R. and Brown J. (1984), 'Newspaper Images of the Victim: A British Study', *Victimology*, **9**, 82–94.

Mawby, R. and Walklate, S. (1994), *Critical Victimology*, London: Sage.

Miers, D. (1980), 'Victim Compensation as a Labelling Process', *Victimology*, **5**, 3–16.

Miers, D. (1989), 'Positivist Victimology: A Critique', *International Review of Victimology*, **1**, 3–22 and 219–30.

Miers, D. (1990), 'Compensation and Conceptions of Victims of Crime', *Victimology*, **8**, 204–12.

Miers, D. (1992), 'The Responsibilities and the Rights of Victims of Crime', *Modern Law Review*, **55**, 482–505.

Miers, D. (1997), *State Compensation for Criminal Injuries*, London: Blackstone Press.

Quinney, R. (1972), 'Who Is the Victim?', *Criminology*, **10**, 314–23.

Reiner, R. and Cross, M. (1991) (eds), *Beyond Law and Order*, London: Macmillan.

Rock, P. (1998), 'Murderers, Victims and Survivors', *British Journal of Criminology*, **38**(2), 185–200.

Scott, R. (1969), *The Making of Blind Men*, New York: Russell Sage.

Sebba, L. (1996), *Third Parties: Victims and the Criminal Justice System*, Columbus: Ohio State University Press.

Shapland, J., Willmore, J. and Duff, P. (1976), *Victims in the Criminal Justice System*, Aldershot: Gower.

Skolnick, J. and Dombrink, J. (1978), 'The Legalisation of Deviance', *Criminology*, **16**, 193–208.

Sudnow, D. (1965), 'Normal Crimes: Sociological Features of the Penal Code in a Public Defender Office', *Social Problems*, **12**, 255–76.

Vrij, A. and Fischer, A. (1997), 'The Role of Displays of Emotion and Ethnicity in Judgments of Rape Victims', *International Review of Victimology*, **4**, 255–65.

Walklate, S. (1989), *Victimology*, London: Unwin Hyman.

Walster, E. and Berscheid, E. (1967), 'When Does a Harm-Doer Compensate a Victim?', *Journal of Personality and Social Psychology*, **6**, 435–41.

Watson, D. (1976), 'Some Conceptual Issues in the Social Identification of Victims and Offenders', in E. Viano (ed.), *Victims and Society*, Washington, DC: Visage Press, 60–71.

Wertheimer, A. (1977), 'Victimless Crime', *Ethics*, **87**, 302–18.

Winkel, F. and Renssen, M. (1998), 'A Pessimistic Outlook on Victims and an "Upward Bias" in Social Comparison Expectations of Victim Support Workers Regarding Their Clients', *International Review of Victimology*, **5**, 203–20.

Ziegenhagen, E. (1978), *Victims, Crime and Social Control*, New York: Praeger.

5   Implications of the International Crime Victims Survey for a Victim Perspective

Jan van Dijk

Introduction

The International Crime Victims Survey and Repeat Victimization

Over the past 20 years a growing number of countries have started crime victims surveys to assess national or local crime problems. Such surveys ask representative samples of the general public about selected offences they might have experienced over a given time. The resulting victimization rates constitute a better indicator of the level of crime than the numbers of crimes reported to, and recorded by, the police. If the research methodology used is standardized, the surveys also offer a new opportunity for the collection of crime statistics which can be used for comparative purposes. The International Crime Victims Survey (ICVS) was initiated in 1987 with this aim in mind. This standardized survey has so far been carried out in 54 different countries under the supervision of an international working group chaired by the author. The data collection took place in three main rounds – in 1988, 1992 and 1996 respectively.[1]

The significance of victim surveys for criminology goes beyond the gathering of better data on the level and distribution of crime; they also provide information about the experiences of victims with the police and other relevant agencies. This feature of the ICVS offers unique opportunities for critical assessments of the way in which national governments deal with victims of crime. This chapter compares the expectations, experiences and judgements of victims from various parts of the world, and explores whether the attitudes of crime victims towards the police differ across world regions. Global findings will be compared with findings concerning victims from industrialized nations, nations with economies in transition (East and Central European nations) and nations with developing economies (Africa, Asia, Latin America).

Several analyses of victimization survey data have shown that, over a given time period, small numbers of all victims account for large proportions of all victimization (Farrell and Pease, 1993; Wittebrood and Nieuwbeerta, 1997; Kleemans, 1996; Mukherjee and Carcach, 1998). Victim recidivism is very common. Many victims are revictimized by the same type of offence within the same year, and often within weeks or months of the last offence. Analyses of the ICVS data confirm that a substantial proportion of victims in all countries are revictimized by any or the same type of crime during the course of one year. Table 5.1 shows the percentage of victims who were revictimized during the remaining part of the same year.

Table 5.1 confirms that repeat victimization is very common worldwide. More than 40 per cent of those victimized are victimized more than once in the course of a year. In Asia a third of victims are multiple victims. In Latin America more than half of all victims are multiple victims. Repeat victimization is also very common for different types of crime in all world regions. The rates are the highest for minor car-related offences and for sexual and violent offences which often show a cyclical pattern. Repeat victimization is not uncommon for burglaries and robberies either: one in five of the victims of these crimes are revictimized during the remaining part of the year.

Repeat victimization, which is the result of the random distribution of incidents, can be analysed by comparing actual frequencies with expected frequencies. Table 5.2 shows, for victimization by 'any crime', by 'burglary' and 'violence against women', how actual frequencies of multiple victimization compare to expected frequencies if each person had an equal chance of being victimized by an incident (the Poisson distribution).

The statistics in Table 5.2 show that the actual distribution differs sharply from what would be expected if victimization was randomly distributed across the population. For example, on the basis of random distribution, about 11 500 respondents ought to have been victimized twice or more by any crime. In reality about 13 500 were revictimized once or more. In the case of burglary and violence against women there are many more repeat victims than can be explained by random distribution. It is especially noteworthy that the number of persons victimized three times or more is also much larger than expected.

Table 5.1 Percentages of victims revictimized by any crime or the same type of crime the same year, overall and per world region: results of ICVS data 1988–1996

	Any Crime	Car Theft	Theft from Car	Car Damage	Motor-cycle Theft	Bicycle Theft	Burglary	Attempted Burglary	Robbery	Personal Theft	Sexual Offence	Assaults & Threat	Violence Against Women
Western Europe	37.3	9.3	19.1	24.9	15.1	15.6	12.8	10.4	14.7	12.7	35.8	28.8	36.6
New World	45.3	14.3	21.9	21.8	5.8	15.0	20.2	19.2	28.0	21.5	41.9	33.6	44.0
Countries in transition	41.6	13.8	35.5	30.4	14.2	10.1	19.7	20.7	19.6	21.0	29.3	29.8	24.8
Asia	30.9	5.1	12.1	30.5	10.0	11.6	23.2	20.5	15.1	20.7	26.2	26.6	33.9
Africa	44.0	16.7	27.7	30.5	19.3	11.0	28.8	29.3	15.7	22.1	38.1	25.7	36.5
Latin America	53.9	12.5	34.7	51.1	0.4	13.0	32.6	34.6	37.5	37.6	43.1	36.5	42.7
Total	41.5	12.22	27.4	30.5	12.5	12.5	20.4	20.6	20.1	20.7	34.3	29.9	33.3

99

Table 5.2   Actual distribution of victimization by crime and expected distribution on the basis of equal chances (Poisson distribution), for 'any crime', 'burglary' and 'violence against women'

	No. of victimizations					
	0	**1**	**2**	**3**	**4**	**5**
Any crime						
actual	94 417	19 758	7 647	3 098	1 462	1 117
expected	78 282	38 865	9 670	1 582	205	14
Burglary						
actual	124 727	3 020	618	168	33	51
expected	123 515	4 995	105	2		
Violence against women						
actual	64 787	826	237	117	31	122
expected	63 618	2 458	45	–	–	–

Determinants of Repeat Victimization

Repeat victimization can be the result of structural vulnerabilities of certain population groups – so-called heterogeneity (see Ellingworth *et al.*, 1997). Known risk factors for criminal victimization include youth, residence in a large city, high income and an outgoing lifestyle (van Dijk and Steinmetz, 1983). People with such characteristics have higher than average chances of being victimized and are therefore also more likely to be repeat victims.[2]

Repeat victimization can also occur because the offender deliberately victimizes the same person again. Examples are spouse abuse, school playground bullying and repeated attacks on ethnic minority shopkeepers by racist gangs. In the case of property offences, the offender who has successfully committed an offence against a particular person may decide to try his luck against the same individual once again.[3] In all the above cases repeat victimization is somehow dependent on the previous victimization(s) and, in the victimological literature, is called 'event dependency'. Whatever the causes of repeat victimization, its statistical prevalence has important policy implications. If victimization signals heightened vulnerability to future victimizations, victims are a priority target group for crime prevention advice. If victims know or suspect that they are being victimized by the same offender(s), they may want the police to intervene by arresting that person. Repeat victims may also be in need of support because of the accumulated effects of their multiple victimization (Winkel 1998); in short, they, more than other victims, might want real protection from the police against a particular offender.

In this secondary analysis of ICVS data, this chapter explores whether repeat victims hold different expectations than one-time victims about what the police can, or should, do for them and whether they evaluate actual police responses differently; the hypothesis is that repeat victims in all countries have special needs. Since the phenomenon of repeat victimization is insufficiently recognized by the police, these special needs of repeat victims are largely neglected and, for this reason a large proportion of repeat victims, one can assume, will be dissatisfied with the police response. The chapter will carry out an exploratory study of repeat victims' attitudes towards the police, using the international data from the 1996 ICVS but, in order to put these international findings in the correct perspective, differences in victims' attitudes across world regions will first be examined.

In the questionnaire from the 1996 ICVS, follow-up questions about experiences with the police were limited to five types of crimes: theft from car, burglaries, robberies, sexual incidents and threats/assaults. In the next section of the chapter, attention will first be given to the experiences of victims of these five types of crime (combined), followed by an analysis of victims of household burglary and violence against women. Household burglary is the most common form of serious crime victimizing ordinary citizens and is also one of the types of property crime with the largest proportion of repeat victims. Victims of violence against women are defined as assaults and/or sexual assaults (rapes, attempted rapes or sexual harassment). Many of these crimes are committed by spouses or ex-spouses and flow from an abusive relationship. Repeat victimization is very common among this group of victims.

The chapter looks respectively at: the rate of reporting to the police; the reasons for reporting; the reasons for not reporting; satisfaction with the police response and reasons for dissatisfaction. It examines experiences of crime victims with victim support agencies and their needs as regards specialized help. In addition, some findings will be presented on fear of crime among crime victims and their assessment of the effectiveness of the police in controlling crime in their neighbourhoods.

Experiences of Victims and Repeat Victims of Five Types of Crime

Reporting to the Police

For most crime victims the police is the single most important agency representing the criminal justice system. In the ICVS several questions deal with the interactions of victims with the police. Victims of all five types of crime were asked whether they or anybody else had reported the incident to the police. Those who had were asked why they reported. Those who hadn't were asked why not. More than one reason could be given. Data are presented on the most frequently mentioned reasons. Table 5.3 shows the results for one time and repeat victims overall and per world region.

First, with respect to regional differences, the results show that victims in the most developed nations are more likely to report to the police. Victims in transitional nations and developing nations are less inclined to report. Among victims of the more affluent industrialized countries the most common reasons for reporting are a belief that crime should be reported and for insurance requirements. Victims in the poorer regions mention recovery of property as their dominant concern, but also more often wish to see the offender caught and sentenced. In these regions more victims also hope to stop what is happening to them and to get help from the police.

One can speculate that the differences can largely be accounted for by the relative prevalence of insurance against criminal losses in the more affluent countries. In Western countries 70 per cent or more households are insured. In most developing countries only between 10 per cent and 20 per cent of the respondents are insured against household burglary. For financial redress victims in developed countries rely on insurance rather than on the police and, since reporting to the police is a requirement for insurance payments, victims in these countries are more likely to report. In the poorer quarters of the world the stakes for reporting victims are higher; for them, successful criminal investigations and the recovery of the stolen property is the only available avenue for redress. In this situation, victims who doubt the efficacy of criminal investigations will more readily refrain from reporting.[4]

As Table 5.3 shows, the experience of one-time and repeat victims differ in many respects. The differences are the clearest among victims from developed countries. As we have seen, victims in this region are more likely to report to the police for insurance reasons. Repeat victims in the affluent West report less often for insurance reasons but are more often inclined to report than one-time victims in order to see the offender arrested and/or to stop what is happening. These findings suggest that repeat victims do, as we supposed, know or assume that the same offender(s) are victimizing them

Table 5.3   Percentages of offences reported to the police and reasons for reporting and non-reporting by one-time and repeat victims of five types of crime overall and in developed, transitional and developing nations

	Overall		Developed		Transitional		Developing	
	Once	Repeat	Once	Repeat	Once	Repeat	Once	Repeat
No. of respondents	5 437	3 419	1 574	745	2 322	1 386	1 541	1 287
No. reporting to police (%)	42.0	37.7	54.9	49.4	40.4	37.9	30.9	30.9
Reasons for reporting (%)								
recover property	43.0	39.7	30.5	21.2	48.9	41.4	55.0	54.6
insurance reasons	23.5	20.7	32.1	24.4	17.7	16.1	19.0	22.9
should be reported	32.2	31.8	38.1	36.1	31.5	32.7	22.2	26.8
want offender caught/punished	37.6	41.6	24.9	29.9	44.7	48.1	47.4	44.3
to stop it	24.1	30.5	19.0	26.5	27.0	30.3	28.2	34.5
to get help	12.4	14.3	9.1	12.1	12.8	14.2	18.0	16.4
Reasons for not reporting (%)								
not serious enough	33.3	24.8	50.4	36.4	31.5	25.7	23.7	18.9
solved it myself	11.1	15.6	12.7	14.2	10.1	15.4	11.4	16.4
inappropriate for police	11.9	14.6	10.2	11.9	12.3	13.7	12.5	16.6
police could do nothing	25.6	22.5	11.7	13.2	29.3	24.8	30.4	24.4
police won't do anything	20.5	27.8	8.3	10.3	19.5	27.8	30.5	35.4
fear/dislike of police	6.3	8.0	2.7	2.4	5.2	5.8	10.3	12.6
did not dare	4.9	6.9	2.7	6.4	5.9	5.6	5.3	8.3

again and again and seek protection from the police against their victimization.[5]

The reporting patterns of repeat victims in developed countries resemble those of victims in developing countries. Like victims in developing countries, repeat victims in developed countries are less inclined to report to the police. This finding suggests that they are less certain that the police can satisfy their needs. Repeat victims in developed countries do not refrain from reporting because they consider their victimization not serious enough; they are more likely than one-time victims to refrain because they feel that the police could not, or would not, do anything. In this respect too, victims from developed countries resemble victims from developing countries.

For repeat victims in developed countries, the stakes seem to be as high as for victims in poorer countries: they feel that the police should prevent a reoccurrence of the crime by arresting the offender. Since this is often beyond the police's capacity, repeat victims are less likely to be satisfied with the police response. The next section tests these assumptions by looking at victim satisfaction with the police response and at the reasons for victim dissatisfaction.

Victim Satisfaction with Police Response

Victims in the developed countries are more often satisfied with the police response. This high level of satisfaction may not only reflect better services, it might also be due to the reporting victims' – notably those reporting for insurance reasons – more modest expectations. Such victims are more likely to complain about their insurance payments than about the police, whereas in less affluent countries police forces suffer the full brunt of victims' frustrations about financial losses. Notably, more victims in the developing world mention that the police treated them incorrectly or impolitely. This result confirms that, in some developing countries, the police are less likely to respect the civil rights of citizens, including those of crime victims.

The statistics given in Table 5.4 show that repeat victims are less often satisfied with the police response in all regions. The differences are most pronounced among the victims, as assumed, from the developed countries. In developed countries, three out of four one-time victims are 'satisfied', against only two out of three repeat victims. Although the reasons for dissatisfaction must be interpreted with caution because of the rather low numbers, in line with the reasons for reporting given by repeat victims in the developed countries, a significant source of discontentment for these victims is that the police did not find the offender. Repeat victims in the developed world are also somewhat more likely to feel badly treated by the police.

Table 5.4 Percentages of one-time and repeat victims of theft from cars, burglary, robbery, sexual incidents and threats/assaults who are satisfied with the police and the reasons for dissatisfaction, overall and for three world regions

	Overall		Developed		Transitional		Developing	
	Once	Repeat	Once	Repeat	Once	Repeat	Once	Repeat
Satisfied	54.4	44.3	75.0	63.5	41.3	36.0	41.6	36.6
Reasons not satisfied								
did not do enough	47.5	44.5	55.8	51.7	38.9	38.7	58.2	48.1
were not interested	36.6	34.5	42.8	32.6	35.8	36.6	33.4	32.8
did not find offender	32.0	35.2	18.9	26.3	38.3	39.9	29.6	33.8
did not recover goods	37.0	29.6	22.1	11.8	42.4	37.1	37.7	29.2
gave no information	17.5	15.5	27.4	14.8	12.5	14.8	20.0	16.6
incorrect/impolite	10.6	14.2	10.9	14.0	7.2	12.6	17.0	16.2
slow to arrive	9.9	11.5	11.4	13.1	9.9	8.3	8.8	14.5

105

These results confirm that the expectations, as well as the experiences, of reporting repeat victims in developed countries resemble those of reporting victims in less affluent countries.

Victim Assistance

Victims of more serious types of crime who had reported to the police were asked whether they had received support from a specialized victim support agency ('agencies to help victims of crime by giving information, or practical or emotional support').

As shown in Table 5.5 more victims in the West receive specialized help than elsewhere. In very few countries in the other regions are specialist services provided by specialist agencies. In Central and Eastern Europe and the developing countries, many more victims would have appreciated such help. Although no mention was made of financial support, some victims might have understood it as such, and this could help explain why support is most often wanted in countries where few victims are covered by insurance.

In the economically developed countries a slightly higher percentage of repeat victims, who reported to the police, received specialized help than one-time victims (this will be discussed further in the sections on burglary victims and victims of violence against women). The need for such help is somewhat higher among repeat victims in developed countries. Elsewhere, very few one-time or repeat victims receive help. The majority of victims in developing and transitional countries would have welcomed such help, regardless of being one-time or repeat victims. Although there is a large gap between the demand and supply of specialized help everywhere, this gap is largest in the less affluent parts of the world.

Repeat victims in developed countries are, as we have seen, more often than other victims dissatisfied with the police and marginally more inclined to be in need of specialized help. These results suggest that repeat victims do not see specialized help by other agencies as a viable substitute for police services.

General Attitudes of Victims

All respondents were asked to give a general judgement on the performance of the police in their area. They were also asked whether the last time they went out they had stayed away from certain streets or areas for fear of crime.[6] Table 5.6 gives the percentage responses of citizens who have not been victimized, who have been victimized once and who have been victimized more often (repeat victims), overall and by world region.

Table 5.5 Percentage of victims who received, or would have appreciated receiving, help from a specialized agency

	Overall		Developed		Transitional		Developing	
	Once	Repeat	Once	Repeat	Once	Repeat	Once	Repeat
Had help from specialized agency	4.1	4.7	7.7	12.3	4.1	3.7	2.5	3.3
Would have found agency useful	67.7	66.5	37.0	43.8	78.2	74.7	71.7	67.6

Table 5.6 Percentage of non-victims, one-time victims and repeat victims thinking police do a good job in controlling crime in their area and avoiding dangerous places after dark

	Overall			Developed			Transitional			Developing		
	None	Once	Repeat	None	Once	Repeat	None	Once	Repeat	None	Once	Repeat
Police do a good job	56.0	41.9	34.4	76.1	67.6	57.4	42.6	29.7	27.9	43.8	31.1	26.7
Fear of street crime	36.3	47.7	55.3	24.3	33.8	44.8	42.8	50.6	51.9	44.4	58.6	65.2

The figures show that citizens in the developed countries are generally more satisfied with the performance of their local police and less fearful of street crime. The comparison between the opinions of non-victims, one-time victims and repeat victims shows a strikingly consistent pattern. Victims are less satisfied with the police and more fearful than non-victims. Repeat victims exhibit all these tendencies to a more pronounced degree than one-time victims.

We have seen that repeat victims are less inclined to report subsequent incidents to the police and that reporting repeat victims are less often satisfied with the police's response. These findings suggest that the reduced level of satisfaction of repeat victims with overall police performance is rooted in negative personal experiences with the police. It is also plausible that repeat victimization experiences generate an increased fear of (street) crime. Considering what we have seen in Table 5.2, the pattern of repeat victimization is such that repeat victims have sound reasons to be more concerned about future victimizations than others. Repeat victims run an increased risk of being victimized again, and at least some seem to be aware of this fact.

The combined results on repeat victimization confirm that repeat victims have special expectations concerning the police, such as arresting the offender and/or offering concrete protection, which the police often fail to meet. Although repeat victims in developed countries more often receive specialized help, this does not act as an adequate remedy for insufficient police services. This conclusion implies that repeat victims will suffer more than other victims from secondary victimization. In the economically most developed countries victim satisfaction is generally at a high level so, in these countries, the special problems of repeat victims are therefore especially pronounced. In developed countries the police are better at satisfying victims because many victims rely on their insurance for financial redress and expect little more from the police than correct treatment and information; however, police forces in developed countries are less successful in satisfying the demands of repeat victims.

The next section will look, specifically, at the results concerning victims of burglary and violence against women.

Experiences of Victims and Repeat Victims of Burglary and Violence against Women

This section compares the reporting patterns and attitudes of victims of burglary with those of victims of violence against women. The comparison attempts to increase our understanding of the expectations and experiences of these two groups of victims *vis à vis* the police.

These two groups of victims are chosen because much of the recent literature on repeat victimization deals with either household burglary (Anderson *et al.*, 1994) or violence against women (Lloyd *et al.*, 1994). The prevalence of repeat victimization cannot easily be overestimated. According to our international data, 24 per cent of the burglary victims and 41 per cent of the violence against women victims were repeat victims within the course of one year.

In the case of burglary, repeat victimization is thought to be partly caused by offenders revisiting targets which they have successfully victimized before. Violence against women is often committed by spouses/partners or ex-spouses/ex-partners. In these cases, the offences are governed by the offender's problems with, or emotions towards, a specific individual. Repeat victimization is not an exception but the rule. In some cases, the use of violence is deeply engrained in the lifestyle of both offender and victim (Genn, 1988). In our data set, 37 per cent of the one-time victims of violence against women knew the offender by name as did 52 per cent of the repeat victims. Of the repeat victims from developed countries 63 per cent knew the offender by name.

Our hypothesis, here, is that repeat victims of burglary and violence against women often report to the police in order to obtain protection against the criminal activities of an individual offender. In the case of repeat burglaries, the victim will suspect having been visited by the same offender. In the case of violence against women, by partners or ex-partners, victims know the offender. If they report the incidents to the police they will typically expect protection and help. One might expect police forces to have difficulties in satisfying the demands of these two groups of repeat victims.

In the following tables, no differentiation will be made between world regions because the numbers of victims per region are too small for systematic presentation. At some points regional data will be cited by way of illustration.

Reporting

The frequency with which victims report offences to the police is strongly related to the type of crime involved. Table 5.7 shows the rates of reporting of burglaries and violence against women respectively. A further differentiation is made between one-time and repeat victims. The latter aspect is discussed at the end of this section.

Table 5.7 shows that both one-time and repeat victims of burglary are twice as likely to report to the police than one-time victims and repeat victims of violence against women. The majority of burglaries are reported to the police and little more than a quarter of incidents involving violence

Table 5.7   Percentages of burglaries and violence against women reported to the police and reasons for reporting and non-reporting

	Burglary		Violence against Women	
	Once	Repeat	Once	Repeat
Reported to the police (%)	61.8	54.7	28.3	26.8
Reasons for reporting (%)				
recover property	53.1	56.5	4.0	0.0
insurance reasons	20.9	17.3	4.7	4.4
should be reported	33.2	24.2	26.0	37.0
want offender caught/punished	42.8	48.5	54.2	43.6
to stop it	23.9	29.3	45.2	57.5
to get help	14.1	16.8	19.2	29.6
Reasons for not reporting (%)				
not serious enough	25.3	21.2	15.6	11.2
solved it myself	11.2	14.1	22.4	18.1
inappropriate for police	8.4	7.8	15.6	26.9
police could do nothing	27.7	26.2	19.8	20.7
police won't do anything	20.8	30.2	14.6	12.9
fear/dislike of police	5.8	2.9	13.8	18.2

against women. Further evidence from the ICVS reveals the reporting rate for burglary is 20 per cent higher in developed countries than in developing countries; the difference between the reporting rates of violence against women of the three regions is no more than 10 per cent.

Victims of burglary quite often seek assistance from the police in recovering property. As I have discussed above, this is most notably the case in developing countries and countries in transition. Many victims wanted the offender to be caught and punished, and many also referred to the moral obligation to report, especially in developed countries. A large number of victims of burglary in the developed countries said that they reported for insurance reasons. In other countries, victims report not to back up insurance claims, but in the hope that their property will be reclaimed from the offender by the police; in other words, they report to the police to recover their property and/or to see the offender arrested and sentenced. In all regions, then, financial considerations play an important role in the expectations of victims of burglary *vis à vis* the police.

If victims of violence against women report to the police, they most often want the offender to be caught and punished and/or to stop what is happening. One in five also mention the wish to receive help. The reasons for reporting are significantly different from those of burglary victims, and the special expectations and concerns of such victims go some way towards explaining the relatively low reporting rate. Victims may doubt the capacity of the police to offer protection against known offenders or even the commitment of the force to respond to such requests properly. Others may hesitate to ask the police to intervene in what they see as problems in their private life.

Burglary victims who did not report their victimization to the police were asked why they did not do so. As previously mentioned, more than one reason could be given. The main reasons for the non-reporting of burglaries was that the incident was not serious enough or that the police could do nothing. The reasons seem to be mainly economic. Victims of violence against women more often mention that they solved the problem themselves and/or found the incident inappropriate for the police. They also, more often than other victims, mention non-reporting because of fear or dislike of the police. Non-reporting of violence against women seems to be governed by uncertainties about the role of the police in these cases.

Repeat Victims

The results concerning repeat victims are interesting for several reasons. Although repeat victims are faced with serious problems, they are slightly less willing to report. The most interesting differences are found between the reasons for reporting. Repeat victims of burglary mention, more than other burglary victims, that they want the police to arrest the offender, stop what is happening and provide help – in short, they report in the hope that the police will offer protection against the offender. The wish for the police to stop the offender and offer help is even more central for repeat victims of violence against women who are somewhat less interested in seeing the offender arrested than one-time victims. As we have seen, many of these victims have intimate relations with the offender, or have had such relations in the past, and may, therefore, be reluctant to initiate criminal proceedings.

The reason for not reporting – 'police won't do anything' – is more often mentioned by repeat victims of burglary than by one-time victims (30 per cent of repeat victims against 21 per cent of one-time victims). This may be due to the fact that these victims may have had disappointing experiences with the police on a previous occasion. Repeat victims of violence against women do not feel this way at all; only 13 per cent mention this reason. However, they do more often mention that they felt that the matter was inappropriate for the police (27 per cent), confirming that a sizeable minority of victims of domestic violence do not want the police to intervene. A remarkable 18 per cent of these repeat victims mention fear or dislike of the police as a reason for non-reporting. The latter reason is the most common among victims in developing countries, particularly some Latin American countries. This result indicates that victims of violence against women in these countries are discouraged from reporting by the prevailing 'macho' police culture.

These results confirm our hypothesis that repeat victims of burglary and, even more, repeat victims of violence against women demand, more than one-time victims of these types of crime, protection and help from the police.

Victim Satisfaction

This section discusses whether repeat victims of burglary and violence against women are more or less often satisfied than one-time victims, with the police response they receive.

As shown by Table 5.8 victims of violence against women are more often satisfied than victims of burglaries with the police response they receive. It is difficult to interpret this result since, first, these groups must have vastly different needs and, second, this result must also be seen in relation to a much lower reporting rate (as discussed above, only one in four victims of violence against women report). The few victims of violence against women who report to the police are somewhat more likely to be satisfied by the services delivered than victims of burglary. This result suggests that at least some police forces succeed in satisfying the special needs of these female victims.

Perhaps the most striking finding of our analysis is that repeat victims of both types of crime are significantly less often satisfied with the police response than one-time victims. However, the reasons for dissatisfaction are based on fairly low numbers and must be interpreted with due caution. This is particularly the case with regard to the results on the satisfaction of victims of violence against women: very few of these cases are reported. Nevertheless, the results available show few remarkable differences, although, notably, a relatively high percentage of victims of violence against women complain about the police being impolite or incorrect. This complaint was most common among victims from the developing world: more than 30 per cent mentioned this.

Table 5.8   Percentages of one-time and repeat victims of burglaries and violence against women who are satisfied with the police response and reasons for dissatisfaction

	Burglary		Violence against Women	
	Once	Repeat	Once	Repeat
Satisfied with response (%)	43.5	29.8	56.8	41.9
Reasons not satisfied (%)				
did not do enough	43.8	36.7	50.2	58.4
were not interested	30.0	36.4	39.7	34.1
did not find offender	39.2	37.5	19.7	36.3
did not recover goods	46.8	36.8	3.6	0.0
gave no information	16.1	13.3	21.5	10.6
incorrect/impolite	9.8	9.1	22.1	28.7
slow to arrive	11.7	17.9	7.2	6.9

The results clearly indicate that repeat victims of both types of crime are often disappointed in the capacity, or willingness, of the police to offer the services they want – that is, protection against the offender.

Victim Assistance

In the 1996 survey, victims of burglaries and violence against women who had reported to the police were specifically asked whether they had received support from a specialized agency. As noted earlier, in most countries few victims had received such help. The figures are variable across offence type. As shown in Table 5.9, victims of violence against women are more likely to receive help than victims of burglary.

The ICVS can provide regional rates, regarding 'assistance', which reveal that 6.6 per cent of burglary victims, in developed countries, received help as did 15 per cent of the repeat burglary victims. Elsewhere in the world these percentages stay below 3 per cent. Of the victims of violence against women in developed countries, 6.6 per cent had received help as had 29.4 per cent of the repeat victims. The relatively high prevalence of actual help for repeat victims in developed countries reflects the existence of special provisions for female victims, such as shelters for battered women and rape crisis centres.

Table 5.9   Percentages of victims of burglary and violence against women who have received victim assistance or would have appreciated such help

	Burglary		Violence against Women	
	Once	Repeat	Once	Repeat
No. of victims	1 435	481	435	286
Have received help from specialized agency	3.3	4.0	5.1	8.8
Would have found agency useful	57.0	64.4	72.8	72.8

The majority of the victims of burglary and violence against women who do not receive help would have appreciated it. Victims in the transitional countries and the developing countries more often express an interest in such services. Repeat victims are slightly more interested, but the differences are small. Repeat victims differ more from other victims in their attitudes towards the services of the police than in their need for specialized help.

Victim Attitudes

Finally, this section briefly compares attitudes concerning local police, fear of street crime and fear of burglary for respondents who have not been victimized in the last five years, with those who have been victimized once last year and those who had been victimized more than once last year.

The results show, in Table 5.10, that citizens who are victimized by either a burglary or violence against women quickly lose confidence in the crime-controlling capacity of their local police. Burglary victims are keenly aware of their increased risks of being burgled (van Dijk *et al.*, 1990) and repeat victims even more so. In line with this, victims are also more likely to use precautionary devices, such as burglar alarms, than non-victims (6.8 per cent of non victims, 12.4 per cent of one-time victims and 13.1 per cent of repeat victims possess an alarm). Victims of violence against women are more fearful of street crime than non-victims. Experiences of victimization by males in private settings often generate generalized feelings of fear, as has been shown in other analyses.

Table 5.10   **Percentage responses of non victims, one-time victims and repeat victims of burglary and violence against women, thinking police are doing a good job in controlling crime in their area and fearing street crime and burglary**

	Burglary			Violence against women (women only)		
	None	Once	Repeat	None	Once	Repeat
No. of victims	51 799	1 435	481	28 294	435	286
Police do a good job	55.5	38.6	28.9	54.5	41.0	32.7
Fear of street crime	37.0	54.0	56.1	47.8	67.6	72.3
Fear of burglary	36.7	61.6	68.1	–	–	–

Conclusions and Policy Implications

Less than half of the victims of conventional crimes report their victimization to the police. Less than one in three female victims of violence do so. Reporting is particularly low in developing countries. The reasons for reporting vary across types of crime and country. In the industrialized countries many victims report crimes to fulfil a condition for claiming insurance money. In countries where fewer people have insurance, victims report in the hope that the police will find the offender and recover their property.

Globally, less than half of the reporting victims are satisfied with their treatment by the police. In the transitional and developing countries the level of satisfaction is even lower. In relation to this, many victims are reluctant to report crimes to the police. This lack of confidence in the police implies that crime victims often have no authority to which to turn and consequently feel alienated. Low reporting rates also impede effective crime prevention and control. The chances of arresting the offenders and getting a conviction largely depend on the information supplied by the victim. If many victims are doubtful whether reporting to the police will do them any good – as is clearly the case in most developing nations – the effectiveness of the police is severely undermined. For more effective criminal investigations the cooperation of victims is essential. This is another reason why the proportion of satisfied victims ought to be used as a performance measure for criminal investigation agencies.

According to the survey, few victims who had reported to the police received specialized help although half of them would, however, have welcomed it. Clearly, there are many unmet needs among the many victims of crime, especially among female victims of violence.

These findings show that the standards for victim assistance and empowerment of the 1985 UN Declaration of Basic Principles of Justice for Victims of Crime and Abuse of Power are far from sufficiently implemented. According to the Declaration, victims must be treated with dignity and respect at all stages of criminal proceedings. They should also be well informed about the proceedings and be allowed to present their views and concerns. In addition, the Declaration stipulates that all necessary forms of support should be made available. In 1998 the Commission on Crime Prevention and Criminal Justice, a functional commission of the Economic & Social Council of the UN, adopted two documents to promote the implementation of the Declaration – the *Guide for Policy Makers* and the *Handbook on Justice for Victims*. These documents will be published by the United Nations Centre for International Crime Prevention (they are also available at www.victimology.nl). In addition, the US Department of Justice has offered to organize training seminars on the use of the *Handbook* for relevant categories of officials.

A better deal for crime victims seems an obvious requirement of national and international crime prevention strategies. In developing countries and countries in transition, the consequences of victimization by conventional crime are often very severe since no financial support is available. International organizations, such as the United Nations, should consider setting up relief funds for the victims of criminal violence in countries where state compensation does not exist. Proposals for such a fund have been made and are the subject of discussion within the Commission mentioned above.

Of great policy relevance is the outcome of evaluations of the effects of better treatment of victims by the police, prosecutors and the courts. In the Netherlands (Wemmers, 1995), the results of one such evaluation show that victims who have been treated better by the police have a more positive attitude towards the police and the system in general. They are also more inclined to feel obliged to respect the law and are therefore less likely to commit crimes themselves; this result confirms the notion that citizens are very sensitive to the procedural justice rendered to them by the police and the judicial authorities. By treating victims better, the criminal justice system helps enhance respect for the law and thereby the prevention of crime. Since almost all citizens are victimized at least once during their lifetime, the impact of adequate victim policies on respect for the law and its institutions cannot be overstated. A better deal for crime victims is the most effective public relations policy the criminal justice system can pursue. It is also a cornerstone of effective crime prevention.

Repeat Victimizations

The ICVS has confirmed the universal prevalence of repeat victimization. It has also documented that repeat victims have special needs which are largely unmet by the police. Repeat victimization is a forceful argument for targeting crime prevention efforts at victims. In several countries, police forces provide crime prevention advice to reporting victims with fairly good results (Winkel, 1987; Boogaard, 1992). Our results suggest that more should be done for repeat victims, especially in developed countries. The findings with regard to repeat victims indicate that repeat victims, even more than other victims, feel neglected by the police. Repeat victims of both property and violent offences are often in urgent need of protection against the activities of known offenders. If they report, they are especially likely to be dissatisfied with the services delivered since, in many cases, the police apparently fail to offer the protection needed. Many repeat victims have no confidence in the usefulness of the police and refrain from reporting.

The poor service delivered to repeat victims are wasted opportunities for successful crime prevention and detection. For the citizens involved these negative experiences have an alienating effect, leading many repeat victims to express a distinct lack of confidence in their local police. Since they tend to be more fearful of crime and, according to ICVS findings not presented here, often live in socially less integrated neighbourhoods, repeat victims are in danger of losing their trust in institutions, and the 'community' in general, as well as their respect for the law. As we have seen, the underreporting of repeat victimization of violence against women is very pronounced worldwide. Not only the victims involved but also their children – and, in fact, society as a whole – would greatly benefit from services which highlight the rejection by society of all forms of domestic violence.

In some countries, most notably in the UK, police forces make efforts to improve their responses to repeat victims of violence against women and burglary (Farrell and Pease, 1993). In 1997 the UK's Norfolk police force was awarded the European Crime Prevention Award in The Hague for a programme offering special protection to victims of violence against women (for example, linking up the women at risk to the local police station through personal electronic alarm equipment). Similarly, the Huddersfield scheme to reduce repeat vehicle theft and burglary victimization is highly acclaimed (Chenery *et al.*, 1997). The most innovative elements of this scheme are the loan of monitored alarms, trackers and covert cameras to repeat victims. The provision of such equipment was found to be effective in terms of protection offered, and it seems a desirable option for repeat victims of burglary everywhere in the industrialized world.

Little thought has yet been given to the implications of repeat victimization for criminal proceedings. The sheer prevalence of the phenomenon underscores the need for victims to have a larger role in the proceedings. Crime victims cannot legitimately be construed as people who had the misfortune to be at the wrong place at the wrong time and thereby having little relevance to the criminal case. In many more cases than previously recognized, the offender has wittingly, or even deliberately, committed several offences against the same victims. While this is obvious in cases of spouse abuse or racist attacks on shop owners, repeat victims are often also involved in cases of burglary or robbery. Prosecutors and judges seem to have little or no awareness of the phenomenon of repeat victimization, let alone of the need to give special consideration to the needs and interests of repeat victims in the proceedings. Coping resources of these victims might be depleted by the reoccurence of stressful events (Winkel, 1998). Such victims may not only need counselling and support but also special assistance in their capacity as witnesses or providers of a victim impact statement. Information on repeat victimization is also relevant for sentencing. For perpetrators of burglaries or robberies, the revisiting of successfully victimized premises might just be a matter of convenience. However, the choice to revictimize the same people shows a lack of compunction which merits the consideration of the courts. In such cases the imposition of generous victim compensation seems particularly appropriate.

By treating all victims more fairly and humanely, the criminal justice system can maintain or restore victims' respect for the law. In so doing, a downward spiral of criminal violence and resentment among victims might be prevented. From this perspective, helping victims is not just a task for welfare agencies and volunteers; it belongs to the core business of police and the courts.

Notes

1   In total more that 133 821 citizens of 15 years and older were interviewed within the framework of the ICVS. Details of the ICVS can be found in van Dijk *et al.* (1990), Alvazzi del Frate *et al.* (1993) and Mayhew and van Dijk (1997). Samples sizes varied between 1000 in developing countries and 2000 in most other countries. In developing countries and most countries in transition the interviews were carried out through face-to-face interviewing. In most developing nations and some nations in transition, the survey was carried out among the inhabitants of the largest city (city surveys). Elsewhere, well-spread samples were drawn from the national population. For a discussion on the methodological aspects we refer to the publications just mentioned see also Block (1993); Lynch (1993); and Stangeland (1995).

The key figures presented here are based on the results of the surveys carried out in 1996 in the course of the third sweep of the survey. This data refers to the experiences of about 60 000 citizens. The data was aggregated into rates for three global regions. The first region is represented by the industrialized (developed) nations and consists of the New World (USA, Canada) and Western Europe (11 countries). The second region, of nations in transition, is Central and Eastern Europe (20 countries). The third region, of developing nations, consists of Asia (China, India, Indonesia and Philippines), Latin America (Argentina, Bolivia, Brazil, Colombia, Costa Rica and Paraguay) and Africa (Egypt, South Africa, Tanzania, Tunisia, Uganda and Zimbabwe).

Respondents were asked to report on incidents of victimization which happened to them or their households over the past five years. In a follow-up question, those who mentioned victimizations were asked whether a victimization took place in the last year. Follow-up questions on reporting to the police and related issues refer to the last victimization by a specific type of crime. In this chapter the analysis is, with some exceptions, limited to victimizations which took place in the previous 12 months.

2   Table 5.2 shows that observed multiple victimization is more frequent than is to be expected on the basis of random distribution. Repeating this comparison between the frequencies of observed and expected multiple victimization for a subgroup of high-risk persons (using the four variables: young, living in a big city, affluent and outgoing), the differences between observed and expected frequencies can be expressed in the K-SZ measure. For the total group under analysis, the K-SZ is 45 6671 (n=128 827; p<0.000). For the more homogeneous high risk group the K-SZ was much smaller but still significant (14 6789; n=7072; p<0.000). This result confirms that repeat victimization is not fully accounted for by the four known risk factors.

3   Repeat victims of violence usually know whether the same offender was the perpetrator. There is some evidence from the British Crime Survey 1992 that many repeat victims of burglary and other property crimes assume their victimization to be the work of the same offender(s) (Chenery *et al.*, 1996).

4   An analysis at the level of individual victims showed that income level is the most important factor related to reporting of crimes. The second most important factor is the perceived seriousness of the offence. Other relevant factors are age, level of education and gender. More affluent, older, better educated and male victims are somewhat more likely to report crimes to the police. In sum, victimizations which are more serious and concern socially established victims are most likely to be reported. The dependent variable of the regression analysis was the decision to report theft from cars, burglary with entry, robbery, sexual incidents and assaults/threats (n=24 081). The variables chosen in the equation were income, seriousness, age, education, gender and lifestyle (outdoor visits). The multiple R was 0.27.

5   The lower proportion of repeat victims who report for car insurance reasons may also be the result of an overrepresentation of poorer, uninsured persons in this group.

6   For an elaboration of these survey questions the reader is referred to previous publications on the ICVS (van Dijk *et al.*, 1990).

References

Alvazzi del Frate, A., Zvekic, U. and van Dijk, J.M. (1993) (eds), *Understanding Crime: Experiences of Crime and Crime Control*, Rome: UNICRI.

Alvazzi del Frate, A. and Patignani, A. (1995), *Women's Victimization in Developing Countries*, Rome: UNICRI.

Anderson, D., Chenery, S. and Pease, K. (1994), *Biting Back: Tackling Repeat*

Burglary and Car Crime, Crime Detection and Prevention Series, No. 58, London: Home Office Police Department.

Block, R. (1993), 'Measuring Victimization's Risk: The Effects of Methodology, Sampling, and Fielding', in A. Alvazzi del Frate, U. Zvekic and J.J.M. van Dijk (eds), *Understanding Crime: Experiences of Crime and Crime Control*, Rome: UNICRI, 163–73.

Boogaard, J.W. van den (1992), *Slachtoffers Van Woninginbraken Benaderd*, Enschede: Universiteit Twente, Faculteit der Wijsbegeerte en Maatschappijwetenschappen.

Chenery, S., Tseloni, A. and Pease, K. (1996), 'Crime which Repeats: Undigested Evidence from the British Crime Survey 1992', *International Journal of Risk, Security and Crime Prevention*, **1**(3), 207–16.

Chenery, S., Ellingworth, D., Holt, J. and Pease, K. (1997), *Biting Back II: Reducing Repeat Victimization in Huddersfield*, London: Home Office, Police Research Group.

Ellingworth, D. *et al.* (1997), 'Prior Victimization and Crime Risk', *International Journal of Risk, Security and Crime Prevention*, **2**(3), 201–14.

Farrell, G. and Pease, K. (1993), *Once Bitten, Twice Bitten: Repeat Victimisation and Its Implications for Crime Prevention*, CPU Paper 46, London: Home Office Crime Prevention Unit.

Genn, H. (1988), 'Multiple Victimization' in M. Maguire and J. Pointing (eds), *Victims of Crime: A New Deal?*, Milton Keynes: Open University Press, 90–100.

Kleemans, E.R. (1996), 'Heraald Slachtofferschap van Het Delict Woninginbraak', *Tijdschrift Voor Criminologie*, **38**(3), 232–44.

Lloyd, S., Farrell, G. and Pease, K. (1994), *Preventing Repeated Domestic Violence: A Demonstration Project on Merseyside*, Crime Prevention Unit Paper No. 49, London: Home Office.

Lurigio, A.J., Skogan, W.G. and Davies, R.C. (1990) (eds), *Victims of Crime: Problems, Policies and Programmes*, London: Sage.

Lynch, J.P. (1993), 'Secondary Analysis of International Crime Survey Data', in A. Alvazzi del Frate, U. Zvekic and J.J.M. van Dijk (eds), *Understanding Crime: Experiences of Crime and Crime Control*, Rome: UNICRI, 175–89.

Mayhew, P. and van Dijk, J.J.M. (1997), *Criminal Victimisation in Eleven Industrialised Countries: Key Findings From the 1996 International Crime Victims Survey*, The Hague: WODC, Ministry of Justice.

Mukherjee, S. and Carcach, C. (1998), *Repeat Victimisation in Australia*, Griffith, ACT: Australian Institute of Criminology.

Roberts, A.R. (1990), *Helping Crime Victims: Research, Policy and Practice*, London: Sage.

Stangeland, P. (1995), *The Crime Puzzle: Crime Patterns and Crime Displacement in Southern Spain*, Malaga: IAIC.

Travis, G., Egger, S. and O'Toole, B. (1995), 'The International Crime Surveys: Some Methodological Concerns', *Current Issues in Criminal Justice*, **6**, 346–61.

van Dijk, J.J.M. (1994), 'Understanding Crime Rates; On the Interactions Between the Rational Choices of Victims and Offenders', *The British Journal of Criminology*, **34**(2), 105–21.

van Dijk, J.J.M. and Mayhew, P. (1992), *Criminal Victimization in the Industrial-*

ized World: Key findings of the 1989 and 1992 International Crime Surveys, The Hague: Ministry of Justice, Directorate for Crime Prevention.

van Dijk, J.J.M., Mayhew, P. and Killias, M. (1990), *Experiences of Crime Across the World: Key Findings of the 1989 International Crime Survey*, Deventer: Kluwer.

van Dijk, J.J.M. and Steinmetz, C.H.D. (1983), 'Victimization Surveys: Beyond Measuring the Volume of Crime', *Victimology: An International Journal*, **8**, 291–301.

van Dijk, J.J.M. and van Kesteren, J. (1996), 'Criminal Victimization in European Cities; Some Results of the International Crime Victims Survey', *European Journal on Criminal Policy and Research*, **4**(1), 9–21.

van Dijk, J.J.M. and de Waard, J. (1991), 'A Two-Dimensional Typology of Crime Prevention Projects: With a Bibliography', *Criminal Justice Abstracts*, **23**(3), 483–503.

Wemmers, J.A. (1996), *Victims in the Criminal Justice System: A Study into the Treatment of Victims and its Effects on their Attitudes and Behaviour*, Amsterdam: Kugler.

Winkel, F.W. (1987), *Politie en Voorkoming Misdrijven*, Amsterdam: Mens en Recht.

Winkel, F.W. (1998), *Repeat Victimization and Trauma-Susceptibility: Prospective and Longitudinal Analyses*, Amsterdam: Free University, Kurt Lewin Institute.

Wittebrood, K. and Nieuwbeerta, P. (1997), *Criminal Victimization During One's Life Course in the Netherlands: The Effects of Routine Activity Patterns and Previous Victimization*, Leiden: Netherlands Institute for the Study of Criminality and Law Enforcement.

Zvekic, U. (1996), 'The International Crime (Victim) Survey: Issues of Comparative Advantages and Disadvantages', *International Criminal Justice Review*, **6**, 1–21.

Zvekic, U. and Alvazzi del Frate, A. (1993), 'Victimization in the Developing World: An Overview of Preliminary Key Findings from the 1992 International Crime Survey', in A. Alvazzi del Frate, U. Zvekic and J.J.M. van Dijk (eds), *Understanding Crime*, Rome: UNICRI, 51–85.

PART II
VICTIMS WITHIN CRIMINAL JUSTICE

6 The New Status of Victims in the UK: Opportunities and Threats

Helen Reeves and Kate Mulley

There has been an enormous growth of new policies and provision for victims and witnesses in the UK over the last five years. On paper, this growth represents a massive improvement in the way in which victims are treated within the criminal justice system. So has the victim/witness agenda been met? Has secondary victimization by a seemingly unsympathetic criminal justice process become a problem of the past? Do victims now have a voice? In this chapter, we will focus on the implementation of these new measures and, in so doing, consider both the opportunities and the threats that this represents.

The present situation in the UK represents a watershed. For the first time victims and witnesses are genuinely central to people's thinking on criminal justice. Victims are now not merely regarded as a source of evidence, but are seen as having a legitimate interest with needs and rights of their own. New groups of people working within criminal justice are coming into contact with victims and witnesses and are required to take their views into account. It is now generally recognized that victims and witnesses should be treated with respect and consideration by all those working in a system which, to a large extent, is dependent upon their cooperation. An increasing recognition of the problems faced by victims – for example, the need for adequate protection and information – has led to a range of new measures, with various solutions now enshrined in legislation or set out in practice guidelines and service standards.

However, we will argue that, although these changes do represent new opportunities for victims, their value will ultimately depend on the way in which they are put into practice. Essentially, how well they work will depend on the approach of the agencies involved in their implementation. Is there a willingness for change? Will additional resources be made available and will existing preconceptions and attitudes be challenged? A change in the culture of the criminal justice system is needed, but whether these new solutions will be able to deliver this change for the benefit of crime victims is yet to be determined. Certain potential dangers have already become apparent and we will be examining these in some detail to see what lessons can be learnt.

Victim Support's Perspective and Agenda for Action

Victim Support is the national charity which offers help to over 1 million crime victims and witnesses each year. Staff and volunteers based in 386 schemes throughout England, Wales and Northern Ireland (Scotland has its own organization) offer information, practical assistance and emotional support to people who have become the victims of crimes ranging from burglary to the murder of a relative. It also runs a Witness Service in every Crown Court in England and Wales, and in a growing number of magistrates' courts, offering information and support to witnesses, victims and their families attending court. Currently, over 17 000 people work for Victim Support, mostly in a voluntary capacity. In 1999 it celebrated its silver jubilee.

By trying to ensure that all individuals have equal access to our services and are equally likely to benefit, Victim Support aims to provide a comprehensive service to all victims of crime, rather than a service which is limited to the small percentage of individuals whose cases progress through the criminal justice system.

As well as being a service-providing organization, Victim Support also works to increase understanding and awareness of the effects of crime and to ensure better recognition of victims' rights. Because of the extent of its contact with victims and witnesses, it is in a unique position to gather information about the impact of crime. It is also able to monitor the introduction of changes to the criminal justice system, examining how they are perceived and used by victims.

The Effects of Crime

Victim Support works with people who have experienced a crisis in their lives. It believes that this experience is essentially different from that of an accident or illness, because it has been brought about intentionally by another person. Victims of crime have been subjected to someone interfering in their lives, and this negative experience may fundamentally alter their view of the world. Resultant feelings of anger, fear and guilt are all common and are both normal and healthy. However, long-term problems may arise if an individual is unable to work through these emotions and form a resolution.

Research into the effects of crime carried out by Mike Maguire and Claire Corbett (1987) found that the emotional impact of crime was, in many ways, more important than the consequent physical pain or financial loss. Seemingly trivial offences could lead to a major trauma. These findings are backed by Victim Support's everyday experience. For example, in 1997 the organization offered support to just under 500 000 people who had been burgled. In most of these cases the offender will never be detected. This means that many victims cannot hope for a resolution through the criminal justice process, and this can leave them feeling both upset and frustrated – feelings which may manifest themselves in anger directed at the authorities which they believe have failed to protect their interests. The service offered by Victim Support aims to help people address their feelings, as well as offering practical help and assistance. Because its services are provided by local people who are giving their time free of charge, it demonstrates concern on behalf of society, helping to counteract the negative impact of the crime. In this way, its approach can be described as truly restorative in nature.

An important part of Victim Support's philosophy is that it offers a community response to crime which can help ameliorate a victim's feelings of anger and disaffection. While respecting the victim's right to make their own decisions, it makes sure that victims have access to the services they need or want, and that they can talk freely and in confidence to someone outside their circle of family and friends. In this way, it hopes to maximize the possibility of an ultimately positive outlook following the crime. The organization's sole aim is to help crime victims and witnesses – it has no other agenda – and it is from this perspective that it approaches the role of the victim within criminal justice. It is also the perspective that we take in discussing the issue in this chapter.

We believe that the state should assist the victim's recovery from the crime as far as possible. However, our experience shows that this rarely happens in practice. All too frequently, an individual's initial negative reaction on becoming a victim of crime is reinforced and intensified by their experience of the criminal justice process. This happens for a number of reasons. In the past, many victims cited a lack of information as their major dissatisfaction. They felt alienated and sidelined. These feelings are compounded when a victim's very involvement in the process places them in danger and yet insufficient steps are taken for their protection. Add to this the additional insult that victims may feel if they are treated unsympathetically and you begin to see why so many victims are dissatisfied and distressed.

Victim Support's Policy Work

The extent of Victim Support's contact with victims and witnesses has helped us identify problems and issues at the earliest stage. We can see how the difficulties experienced by victims of crime extend well beyond the trauma of the initial offence. Once problems have been identified through our local work, we have carried these issues forward by national research, campaigns and policy development.

Over the years, Victim Support has commissioned and conducted a range of internal research projects. Most recently we looked at the experiences of women who report rape and the treatment of child witnesses at court in two research reports. The first, entitled *Women, Rape and the Criminal Justice System* (Victim Support, 1996a) looked at the experiences of over 1000 women who reported rape and highlighted the problems they faced during the criminal justice process. The report identified three main areas of concern: a lack of information; the need for protection in the community from the offender; and the way these women were treated when they were called to give evidence at court. The second report, *Children in Court* (Victim Support, 1996b) provided an analysis of children's experiences as witnesses in the Crown Court and demonstrated the wide variations in practice in the way in which child witnesses are treated.

We have also set up a number of interagency working parties to consider specific issues. For example, in 1990 we convened a National Inter-Agency Working Party on Domestic Violence with a remit to review the type and extent of service provision currently available to victims of domestic violence and to produce recommendations as to how these should be coordinated and extended throughout the UK. The working party's report was launched in 1992 to widespread public acclaim, and many of its recommendations have since been adopted (see Victim Support, 1992). In 1994, following feedback from local schemes, Victim Support convened an independent working party to look at the support available to the families of road death victims. We had become increasingly concerned that the grief and distress caused to these families was all too often exacerbated by the formality of the procedures which had to be followed and by the lack of information or support provided. Again, the working party produced a substantial report of its findings (Victim Support, 1994).

As well as convening working parties and carrying out internal research projects, Victim Support has extensive contact with government bodies and with the main professionals who operate in the criminal justice system. We are frequently invited to sit on external working parties and national committees and to contribute to training programmes and consultations. Amongst others, we are members of the Victims' Steering Group (the body which is responsible for monitoring implementation of the Victim's Charter), the Health and Safety Executive's Inter-Departmental Committee of Violence to Staff, the Witness Care Sub-Group of the Trials Issues Group, the NACRO Race Issues Advisory Committee, the Racial Incidents Standing Committee and the Interdepartmental Working Group on the Treatment of Vulnerable or Intimidated Witnesses in the Criminal Justice System.

As a result, Victim Support has developed a large body of policy. In February 1995, we drew all our policies together in the paper *The Rights of Victims of Crime* (Victim Support, 1995). This document contains a statement of the rights to which Victim Support believes all victims of crime are fundamentally entitled. It focuses on the experiences of crime victims and witnesses within the criminal justice system, concluding that the state's concern to deal with the offender while at the same time protecting his/her human rights needs to be matched by a similar concern for the victim. We believe that, by reinstating the victim in the criminal justice process, the state must undertake certain responsibilities which can be grouped under five main principles:

- *Compensation*. Victims should be entitled to receive compensation so that they are in approximately the same financial position as they were before the crime.
- *Protection*. Victims and witnesses should be protected in any way necessary. By participating in the criminal justice process victims may place themselves in danger of intimidation or harassment, especially where they are the key witness to a case. For example, our survey, *Women, Rape and the Criminal Justice System* (Victim Support, 1996a) found that one in every three of the Victim Support Schemes which took part said that they were in touch with women who had experienced intimidation or harassment subsequent to reporting the offence. One woman was later murdered by the man who raped her. Unless victims and witnesses are offered protection, backed up by adequate resources to ensure their safety, they can not be expected to give their best evidence in court. As well as physical protection, we also believe victims have the right to expect a degree of psychological protection – for instance, the right to privacy.
- *Services*. Victims have the right to receive respect, recognition and support. Victims and witnesses are entitled to receive services from an organization which is dedicated to their needs. Yet, although the services provided by Victim Support can make a substantial contribution

in assisting the victim's recovery, they are not in themselves sufficient. It is essential that the experience of respect and support is
reinforced by all the professionals with whom the victim comes into
contact. Confidence in the criminal justice system depends to a large
extent on the way people are treated when they are required to take
part.

- *Information*. Victims have the right to receive clear information about
the progress of their case, about the procedures being followed, about
their role in this process and about any rights they may have. They
should also receive an explanation of any decisions made in the case,
ideally by the person responsible for taking that decision. Lack of
timely information is the most common complaint we hear voiced by
crime victims, undermining their satisfaction with the whole process.
As well as receiving insufficient information, victims also complain
that they have no opportunity to contribute themselves. Frequently,
victims have information on the circumstances of a crime – often not
strictly evidence, but still relevant – and yet no-one is interested. This
can lead to victims sitting in court feeling as though the case has
nothing to do with them, resulting in enormous frustration and an
unsuccessful outcome from the victim's point of view. We believe
that victims should have an opportunity to give a statement in their
own words about the full financial, physical and emotional consequences of the crime and about any fears they may have about retaliation. This statement should be taken into consideration whenever
decisions are made about the case, including cautioning, charging and
bail.

- *Responsibility*. Victim Support firmly believes that victims should be
free of the burden of decisions relating to the offender. This responsibility lies with the state and should not be placed on the victim. As an
ordinary citizen, the victim may have a responsibility to give information, and they may also have other opportunities to make a positive
contribution – for example, in mediation – but this should not be
confused with the state's ultimate responsibility to deal, and to be
seen to deal, with the offender. This point will be discussed in some
detail when we consider the implementation of restorative justice
initiatives.

New Opportunities for Victims: An Overview of Developments

Victim Support's publication of *The Rights of Victims of Crime* (1995) set
the agenda. It identified a range of common problems and then spelt out

solutions to them. Since the publication of that report the status of victims in the UK has dramatically improved. One by one, the rights identified as applying to all victims of crime have been recognized and acted on. We will now consider the major developments which have taken place over the past few years, highlighting the opportunities they represent for victims of crime

In 1990 the Home Office published the first *Victim's Charter* (1990) which attempted to set out the rights and standards of service which crime victims could expect to receive. Although the Charter contained little new information, and no guidance on what to do if its standards were not met, the fact that it referred to victims as having rights represented an important principle in itself. It was a major landmark in that it confirmed, for the first time, that there was a problem to be addressed. *The Courts Charter* (Lord Chancellor's Department, 1992) set out a series of modest provisions for victims and witnesses regarding court waiting times, the listing of cases and the opportunity to receive information about the process of the case.

In 1993 Victim Support published the report of an independent working party on compensation (Victim Support, 1993), which called for changes in the state-funded criminal injuries compensation scheme and recommended that it be replaced by a tariff system (to speed up the processing of cases and to provide more parity in the awards made), backed by adequate benefits to cover loss of earnings. The Criminal Injuries Compensation Act 1995 introduced a new tariff scheme, which came into effect in April 1996. The Act represents an improvement on the preceding scheme, although some problems persist.

However, it was not until the second Victim's Charter was published in June 1996 that victims received any substantial improvement in their status (Home Office, 1996a). This Charter focused on the victim's right to information, placing a responsibility on the police to give victims information at every stage in the process. New leaflets and information packs were produced and new rights for victims attending court were spelt out. For the first time it was agreed that witnesses are entitled to a pre-trial familiarization visit (to look round the court before the trial) and to receive support at court, as well as to wait separately from the defendant. The service standards set out in the Charter are enforceable, with complaints procedures listed and compliance with the standards monitored by the agencies concerned and reported back to the Victims Steering Group. The Charter also established two pilot projects: the 'One Stop Shop' for keeping victims informed about their case and 'victim statements' whereby victims are offered the opportunity to provide information about the full effects of the crime. These two pilot projects are the subject of evaluation (Hoyle *et al.*, 1998).

The *Statement of National Standards of Witness Care in the Criminal Justice System,* published by the Witness Care Sub-Group of the Trials

Issues Group (1996), represents a major breakthrough in the way in which witnesses are treated at court, by providing guidance for local criminal justice agencies to help them improve their services. For example, it states that the time witnesses are kept waiting at court should be kept to a minimum and recommends that standby arrangements (somewhere away from the court building) should be available for particularly vulnerable witnesses, such as children, while waiting to give evidence. Sensitive cases should be identified early so that fixed dates can be arranged with any special provisions, such as the use of a screen while giving evidence, agreed in advance. In addition, unless necessary for evidential purposes, witnesses' addresses should not be read out in open court. All these proposals demonstrate a greater understanding of the needs of victims and witnesses and a new willingness to take them into account.

By 1996 there had been substantial recognition of victims' rights to information and improvements in the way victims are treated when they are called to give evidence, but one basic right – the need for protection – had still received very little attention and was not identified as a priority until 1997. The Protection from Harassment Act 1997, originally conceived to deal with the problem of 'stalking' (Home Office, 1996b), established two new criminal offences: causing harassment, alarm or distress; and causing fear of violence. These offences are intended to cover repeated incidents which, although they may be of a minor nature in themselves, when considered cumulatively can build up to make life intolerable. Such incidents may well be a feature of domestic abuse, racial harassment or neighbour disputes and were not previously sufficiently covered under the criminal law. This often meant that victims would have to wait until either a civil order had been breached, or a more serious crime had been committed against them, before they were able to seek protection. The Act also introduced a civil measure to deal with harassment and a new hybrid remedy whereby a breach of the civil order becomes a criminal offence. By allowing the civil and the criminal law to be used in conjunction with each other the protection which the Act is able to offer should be vastly increased.

The Crime and Disorder Act 1998 also has significant implications for victims. The Act is aimed at reducing offending and helping create safer communities. To achieve these aims it proposes a series of changes to the youth justice system which could lead to a significant shift in the role of victims. The new youth justice provisions provide for victims to be formally consulted and involved at every stage. Under the Act, cautions will be abolished and replaced with a system of reprimands and final warnings. Reparation orders will be introduced whereby young offenders can be ordered by the court to make reparation to the victim, if the victim wants this to happen, or to the community if the victim does not want direct reparation. Reparation may take the form of an apology or repairing any damage for which the offender was responsible. The victim's involvement is voluntary.

On entering office in 1997, the Labour government stated its intention to help vulnerable and intimidated witnesses by setting up an interdepartmental group to look at all the stages of the criminal justice process from the reporting of a crime, through to the investigation and pre-trial procedures, to the trial itself and the array of post-trial issues. Victim Support was the only voluntary agency represented on the group. In June 1998 the group published its report *Speaking Up for Justice* complete with a series of 78 very wide-ranging recommendations (Home Office, 1998a). It aims to increase access to justice and lists the special measures which can be brought into force to enable children, people with intellectual disabilities or physical and mental illnesses to report crime and help them give their best evidence at court. It attempts to address the problem of witness intimidation, realizing that witnesses need protection in the community both before and after appearing at court. Some of the issues tackled in the report are contentious – for example, whether the defendant has the right to face their accuser in court. It recommends that, in certain circumstances, adult witnesses should be able to give evidence from behind a screen or via a closed-circuit television link and looks at the use of video and prerecorded evidence. Procedures during rape trials come under close scrutiny with the report recommending that the cross-examination of witnesses should be conducted with dignity and respect, and that the law should be clarified as to when a victim's previous sexual history is relevant and admissible as evidence. One of the most controversial recommendations is that defendants in rape cases, and some other cases such as 'stalking', should be banned from cross-examining the victim. At the time of writing, the report has been sent out for consultation, with the government indicating its broad support for the recommendations.

The report of the *Review of the Crown Prosecution Service* (CPS), chaired by the Rt Hon Sir Iain Glidewell (1998), also contains recommendations which, if implemented, will have direct implications for victims and witnesses. The report recommends that the CPS take overall responsibility for providing information and, where desired, an explanation to victims about any decisions it has taken in the case. It was felt that leaving this responsibility with police officers placed an unfair burden on them, especially if the officer had not understood, or was not in agreement with, that decision. The report states that, in most cases, this responsibility will constitute providing written notification to the victim, with the offer of an interview with a CPS lawyer if an explanation is asked for. This provision works against the principle set out in the 'One Stop Shop' project in the 1996 Victim's Charter, that there should be a single point of information for victims, but it does mean that victims will be entitled to receive an explanation from the agency responsible for the decision in question.

Threats: Dangers Identified in the New Measures for Victims

All the new developments outlined above represent a cause for celebration. To an extent Victim Support's policy agenda is being met, with each of the five principles identified in *The Rights of Victims of Crime* report receiving attention. Victims' issues are now firmly on the political agenda, but does this mean that victims and witnesses are feeling the benefit? Have all their needs been met? Many of these new provisions have yet to be implemented, and it is in their implementation that problems can arise.

The Limitations of Legislation

There is an assumption that, because a law is on the statute book, it is somehow effective or enforced, yet this is not always the case. Legislation may be ineffective for a number of reasons. The interpretation of the law may be reliant on the discretion of key individuals, an Act's provisions may not be brought into force, or it may be little known and used.

For some time, concerns have been expressed about court practice in permitting complainants in rape cases to be cross-examined about their previous sexual history. The interim report of a research study being conducted on behalf of the Home Office cites the fear of aggressive, humiliating and irrelevant questioning in court as the largest single factor in making women decide to withdraw their complaints (Harris and Grace, 1999). Certainly, several high-profile cases have added to this fear, but high drop-out and attrition rates in rape cases have been a problem for some time. Official crime statistics reveal that the conviction rate for rape has drastically declined over the past 20 years, falling from 33 per cent in 1979 to 11 per cent in 1993 and to 9 per cent by 1997.

However, this problem has already been specifically addressed in legislation. Section 2 of the Sexual Offences (Amendment) Act 1976 states that at rape trials

> ... except with the leave of the judge, no evidence and no question in cross-examination shall be adduced or asked at the trial, by or on behalf of any defendant at the trial, about any sexual experience of a complainant with a person other than that defendant.

The issue of cross-examination of rape victims on their previous sexual history was raised as a specific problem by the Interdepartmental Working Group on the Treatment of Vulnerable or Intimidated Witnesses. The report concluded that 'there is overwhelming evidence that the present practice in the courts is unsatisfactory and that the existing law is not achieving its purpose' (Home Office, 1998a: 69).

So why is there a common perception that rape complainants are still unfairly questioned on their previous sexual history, and that in many rape trials it seems that the complainant's reputation is on trial? One of the reasons why the Act is perceived to have failed is because it allows the use of discretion by judges, which means that witnesses can never be sure before attending the trial whether or not they will face humiliating and intimate questions about their personal lives. Publicity arising from cases where this has happened results in many, if not most, women being even more worried than they should be. The Working Group recommended that the current law should be amended to provide for a more structured approach to decision-making and to set out clearly when evidence on a complainant's previous sexual history may be admitted into evidence. It will be interesting to see how this proposal is developed and whether a workable solution can be found.

The Protection from Harassment Act 1997 is important new legislation for victims. But, again, its effectiveness should not be taken for granted. Figures for its first year of operation (*Hansard*, June 1998) show that of 504 prosecutions under the Act there were 247 convictions. What is not so easy to ascertain is how appropriately the provisions in the Act are being used. Is it tackling 'stalking' and harassment? One of the problems in drawing up the legislation was how to define harassment. It was argued that because such a wide range of behaviour needed to be covered, with new behaviours being added as they arose, it was better not to include any absolute definition but rather to define harassment by the effect that actions had on the victim, where the alleged offender knew, or ought to have known, that their course of conduct amounted to harassment. While Victim Support welcomed the weight which was given to the effects on the victim, by leaving the definition open so as not to rule out certain behaviours, behaviours correspondingly could not be ruled in. Again, the interpretation of the Act will, to a large extent, depend on the discretion of key individuals. Will prosecutions be sought in all the relevant cases? Will judges and magistrates be sufficiently aware of the impact that certain behaviours can have on victims? Will the provisions of the Act be consistently applied throughout the country? Only time will tell.

One final observation on the implementation of this legislation relates to the new hybrid remedy; by providing for a breach of the civil order to become a criminal offence the protection afforded by the Act should be greatly enhanced. Yet even when the proposals were sent out for consultation there was already concern about how the civil and criminal provisions would work together. It was undecided whether complainants would be able to receive protection from a civil order while they are waiting for a criminal case to go to court, a process which could take up to a year. Most of the provisions in the Act came into force in 1997, but those setting out procedures for a criminal breach of civil injunction remain unresolved at the end of 1998. We hope a way can be found to make this most important aspect of the legislation work.

People also need to be aware that relevant legislation exists. This is a particular problem with the civil law in that it limits the protection it is able to provide. There are a variety of provisions available for personal protection – for example, for victims of domestic assault – yet the law in this area is confusing. Women seeking protection from domestic violence need to have access to good (and free) legal advice.

This problem of a lack of knowledge applies generally. Many of the provisions aimed at improving the situation of victims and witnesses are little known, with the consequence that they can become a resource only for a well-informed, or well-supported, minority. For example, the two Victim's Charters were never widely distributed or automatically made available to members of the public. Obviously, it is in this area that organizations such as Victim Support have an important role to play, making sure that, where rights do exist, people know what they are and how to exercise them.

A Change of Culture in the Criminal Justice System

All the criminal justice agencies exist within the context of a system which is geared towards dealing with offenders. This philosophy influences all their working practices, including any new measures which are subsequently introduced. Many criminal justice agencies now have new responsibilities for consulting and informing victims and witnesses, which can lead to a possible conflict of interest with their existing duties and responsibilities. Moreover, these professionals are not necessarily trained to deal with victims of crime and may not welcome this new area of work. Generally, when, for example, the CPS or the Probation Service are asked to contact victims and witnesses, it is assumed that this work is resource-neutral and no additional moneys are made available. Yet these agencies have other responsibilities, and providing services for victims of crime is not their central purpose. All these factors will affect implementation, determining whether the spirit of these new measures is translated into practice. The criminal justice establishment may take on new ideas, but in implementation may convert them to work towards meeting their more traditional ends.

As mentioned earlier, *The Review of the Crown Prosecution Service* (Glidewell, 1998) recommends placing new responsibilities on the CPS to inform victims of their decisions – for example, giving the reasons for discontinuing a prosecution. It already has a responsibility to offer a face-to-face interview to relatives in fatal cases where a prosecution has been discontinued. It is important that these families receive a sympathetic and sensitive explanation from the agency responsible for the decision, since if people are merely provided with basic information they may feel frustrated or draw their own conclusions about how a decision has been reached. Some officers are very good at this work, demonstrating a genuine sympathy with victims and witnesses, but they have not been trained or selected for this role. They have no professional background in meeting victims or contacting bereaved relatives and yet will have to deal with a whole range of human emotions – anger, guilt and distress – and deal with these raw emotions positively and non-judgementally. Training and support are needed, and this will require additional resources.

The Probation Service is another agency with new responsibilities for liaison with victims. They now have a duty to contact victims about the release of offenders sentenced to imprisonment on a conviction for a serious sexual or violent offence. Victim Support and the Association of Chief Officers of Probation (ACOP) have worked in close liaison, producing a joint statement on how to approach this work (ACOP/Victim Support, 1996). It had been hoped that the probation officer working with the offender in the case would contact victims so that they could provide a full, free flow of information to help the victim come to terms with the situation. However, this is not happening because of a perceived clash of interests and the probation officer's duty of confidentiality to the offender. In some areas, therefore, victims have to see a separate officer who, although specially trained for this role, may not have access to the same depth of information.

A lack of clarity about new roles can also lead to the introduction of inappropriate services or working methods. In the 1980s the police came under a great deal of criticism for their perceived insensitive treatment of rape complainants. In response, they made enormous improvements to their working practices, updating procedures, improving facilities and introducing new training programmes.

In certain parts of the country the police have introduced a 'chaperone' system, whereby rape complainants are allocated a specially trained, dedicated officer who is intended to act as a contact point throughout the investigation. The aim of this system is to ensure that the victim is kept informed of developments and can build up a relationship with one officer, rather than having to deal with a different individual each time. While the system represents a great improvement in witness care, the way in which it has been implemented has led to some unforeseen problems. In some cases, the one-to-one relationship established under the chaperone system has gone further than originally intended, with victims becoming very dependent on one police officer and looking to have all their support needs met through the police. This can be problematic when that officer is required to move on to other duties: also, when the police investigation concludes, the relationship will come to an end and yet many victims need support for a much longer period – sometimes for years. In addition, the police are not, and can never be, a confidential service since they have a duty to use information which comes to them and all their records are technically disclosable to the defence. They cannot act as independent agents. Obviously, the particular limitations of the police role must be made clear to victims from the outset. While the police intention in helping rape victims is to be applauded, the implementation of these improvements requires careful monitoring and, as with other services, boundaries have to be firmly established from the beginning.

New Obligations for Victims

In some cases, initiatives which were designed to offer increased opportunities for victims and witnesses can in fact represent new obligations. The proposed introduction of restorative justice initiatives and the trial of 'Witness Statements', introduced under the second Victim's Charter, represent cases in point.

The Crime and Disorder Act 1998 introduces elements of restorative justice into the youth justice system. Under this Act victims should be involved, consulted and considered at practically every stage. Written reports will be produced on the victim's point of view and new reparation orders will be introduced.[1] However, mediation and reparation were not listed among the five key principles in Victim Support's policy paper (1995). Why was this? Mainly because they were not regarded as a priority. We believe that the five principles listed – information, protection, services, compensation, and freedom from the burden of decisions relating to the offender – all have to be addressed first. Without these conditions in place victims are not in a position to make a realistic decision about participation in mediation initiatives. For example, if an individual is not safe, possibly the subject of intimidation – then their choice to accept reparation from the offender is not a real one. Similarly, if insufficient support or information is available, the possible benefits of participating in mediation will be severely limited, or even negated, for the victim.

Furthermore, mediation and reparation schemes are not necessarily the best use of increasingly scarce resources, particularly as such schemes are only open to victims in cases where the offender has been detected. New schemes focusing on mediation or restorative justice may, in fact, distract from the provision of more general support. Victim Support would like to be involved in mediation initiatives in order to represent victims' interests and provide personal support through the process if this is desired, but such involvement is taking very limited resources away from our other more essential services which are available to all victims, not just those whose offender is under consideration.

Approaching victims to participate in restorative justice initiatives can be very liberating in that it allows victims of crime to confront the offender and to have their say. However, it could also be experienced as an additional burden in the form of unwanted contact with, or even responsibility for, the offender. Although participation in such schemes is voluntary, with victims free to choose not to meet the offender or receive reparation, giving them the choice to become involved – particularly where this involvement may affect the type of sentence/punishment meted out – can place the victim in a difficult position. They may feel guilty if they choose not to participate and yet anxious if they do. Refusing to participate could leave victims open to possible threats and intimidation or believing that this may be the case. This concern is compounded when you consider that victims may feel that they *ought* to participate in the new provisions for the treatment of young offenders, particularly if they are asked to do so by a police officer. Obviously, the way this choice is put to them will be of vital importance, and officers will need to be trained for this role. A stated aim of the Crime and Disorder Act is to speed up the youth justice process. Yet, if victims are to be increasingly involved – in fact 'consulted at every stage' – they will need sufficient time to consider their options or seek advice. A concern is that trying to speed up the process carries the risk of drastically reducing victims' thinking time, so that some may end up feeling bulldozed into cooperating.

Historically, mediation and reparation schemes have been criticized for placing the interests of offenders at centre stage and for not paying enough attention to the interests of victims (see Davis *et al.*, 1988; Young, 1989). Certain restorative justice initiatives, such as proposals for the use of Family Group Conferences in some police force areas, are far more victim-focused, adopting a more sophisticated approach and employing the skills of independent and professional mediators (see Young, Chapter 11 in this volume). However, the measures in the Crime and Disorder Act will need to attract sufficient resources to ensure that they are of a high quality rather than a mere paper exercise which only pays lip service to the views of victims.

If people are consulted, but that consultation takes the form of a standard letter with little opportunity to ask questions, then the process may be damaging to victims. It may lead to increased levels of anxiety or guilt, or re-open the emotional wound occasioned by the initial offence. On the other hand, if the consultation is carried out sympathetically, with choices put to victims in a clear and non-judgemental manner, it could be of great value. The primary objective of the Crime and Disorder Act is to tackle crime and disorder to create safer communities. The Home Office guide to the Act (1998b) does not refer to the needs of victims or to the victim's perspective. It must not be assumed that an offer of consultation or reparation will automatically be of benefit to victims. All such intervention must be tested and their effects measured. Will the individuals who choose not to participate also be offered support and information? Will refusals be monitored? For the measures in the Act to be of real assistance, sufficient training, time and resources must be allocated for their implementation.

The 1996 Victim's Charter introduced the use of 'victim statements' in a series of pilot projects. This initiative should give victims an opportunity to make a statement about the full effects which the crime has had on them. It was envisaged that these statements would become a valuable source of information for the police and CPS, helping them make decisions during the management of the case. For example, information about fears of a repeat attack or threats could be taken into account when asking for specific bail conditions. Victim Support did, however, voice concern over whether these statements should be used to influence sentencing. As well as not being convinced of the inherent fairness of such an approach, it was also felt that it might give rise to unrealistic expectations or expose victims to intimidation, retaliation or guilt.

It has been argued, for example by Edna Erez in Chapter 8 of this volume and her earlier (1994) work on 'victim impact statements' in the United States, that the act of giving such a statement is of benefit to victims, in that the very process of being asked to give information and express their views is of therapeutic value: 'Victim involvement and the opportunity to voice concerns are necessary for victim satisfaction with justice, psychological healing and restoration' (Erez, 1994: 19). However, she also recognizes the possible problem of heightened expectations being unfulfilled, especially if these expectations are unsubstantiated in the first place. The value of 'victim statements' will be determined by how they are used and how this use fits with the expectations which have been attached to them.

The 'victim statements' being piloted in the UK differ significantly from 'victim impact statements' used in other parts of the world, significantly in the United States. 'Victim impact statements' take a variety of forms but, in essence, are provided after the verdict, for the purpose of sentencing. 'Victim statements', on the other hand, are taken at the beginning of the process and are intended to inform decisions taken throughout the duration of the case. Their purpose is: to alert the authorities to any continuing risk to the victim; to enable the professional parties involved in the case to take the victim's interests into account; to provide the prosecutor with information which could be used to refute misleading statements made by the defence during mitigation; and where additional, relevant, information is available, to enable the prosecutor to provide this to the court at any appropriate stage.

At the time of writing, the results of research into the pilot projects have not yet been published[2] (see Hoyle *et al.*, 1998); nationwide implementation will depend on the outcome of the pilots. The research will need to consider both how 'victim statements' are being offered and how they are being used, as this will affect their usefulness and the victim's subsequent satisfaction. We have already heard various reports of how these statements have been offered. In some cases, it has been implied that, by making a statement, the victim is likely to have an influence over sentencing, yet there is no evidence to support this assertion. Currently, the standard letter which is sent out with the statement form is very ambiguous, leaving victims unsure, from the outset, how their information will be used. Moreover, since any information contained in the statement will be made available to the defence, this must be made clear to victims from the outset, as it may well influence the type of information given or even whether the victim decides to give a statement at all. We will also need to see detailed monitoring of how these statements have been used by the authorities they were designed to inform. Who actually sees them? It may well be that whether these statements are used as originally intended will depend on the clarity of the objectives and whether or not these are shared by all the people charged with the task of implementation. At the moment, there appears to be a great deal of confusion about who or what 'victim statements' are for.

Remedies for Victims: Hidden Dangers

Even those remedies designed solely for the assistance of victims need careful monitoring to ensure that they consistently meet their stated objectives. Compensation orders have been available since the 1970s and, from 1988, the courts have had a duty to consider making a compensation order in every case involving death, injury, loss or damage. Compensation orders were introduced specifically as a measure to help victims of crime. They should be effective in offering financial redress, but unfortunately the way in which the system has been set up often means that they can prove less than satisfactory in practice. For instance, the payment of a compensation order depends very much on the offender's means; thus, if an offender is sentenced to imprisonment, the payment of compensation becomes increasingly unlikely. If a compensation order is not paid, or is reduced on account of the offender's reduced means, then it may be paid to the victim in very small instalments over a considerable period of time: the victim's means, or immediate needs, are not taken into account. This process can be extremely damaging to victims. A paltry weekly payment is of little practical use but can serve as a constant reminder of the offence, making it more difficult for victims to put the crime behind them. Late or missed payments become a source of annoyance. All this can lead to victims feeling increasing anger towards both the offender and the criminal justice system as a whole.

For some years, Victim Support has called for compensation orders to be paid to victims immediately and in full by the court, with the money then recovered from the offender. Any delay or default in payment would then be borne by society as a whole rather than the individual victim.

Conclusions

In this chapter we have outlined Victim Support's policy agenda and tried to demonstrate how, to a large extent, this agenda has been picked up and acted upon. However, we have also tried to illustrate how some of the new measures for victims may not, in practice, be as effective as was originally intended. So why is this the case and what can be done about it?

One explanation is that while the 'victim agenda' is a political priority, when it comes to implementation, victims' interests become hijacked by the traditional criminal justice agenda. After all, the criminal justice system was established to deal with offenders, and this outlook permeates all its responses. It is easy to see how victims' issues, as a popular political cause, have been picked up and moulded to support different philosophies on how best to deal with offenders: punishment or rehabilitation. Neither of these approaches are victim-focused and yet both can be seen to have used 'the victim's perspective' to further their own ends. Campaigners for tougher sentences have used statements made by individual victims of crime as if they represent the views of 'all' crime victims. In fact, victims' views on sentencing seem to be as varied as that of any other cross-section of the general public. Alternatively, supporters of a more restorative justice system can place unfair expectations on victims – for example, by asserting that they have a responsibility to 'educate' the offender and help them to understand the effects of their crime. Why should victims be so burdened? Surely this is a responsibility for society as a whole.

So how can we ensure that procedural and legislative changes designed to help victims actually do so? First, there must be absolute clarity about the aims of any of these new measures. If there are other objectives besides those of helping the victim, these must be relayed honestly to victims so as to inform any decisions they may make. Many victims are strongly motivated to use their negative experience for the benefit of society, to ensure that some positive outcome results from their suffering. If crime reduction and the re-education of the offender are the primary aims, this should be relayed to the victim when asking for their cooperation – indeed, many victims would be pleased to support these ends. In addition, objectives should be specific, rather than assuming that certain types of intervention are likely to be helpful. Are mediation/reparation schemes for the benefit of the victim, the defendant, or society as a whole? It is not sufficient to say 'all three'. We must analyse both what such schemes are intending to achieve and exactly how they are going to do it. If objectives are unclear from the outset then it is all too easy for such schemes to change in emphasis according to the views of the individuals responsible for their implementation.

Second, time must be taken to ensure that intentions are communicated accurately to all those concerned. As can be seen with the 'victim statement' pilots, accurate information must be given to victims about the purpose of the statements and how they will be used, thus ensuring that expectations are not unfairly raised. If 'victim statements' are unlikely to influence sentencing, this should never be implied as a means of securing victims' cooperation. The police and CPS also need to know what these statements are for and how they are meant to use them. Communication of boundaries and limitations is also essential and, as with the police 'chaperone' system, time must be taken to ensure these boundaries are understood.

Where organizations are expected to take on a new role they must receive training to help them do so. Such training should equip individuals not only with new skills but with a means of challenging commonly held assumptions and working practices. The provision of victim awareness training should help agencies working within criminal justice look at issues from a different perspective and consequently help them better judge the consequences of their actions. Putting these safeguards in place will not be resource-neutral, so adequate resources must be allocated so that new procedures can be implemented effectively. This should also encourage the agencies involved to approach this type of work with more enthusiasm.

We believe that there will always be a role for a specialist agency whose sole purpose is to represent the interests of crime victims. Victim Support, by working to promote victims' rights draws on our extensive contact with victims and witnesses to keep track of new developments, to identify problems as they arise and to lobby to ensure that victims' interests remain central and are not hijacked for any other purpose. Obviously, we are also there to provide a service, to help alleviate the effects of crime and to reduce the pain of crime. However well attuned to victims' interests the criminal justice process becomes, this service will still be necessary.

There is an enormous motivation for change. The past treatment of victims and witnesses has become widely recognized as unacceptable, and a shift in culture has taken place, with victims' interests now nearing the top of the political agenda. This new agenda for action represents an enormous opportunity. All those working with victims of crime and within the field of criminal justice now have a duty to work towards turning this opportunity into a new reality.

Notes

1   These are currently being piloted and evaluated in various designated sites throughout the country.
2   The research has subsequently been published and is discussed in the chapters by Ashworth and Erez in this volume.

References

Association of Chief Officers of Probation (ACOP) and Victim Support (1996), *The Release of Prisoners: Informing, Consulting and Supporting Victims*, Joint Statement, London: ACOP/Victim Support.

Davis, G., Boucherat, J. and Watson, D. (1988), 'Reparation in the Service of Diversion: the Subordination of a Good Idea', *The Howard Journal*, **27**(2), 127–34.

Erez, E. (1994), 'Victim Participation in Sentencing: And the Debate Goes On', *International Review of Victimology*, **3**(1/2), 17–32.

Glidewell, I. (1998), *The Review of the Crown Prosecution Service: A Report*, Cmnd. 3960, London: HMSO.

Harris, J. and Grace, S. (1999), *A Question of Evidence? Investigating and Prosecuting Rape in the 1990s*, Home Office Research Study 196, London: Home Office.

Home Office (1990), *The Victim's Charter: A Statement of the Rights of Victims of Crime*, London: Home Office.

Home Office (1996a), *The Victim's Charter: A Statement of Service Standards for Victims of Crime*, London: Home Office.

Home Office (1996b), *Stalking the Solutions: A Consultation Paper*, London: Home Office.

Home Office (1998a), *Speaking Up for Justice*, Report of the Interdepartmental Working Group on the Treatment of Vulnerable or Intimidated Witnesses in the Criminal Justice System, London: Home Office.

Home Office (1998b), *Guide to the 1998 Crime and Disorder Act*, London: Home Office.

Hoyle, C., Cape, E., Morgan, R. and Sanders, A. (1998), *Evaluation of the 'One Stop Shop' and Victim Statement Pilot Projects*, A Report for the Home Office

Research Development and Statistic Directorate, Bristol: Department of Law, University of Bristol.

Lord Chancellor's Department (1992), *The Courts Charter*, London: HMSO.

Maguire, M. and Corbett, C. (1987), *The Effects of Crime and the Work of Victim Support Schemes*, Aldershot: Gower.

Trials Issues Group (1996), *Statement of the National Standard of Witness Care in the Criminal Justice System: Taking Forward Standards of Witness Care Through Local Service Level Agreements*, London: Home Office.

Victim Support (1992), *Domestic Violence*, Report of a National Interagency Working Party Convened by Victim Support, London: Victim Support.

Victim Support (1993), *Compensating the Victim of Crime: Report of An Independent Working Party*, London: Victim Support.

Victim Support (1994), *Support for the Families of Road Death Victims:* Report of An Independent Working Party Convened by Victim Support, London: Victim Support.

Victim Support (1995), *The Rights of Victims of Crime: A Policy Paper*, London: Victim Support.

Victim Support (1996a), *Women Rape and the Criminal Justice System*, London: Victim Support.

Victim Support (1996b), *Children in Court: Research Report*, London: Victim Support.

Victim Support (1998), 'Restorative Justice and Victim Support', *Victim Support Magazine*, (67), Summer.

Young, R. (1989) 'Reparation as Mitigation', *Criminal Law Review*, 463–72.

7 Victims and Criminal Justice: Creating Responsible Criminal Justice Agencies

Joanna Shapland

A Criminal Justice Separate from Victims and Offenders?

If one were to look back 20 years – to take off the dusty shelves a book or an official government report about victims' needs in criminal justice[1] – one would read about the necessity of supporting victims during their progress through criminal justice, about providing them with information, about whether statutory agencies should have a victim perspective, about different kinds of compensation, about mediation and reconciliation, and about vulnerable victims. Yet the most recent government statement of policy for all victims of criminal justice in England and Wales, the 1996 Victim's Charter (Home Office, 1996), sets out very similar kinds of cocnerns. It indicates standards of service so that, *in future*, victims will be able to expect:

- a crime they have reported to the police will be investigated and that they will receive information about what happens
- the chance to explain how the crime has affected them so that their interests be taken into account
- if they have to go to court as a witness, that they will be treated with respect and sensitivity
- to be offered emotional and practical support.

It is clear that there has been little change in the problems that victims experience in relation to criminal justice over that time period. This is strange – although we would not expect the needs of victims necessarily to change, we might expect that, in 20 years, some of the solutions might have been produced.

If we examine these difficulties more closely, we can see that they are characterized by the need for criminal justice agencies to reach out and respond to victims. In the same way as earlier government reports, the Victim's Charter assumes a separation between criminal justice and victims. The business of criminal justice agencies in their duties towards criminal justice is seen as almost self-contained. The core aims, performance measures and initiatives of the principal criminal justice agencies stress the need for effective and efficient processing of cases and the accompanying requirements for the construction of stronger and more automatic links between agencies. Those standing outside the mainstream flow of cases through the system from police to sentencer tend to be viewed as problems to be managed, rather than as integral parts of justice. They are less controllable, prone to produce unwarranted delay or make difficult decisions, and persons to whom strictly defined services will have to be offered. These outsiders are offenders, defence lawyers, witnesses and victims. Throughout the 20 years, criminal justice has been seen as separate from victims, with victims being a rather annoying group which stand apart from justice, but to whom we now need to consider creating some kind of response and making some concessions. There is little idea that victims are fundamentally woven into justice – that justice incorporates both victims and offenders.

It is this idea of separation between victims and criminal justice that I want to examine in this chapter. I shall do so in the context of the report of the JUSTICE Committee,[2] *Victims in Criminal Justice* (JUSTICE, 1998), which I chaired.[3] The Committee looked at the whole process of criminal justice from the point at which an offence had been reported to the police and recorded by them, through investigation by the police, pre-court prosecution decisions, mediation and diversion schemes, court processes and parts of the penal system affecting victims, including conditional release.

Some light may be thrown on this phenomenon of separateness by thinking about offenders. Much of what I have argued in relation to victims could be also said about the 1990s in relation to offenders. Although, clearly, there are defined roles for the offender in criminal justice, the daily interaction between justice and offender, its nature, effectiveness and the limits which should be put on it have not been the subject of much attention. Within criminal justice, we tend to talk about cases, about outcomes or disposals, rather than about offenders. This is also rather odd, given that all the statutory institutions and agencies of criminal justice have, as their central focus, tasks concerning offenders.

The lack of concentration on offenders and the relative failure to implement uncontroversial measures in relation to victims (such as informing them of the case's progress), seems even stranger given the changes to public services in England and Wales over the same time period. The public sector has been encouraged, bullied or forced into a culture where value for money is vital and performance (and pay) are measured on the basis of numerical indicators of activity and their cost (if not yet their outcomes). The services sector has been held up to the public sector as a model to be admired in its attention to its customers and their wants. The whole idea of charters has been lifted into the public sector to provide definable standards for service to members of the public. However, although we may be able to claim back compensation if our trains are late, standards for victims have been slow to emerge (or be implemented). Standards for offenders are still a concept to be wrestled with in many parts of the criminal justice system.

Integrity in Criminal Justice

The JUSTICE report argues that this is wrong. It considers that criminal justice will have no integrity if it does not recognize and consider the role of victims and the services it needs to offer victims. The same applies in respect of its duties towards offenders. The concepts of integrity and accountability in criminal justice are crucial to the philosophical basis underpinning the Committee's recommendations. What is meant by integrity? For the JUSTICE Committee, it means that every agency in a justice system should comply with standards which are publicly stated and which are, by that society at that time, judged to be fair (Recommendation 1.2:23). In relation to offenders (the context in which this is normally argued in criminal justice), for example, the agents of crime control, such as the police, must only have powers to secure convictions if those powers are clearly known and are fair. Equally, those who deal with the criminal justice process, such as judges or lawyers, must avoid wrongful convictions and must not allow state officials to take advantage of any breaches of fair standards. Of course, much of JUSTICE's work has been devoted to setting out those standards and taking on casework where they appear to have been breached.

Integrity is similarly applicable to victims. Hence the report argues that:

> The victim, whose rights as a citizen have been violated by the commission of a crime, must be accorded proper concern and respect in any procedures in which he or she participates. There must be standards for those procedures, adhered to by the criminal justice agencies, and publicly known. Moreover, such standards must be fair. (JUSTICE, 1998: 23)

Although this book is centrally concerned with victims' role in criminal justice, I think it is necessary to stress that attention by the criminal justice system to victims does not, and should not, presume any lessening of attention to offenders. Indeed, what would benefit victims (such as, for example, knowing where to go at court, where to sit in court, and what the procedures are about) is often identical to what would be helpful for offenders. As the JUSTICE report indicates:

> What is vital is that the interests of each person who is participating in criminal justice, and the ways in which these are expressed in standards embodying rights and services, can be perceived as fair. (JUSTICE, 1998: 23)

It is important to spell out, however, that a justice system with integrity – one with equitable standards for all participants – is not one in which the implementation of those standards means that everyone should have exactly the same service delivered in exactly the same way. People participating in criminal justice are different people, fulfilling different roles and with different needs. So, for example, child witnesses and disabled witnesses have different needs in relation to attendance at court, in relation to the services provided at court and in relation to the architecture of the courthouse. Support for witnesses includes a variety of provision, from emotional support and providing factual information (useful to many) to support in relation to intimidation or in relation to enabling those with no money to get to court.

Integrity and Victims: Responsibilities and Legitimate Expectations

The concept of integrity needs to be drawn out further. With regard to victims, one essential element is that the JUSTICE Committee saw both victims and criminal justice agencies as each having both responsibilities and rights in relation to each other. In this formulation, rights and responsibilities are the two sides of the same coin and so are inextricably linked. The responsibilities of victims are the expectations (or rights) which the criminal justice system can have of victims. The responsibilities of agencies are the expectations (or rights) which victims can have of the criminal justice system.

Victims' Responsibilities to Criminal Justice: The Expectations that Criminal Justice has of Victims

Victims in fact already have many responsibilities within criminal justice. These include helping with the investigation of the case, providing evidence through making statements to the police and giving evidence in court. There have been recent proposals to increase these responsibilities in England and Wales, including asking victims for their views on whether offenders should be released from prison after long prison sentences or as conditional release on licence.[4] Proposals for restorative justice measures, including family group conferencing, will produce additional responsibilities. It is important that these responsibilities are acknowledged.

By emphasizing that victims already have responsibilities to criminal justice, I am not suggesting that victims should have *full* responsibility. Much of the concern about 'victims' rights' on the part of English and Welsh policy-makers and criminal justice agencies has been that this would allow victims to take full responsibility for the discretionary decisions about prosecution, conviction and sentence, which they – and I – would argue are properly the remit of the police, prosecution, judiciary and jurors. I think it is very important that the victim is clearly not given the responsibility as to whether the offender should be charged, prosecuted, convicted or sentenced. So does the JUSTICE report. In fact, the report disparages the tendency of the police to ask the victim to indicate whether they will 'press charges' in domestic violence cases, because that is effectively asking the victim to take a police/prosecution decision (Recommendation 2.9).

However, leaving the responsibility for taking decisions about what is to happen to the offender to criminal justice agencies should not blind us to the responsibilities we are still placing on victims. Making statements to the police, attending identification parades, or attending court to give evidence is often stressful, takes up time and causes inconvenience. There is also clearly an obligation on victims to undertake them – in the case of giving evidence, a legal obligation which is enforceable by imprisonment.

Rights for Victims?

Correspondingly, many have argued for rights for victims. Some of these rights, such as the right to information, are now universally acknowledged as matters of good practice. Many are acknowledged in the 1996 Victim's Charter. The Charter itself does not refer to 'rights', but instead to the 'standards of service' victims can expect in relation to the agencies represented on the national Victims Steering Group, which compiled the Charter. This is in accordance with its overall philosophy, which is to see victims as a separate group to which criminal justice owes some services (information, consultation and support). It does not accord victims the legitimacy of a status within criminal justice whereby they would be able to demand their proper place (as opposed to receiving an apology, or maybe even compensation, if they did not receive the service designated as proper for victims by criminal justice).

The word 'rights' itself has been very controversial in England and Wales where, as in the Charter, a service model of delivering services to victims has often been the preferred path. The choice of language between 'rights', 'standards' and 'services' does highlight power differentials, as well as differences in the ways in which people can try to enforce any right/service they have not obtained. However, the advent of charters has started to open up a middle way between the opposed poles of the rights versus services debate which often descended to a rather sterile and terminological level in the 1970s and 1980s. Although there are considerable concerns about the effectiveness of charters,[5] they do embody the sense that citizens (and victims as citizens) can, and should, have expectations of official agencies, whilst the older services model stemmed from the rather paternalistic idea that agencies should do good to those who were poor, victimized, hurt and so on (see Shapland, 1986). In the terms of van Dijk's (1983) typology of victim-oriented policy initiatives, charters fall under the heading of a re-tributive or criminal justice ideology rather than the heading of a welfare state initiative. Standards and charters indicate that the idea that individuals should have legitimate expectations of official bodies (including the criminal justice agencies) is no longer strange.

The debate in the 1990s is, in fact, often not about the *content* of the 'rights', 'services' or 'service standards'. Victims' needs of criminal justice have become so well known that there is little debate about the need for information, consultation or support (even though it seems difficult to make it happen in practice). The debate is about how they should be delivered and what mechanisms should be provided as accountability to the victim.

Hence, as the JUSTICE report argues, the procedure is often called a 'right' when the individual has the ability to enforce its delivery through being an active participant in the process (a 'right' to be heard at court and so on).[6] The same element may be called an 'expectation' or a 'legitimate expectation', when the individual is given means of enforcement which are not active, procedural rights during the process (for example, through complaints – the Victim's Charter's preferred mechanism for accountability – or through an ombudsman or civil negligence process). In the past the words, 'the agency's duty' or a 'service to victims' have often been used when no explicit standards have been set and no mechanism for accountability set up.

Legitimate Expectations of Victims

The JUSTICE Committee's terminology, being based on the idea that the criminal justice system should have integrity in its relations with victims, was that of victims' *legitimate expectations*. This accords with the notion that these expectations should lead to publicly known standards and clear mechanisms for delivery of services by agencies to meet them.

What are the legitimate expectations that victims can have? Lists, like definitions, always create controversy, and the list produced by the JUS-TICE Committee cannot be regarded as all-encompassing. However, as the Committee suggests, it could provide a yardstick against which proposals for change in criminal justice could be measured. It can also form a basis for evaluation of the current service being provided.

The JUSTICE Committee list of the legitimate expectations is (1998: 28–29):

1. appropriate acknowledgement of the role and responsibilities of the victim within each criminal justice process and by each institution, agency or individual involved in those processes, including, where relevant, timely consultation on decisions, but not expecting victims to take responsibility for decisions which are properly the remit of a criminal justice institution or agency;
2. support and assistance for victims in relation to the effects of the offence and in discharging all responsibilities placed on them in relation to criminal justice;
3. information and explanation as to what is happening to the case;
4. means to ensure timely and accurate provision of information to relevant criminal justice institutions and agencies about the offence and its effects on victims;
5. being made aware of what is expected of them at each stage (when they will be needed, where they go, what will happen);
6. making the safety of victims and of those close to victims a major factor in relation to decisions in criminal justice and, where relevant, civil justice processes; in particular, provision of a safe environment for victims on the premises of all criminal justice institutions;
7. minimisation of further damage or harm to victims through criminal justice procedures;
8. compensation and alleviation of the effects of the offence, as well as mini-misation of cost to victims in assisting criminal justice.

If we look, for example, at new proposals for restorative justice, it is important that these schemes ensure that victims are informed about what is happening, about any contract made with the offender, and about the outcome if the case is referred back to the police, prosecution or court. Equally, the safety of victims needs to be made a major consideration both during the mediation or conferencing, and after it. If victims are asked to attend conferences, then they need to be paid travelling expenses, in the same way as if they were asked to attend court to give evidence.

The Responsibilities of Agencies – Legitimate Expectations of Victims

What then are the responsibilities of agencies? Well, it's quite simple. The responsible agency has the duty of meeting the legitimate expectations of victims (and, of course, those of offenders). The important difference from current practice is that these are responsibilities placed on each and every relevant agency in criminal justice. It would not be possible for an agency to argue that it is not their responsibility to do this particular thing (such as providing information), but that of another agency.

So, for example, it would be the courts' job to ensure the safety and freedom from intimidation of all individuals on court premises. In the past, that task has largely been performed by the police. However, pressure on police resources in England and Wales has meant that the police have largely withdrawn from that task,[7] though if police officers are present to give evidence and an incident occurs they will help. Courts now generally employ private security to help court staff with security (Shapland and Bell, 1998), although, in the Crown Court, it is primarily the Witness Service (volunteer witness support staff) who staff the information desk and may notice instances of intimidation. The importance of assigning responsibility on court premises to the court is that it becomes clearly seen to be not the police's responsibility, nor that of witness support, but the responsibility of the court. The court would have the responsibility of ensuring that it employs sufficient and sufficiently trained security staff, that all ushers and other employees know what to do in an emergency, and that there is a clear reporting point and actions to take if there appears to be intimidation, whether that be in the courtroom, in the corridors or in the restaurant.

Why does this matter? The changes in public sector administration in the last decade have improved, and been made more detailed, the financial accountability of public sector agencies to central government. The tools for this are the linking of work done to budget lines and the measuring of work in terms not just of job specifications, but also by performance indicators. The Milton Keynes Criminal Justice Audit (Shapland *et al.*, 1995; 1996)[8] showed clearly that the core tasks, and hence the budget lines of criminal justice agencies, have been defined in terms of processing offenders. Work with victims has not been defined as a core task for most criminal justice agencies (with the obvious exception of the police) and, as a result, it has been extremely difficult for agencies to devote time and personnel to work relating to victims, either in terms of delivering services or even in terms of formulating the best way of delivering such services or standards which victims should be able to expect. It is only by clearly assigning responsibility to *each* agency for those aspects of criminal justice through which it has any dealings with victims that it will be possible to identify its tasks and its necessary budget lines.

It is because such responsibilities are not currently clearly defined and accepted that agencies tend to begrudge providing services for victims. Given the existing financial constraints in the public sector, it is entirely natural that an agency will not want to develop services (let alone services to a prescribed standard) for what it may see as a new client group. It will feel that it is having enough difficulty in performing what are defined as its current core tasks (of processing cases/offenders). It is only if it becomes clear that every agency that has contact with victims (or offenders) has responsibility towards them that this reluctance will decrease.

Hence the JUSTICE Committee argues that every criminal justice agency which has any direct dealings with victims *or* which takes decisions which affect victims or which produces information which victims can legitimately expect needs to take responsibility for these contacts. Moreover, the way in which the agency is funded and the ways in which its performance are judged must also mirror those responsibilities. This is the concept of the 'responsible agency'.

In putting this responsibility on each agency, I do not mean that each item or service for which the agency is responsible has to be delivered by that agency. Court staff may not have the skills or training to provide witness support. It is also possible to argue that such support should be provided by an independent body, so that witnesses are not frightened of confiding their fears or concerns. In this instance, it may be better for a body such as Victim Support to be contracted to provide witness support services to the courts service. However, if the courts are to be responsible agencies, in the JUS-TICE terminology, then the contracting would need to be done directly by the courts service and by individual magistrates' court committees, rather than through a national Home Office grant, as is the case currently for the Witness Service in the Crown Court.

Similarly, it may be more suitable for one agency to coordinate the provision of information to victims. The 1996 Victim's Charter recommended that this agency should be the police, and pilot schemes were set up to attempt this as a 'One Stop Shop' for serious offences (Hoyle *et al.*, 1998).[9] The Glidewell (1998) report[10] recommended that it should be a task of the Crown Prosecution Service. I would argue that both the police and the Crown Prosecution Service (and the courts) have a responsibility to ensure that information about their decisions is passed to victims. If national coordination cannot be achieved to make one agency responsible for all information provision, then the responsibility remains with all three agencies which will need to undertake it, for all victims, themselves. This example indicates that adopting the concept of the responsible agency might also encourage cooperative action. The strain on each agency's budget would be considerably reduced if agreement could be reached and effective steps taken to ensure that information provision could be done by one agency, rather than by sending three letters to the victim.

Given the longstanding difficulties in achieving effective services to victims, I might be accused of being naive in presuming that a simple change to make agencies responsible for all the ways in which they come into contact with victims might do the trick. However, it is important to realize that the concept of the responsible agency is in fact a revolution in criminal justice philosophy, even though it will lead directly to practical applications which are easy to implement. The revolution is one of philosophy, principle and attitude, not an unattainable goal.

The Impoverishment of Criminal Justice through Emphasizing the Solomon Model of Discretionary Decision-making

Why is the concept of the responsible agency a revolution in philosophy and attitude? I think it is because our view of criminal justice has become too cramped and too impoverished. Gradually, we have constrained our horizons of what criminal justice might be.

We need first to recognize that our so-called criminal justice system is not a system at all, in terms of a unitary coalition of agencies all striving towards the same goals and having identical aims. That is now seen as a truism. In 1988 I compared it to the medieval barony system (Shapland, 1988), whereby each baron or criminal justice agency jealously guarded its piece of criminal justice processing, only negotiating reluctantly with others. Since then, the pressures towards value for money and specific performance indicators for each agency have increased their isolation from each other. It is only recently (for example, in the work of the Trial Issues Group[11]), that it has been realized that overall performance from the system (in relation to delays or services to victims) will not result from specific agency performance measures unless those performance measures are coordinated across agencies towards overall system goals. The current pressure towards fast-tracking of cases involving persistent young offenders, and reducing delays in general, has had to adopt this process of setting overall aims and then breaking them down into tasks for each part of the system.

It is, however, important to realize that this is not a problem unique to the UK. Wherever performance measures for individual agencies have been emphasized (for example, in New Zealand, where each chief executive in charge of each government department has annual contracts, examined by parliament, to deliver specified services), there is a difficulty of coordinating action across agencies or departments. Moreover, it is a problem endemic in criminal justice worldwide. We in the UK do not have our current plethora of agencies and departments purely for historical reasons, or because we have a common law/Anglo-Saxon legal system. They exist because it is seen as increasingly essential that investigative, prosecutorial and judicial functions be independent, to prevent abuses of power; this has resulted in a need for at least three government departments/supporting agencies.

Although providing a coordinated service to victims will therefore be difficult, the fief-like tendency of the criminal justice system does not explain why there has been such a concentration on delays, for example, rather than on victims. It seems to me that the reason for this, and the reason why the concept of the responsible agency is a revolution, is the growing concentration of both individual agencies and the whole system on discretionary decision-making about the offender. Elsewhere I have referred to this tendency as the Solomon model (Shapland, forthcoming).[12]

The Solomon model of criminal justice focuses almost entirely on the adequacy and speed of the discretionary decisions taken by the police (to charge/summons), the prosecution (to prosecute or divert) and the judiciary (on bail, conviction and, particularly, sentencing). Criminal justice is seen as decision-making, with the active participants being the decision-maker and the person on whom decisions are made (the offender). In practice, the offender is often as much a non-player as the victim, since active negotiations over these decisions tend to take place with his or her legal representative, rather than with the offender personally. Legal representatives are supposed to relay decisions and allow input by the offender, though several pieces of research have cast doubt on the extent to which legal representatives give defendants an opportunity to consider such decisions, particularly at busy magistrates' courts (Jackson *et al.*, 1991; McConville *et al.*, 1994).

The Solomon model emphasizes proper processing of the offender's case, according to due process. Recent concentration in England and Wales on fast-tracking, judge management of cases and minimizing delay is all in accordance with the Solomon model. The emphasis of the English and Welsh criminal justice system on processing was seen in the Milton Keynes Criminal Justice Audit (Shapland *et al.*, 1995; 1996), which found that this accounted for much of the post-investigation cost of the system because criminal justice agencies were spending their time trying to take the right decisions about what should happen to the offender. Both speedy processing and good discretionary decision-making require the right information to be put before the decision-maker at the appropriate time. As a result, the Solomon model of criminal justice relegates victims (and also offenders) to the status of information providers for decisions, rather than people in whom the criminal justice system should be interested in their own right. The Milton Keynes audit showed that contacts with victims and offenders were to obtain information about them or the offence which decision-makers needed, rather than to consider why the offence was committed, or what would be the most effective way to prevent it from reoccurring, or to offer support or redress to victims. I would argue that this concentration on the Solomon model as the epitome of criminal justice has impoverished our view of justice – and thereby also excluded victims.

Criminal Justice as Public Service

The JUSTICE Committee (1998) looked at similar questions from the point of view of the different accountabilities of criminal justice agencies. It argued that, at each stage of the criminal justice process, there are responsibilities owed by the relevant agencies to society itself, to government through ministries and agencies (as the executive embodiment of the state) and to individuals participating in the creation of criminal justice for that case in that location. Proper decision-making can be viewed as one of the responsibilities owed to society. The last few decades have emphasized the financial and processing accountabilities of professionals and agencies to ministers and to government generally. However, this focus on state-directed responsibilities which are centrally directed has tended to divert attention away from the responsibilities of criminal justice to individuals and communities.

The realization that criminal justice had become something which was too inward-looking and too focused on meeting targets imposed by ministers and the executive, spurred by consumerism, has resulted in a new direction in the last few years towards the specification of service delivery to 'users'. Users are generally taken to mean both those private individuals who are required to take part in that stage (at court or in the police station) and also professionals who are not on their home territory in that agency (professionals from other fiefs). As the JUSTICE Committee says:

> More recent formulations of criminal justice as including the idea of delivering services to users and to clients are … a considerable improvement on the earlier idea, prevalent in the first half of this century, that criminal justice was something done by such people as judges and police officers, with lay people being immaterial to this process. Service at least indicates the existence of two parties – the service deliverer and the receiver of the service, with the possibility of comment by receiver to deliverer. (JUSTICE, 1998: 111–12)

However, the JUSTICE Committee argued that service delivery is still too limited a goal for criminal justice. The problem with being satisfied with service delivery, however high the standards, as the means by which criminal justice interacts with lay people, is that it fixes attention on those services alone. So, for example, witness support would be examined in terms of the service provided by those appointed to deliver it, rather than being considered as part of all court personnel's duties. Views on the adequacy of witness support might be limited to the results of questionnaires to users asking about contact with, and the services of, the Witness Service, rather than encompassing the response of the police to the likelihood of intimidation, the adequacy of the information on how to find the court on the court leaflet, the provision of information desks and child care, and so on.

If the relationship between criminal justice and victims/witnesses/offenders is defined solely in terms of the provision of services then, as the JUSTICE Committee argued, the services which are provided by agencies and institutions will increasingly become defined by them, with those receiving the services at best reactive partners (complaining if the services are inadequate, suggesting new ones for the agencies and institutions to agree with or disregard) and, at worst, passive recipients of whatever the agencies and institutions have decided should happen.

The JUSTICE Committee contrasted this with the idea of criminal justice as *public service*. Criminal justice as public service incorporates the acknowledgement of the multiple accountabilities and responsibilities of criminal justice agencies and institutions, as well as those of victims, witnesses and offenders. Hence each step in criminal justice would need to be seen as incorporating several responsibilities to different parties, all of which need to be discharged in different ways. The list of responsibilities and accountabilities includes (1998: 112):

1. financial and service delivery responsibility to the head of that agency or institution, to ministries and ultimately to Parliament, for the adequacy of the decisions taken and services delivered;
2. procedural responsibility to those involved in that step and in subsequent steps (for example, to ensure that adequate information is passed to all the agencies and institutions involved in that step, and to those involved in the next or subsequent steps);
3. accountability to the community and to society for the propriety and adequacy of the decisions taken and services delivered;
4. responsibility to all lay people who have been involved in that step for the propriety and adequacy of the decisions taken and services delivered.

This is a much wider set of responsibilities than those embodied in the Solomon model (which would emphasize the second and third sets of responsibility above, with a focus on accountability to society generally), or those related to the public sector reforms relating to value for money, effectiveness and efficiency (which emphasize the first set of responsibilities). Of course, both the Solomon model and the public sector reforms have weight. Discretionary decision-making is a crucial part of criminal justice; ineffective and unreachable criminal justice, which does not produce decisions for months, is not justice.

However, accountability to government, to society in general and to other agencies does not produce the transparent, relevant criminal justice which people in local communities can see is applicable to them, to their need for security from crime, and to the resolution of their disputes. Many years ago, Christie (1977) stressed the tendency of criminal justice professionals to take away people's disputes into closed, professional discourse and fora. His original complaint was the overprofessionalization of justice and the focus on processing. Although that is still, as we have seen, a dominant tendency, my concern here is that the welcome addition of financial and service delivery accountability to the executive (the 'centre') does not address the equal need for accountability to local people and communities (the 'periphery'). Service delivery and service standards may be excellent but, unless they are relevant to people's concerns and seen to be relevant to people's concerns, local people will still feel disenfranchised and unwelcome.

As media and public attention to 'law and order' and the 'problem of crime' has increased in England and Wales, so people will feel that the criminal justice system should respond to their concerns. One consequence of that is the pressure for politicians and criminal justice responses to be seen to be tough, with a consequent move towards, initially, under the last Conservative government, a more ideological criminal justice policy (as Garland (1996) has argued) and subsequently, I would suggest, a more populist, pragmatic and rather self-contradictory one. Currently, criminal justice policy in England and Wales is seeking to marry toughness with effectiveness. This can cause difficulties when effectiveness, in terms of prevention of re-offending, suggests the adoption of more liberal measures. It causes further difficulties when a government which is well aware of the limitations of state action on crime still has to retain a tough image of being able to do something about it. It is a difficult balancing act.

However, even if the balance is successfully struck, toughness and effectiveness are useless if the target of the toughness is not the one about which people are concerned or if the crime reduction is not apparent to local people. Similarly, a criminal justice which speaks only to itself in its own courtrooms will not seem relevant to most local people.[13] I would, therefore, argue that the JUSTICE Committee's fourth accountability – that to the lay people involved in the case for the propriety and adequacy of the decisions taken and services delivered – is crucial to both the legitimacy of criminal justice and the acceptability of criminal justice policy. It is that fourth accountability which addresses the key concerns of victims – for information, explanation, consultation, support and a welcome in criminal justice. It is also this accountability which creates the open, transparent, just criminal justice that is so important where there is greater suspicion of criminal justice personnel or governments.

Criminal justice as public service transcends the Solomon model to bring in the concerns of victims, witnesses and offenders. It should be stressed that it is not the substitution of local justice for national justice (in the sense that each town would have its own ideas of what would be fitting punishment). Nor is it in any way a return to 'mob rule' or the 'vindictive victim'.[14] The values on which criminal law is based and sentencing occurs would continue to be those decided by parliament and interpreted through case law and precedent. But there would be an obligation on those practising criminal justice to explain their decisions and to welcome those who bring their cases to be dealt with through the criminal justice process – in other words, to make criminal justice accessible and visible.

Criminal justice as public service reaches so far beyond the idea of service delivery that I think it could fairly be called a revolution. It would suggest that local courts should reach outwards to their local communities in the ways in which prisons in England and Wales have started to do. It might promote a clustering of justice facilities for the public around courthouses, including local prosecution offices (so that victims and witnesses could be consulted by prosecutors), duty solicitor/law centre offices, mediation services, debt counselling, victim support and legal advice centres. The local courts/law facilities would encourage open days and discussion in local schools and colleges about the use of the law and about the operation of civil and criminal justice. They would be open to, and welcome, the public, because they were there to serve that area and to make criminal justice accessible to that community. What is now seen as court administration would be a central part of public service, to be undertaken by judges, prosecutors and police working together with administrative staff. The courts would be there for the people, rather than the people being there for the courts. In this view of criminal justice, there would be no separation between criminal justice agencies and victims. Both victims and offenders would be central to criminal justice.

Notes

1 For example, the recommendations on victims in criminal justice contained in the 1985 Recommendation of the Select Committee of Experts on the Victim and Criminal and Social Policy of the Council of Europe.

2 Given the heightened salience of questions concerning the role of the victim in criminal justice in the UK in the 1990s, particularly in relation to providing information to

victims, the possibility of victim impact statements being used at court and in conditional release, and the needs of vulnerable victims, JUSTICE decided in November
1994 to form a committee on the role of the victim in criminal justice. Its wide remit
covers: the position of victims of crime in relation to the criminal justice process; the
role which they should expect and be expected to play in the various stages of that
process; the extent, if any, to which they should influence decisions which are taken
with reference to defendants and offenders; their relationship with the services, profes-
sions and institutions concerned; and to make recommendations.

3   This chapter, however, takes the ideas in that JUSTICE report somewhat further.
Obviously, neither the members of the committee nor JUSTICE itself can be held to
agree with, or be responsible for, the views expressed in this chapter.

4   Home Office (1995b); Association of Chief Officers of Probation (1996).

5   Fenwick (1995) has, quite correctly in my view, questioned whether the Victim's
Charter standards can be related to performance or whether they are merely expressions of intention which cannot be enforced and on which victims cannot rely.

6   This is difficult to reconcile with the English and Welsh criminal justice process, in
which, as I have argued above, the victim has responsibilities, but is only rarely
currently an active decision-making participant.

7   Unless there is a clear threat of violence and the local police commander decides to
detail officers for a specific case (for example, in relation to drug gangs).

8   The Milton Keynes Criminal Justice Audit was undertaken on behalf of the Youth
Crime Strategy Group, comprising the agencies involved in youth justice in Milton
Keynes, a rapidly growing town north of London, which had a population of around
250 000 at the time of the audit. The experiences of the criminal justice agencies
highlighted the absence of a local coherent strategy for dealing with crime committed
by young people. Each agency felt constrained by lack of resources and no single
agency could impact on the situation alone. The aim of the audit was to display to all,
transparently, how the resources of criminal justice were being used and hence reveal
its effective priorities.

9   See http://www.homeoffice.gov.uk/rds/publf.htm for publication by Hoyle *et al.* (1998).

10   The *Review of the Crown Prosecution Service*, commissioned by the Attorney-General,
was presented to the House of Commons by Sir Iain Glidewell in 1998.

11   The National Trial Issues Group and its associated local Groups was formed by the
Home Office to take forward recommendations on reducing delays and increasing the
efficiency of the criminal justice system, made by the Masefield Scrutiny team (see
Home Office, 1995a). The Scrutiny team looked across the whole criminal justice
system, focusing particularly on pre-trial interactions between police, prosecutors and
courts, and on the needs of victims and witnesses. A sub-group of the Trial Issues
Group has since been implementing the recommendations of the Scrutiny team and
further tasks (from, for example, the Home Office review of the needs of vulnerable
witnesses) relating to the needs of victims and witnesses. The Trial Issues Group
comprises the Bar, court service, Crown Prosecution Service, Home Office, Justices'
Clerks Society, Lord Chancellor's Department, Magistrates' Association, the police
service, the prison service, the probation service and a private sector member. Victim
Support is a member of the subgroup on victims and witnesses.

12   Although the actual case in which Solomon delivered his famous judgment would best
be characterized as a civil case in the family court.

13   Except possibly in relation to major and horrific crimes, such as murder and sexual
assault, which people see as well beyond their control and which they regard as being

committed by offenders who come from outside their own community or by offenders who are not 'people like us'.
14 Although it should be stressed that, in England and Wales, as successive British Crime Surveys have shown, the vindictive victim is a rarity.

References

Association of Chief Officers of Probation (1996), *Position Statement on Victims: Probation Services and the Victims of Crime*, London: ACOP.

Christie, N. (1977), 'Conflicts as Property', *British Journal of Criminology*, **17**(1), 1–15.

Fenwick, H. (1995), 'Rights of Victims in the Criminal Justice System: Rhetoric or Reality?', *Criminal Law Review*, 843–53.

Garland, D. (1996), 'The Limits of the Sovereign State: Strategies of Crime Control in Contemporary Society', *British Journal of Criminology*, **36**(4), 445–71.

Glidewell, I. (1998), *Review of the Crown Prosecution Service: A Report*, Cmnd. 3960, London: HMSO.

Home Office (1995a), *Administrative Burdens on the Police in the Context of the Criminal Justice System*, London: Home Office.

Home Office (1995b), *National Standards for the Supervision of Offenders in the Community*, London: Home Office.

Home Office (1996), *The Victim's Charter: A Statement of Service Standards for Victims of Crime*, London: Home Office.

Hoyle, C., Cape, E., Morgan, R. and Sanders, A. (1998), *Evaluation of the 'One Stop Shop' and Victim Statement Pilot Projects*, A Report for the Research and Statistics Directorate, London: Home Office.

Jackson, J., Kilpatrick, R. and Harvey, C. (1991), *Called to Court: A Public Review of Criminal Justice in Northern Ireland*, Belfast: SLS.

JUSTICE (1998), *Victims in Criminal Justice*, Report of the Committee on the Role of the Victim in Criminal Justice, London: JUSTICE.

McConville, M., Hodgson, J., Bridges, L. and Pavlovic, A. (1994), *Standing Accused: The Organisation and Practices of Criminal Defence Lawyers in Britain*, Oxford: Clarendon Press.

Shapland, J. (1986), 'Victims and Justice: Needs, Rights and Services', in J. van Dijk, C. Haffmans, F. Ruter, J. Schutte and S. Stolwijk (eds), *Criminal Law in Action*, Arnhem: Gouda Quint, 393–404.

Shapland, J. (1988), 'Fiefs and Peasants: Accomplishing Change for Victims in the Criminal Justice System', in M. Maguire and J. Pointing (eds), *Victims of Crime: A New Deal?*, Milton Keynes: Open University Press, 87–194.

Shapland, J. (forthcoming), 'Victims and Criminal Justice: A Public Service Ethos for Criminal Justice?', in J. Jackson and S. Doran (eds), *The Judicial Role in Criminal Proceedings*, Oxford: Hart Publishing.

Shapland, J. and Bell, E. (1998), 'Victims in the Magistrates' Courts and Crown Court', *Criminal Law Review*, 537–46.

Shapland, J., Hibbert, J., I'Anson, J., Sorsby, A. and Wild, R. (1995), *Milton Keynes Criminal Justice Audit: Summary and Implications*, Sheffield: Institute for the Study of the Legal Profession, The University of Sheffield.
Shapland, J., Hibbert, J., I'Anson, J., Sorsby, A. and Wild, R. (1996), *Milton Keynes Criminal Justice Audit: The Detailed Report*, Sheffield: Institute for the Study of the Legal Profession, The University of Sheffield.
van Dijk, J.J.M. (1983), 'Victimologie in Theorie en Praktijk: Een Kritische Reflectie Op De Bestaande En Nog Te Creëren Voorzieningen Voor Slachtoffers Van Delicten', *Justitiële Verkenningen*, **6**, 5–35.

8   Integrating a Victim Perspective in Criminal Justice Through Victim Impact Statements

Edna Erez

Introduction

One of the features that characterises recent developments in criminal justice is, to use Wolfgang's (1982) phrase, a move from 'individualization of the offender to individualization of the victim'. In countries around the world, this move has been manifested in numerous victim-oriented reforms in criminal law and procedures. They include provisions concerning victims' financial, psychological, medical and justice needs resulting from the victimization and its aftermath, as well as the criminal justice response to crime (Sebba, 1996).

The most controversial and resisted victim-oriented reform has been provisions to include victim input in criminal justice proceedings. This legislation, which was the culmination of a long campaign to improve the treatment of crime victims by the justice system, was aimed at reducing victims' frustration with, and alienation from, a legal system in which they have had neither a status nor a voice in the processing of their offenders. Providing victims with rights for input into proceedings was expected to reduce victim alienation, increase their satisfaction with justice and sense of fair treatment, and restore their dignity (Erez, 1989; Kelly and Erez, 1997).

The experience of the past decade with victim input rights has shown that, despite claims by victim advocates concerning the reform's potential to improve the system, as well as warnings by legal scholars and practitioners about the dangers of including a victim voice in an adversarial justice system, the reform has had little effect on the criminal justice system and on victims' satisfaction with it.

This chapter provides the background behind attempts to integrate a victim voice in criminal justice through victim impact statements. It presents the continuing controversy around this reform, and the research findings which uncovered the multifaceted and complex dynamics of adjudication in an adversarial criminal justice system which are responsible for the reform failure to transform court practices. The chapter concludes with a call for providing victims with a meaningful voice in adversarial legal proceedings. As the reviewed research suggests, such a voice can empower victims and simultaneously enhance justice in adversarial legal systems.

The Background

Victims' right to input into sentencing can be traced to the efforts of two major movements. In criminology, the 1970s were marked by a strong movement to replace the individualized treatment or rehabilitation model, with a 'just deserts' or justice model of sentencing. Enshrined in the principle of proportionality, the justice model was expected to reduce the sentence disparity that characterized the individualized treatment model (see, for example, American Friends' Service Committee, 1971; Fogel, 1975). In the justice model, two factors determine the penalty: crime seriousness, measured by the harm suffered by the victim; and offender culpability, determined by the type of *mens rea* (criminal intent) and the degree of moral turpitude in the commission of the offence. Culpability has a limiting effect on punishment when the harm inflicted by the offender was unforeseen, and it has an aggravating effect if the crime was committed in a particularly heinous or atrocious manner. The 'just deserts' philosophy and principles have been adopted in sentencing legislation in the UK, the USA, and Australia (US Sentencing Commission, 1987: 1.2; von Hirsch and Ashworth, 1992).

Paralleling the concern with 'just deserts' was the rise of a vocal victims' movement seeking to improve the plight of victims in the criminal justice system, and rectify their traditional lack of voice in legal proceedings. Activities on behalf of victims resulted in legislation which mandated rights of compensation from the state, restitution from the offender, support or counselling services, and victim participation or input into sentencing (Erez, 1989). The right of input is commonly known as a victim impact statement (VIS).[1] A VIS is a statement made to inform the judge of any physical or psychological harm, or any loss or damage to property, suffered by the victim as a result of the crime. Because the justice model considers harm as a measure of crime seriousness, a statement about the injury and loss suf-fered by the direct victim seemed logical and warranted (Erez and Sebba, 1999). The combined effect of these two movements on sentencing has been a shift from individualization of the offender to individualization of the victim (ibid.).

Both reforms – the 'just deserts' approach to sentencing and mandating victim input into sentencing – were highly controversial.[2] Supporters of victim participatory rights suggested that input would serve as a recognition of a victim's wish for party status (Hall, 1991) or individual dignity (Henderson, 1985), and would remind judges, juries and prosecutors that behind the 'state' is a real person with an interest in how the case is resolved (Kelly, 1987). Information on victim harm would enhance proportionality and accuracy in sentencing (Goldstein, 1984; Erez, 1990), and advance the various aims of punishment (Talbert, 1988).

Supporters have argued that participatory rights will have various thera-peutic benefits to offenders and victims. Therapeutic jurisprudence suggests that victim input will help perpetrators understand the effect of their action on their victims, develop empathy for them and thus accomplish offender rehabilitation (Wexler and Winick, 1996; Wiebe, 1996). Participation and input will also promote victims' psychological healing (Erez, 1990; Wiebe, 1996). Procedural justice theory suggests that presenting their side to deci-sion-makers will provide victims with 'process control' (Tyler, 1988), and enhance their satisfaction with justice, regardless of the outcome (Lind and Tyler, 1988). In contrast, a criminal justice system that provides no opportu-nity for victims to participate may exacerbate the feelings of helplessness and lack of control that arise as a result of a crime (Kilpatrick and Otto, 1987). Allowing victim input will also provide victims with an equal right to be heard by the court and thus enhance fairness for them (President's Task Force on Victims of Crimes, 1982: 76; Sumner, 1987).

Opponents of victim input rights criticized the law for challenging the general conception of crime as a violation against the state rather than individual victims, and for undermining fundamental principles of an adversarial legal system, including the rights of defendants (Ashworth, 1993). They also claimed that emphasizing victim harm over offender culpability may violate traditional sentencing principles that do not penalize offenders for unforeseen results (ibid.). Others raised potential detrimental effects which victim input might have on sentencing: unacceptable pressures on the court in high-profile cases (Rubel, 1986), particularly in capital cases tried in US courts (Bandes, 1996); substitution of the victim's subjective ap-proach for the objective one presumably practised by the court (Victorian Sentencing Committee, 1988); and threats to sentence uniformity which would undermine the 'just deserts' approach to punishment. Sentence disparity, it was argued, is likely to ensue when similar cases are disposed of differently, depending on the availability or thoroughness of the VIS (Hall, 1991) or the 'the resiliency, vindictiveness or other personality attributes of the victim' (Grabosky, 1987: 147).[3] This issue is of particular concern in capital cases in the USA (Sebba, 1994), where it has been argued that empathy with the victim and other 'right emotions' which VISs commonly invoke may lead to arbitrariness and prejudice in the imposition of a death sentence (Bandes, 1996). Some have concluded that victim input in general lacks probative value in a system of public prosecution and is likely to be highly prejudicial (Hellerstein, 1989).

The legal profession, in particular, mobilized to oppose reform measures that were imposed from the outside, challenged established legal traditions about victims' role in criminal justice and threatened routine court practices (see, for example, Australian Law Reform Commission, 1987; Victorian Sentencing Committee, 1988). Legal scholars were also quick to point out the regressive ideological underpinning of the reform (Henderson, 1985; Bandes, 1996), its inherent legal contradictions (Ashworth, 1993) and the limits of the reform in many jurisdictions (Hellerstein, 1989). Victim input rights have been particularly criticized for their presumed alliance with, or exploitation by, 'law and order' campaigns. Opponents have argued that victims' anguish has been mobilized into support for a conservative ideology, and that the attempt to integrate victims into the process may be a way of accomplishing the goal of harsher punishment (Henderson, 1985; Hellerstein, 1989). One legal scholar has attributed recent penological trends, which demonstrate increases in the severity of punishment, to attempts to integrate a victim voice in criminal justice, and warned against 'victims in the service of severity' (Ashworth, Chapter 9 in this volume).

Victims' psychological welfare has also served as grounds for objections to input rights. Some have argued that participatory rights may create expectations that are not, or cannot, be met (Fattah, 1986; Ashworth, 1993). Victims who feel that their input has been ignored by judges may become embittered and resentful (Henderson, 1985). In the UK, Victim Support activists have argued that allowing victim input will have adverse effects on victims, as it will return the burden of responsibility for decisions concerning offenders to victims. According to Victim Support, crime victims do not want this burden; therefore, victim input should be presented only to prosecutors in preparation of their cases rather than directly to judges (Victim Support, 1995).

Objections from a managerial perspective were also raised. Potential adverse effects of victim participation include delays, longer trials and additional expenses for an already overburdened system (see, for example, Australian Law Reform Commission, 1987; Miers, 1992). Some claimed that the reform may not be effective in terms of cost-benefit, and that victim input would add very little useful or novel information which is not already available to the court (Australian Law Reform Commission, 1987) or taken into account in the definitions of offences and of mitigating or aggravating circumstances (Ashworth, 1993).

These debates reveal three major tensions which have become arenas in the implementation of victim input rights: first, a tension exists between the preservation of traditional conceptions of the adversarial legal system and the provision of victims' participatory rights. In this context, one legal scholar has predicted that efforts to define a role for the victim would meet great resistance from the principal actors in criminal processing: the prosecutor, the defence counsel and the judge. To them, attempts to integrate victims would only 'formalize a relationship with the victim which already exists, or which prosecutors and judges have decided for good reason should not exist' (Goldstein, 1984: 242). The research discussed below confirms this prediction and reveals the strategies or 'neutralization techniques' invoked by legal practitioners to avoid implementing victim input legislation.

A second tension was created by attempts to accommodate victim input rights within an emerging ideology of managerial justice (Douglas *et al.*, 1994) which places a high premium on speed, costs and efficiency. This ideology of administrative rationality and technocratic justice (O'Malley, 1984) has transformed the courts into modern businesslike administrative agencies concerned with productivity and cost-effectiveness in the delivery of their 'services' (Heydebrand and Seron, 1990). This managerial approach has also contributed to the reform's failure to provide victims with the expected benefits of a voice, as well as to court inertia in the processing of crime and criminals.

Lastly, a tension has emerged between the demands to provide victim input rights and attempts to increase sentence uniformity and reduce its severity. The two movements that coalesce in this reform – the 'just deserts' and victim participatory rights – may, in fact, pull in different directions: uniformity and predictability in sentencing versus specificity of penalty according to victim harm (Erez and Sebba, 1999). This tension has also served as grounds for practitioners' reluctance to consider victim input. Interestingly, both sides of the debate have used victims' welfare as an argument to buttress their position.

In the following section recent research findings addressing the issues at the core of these tensions will be presented: the effects of victim input on court outcomes and processes, on the traditional conception of the adversarial legal system including defendants rights, and on victims' welfare and satisfaction with justice.

Assessing the Effects of VIS on Criminal Justice

Effects on Court Outcomes and Practices

The effect of victim impact statements on court outcomes and processes has been addressed by quantitative analyses (Erez and Tontodonato, 1990; 1992; Davis and Smith, 1994), as well as by qualitative research (Hillenbrand and Smith, 1989; Henley *et al.*, 1994; Erez and Rogers, 1999).

Quantitative studies in various jurisdictions and countries included comparisons of sentencing outcomes before and after the passage of the legislation mandating victim input (Erez and Roeger, 1995a) and comparisons of cases with and without a VIS, controlling for all other variables presumed to affect court outcomes either statistically (Erez and Tontodonato, 1990; Erez and Roeger, 1995a) or experimentally, through random assignment of cases to control and treatment groups (Davis and Smith, 1994). These studies have tested the hypothesis that VISs have a harshening effect on sentencing by examining the correlation between the presence of VISs in the file and harsher sentences, and between the absence of a VIS and sentence leniency. They did not address the content of the VIS and its effects on sentencing outcomes.

Quantitative studies, whether they were correlational (Erez and Tontodonato, 1990; Douglas *et al.*, 1994; Erez and Roeger, 1995b) or experimental (Davis and Smith, 1994), did not identify any significant effects of VISs on sentence outcomes. They reported various implementation problems (for instance, prosecutors did not receive VISs, VISs were perfunctory or were not read by officials) which were presumed to be the reason for the reform's minimal impact (Davis and Smith, 1994; Sebba, 1996).

Qualitative studies on the effect of VISs offered either survey data about court officials' experiences with, and impressions of, the reform's impact (Hillenbrand and Smith, 1989; Henley *et al.*, 1994) or in-depth interviews of legal professionals (Erez *et al.*, 1994; Erez and Rogers, 1999; Erez and Laster, 1999). These studies confirm the finding that, overall, the reform has had little impact on court outcomes and processes, although the interview data confirm the hypotheses (Erez, 1990; Sebba, 1996) that victim input does have some effects on sentencing outcomes – effects that are concealed and are washed out in aggregate studies. The interview data also identified the strategies which legal professionals employ to minimize victim input and the 'techniques of neutralization' (Sykes and Matza, 1956) they invoke to discard VISs and resist a meaningful implementation of the mandate to consider them (Erez and Laster, 1999).

Studies that surveyed court officials (Hillenbrand and Smith, 1989; Henley *et al.*, 1994) found that the majority favoured the *principle* of considering victim impact in sentencing decisions, and that few officials believed that VISs created or exacerbated managerial problems in the criminal justice process. Indeed, most judges and prosecutors thought that VISs improved the quality of justice – for example, by influencing restitution awards (see also Shapland *et al.*, 1985) or by having some impact on the sentence. Practitioners did not identify any operational problems (such as slowing down the process), nor did they report challenges of victim input by the defence. Yet, despite their expressed sympathy for victims, these studies suggest that judges and prosecutors mostly paid lip service to victim input (Henley *et al.*, 1994; see also Erez and Rogers, 1999). They expressed doubts about the potential of VISs to change, in any way, routine disposi-tions in the majority of criminal court cases and speculated about problems that may arise from discovery issues, from victim exaggeration of monetary loss, injury, or psychological harm, and from the prospects of victim input providing any new information which is not already available from the file. They also intimated that victim input needs to be taken with 'a grain of salt' (Erez *et al.*, 1994; Henley *et al.*, 1994).

Legal practitioners' distrust of victims and their input, and the strategies they employ to minimize them, clearly emerged from studies which used in-depth interviews of legal professionals (Erez and Rogers, 1999; Erez and Laster, 1999). The interview data also provide support for the hypothesis of differential effects of the VIS content on sentencing outcomes.

Legal occupational culture provides two mechanisms for excluding vic-tim input: typification, or the notion of the 'normal' victim, and 'objec-tivity'. Analogous to the concept of 'reasonable man' applied to defendants, practitioners use the concept of the 'normal victim' to evaluate the veracity and credibility of victim input. Victim reactions that are not perceived as typical are often viewed as exaggerated, illogical and unbelievable by all legal professionals, particularly defence attorneys (Erez and Rogers, 1999). Although few highly experienced practitioners could recognize variations in 'normal' victim reactions, most legal professionals were willing to accept only a narrow range of 'normality' in victim harm and would not tolerate a victim's apparently extreme or excessive reaction to a crime. Overall, the majority of the accumulated 'typical' victim experiences serves to reduce professionals' preparedness to accept as genuine or truthful a reaction that is out of the 'normal' or expected range of experience (see also Sudnow, 1965; Frohmann, 1992). This typification phenomenon has contributed signifi-cantly to professionals' rejecting individual reactions to crime and ignoring victims' input (Erez and Rogers, 1999; Erez and Laster, 1999).

Another feature of legal occupational culture often invoked when practi-tioners reject victim input is 'objectivity'. Objectivity is a normative ideal in law. It is the legal apologetic that defends against the use, or acknowledgment, of affect or standpoint in the perception and construction of legal events or decisions. Judges claim, or are presumed, to examine cases that come before them in an 'objective' fashion, detached from any emotional baggage that the human stories in the criminal cases often carry. The belief in the 'objective' application of law in sentencing decisions allows judges to define unusual victims' stories of crime impact as 'subjective' – and hence irrelevant – and to ignore any victim input which they deem 'out of the ordinary' or outside the legal professionals' routine experience with this crime (ibid.). Despite a growing tendency in the law to recognize subjective experiences (Laster and O'Malley, 1996) and a recognition that objectivity is problematic when interpreting and applying legal rules (Rogers and Erez, 1999), legal professionals still describe their routine case dispositions as 'objective'. Likewise, they use the presumed 'subjectivity' and emotionality of victim input as a reason for denying its legitimacy, despite serious questions raised by feminists and others as to whether subjective experiences can be presented in an 'objective' manner (Erez, 1999) and a recognition that emotions underlie rational, logical, legal decisions (Bandes, 1996). Furthermore, the data suggest that perceptions of 'objectivity' held by legal professionals are themselves subjective, and are influenced by factors such as political positioning, professional roles, proximity to victims or prior life experiences (Rogers and Erez, 1999).

The practitioners who mentioned the importance of objectivity often offered the apology that victims have various motives, or built-in incentives, to lie or exaggerate their injuries – namely, the penalty the offender would receive (victims were presumed to be vindictive), or financial gain, including the size of a compensation order a victim would be awarded (victims were presumed greedy) (Erez and Rogers, 1999). The 'denial of the victim' and 'denial of the injury' were part of the repertoire of 'techniques of neutralization' (Sykes and Matza, 1956) judges used to justify minimizing or ignoring victim input. Other techniques practitioners invoked to discard victim input included: 'resort to higher loyalty'- the obligation of judges to clear court dockets and move cases along, or avoid departures from the tariff; 'denial of responsibility'- the VISs judges received were perfunctory or useless; and 'condemning the condemners' – dismissal of the reform as a political move to win support, election, or government succumbing to political pressures by vocal feminists and victim groups (Erez and Laster, 1999).

Victim input has nonetheless had some effects on sentencing. Most often these were cosmetic changes, as judges often quoted in sentencing remarks victim statements about suffering, attempting to, in the words of the judges, 'to bring home to offenders the harm they inflicted on victims' (Erez and Rogers, 1999: 231). But, in a few cases, victim input did impact on sentencing outcomes. Legal professionals who were asked to provide specific instances in which they thought a sentence was changed or reconsidered based exclusively on victim input offered examples suggesting that victim input may lead to both more severe and more lenient sentences. Crimes committed in a particularly cruel manner, or offences which caused prolonged suffering to victims, or longlasting consequences, led to more severe sentences, whereas complete recovery, a forgiving victim or circumstances which suggest that the harm was wrongly attributed to the offender led to more lenient outcomes (ibid.). Contrary to arguments that victim input leads to punitiveness and sentence harshness, these findings suggest that VISs enhance proportionality and accuracy in sentencing.

The minimal role that victim input plays in sentencing is also evident in the limited extent of its impact on court schedules and proceedings. Allowing victims a voice in sentencing has not resulted in longer trials or mini-trials on the content of the VIS. Practitioners conceded that it is very rare to have a victim called to testify about their input, as such a move may have adverse effects on the sentence. At most, including the VIS has added a few minutes to sentencing as, in the words of the practitioners, 'it takes only few minutes to read the impact materials' or 'it takes two to three minutes to digest the statements' (ibid.: 232–3). Many legal professionals commented that, on the whole, the VIS reform had actually saved court time, as the information on victim harm was readily available from the VIS rather than spread all over the file (Erez *et al.*, 1994). The English pilot project also found that the victim statements included new information which was not already available from other sources (Hoyle *et al.*, 1998: 28).

Effects on the Conceptions of Justice in an Adversarial System and Defendants' Rights

Providing victims with a voice in the form of victim impact statements has not affected fundamental principles underlying the adversarial legal system. The research suggests that the VIS has not transformed victims into parties to proceedings, nor has it compromised defendants' rights. Studies of jurisdictions which use VISs demonstrated that victims do not use the VIS as an opportunity to make inflammatory, unjustified prejudicial statements about the defendant (Cassell, 1999) or to subject offenders to 'unfounded or excessive allegations, made from the relative security of VIS' (Ashworth, 1993: 507). In most jurisdictions, victims do not prepare their own statement; their input is filtered or 'edited' by the specific agency responsible for the preparation of the VIS. 'Retelling' victims' stories for legal consumption often 'sterilizes' (Delgado, 1989) them and takes the power out of victim stories to the extent that judges often note that the VISs they read are mild compared to what they would have expected in light of the offence involved. The effect of 'retelling' harm – utilising what legal professionals call a 'clinical' approach to harm (Erez *et al.*, 1994) – eliminates individual victims' idiosyncrasies, suppresses unusual attributes of the injury and, in the words of one judge, results in 'a generous understatement of victim harm' (Erez and Rogers, 1999). In general, studies show that when victim information is mediated by justice agents, the 'construction of stories' is affected both by resource considerations and by the goals and priorities of the agency involved; consequently, loss or distortion of critical details of the harm is highly likely (Douglas *et al.*, 1994; Erez and Rogers, 1999). Furthermore, the recent English study of victim statements, which compared the relative advantage of self-prepared statements and those prepared by the police, suggested that both methods tend to understate, rather than overstate, the impact of offences, and that victim statements do not encourage exaggeration, inflammatory statements or vindictiveness (Hoyle *et al.*, 1998: 28).

Research also suggests that the VIS reform has not promoted changes in sentencing principles. Legal professionals, in a jurisdiction which mandated consideration of a *particular* victim harm, emphasized that the purpose of instituting the VIS was to give victims a voice, not to restructure sentencing priorities. They reiterated the importance of offender culpability over harm in imposing penalties, and reported that, in their sentencing decisions, they do not consider victim harm as the overriding criterion in sentencing (Erez *et al.*, 1994). Although they conceded that, in a few cases, victim input has caused them to reconsider a sentence and make it proportional to the harm inflicted on the victim, these were cases in which the offender culpability was firmly established (Erez and Rogers, 1999).

Research suggests that victim input has the potential of improving 'justice' – of making sentences more commensurate or proportional – in an adversarial legal system which conceptualizes the trial as a combat between the prosecution and the defence. One of the major challenges in criminal justice sentencing is forming a fair and accurate picture of crime and its consequences to guide decision-makers in their difficult task. The prosecution has its priorities and constraints when prosecuting offenders. More often than not, its organizational interests are opposed to those of the victim, and prosecutors may not be interested in disclosing the full scope of the crime impact (Goldstein, 1982). Research confirms that judges are sometimes unaware of the harm victims sustained as a result of the crime, because the information was not included as part of the file, either intentionally (due to bargaining considerations, or other priorities of the agencies charged with preparing the statements), or unintentionally (due to staff underestimating the importance of the information, incompetence or laziness, or lack of resources) (Erez and Rogers, 1999).

Direct input from victims may guarantee that legal professionals become aware of the injuries sustained in a particular case, as well as help them become acquainted with the short- and long-term effects of various crimes. Research shows that legal professionals who have been exposed to VISs have commented on how uninformed they were about the extent, variety and longevity of various victimizations, and how much they have learned from properly prepared VISs about the impact of crime on victims (Erez and Rogers, 1999; Cassell, 1999).

Arguments that allow victim input may result in 'unequal justice' (due to variation in victim persuasiveness, vindictiveness or other personal attributes), equally apply, according to one Australian judge, to any other aspect of the case (Erez *et al.*, 1994). In the USA these sentiments have been expressed in Justice White's powerful dissenting argument in *Booth* v. *Maryland*, stating that 'No two prosecutors have exactly the same ability to communicate the facts ... but there is no requirement that the evidence and argument be reduced to the lower common denominator' (482 US at 518). And, given that most justice systems allow almost unlimited mitigation evidence on the part of the defendant, an argument for equal justice requires that victim statements about harm be allowed as well (Cassell, 1999).

Effects on Victims' Welfare and Satisfaction with Justice

The cumulative knowledge acquired from research in countries with different legal systems and in various jurisdictions suggests that victims often benefit from participation and input. With proper safeguards, the overall experience of providing input can be positive and empowering. Research conducted in the USA and Australia on victims of various felonies, where a VIS is relevant (that is, a personal harm or loss was suffered by a specific victim), suggests that victims are interested in having a voice (Erez and Tontodonato, 1992; Erez *et al.*, 1994). The victims in these studies did not report feeling burdened or pressured by providing input, and by knowing that their input had been conveyed to decision-makers. On the contrary, they expressed a wish to be heard and their input to be considered by judges. Research on victims in continental legal systems who served as a party to the prosecution (as continental legal procedures allow) were highly satisfied with this role in the proceedings, and their level of satisfaction with justice was positively correlated with the amount of their participation (Erez and Bienkowska, 1993). The recent experiment with victim statements in England confirms that the opportunity to provide input on the crime impact is a positive experience for most victims (Hoyle *et al.*, 1998: ch. 4). The literature on procedural justice provides theoretical explanations for these findings (Lind and Tyler, 1988). According to procedural justice theories, litigants' satisfaction with justice and sense of fairness of the outcome is more affected by the procedures in which decisions were made rather than by the outcomes. Proceedings which provide victims with a voice or 'process control' enhance their satisfaction with justice and sense of fair treatment.

Research in adversarial legal systems also suggests that the majority of victims of personal felonies wished to participate and provide input, even when they thought their input was ignored or did not affect the outcome of their case (Erez *et al.*, 1997; Hoyle *et al.*, 1998). Victims have multiple motives for providing input, and having a voice serves several functions for them: for some, input restores the unequal balance between them and the offender, particularly in cases in which the victim did not have an opportunity to testify or be heard because they were resolved by a plea (Konradi, 1997). Survivors of murder victims, particularly parents, whether in Florida, USA (Shapiro and Weinstein, 1995) or Jerusalem, Israel have articulated a compelling need to provide input and represent the interests of their beloved one in the case. Mr Eyal, a father whose daughter was murdered, reported in an interview to the Israeli newspaper, *Maariv*, that he has had nightmares that 'the trial will take place and I will not be notified and able to participate' (*Maariv*, 18 December 1998). He noted that it is imperative for justice that he has the opportunity to tell how the event has affected the family. Victim impact statements by relatives of the victims of the Oklahoma City bombing expressed similar sentiments (Cassell, 1999).

The literature in the growing field of therapeutic jurisprudence supports the proposition that having a voice may improve victims' mental welfare and documents the harmful effects that feeling silenced and external to the process may have on victims (Wexler and Winick, 1996; Hora and Schma, 1998). Providing input helps victims to cope with the criminal justice experience. Victims who filled out VISs claimed that they felt relieved or satisfied after providing the information (Erez *et al.*, 1994). The recent research in England confirms that the majority of victims who made a statement reported that the experience made them feel better, and 'the cathartic effect of recording the impact had been an end in itself' (Hoyle *et al.*, 1998: 32).

Recent research on the attitudes of rape victims to participation in criminal justice (Konradi, 1997) provides more textured insights into victims' psychological, internally oriented benefits of having a voice. The majority of the victims sought procedural justice and over half of them felt that input would assist with achieving substantive justice. For most of the victims, filing out a VIS is a civil duty that they consider important for reaching a just sentence. Many victims also want 'to communicate the impact of the offense to the offender' (Erez *et al.*, 1997; Konradi, 1997). Through participation and input, victims wanted to engage the criminal justice process. Many echoed the words of Nils Christie (1977) in their wish to assert 'ownership of the conflict' which they felt was misappropriated from them in the name of the state. Others wanted to reduce the power imbalance they felt with the defendant (Shapiro and Weinstein, 1995), resolve the emotional aspects of the victimization, achieve emotional recovery or achieve formal closure. This was particularly true for victims whose violators pleaded guilty and the victims never had the chance to be involved in the justice process. Many victims also wanted to remind judges of the fact that behind the crime is a real person who is a victim (Konradi, 1997; Kelly, 1987). The recent experiment in England confirms that victims have various expressive, instrumental and procedural reasons for providing input (Hoyle *et al.*, 1998).

Research also suggests that the overwhelming majority of victims want their VISs to be used in sentencing, mostly to guarantee that the judges know their side of the story.[4] Judges who were asked whether the VIS reform can lead to disparity in sentencing because of some victims declining to submit an impact statement responded that they have rarely encountered a victim who declined to do so (Erez *et al.*, 1994: ch. 2). Victims who fear retaliation from the offender may avoid the criminal justice system altogether; but, once they have mobilized the system, a request from officials to provide input about the harm they sustained is not documented to be a burden (Erez *et al.*, 1994: Konradi, 1997). Only a small percentage (less than 10 per cent) of victims expressed some fear about providing input for impact statements (Erez *et al.*, 1994; Hoyle *et al.*, 1998).

Research suggests, however, that a substantial proportion of victims who provided input for sentencing were not aware that they had done so (Erez and Tontodonato, 1992; Erez *et al.*, 1997). In the aftermath of the crime, victims are interviewed by various law enforcement agents and cannot distinguish between the purposes of these questionings. This problem was also documented in the recent pilot project with victim statements in England (Hoyle *et al.*, 1998). Studies also confirm that providing input may be associated with victims' lower satisfaction with justice. Many of those who thought their input was ignored showed a lower level of satisfaction with justice because of raised expectations (Erez and Tontodonato, 1992; Erez *et al.*, 1997; Hoyle *et al.*, 1998).

The potential problem of heightening victim expectations can be resolved by explaining to victims that the VIS is only one of the factors judges use to determine the type and severity of penalties. Research has confirmed that victims who receive explanations of the proceedings are satisfied with the outcome, regardless of its nature, and there is no reason to doubt that such explanations could be effective in preventing heightened expectations and subsequent disappointment. Properly administered VIS schemes may also make victims aware that they are being given an opportunity to have a voice, which in turn would help them overcome their sense of powerlessness and lack of control. Victims can also receive indirect benefits from providing input. Victims derive significant satisfaction from judges paying attention to their input by citing victims' own phrases from their impact statements in judicial sentencing comments, as judges often do when a statement is available (Erez and Rogers, 1999). Victim advocates in the USA and Australia confirm that victims feel that the harm they sustained was validated when judges' remarks cite their input, and they are highly satisfied with justice when they read sentencing comments in which judges quote their impact statements (Erez, 1999). The recent pilot project in England also documents that victims whose statement was read in court were very pleased with the experience (Hoyle *et al.*, 1998).

Concerns about challenges to victims' input mounted by the defence and about exposing victims to unwanted cross-examinations on the content of their statements also did not materialize. The legal professionals explained that challenging claims of mental harm was 'not a good move for tactical reasons' (Erez and Rogers, 1999): Challenging a statement requires that the victim be called to testify and crossed-examined about his or her input. This is a risk that defence lawyers are generally unwilling to take, because of its likely adverse effect on the sentence. On the other hand, challenges of monetary issues were usually settled by counsels' agreement that the inflated claims are withdrawn as, in the words of practitioners, 'it is not worth spending hours of court time on a difference of few dollars' (Erez *et al.*, 1994).

Conclusion

Despite the high hopes of victim rights advocates, and the misgivings of opponents of victim participation, the inclusion of victim input in proceedings during the 1990s has had little effect on the criminal justice system and on victims' satisfaction with it. Research suggests that victim impact legislation has failed to transform court practices, and victims' feelings about them, in most of the ways prophesied by the reform critics or supporters. Court inertia seems to result from the legal professionals' strong resistance against accepting victims as a legitimate party in the proceedings and practitioners' reluctance to recognize any value in victim input. Reforms which introduce changes into existing court routines by legislative fiat have only limited success if they do not address legal occupational culture, organizational structure and priorities, and incentives underlying the dynamics of courtroom group work.

The research suggests, however, that there is every reason to include, and no reason to fear, integrating a victim voice through victim impact statements. The VIS practice has demonstrated potential benefits to the justice system as well as to victims. Having a voice can empower victims and improve their views on the fairness of proceedings. With proper safeguards, the practice can also increase victims' sense of control over the process, and consequently their satisfaction with justice. Victim input also ensures that the sentencing judges become aware of the extent of harm sustained by victims, and generally informs them about long- and short-term effects of crime on victims. Accurate information on victim harm can enhance justice in adversarial legal systems, particularly in terms of sentence proportionality. Although it might be argued that the number of cases in which the VIS makes a difference in the outcome (that is, result in either lighter or more severe sentence) is small, to the victims and offenders involved, and to the justice system as a whole, this small probability makes all the difference.

Some time ago a noted American legal scholar commented that:

> We need to move beyond notification and information to victims, even beyond a mere right of 'allocution' to a genuine right of victims to participate as parties in those parts of the process where the adversary system is not working and where they can make a special contribution, or where they have a special stake … . (Goldstein, 1982: 561)

So far, this has largely been a lone voice among legal scholars and practitioners–defenders of the old order. The research reviewed here suggests that the balance of evidence in the debate surrounding the VIS tips towards inclusion, rather than exclusion, of victims. Furthermore, a close examination of objections to including victim input suggests that they are so lacking in merit that it is difficult to see them as anything but a design to conceal some other hidden agenda (Cassell, 1999).

Yet, to institute a meaningful reform in the area of victim participation, it is important to win the cooperation of the legal professionals involved in adversarial justice: prosecutors, judges and defence lawyers. These players have various professional and organizational incentives to resist victim input and ignore the mandate to incorporate victims in proceedings (Erez and Laster, 1999). The problem of the VIS reform, it seems, has not been the VIS itself or its presumed effects on defendants, victims or proceedings, but rather the hostile environment in which the reform has been implemented. To date, legal professionals have been armed with ample unsubstantiated reasons to excuse and justify their reluctance to comply with the VIS reform and to recognize victim input as a viable component in criminal adjudication. The research demonstrates, however, that including victim input does not disturb the old order; rather, it can build and improve on it. It is time for defenders of this order to re-examine their views of victims as 'barbarians at the gates that must be kept out at all costs' (Cassell, 1999). Otherwise, the time-honoured legal tradition of treating victims as invisible is going to be with us for a very long time.

Notes

1   Some jurisdictions have gone further and allowed victims to make statements of opinion concerning the offender's sentence, either in writing or in open court (McLeod, 1986). This chapter will address only written victim statements rather than allocution rights, as the latter are not practiced in many jurisdictions within and outside the USA.
2   The 'just deserts' model was criticized for its theoretical underpinning (for example, Braithwaite and Pettit, 1990), penological effectiveness and justification (for example, Cullen and Gilbert, 1982), unsubstantiated assumptions concerning the capacity of formal law to incorporate subtle nuances of seriousness (for example, Zimring, 1981) or ability to separate an offence from an offender (for example, Gross, 1979), and the inevitable variations in sentencing when statutory definitions of crime consist of broad categories (for example, Gross and von Hirsch, 1981). In terms of criminal justice operation, the adoption of the 'just deserts' model has been criticized because it imposes a 'tariff' on sentencing and highly restricts judges' discretion in imposing penalties.
3   The US Supreme Court reflected these sentiments in *Booth* v. *Maryland* (482 US 496 (1987)) when it outlawed the use of victim impact statements in capital cases. This decision was later overturned in *Payne* v. *Tennessee* (111 S. Ct. 2597 (1991)). For implications of these cases for VISs see Sebba (1994).
4   Victims often state that they provided input on the crime impact to ascertain that 'justice is done'. They also assume or expect that their impact statement will influence sentencing outcomes (Erez *et al.*, 1994; Hoyle *et al.*, 1998). This pairing of 'justice' with the level of harm victims sustained is not surprising and may reflect a 'just deserts' approach to punishment, which views crime seriousness and commensurate punishment as related both to the level of harm sustained and to offender culpability.

References

American Friends' Service Committee (1971), *Struggle for Justice*, New York: Hill and Wang.
Ashworth, A. (1993), 'Victim Impact Statements and Sentencing', *Criminal Law Review*, 498–509.
Australian Law Reform Commission (1987), *Sentencing*, Report No. 44, Canberra: AGPS.
Bandes, S. (1996), 'Empathy, Narrative and Victim Impact Statements', *The University of Chicago Law Review*, **63**(2), 361–412.
Braithwaite, J. and Pettit, P. (1990), *Not Just Deserts*, Oxford: Clarendon Press.
Cassell, P.G. (1999), 'Barbarians at the Gates?: A Response to the Critics of the Victims' Rights Amendment', *Utah Law Review*, 479–544.
Christie, N. (1977), 'Conflicts as Property', *British Journal of Criminology*, **17**(1), 1–15.

Cullen, F.T. and Gilbert, K.E. (1982), *Reaffirming Rehabilitation*, Cincinnati: W.H. Anderson.

Davis, R.C. and Smith, B. (1994), 'The Effect of Victim Impact Statements on Sentencing Decisions: A Test in an Urban Setting', *Justice Quarterly*, **11**(3), 453–69.

Delgado, R. (1989), 'Storytelling for Oppositionists and Others: A Plea for Narrative', *Michigan Law Review*, **87**, 2411–41.

Douglas, R., Laster, K. and Inglis, N. (1994), 'Victims of Efficiency: Tracking Victim Information Through the System in Victoria, Australia', *International Review of Victimology*, **3**, 95–110.

Erez, E. (1989), 'The Impact of Victimology on Criminal Justice Policy', *Criminal Justice Policy Review*, **3**(3), 236–56.

Erez, E. (1990), 'Victim Participation in Sentencing: Rhetoric and Reality', *Journal of Criminal Justice*, **18**, 19–31.

Erez, E. (1994), 'Victim Participation in Sentencing: And the Debate Goes On', *International Review of Victimology*, **3**(1–2), 17–32.

Erez, E. (1999), 'Who is Afraid of the Big Bad Victim? Victim Impact Statements as Victim Empowerment and Enhancement of Justice,' *Criminal Law Review* 545–56.

Erez E. and Bienkowska, E. (1993), 'Victim Participation in Proceedings and Satisfaction with Justice in the Continental Legal Systems: The Case of Poland', *Journal of Criminal Justice*, **21**, 47–60.

Erez, E. and Laster, K. (1999), 'Neutralizing Victim Reform: Legal Professionals' Perspectives on Victims and Impact Statements', *Crime and Delinquency*, **45**(4), 530–53.

Erez, E. and Roeger, L. (1995a), 'Crime Impact v. Victim Impact: Victim Impact Statements in South Australia', *Criminology Australia*, **6**(3), 3–8.

Erez, E. and Roeger, L. (1995b), 'The Effect of Victim Impact Statements on Sentencing Outcomes and Dispositions', *Journal of Criminal Justice*, **23**, 363–75.

Erez E. and Rogers, L. (1999), 'Victim Impact Statements and Sentencing Outcomes and Processes: The Perspectives of Legal Professionals', *British Journal of Criminology*, **39**(2), 216–39.

Erez, E., Roeger, L. and Morgan, F. (1994), *Victim Impact Statements in South Australia: An Evaluation*, Series C. No. 6., August, Adelaide: South Australian Attorney-General's Department, Office of Crime Statistics.

Erez E., Roeger, L. and Morgan F. (1997), 'Victim Harm, Impact Statements and Victim Satisfaction with Justice: An Australian Experience', *International Review of Victimology*, **5**, 37–60.

Erez, E. and Sebba, L. (1999), 'From Individualization of the Offender to Individualization of the Victim', in W. Laufer and F. Adler (eds), *Advances in Criminological Theory*, New Brunswick, NJ: Transaction, 171–98.

Erez, E. and Tontodonato, P. (1990), 'The Effect of Victim Participation in Sentencing on Sentence Outcome', *Criminology*, **28**(3), 451–74.

Erez, E. and Tontodonato, P. (1992), 'Victim Participation in Sentencing and Satisfaction with Justice', *Justice Quarterly*, **9**, 393–427.

Fattah, E.A. (1986) (ed.), *From Crime Policy to Victim Policy*, London: Macmillan.
Fogel, D. (1975), *'We Are Living Proof...': The Justice Model for Corrections*, Cincinnati: W.H. Anderson.
Frohmann, L. (1992), 'Discrediting Victims' Allegations of Sexual Assault: Prosecutorial Accounts of Case Rejections', *Social Problems*, **38**(2), 213–26.
Goldstein, A.S. (1984), 'The Victim and Prosecutorial Discretion: The Federal Victim and Witness Protection Act of 1982', *Law and Contemporary Problems*, **47**, 225–48.
Goldstein, A.S. (1982), 'Defining the Role of the Victim in Criminal Prosecution', *Mississippi Law Review*, **52**, 515–61
Grabosky, P.N. (1987), 'Victims', in G. Zdenkowski, C. Ronalds and M. Richardson (eds), *The Criminal Injustice System*, Vol. 2, Sydney: Pluto Press.
Gross, H. (1979), *A Theory of Criminal Justice*, New York: Oxford University Press.
Gross, H. and von Hirsch, A. (1981) (eds), *Sentencing*, New York: Oxford University Press.
Hall, D.J. (1991), 'Victims' Voices in Criminal Court: The Need for Restraint', *American Criminal Law Review*, **28**(2), 233–66.
Hellerstein, D.R. (1989), 'Victim Impact Statement: Reform or Reprisal?', *American Criminal Law Review*, **27**, 391–430.
Henderson, L.N. (1985), 'The Wrongs of Victims' Rights', *Stanford Law Review*, **37**, 937–1021.
Henley, M., Davis, R.C. and Smith, B.E. (1994), 'The Reactions of Prosecutors and Judges to Victim Impact Statements', *International Review of Victimology*, **3**, 83–93.
Heydebrand, W. and Seron, C. (1990), *Rationalizing Justice: The Political Economy of Federal District Courts*, New York: State University of New York Press.
Hillenbrand, S.W. and Smith, B.E. (1989), *Victim Rights Legislation: An Assessment of its Impact on Criminal Justice Practitioners and Victims*, Report of the American Bar Association to the National Institute of Justice, Washington, DC: American Bar Association.
Hora Fulton, P. and Schma, W.G. (1998), 'Therapeutic Jurisprudence,' *Judicature*, **82**(1), 9–12.
Hoyle, C., Cape, E., Morgan, R. and Sanders, A. (1998), *Evaluation of the 'One Stop Shop' and Victim Statement Pilot Projects*, A Report for the Home Office Research Development and Statistic Directorate, Bristol: Department of Law, University of Bristol.
Kelly, D.P. (1987), 'Victims', *Wayne Law Review*, **34**, 69–86.
Kelly, D.P. and Erez. E. (1997), 'Victim Participation in the Criminal Justice System', in R.C. Davis, A.J. Lurigio and W. Skogan (eds), *Victims of Crime*, (2nd edn), Thousand Oaks, CA: Sage, 231–44.
Kilpatrick, D.G. and Otto, R.K. (1987), 'Constitutionally Guaranteed Participation in Criminal Justice Proceedings for Victims: Potential Effects of Psychological Functioning', *Wayne Law Review*, **34**, 7–28.
Konradi, A. (1997), 'Having the Last Word: An Examination of Rape Survivors'

Participation in Sentencing', paper presented at the Annual Meeting of the Society for the Study of Social Problems, Toronto, 8 August.

Laster, K. and O'Malley, P. (1996), 'Sensitive New Age Laws: The Reassertion of Emotionality in Law', *International Journal of the Sociology of Law*, **24**, 21–40.

Lind A. and Tyler, T.R. (1988), *The Social Psychology of Procedural Justice*, New York: Plenum Press.

McLeod, M. (1986), 'Victim Participation at Sentencing', *Criminal Law Bulletin*, **22**, 501–517.

Miers, D. (1992), 'The Responsibilities and Rights of Victims of Crime', *Modern Law Review*, **55**, 482–505.

O'Malley, P. (1984), 'Technocratic Justice in Australia', *Law in Context: A Socio-Legal Journal*, **2**, 31–49.

President's Task Force on Victims of Crime (1982), *Final Report*, Washington, DC: US Government Printing Office.

Rogers, L. and Erez, E. (1999), 'The Contextuality of Objectivity in Sentencing Among Legal Professionals in South Australia', *International Journal of the Sociology of Law*, **27**(3), 267–86.

Rubel, H.C. (1986), 'Victim Participation in Sentencing Proceedings', *Criminal Law Quarterly*, **28**, 226–50.

Sebba, L. (1994), 'Sentencing and the Victim: The Aftermath of Payne', *International Review of Victimology*, **3**, 141–65.

Sebba, L. (1996), *Third Parties: Victims and the Criminal Justice System*, Columbus: Ohio State University Press.

Shapiro, M.J. and Weinstein, M. (1995), *Who Will Cry for Staci? The True Story of a Grieving Father's Quest for Justice*, New York: Onyx.

Shapland, J., Willmore, J. and Duff, P. (1985), *Victims in the Criminal Justice System*, Aldershot: Gower.

Sudnow, D. (1965), 'Normal Crimes: Sociological Features of the Penal Code in a Public Defender Office', *Social Problems*, **12**, 255–77.

Sumner, C.J. (1987), 'Victim Participation in the Criminal Justice System', *Australian and New Zealand Journal of Criminology*, **20**, 195–217.

Sykes M. and Matza D. (1956), 'Techniques of Neutralization: A Theory of Delinquency,' *American Sociological Review*, **22**, 664–70.

Talbert, P.A. (1988), 'The Relevance of Victim Impact Statements to the Criminal Sentencing Decisions', *UCLA Law Review*, **36**, 199–232.

Tyler, T.R. (1988), 'What is Procedural Justice? Criteria used by Citizens to Assess the Fairness of Legal Procedures', *Law and Society Review*, **22**, 103–35.

US Sentencing Commission (1987), *Sentencing Guidelines and Policy Statements*, Washington, DC: US Sentencing Commission.

Victim Support (1995), *The Rights of Victims of Crime: A Policy Paper*, London: Victim Support.

Victorian Sentencing Committee (1988), *Sentencing: Report of the Committee*, Melbourne: Attorney-General's Department.

von Hirsch, A. and Ashworth, A. (1992) (eds), *Principled Sentencing*, Boston: Northeastern University Press.

Wexler, D. and Winick B. (1996), *Law in a Therapeutic Key*, Durham, NC: Academic Press.

Wiebe, R.P. (1996), 'The Mental Health Implications of Crime Victims' Rights', in D. Wexler and B. Winick (eds), *Law in a Therapeutic Key*, Durham, NC: Carolina Academic Press, 213–241.

Wolfgang, M.E. (1982), 'Basic Concepts in Victimology Theory: Individualisation of the Victim', in H.J. Schneider (ed.), *The Victim in International Perspective*, Berlin: De Gruter, 47–58.

Zimring, F.E. (1981), 'Making the Punishment Fit the Crime: A Consumer's Guide to Sentencing Reform', in H. Gross and A. von Hirsch (eds), *Sentencing*, New York: Oxford University Press, 327–24.

9   Victims' Rights, Defendants' Rights and Criminal Procedure

Andrew Ashworth

This is a confusing time for criminal justice.[1] The governments of many countries are passing laws to increase sentencing severity, and the number of jurisdictions that have mandatory minimum sentences seems to grow each year. Whether the explanations lie in deep popular feelings of insecurity associated with the postmodern condition (Bottoms, 1995), or in the exploitation of populism to assist vote-winning (von Hirsch, 1998: ch. 9) or even to enhance the perceived legitimacy of governments in the face of apparently intractable problems of law-breaking (Garland, 1996), the movement towards penal severity is much in evidence. But it is not universal (Weigend, 1997; Albrecht, 1997), nor is it the only movement that is making headway in the twilight of the twentieth century. This book, and the conference which preceded it, are testimony to the growing worldwide responses to what the organizers have termed 'the victim perspective' in criminal justice. There is great diversity in the nature of these responses: to mention but a few, there are the family group conferences in New Zealand (Morris *et al.*, 1993; New Zealand Ministry of Justice, 1995) and in some Australian states (Braithwaite and Mugford, 1994; Hudson *et al.*, 1996), which vary considerably among themselves in organization, procedure and purpose; in the United States a particular form of 'victims' rights' lobby has gained ground (Erez, 1994; Mosteller, 1997), although there are also some schemes for victim–offender mediation (Umbreit, 1994); and in many European countries the emphasis has been on securing payments from offender to victim (Kaiser *et al.*, 1991).

In some countries the two movements – towards greater penal severity and towards integrating a victim perspective – seem to go hand-in-hand.

The United States provides examples of such a phenomenon, with some victims' organizations that are punitively oriented and with claims that the true goal of some constitutional amendments is to benefit the prosecution rather than to establish victims' participatory rights (see Mosteller, 1998). But in other countries the two movements operate simultaneously, in separate spheres and in apparent contradiction. Thus in England and Wales two indices of the growing severity of sentencing are the burgeoning prison population (in round figures, an average of some 39 000 in 1971, some 44 000 in 1993 and over 65 000 in 1999) and the introduction of mandatory life imprisonment for the second serious offence under the Crime (Sentences) Act 1997 (Cavadino and Dignan, 1997a: chs 4 and 5; Ashworth, 1997). Yet recent decades have also seen a significant trend towards diversion from prosecution, with the number of offenders cautioned rising from 104 000 in 1981 to 191 000 in 1996 (while the number convicted of indictable offences fell from 464 000 to 301 000 over the same period). Diversion has become the principal approach to dealing with young offenders, and the Crime and Disorder Act 1998 introduces a new procedure which, among other things, draws in some elements of restorative justice as a mainstream response to youth offending (see Home Office, 1997: 16–17).[2] Much emphasis has been placed on the anticipated effectiveness of the new procedures in reducing re-offending among young offenders, rather than on the value to victims of allowing them to participate in the process or on the possible pressures and demands on victims.[3]

So the two different political relationships between escalating sentence severity and developing restorative justice point to two different dangers, which we might call 'victims in the service of severity' and 'victims in the service of offenders'. Each of them can be seen as forms of victim prostitution (cf. Miers, 1992), which ought to be exposed and opposed. More broadly, these dangers remind us of the need to ensure that the growing interest in promoting the victim perspective should not reduce our vigilance about proper standards and safeguards in criminal justice.

In this chapter I will focus on three out of the many issues arising in this area. First, to what extent should there be procedural protections for victims and other witnesses in court? Second, to what extent do schemes of restorative justice attain proper standards of procedural and substantive fairness? And, third, how strong are the arguments for granting procedural rights to victims?

Victim-complainants as Witnesses

There are some provisions in the ethical codes of the legal profession, and some appeal court decisions, on the limits of proper cross-examination of witnesses. Thus paragraph 610(e) of the General Council of the Bar's *Code of Conduct for Barristers* states that a barrister at court 'must not make statements or ask questions which are merely scandalous or intended or calculated only to vilify or to annoy either a witness or some other person'. Annexe H to the Code, added to give greater guidance on ethics in criminal cases, tackles the question of how far the defence may go in cross-examination of prosecution witnesses, stating that counsel 'is entitled to test the evidence given by each individual witness ... Further than this he ought not to go.'[4] In a Crown Court trial the judge is expected to intervene to prevent lines of questioning that breach this rule or are otherwise oppressive.[5] This, however, must be seen in the context of an adversarial system of criminal justice in which defence lawyers are expected to test the prosecution case to the full (see Luban, 1993; Blake and Ashworth, 1998; Ashworth, 1998: ch. 3). Most judges have been 'socialized' into such a system and, while there is growing recognition of the special needs of child witnesses, it does not appear that many judges are willing to control cross-examination by counsel in other cases.

Research conducted in English courts shows the extent to which witnesses are subjected to treatment that they (and many other non-lawyers) view as oppressive. Paul Rock's study of an English Crown Court offers many examples of insulting, intrusive and degrading cross-examination (Rock, 1993: ch. 2). Sue Lees (1997) raised the profile of victimization through cross-examination in rape trials by presenting evidence of the humiliating and degrading cross-examination of many rape complainants. Research by Victim Support (1996: 25, 41, 56) gives accounts of why some rape victims feel that defence counsel 'revictimized' them through 'savage' cross-examination, to which neither prosecuting counsel nor the judge raised any objection. And David Brereton (1997) has shown that the defence tactic of trying to discredit prosecution witnesses by intrusive and humiliating questions is to be found in assault trials no less than in rape trials.

In my limited experience, the response of many barristers to research of this kind takes one of two tacks. The first is to deny the findings, claiming either that the samples are too small or that 'in my whole career I have never come across cases of that kind'. That response is troubling in its insensitivity. The second response is to argue that questioning of this kind flows from the logic of the adversarial model. A defence lawyer is ethically obliged 'to promote and to protect fearlessly and by all proper and lawful means his [or her] lay client's best interests',[6] in order to ensure that the presumption of innocence is adequately reinforced. But does it follow that this licenses the defence lawyer to mount all kinds of personal attacks on prosecution witnesses, subject to the trial judge ruling out questioning which is thought to cross the threshold of the oppressive? Is it true that the only way to ensure that a defendant has a fair trial, with full and fearless representation, is to attempt to discredit prosecution witnesses in a degrading way?[7] Too often it is assumed that the logic of the adversarial process prevents negative answers to those two questions; instead it is important to re-examine fundamental concepts such as relevance, and to consider the role of myths and prejudices (about rape, in particular) in sustaining particular attitudes about what is appropriate (Baird, 1998: ch. 1).

What, in this context, is a fair trial? It could be argued that we have here a classic conflict between two sets of rights, those of the defendant (bolstered by the presumption of innocence) and those of witnesses (including victims). Even this starting point is not uncontroversial, because there are those who decline to recognize any rights of witnesses at a criminal trial. In this context it is good to see that the recent Home Office report on vulnerable and intimidated witnesses includes this declaration:

> Witnesses are performing a public duty and should be treated with dignity and respect when giving evidence in court. While recognising the need to ensure that defence counsel is able adequately to test the evidence against their client, the Group recommends that the Lord Chief Justice should be invited to consider issuing a Practice Direction giving guidance to barristers and judges on the need to disallow unnecessarily aggressive and/or inappropriate cross-examination. (Home Office, 1998: para. 8.53)

This is an important statement of principle, which barristers and judges should be slow to dismiss either as 'mere political correctness' or, worse, as simply a confirmation of the existing position. But what is its theoretical foundation? Do witnesses have any rights, to be set against the defendant's right to a fair trial?

The foundations can be located in judgements of the European Court of Human Rights, a provenance made all the more important by the enactment of the Human Rights Act 1998. The European Convention on Human Rights (ECHR) is well known for its declaration of the right to a fair trial, and for the list in Article 6.3 of five distinct rights of defendants in criminal cases. So how does the notion of rights for mere witnesses emerge from this framework?

The right to a fair trial, declared by Article 6.1, is a general right, of which the five rights of defendants in Article 6.3 are non-exhaustive examples. One of the five rights is that in Article 6.3(d): a defendant's right 'to examine or have examined witnesses against him'. In two recent cases, the European Court of Human Rights has had to consider whether a trial can be fair if witnesses for the prosecution remain anonymous and do not give evidence in open court – a context slightly different from the theme of this chapter, but raising similar fundamental issues. In *Doorson* v. *Netherlands*

((1996) 23 EHRR 330) the Court held that the trial was not unfair when two prosecution witnesses remained anonymous and were questioned by the judge in the presence of counsel (but not the accused), whereas in *Van Mechelen* v. *Netherlands* ((1998) 25 EHRR 657) the Court held that the trial was unfair when 11 police officers gave evidence for the prosecution, remained anonymous and were questioned by the judge whilst prosecuting and defence counsel were kept in another room, with only a sound link to the judge's chambers. We are not here concerned with the detailed points in these cases but, rather, with the principle of allowing a defendant's 'normal' rights to be curtailed in the interests of witnesses. In both cases it was feared that the witnesses and their families would be subjected to reprisals if their anonymity was not preserved. There is no express reference in the European Convention to the rights of witnesses, so how did the Court arrive at its judgement in *Doorson*? This is the key passage:

> It is true that Article 6 does not explicitly require the interests of witnesses in general, and those of victims called upon to testify in particular, to be taken into consideration. However, their life, liberty or security of person may be at stake, as may interests coming generally within the ambit of Article 8 of the Convention. ... Contracting States should organise their criminal proceedings in such a way that those interests are not unjustifiably imperilled. Against this background, principles of fair trial also require that in appropriate cases the interests of the defence are balanced against those of witnesses or victims called upon to testify. ((1996) 23 EHRR at 358, para. 70)

In this case the Court conceded that the anonymity of the witnesses presented difficulties for the defence, but held that the defence had been able to ensure that all necessary questions were put to the witnesses and counsel had an opportunity to observe their answers. The decision to exclude the defendant himself was based on reasonable grounds, and was counterbalanced by ensuring that the defence had the opportunity to have the witnesses examined. In *Van Mechelen*, on the other hand, the Court argued that the position of police officers is somewhat different from that of ordinary members of the public (the giving of evidence in court being one of their duties) and that both the defendants and their counsel were wrongly prevented from observing the witnesses' demeanour during questioning.[8]

These decisions establish the significance of the rights of all witnesses in criminal proceedings. Of course there is no complete account of what those rights are, because they are nowhere spelt out in the European Convention itself.[9] Indeed, one of the respects in which the incorporation of the European Convention into United Kingdom law is a mixed blessing is the absence of any clear statement of victims' rights, or the rights of witnesses.

But the idea of witnesses' rights is not confined to the European Court. It has found recognition in a high-profile decision of the Court of Appeal, in a case where the defendant had, in person, questioned the complainant in a rape case in an intimidatory and humiliating manner. The Lord Chief Justice, Lord Bingham, stated that:

> It is the clear duty of the trial judge to do everything he can, consistently with giving the defendant a fair trial, to minimise the trauma suffered by other participants … [T]he judge should, if necessary in order to save the complainant from avoidable distress, stop further questioning by the defendant or take over the questioning of the complainant himself. If the defendant seeks by his dress, bearing, manner or questions to dominate, intimidate or humiliate the complainant, or if it is reasonably apprehended that he will seek to do so, the judge should not hesitate to order the erection of a screen, in addition to controlling questioning in the way we have indicated. (*Brown (Milton Anthony)*), [1998] 2 Cr. App. R. 364, at 391)

Although this case concerned a defendant who represented himself, the recognition that witnesses have interests that ought to be safeguarded is surely of general application. Of course, that is only a first step. The second step is to consider the points at which they conflict with the traditional procedural and evidential apparatus of a fair trial. And the third step is to consider how to maximize both the fairness of the trial (for the defendant) and the protection of the witness, using the well known principle that all alternative methods should be considered before any diminution of rights is contemplated.[10] English courts have, for example, been rather reluctant to authorize the use of screens, and therefore Lord Bingham's reference to this possibility in the above passage was significant.

The government has decided not to rely on judicial regulation in all these matters and Parliament therefore passed the Youth Justice and Criminal Evidence Act 1999, Part II of which contains several provisions for the protection of witnesses, based on the 1998 report *Speaking Up for Justice* (Home Office, 1998). The Act contains three sets of relevant sections. The first of these defines two categories of 'witnesses eligible for assistance' – those who are vulnerable through age or personal circumstances, and those who are likely to suffer through fear or distress. In all these cases a court should consider the appropriateness of special measures, such as screening, the giving of evidence by live link, the giving of evidence *in camera*, the removal of wigs and gowns, the admissibility of videorecorded evidence in chief, the admissibility of videorecorded cross-examination and the examination of the witness through an intermediary (sections 16–33).

The second set of sections provides for the protection of witnesses from cross-examination by the accused in person – a problem that has occurred in cases where a defendant represents himself.[11] The provisions (sections 34–40) will require a court, when a particular witness falls within a protected category and other conditions are fulfilled, to make arrangements for the representation of the defendant for the purpose of the cross-examination. Such provisions do not infringe a defendant's rights under Article 6.3(c) of the ECHR.[12]

The third set of sections was the focus of considerable parliamentary debate in 1999. It concerns the much publicized issue of cross-examining rape complainants about their previous sexual history with persons other than the defendant. Over 20 years ago the Heilbron report concluded that evidence of a complainant's sexual history should be admitted only rarely:

> In contemporary society sexual relationships outside marriage, both steady and of a more casual character, are fairly widespread, and it seems now to be agreed that a woman's sexual experiences with partners of her own choosing are neither indicative of untruthfulness nor of a general willingness to consent. (Home Office, 1975: para. 131)

The Heilbron report led to the enactment of s. 2 of the Sexual Offences (Amendment) Act 1976. There is considerable disagreement about the effect of this section: some judges and barristers argue that it is working well and that judges rarely give leave to allow the cross-examination of complainants under s. 2, whereas the Home Office report concluded that the section's restrictive aim has not been fulfilled in practice and that leave is given more frequently than it ought to be (Home Office, 1998: paras 9.63–9.64; see, further, Baird, 1998: ch. 2; Temkin, 1993; Ellison, 1998). The Home Office report took the view that a judicial Practice Direction would be insufficient to tug the courts back to the restrictive approach intended by Heilbron, and so the Youth Justice and Criminal Evidence Act, s.41, replaces s. 2 with a more detailed and more restrictive provision. Without going into detail here, the new provision retains elements of judicial discretion but will attempt to structure it more tightly. Whether the new law will give proper protection to rape complainants will depend, to a large extent, on whether there is also a change of culture and attitude among barristers and judges dealing with these cases. There must be fresh scrutiny of assumptions about relevance: exactly when and why is a complainant's sexual history with other people relevant (see McColgan, 1996)? As a judge of the Supreme Court of Canada put it:

> The content of any relevancy decision will be filled by the particular judge's experience, common sense and/or logic. ... There are certain areas of enquiry where experience, common sense and logic are informed by stereotype and myth ... . This area of the law – i.e. sexual history evidence – has been particu-

larly prone to the utilization of stereotype in determinations of relevance. (L'Heureux-Dube, J, in *Seaboyer* (1993) 83 DLR (4th) 193, at 228)

Unless some judges and barristers prove willing to recognize that they may have been motivated by stereotypes in the past, it will be easy for the courts to slip back into their old ways after the enactment of the new law.[13] The judges may well claim to be the guardians of fairness in trials, but they need to reconsider what is fair.

The above summary of the Act's provisions, although brief, shows that some of the important issues about the treatment of complainants and other witnesses in court are now being tackled. Other reforms for the protection of witnesses should also be considered. Victim Support has highlighted the need to extend the Witness Service from the Crown Court to all magistrates' courts, and has called for proper funding to support victims and other witnesses in this way.[14] The recent JUSTICE report makes further recommendations for improved facilities and support for victims and witnesses at court (JUSTICE, 1998: ch. 3; see also Shapland and Bell, 1998). It also makes the valuable point that witnesses might be better prepared for cross-examination by being told what to expect and why it is necessary to test their evidence. If the presumption of innocence is to be more than mere rhetoric, it means that the defence should test the prosecution evidence to try to show that it does not meet the standard of reliability and proof required. However, as the committee recognizes, this does not remove the need for controls on unduly aggressive cross-examination (JUSTICE, 1998: 51–55), and this is a problem that has not yet received proper recognition and attention.

Restorative Justice and Standards of Fairness

In order to clear a path towards the precise issue for discussion, it is now necessary to make some preliminary remarks about restorative justice. As has rightly been emphasized by Lucia Zedner (1994) and by James Dignan and Michael Cavadino (1996: 153), we should take care to distinguish between procedural rights for victims and systems of restorative justice. They may go together, but equally they may not. It is quite possible to grant extensive procedural rights to victims (for example, the right to submit a victim impact statement and the right to make a sentencing proposal) within the framework of what remains a 'conventional' punitive system, but such developments do not necessarily convert a punitive system into a restorative one, as several US jurisdictions demonstrate. Equally, but perhaps more rarely, it is possible to develop a system of restorative justice that does not grant substantial rights to victims – for example, by requiring the courts to impose restorative measures rather than leaving them to be determined by victims.[15] The question of procedural rights for victims will be left for the next section of this chapter: here, I will concentrate on restorative justice.

Many different forms of response to crime march under the banner of 'restorative justice' (or reparative or restitutive justice). Three of the key features are:

1   the goal of 'restoring' the victim, by way of apology and/or compensation from, or reparation by, the offender;
2   the further goal of 'restoring' the wider community; and
3   the participation of the victim in the process whereby the response to the offence is determined.

All these matters will be discussed in greater detail in the other chapters of this volume, and so I will move on immediately to the issue of standards, limits and safeguards. Several points concern me. I am aware that many schemes of restorative justice attempt to deal with some of these, but my purpose is to raise the profile of the questions of principle.

First, what exactly is the nature of the 'wider community interest' in crime and sentencing and how should it be satisfied within a restorative scheme? Some restorativists talk as if the whole issue should be settled between the victim and the offender, but that is unacceptable for all but minor offences. The diversion of cases from formal criminal processes is a sound objective for non-serious offences (see Ashworth, 1998: ch. 5), particularly those committed by young offenders. But what of relatively serious offences? In his famous lecture advocating greater involvement of victims in the resolution of conflicts, Nils Christie (1977: 8) did not neglect to mention the wider community's interest in how an offender is dealt with. John Braithwaite and Philip Pettit regard crimes as offences against both the victim and the interest of the community in the security that helps to constitute 'dominion' (Braithwaite and Pettit, 1990; Pettit and Braithwaite, 1993).[16] Lode Walgrave refers to harm to the 'fundamental values of society' (1995: 234–35). The question is how the conception of the wider community interest held by restorativists differs from that held by, for example, just deserts theorists. James Dignan and Michael Cavadino are right to point to 'the social and moral implications that more serious offences have for the whole community' (1996: 169), but what does this mean in practical terms? By what parameters should the community's response be determined? Is it a question of assessing harm and culpability, as in just deserts theory? Or are there other dimensions, such as social protection and crime prevention?

One of the difficulties of the Braithwaite–Pettit approach is that their writings are so opaque on this issue that no firm limits are set to the use of coercion to ensure community security.[17] In arguing that courts should take account of 'how far the offender is capable of offending again' and of 'how common that offence has become in the community', they appear to support the imposition of incapacitative sentences and of deterrent sentences (for individual or general preventive reasons) in some cases (Pettit and Braithwaite, 1993). All restorativists should consider and clarify their position not only on these issues, but also whether restorative justice applies only to non-serious crimes, how it relates to formal court proceedings and, if it is to extend to serious crimes, how the 'public interest' element is constructed. Just deserts theorists argue in favour of the principle of proportionality, for one thing because it is fair to offenders by ensuring that they are not punished beyond what is proportionate to the seriousness of the offence. Critics may argue that the notion of proportionality is indeterminate, politically contingent and so forth but, having made these points, there are still arguments in favour of some concept of proportionality as showing a basic respect for defendants as autonomous individuals and placing limits on state power (see Lacey, 1988: 194–95). It is also important to ensure that, in any system which retains a 'conventional' or punitive approach for serious crimes but which has restorative justice for less serious offences, the 'public interest' element in restorative disposals remains in line with those other sentences.

The first issue, then, of what principles should determine the court disposal (sentence) that is appropriate to the interests of the community, public or state,[18] shades into a second question: what limits are set on the magnitude and type of sentence that can be imposed on individuals in the wider public interest? Michael Cavadino and James Dignan are prominent among the few restorative writers who have faced these two questions in a concrete way, without resorting to airy phrases. Their approach is based on the proposition that victim satisfaction and victim empowerment should be major objectives of the criminal process (Cavadino and Dignan, 1997b: 237, 241 and 245). From this starting point they develop an argument that has negative and positive components. The negative part is their attack on what they term 'strict proportionality' – the view that the achievement of proportionality of sentence ought to be the primary aim of courts. Their characterization of this view is stricter than most just deserts theorists would wish – for example, they do not refer to the 'limited substitutability' approach to non-custodial penalties (Wasik and von Hirsch, 1988) – but there is a fundamental difference between the just deserts approach and that which they favour: the view that proportionality is more important than victim satisfaction, victim empowerment and reintegrative shaming. Their own preference is to give rein to those policies within a framework of limiting retributivism. In such a framework, proportionality would be relevant in two ways:

... firstly in setting the upper and lower parameters within which the overall amount of compulsory reparation and any additional punishment is to be determined; and secondly in acting as a 'default setting' where informal offence resolution proves impossible or is inappropriate. (Cavadino and Dignan, 1997b: 247)

Leaving aside the details of Cavadino and Dignan's theory, the important point for present purposes is that they take the issue of limits seriously, without resorting to vague phrases of the kind found in some other restorative writings. They assign a more attenuated role to proportionality than I would prefer, but its role in their theory is still significant. This is important at a time when concepts of risk are becoming central to much penal policy, and when notions such as 'community safety' can turn out to involve the taking of harsh measures against individuals (Crawford, 1997). One lesson from the heyday of rehabilitation is that a penal rationale that fails to place sensible limits on power – be it the power of the state, its officials or whoever else is determining the actual extent of intervention in the lives of offenders – may lead not only to substantive unfairness but also to excesses and abuse, carried out behind a mask of benevolence. Such tendencies must not be overlooked during the revival of restorativism.

The third issue of principle arises from conflicts among the various interests relevant to the resolution of a case. The victim has interests in reparation, compensation and perhaps in expressing concern about the offence and its effects. There may be secondary or indirect victims, such as family, friends, colleagues and so on. There is also the wider community or public interest. In an ideal case it will be possible to take account of all interests harmoniously. But there will be awkward cases for which some sense of priority will be required. 'Conventional' or punitive systems resolve these questions in various ways. Thus in England and Wales an order for the offender to pay compensation to the victim has priority over a fine, and may coexist with a custodial sentence where the offender has sufficient funds; but where a custodial sentence is thought necessary in the public interest, and this effectively prevents the offender from paying compensation to the victim, it is the victim who loses out (Ashworth, 1995: 256–61). What does restorative theory say about the resolution of these conflicts? Similarly, where (as is usually the case) an offender has limited financial resources, for how many years should an offender be required to make payments to the victim: should there be a limit (as there is for the payment of fines), or should the model of the civil law be followed and no limit imposed? What approach should be taken if the offender's only source of funds for paying compensation to the victim is the house in which he and his family live? My purpose is not to suggest that all non-restorative systems of criminal justice have satisfactory answers to these questions, but rather to highlight the need for a principled consideration of the limits of the obligations to which offenders may be subjected – in restorative systems no less than others. It is insufficient to declare that there must be a compromise and that the task is to strike 'an appropriate balance between the personal interests of victims and the wider social and public interest' (Dignan and Cavadino, (1996: 172): the language of balance is a mere fudge unless decisions have been made on a reasonably clear and principled weighting of the interests that come into play.

The issues of principle raised above do not apply with equal force to all forms of restorative justice. Where offences are non-serious it may be in both the defendant's and the public's interest to divert the case from formal criminal processes. However, even here, one problem is to ensure that the victim does not lose as a result of the diversion and, whereas the new law on the diversion of young offenders under the Crime and Disorder Act 1998 has restorative elements, there is still no legal basis for reparation or compensation to the victim when an offender aged 18 or over is cautioned. Turning to offences that cannot be regarded as non-serious, it seems to be accepted that the 'wider community interest' or 'public interest' must be satisfied, and this may involve the imposition of coercive measures on offenders. If restorative approaches are put forward as an appropriate response to serious offences, the questions raised above must be confronted. It would be wrong for burdens imposed in the name of the wider community to be disproportionate, unless strong justifications could be advanced. The need for safeguards against undue severity does not disappear if a system is called 'restorative' or if it is (currently) operated by benevolent people.

Procedural Rights for Victims

The question of procedural rights for victims is related to, but not dependent on, the issues just considered. It is not dependent on them because the question can also arise in the context of a 'conventional' or punitive system. Various US jurisdictions have been trail-blazers in the right to submit a victim impact statement and the right of allocution (to make a statement on sentence) but, in other respects, the systems are fairly conventional. In England and Wales, too, the system is broadly a conventional court-based one. But before examining the arguments in that context, let us consider victim involvement in restorative approaches to criminal justice.

One of the driving forces behind restorative justice is the belief that victims have been wrongly marginalized by, or even excluded from, the conventional criminal process. Even if courts are required to consider, in all cases, the making of a compensation order in favour of the victim,[19] that still does not assure to the victim a right to be heard in court in English courts, although it does in many continental European systems that are otherwise 'conventional' in their approach (see Kaiser *et al.*, 1991). However, victim participation is now urged by many, including restorativists, and it brings with it the notions of involvement and negotiation. What exactly are the reasons for arguing in favour of this participation?

First, it can be argued that it is only right that the victim should be able to participate, because the crime (or invasion of interests) has been committed against her or him, as well as against the wider community. This is not to say that the crime is solely or chiefly against its direct victim, but that a significant wrong has been suffered by that person.[20] If it is accepted that a proper purpose of sentencing is to ensure that the offender pays compensation or makes reparation to the victim, then the appropriateness of the victim having some role – such as the right to submit an impact statement – is easily established.

Second, it can be argued that allowing the victim to express her or his thoughts about the offence may assist 'reintegration' or the process of coming to terms with what has happened. This is more questionable as a justification, since there may be other, more effective or more appropriate methods of achieving the same result. Various forms of victim support might, for example, be no less effective than some form of participation in proceedings.[21] The question to be answered is whether it should be one of the purposes of post-offence 'proceedings' to help the victim to get over the crime, as well as assuring material compensation or reparation. In 'conventional' criminal justice systems the tendency would be to treat this as a matter for services of support to victims,[22] whereas many restorativists would argue that this should be seen as part of any conference or restorative procedure. There is a need for arguments to establish this.

Third, there is an unashamedly pragmatic reason, repeated recently by the JUSTICE Committee. The criminal justice system depends on the cooperation of victims, as witnesses especially (JUSTICE, 1998: 4), and for that reason it ought to make them feel that they have a contribution to make to the sentencing process. This, in blunt terms, is to use victim participation as a 'sweetener'. The question, again, should be whether there are more efficient and more appropriate means of recognizing the importance of victims' contribution to criminal justice.

For all that Michael Cavadino and James Dignan assert that victim satisfaction and empowerment should be aims of criminal justice, because this is 'to the benefit of the community' and therefore advances the 'public interest' element in sentencing,[23] they retain proportionality as a limiting factor, as we have seen. In their preferred 'Integrated Restorative Justice' model they would also restrict the victim's right of participation to the issue of what compensation or reparation should be expected from the offender, and they go on to suggest that others (in serious cases, a court) should determine the proper response to the 'public' aspect of the offence (Cavadino and Dignan, 1997b: 246–48). In this way their position promotes victim participation while also safeguarding the interests of offenders and of the wider community. Unfortunately, the same cannot be said of some variations of conferencing or restorative justice.

If we return to 'conventional' systems of criminal justice such as the English, ought victims to have the right to submit a victim impact statement to the court, or even to make a statement to the court on sentence? In the previous paragraphs some instrumental reasons for greater victim involvement were discussed in the context of restorative justice. Do these reasons have any force in a conventional system? The first – the direct harm to the victim – remains relevant in the context of compensation. The third – persuading victims to cooperate in bringing offenders to justice – remains problematic: are there not different, more appropriate and more effective ways of achieving this? As for the second reason – assisting the reintegration of the victim – this also raises questions of effectiveness. One finding of the recent English experiments with 'victim statements' is that many of the 30 per cent of victims who opted to make such a statement did so because they believed it important that the offender and others knew what impact the crime had had on them (Hoyle *et al.*, 1998). However, some of the victims who made statements found that their hopes about the influence of their statement were dashed: 'most victims did not know the use to which their VS had been put, and few believed that it had much effect on charge or sentence even though this had been the hope of many' (Hoyle *et al.*, 1998; cf. Erez and Tontodonato, 1992; Erez *et al.*, 1997; Erez, Chapter 8 in this volume). Moreover, there is the question of how many victims really want this degree of involvement. That is not the same as the question of the proportion of victims taking part in participatory schemes: as Victim Support has argued, it is the state's responsibility to shoulder the burden of decision-making in criminal justice and there are dangers in moving towards arrangements which place expectations, let alone burdens, on victims (Victim Support, 1995: 8 and 15). Victim Support does not oppose experiments with victim impact statements relating to compensation and reparation, but it wisely shows greater concern for safeguards than for restorative evangelism.

What other arguments tell against the introduction of victim impact statements into 'conventional' criminal justice systems? I will not develop here those which I have set out elsewhere, but there may be problems in how to test the accuracy of claims made in the statements, especially when the defence disagree with some of them,[24] as well as problems over the extent to which courts may properly take account of unforeseen victim effects when sentencing an offender (problems that may be even greater in a 'conferencing' system).[25] A critical comment on those arguments may be found elsewhere (Erez, 1999). As for allowing a victim statement on sentence, it is one thing to argue (as do Cavadino and Dignan) that this may be appropriate where the court has to decide on compensation or reparation, for those are indeed matters of direct concern to the victim, but it is quite another to suggest that a victim statement is appropriate on any other aspect of sentencing. Indeed, that would be wrong in principle because: first, this should be a matter of public interest (in parallel with what restorative theorists refer to as 'restoration of the community' – see above) on which the victim has no particular claim to be heard; second, because it would be unfair if sentences on offenders varied according to whether a particular victim is forgiving or vengeful – and, indeed, the European Commission on Human Rights has recognized this point when dealing with an application from a murder victim's family (*McCourt* v. *UK* (1993) 15 EHRR CD110); and, third, because it would be unfair for the response to the offender's crime to depend on whether or not the victim chooses to be involved in this way. Even where victims' hopes are not raised about the possible influence of their statements there may also be practical problems, because victims cannot be expected to know about the range of available sentences or about legal limitations and policy statements on their use.

Conclusions

In this chapter I have tried to tackle three aspects of the victim perspective on criminal justice which are relevant to current debates, whilst recognizing that there are so many variations of restorative justice in theory and in practice that some of my criticisms will not apply to some of them. My argument has been that the protection of victims and other witnesses at court is inadequate and that there is a need for a fresh and urgent look at the way in which court proceedings are conducted. Some basic concepts in cross-examination need to be reappraised, and that reappraisal should then be used to change attitudes within the Bar and the judiciary, as well as to change the law. But when it comes to current moves towards restorative justice, my concern is that the boot may be on the other foot. Not only is there the danger that victims will be transformed from 'court fodder' under 'conventional' systems to 'agents of offender rehabilitation' in some conferencing systems, but it is also important that greater attention be paid to the protection of defendants' rights. The interests of the wider community ought to be taken into account, too, but it is essential to establish firm and reasoned limits on the extent to which state power can be exercised over offenders in the name of restorative (or republican) justice. These themes extend to the third issue, on which it was argued that victim participation in decisions about offenders should be confined to matters of legitimate concern to the victim, and should not spill over into areas of public interest, even within restorative processes.

Notes

1   I am grateful to Jim Dignan, David Faulkner, Carolyn Hoyle, Jill Peay and Richard Young for comments on a previous draft, and to other conference participants for further points. Even the sharpest criticisms were helpful.
2   For a discussion of the new law, see Fionda (1999) and Dignan (1999).
3   See the remarks of Helen Reeves at the 1997 AGM of Victim Support, reported at (1997) *New Law Journal*, **147**, 1767.
4   General Council of the Bar, *Code of Conduct for Barristers* (1990, with updating in Amendment 5, 1997), Annexe H, para. 13.5.
5   See, for example, *Kalia, Kalia et al.* (1974) 60 Cr. App. R. 200 at 209–11, citing Lord Hanworth, MR in the Court of Appeal in *Mechanical and General Invention Co. Ltd.* v. *Austin* [1935] AC 346 at 359:

> Cross-examination is a powerful and valuable weapon for the purpose of testing the veracity of a witness and the accuracy and completeness of his story. It is entrusted to the hands of counsel in the confidence that it will be used with discretion … not forgetting at the same time the burden that is imposed upon the witness. We desire to say that in our opinion the cross-examination in the present case did not conform to the above conditions, and at times it failed to display that measure of courtesy to the witness that is by no means inconsistent with a skilful, yet powerful, cross-examination.

These words were spoken in a civil case; the fact that they were followed in a criminal case confirms that respect for witnesses there should be no different, despite the higher standard of proof.
6   General Council of the Bar, *Code of Conduct for Barristers*, para. 203(a).
7   It may be worth mentioning that some defence lawyers may attempt to discredit prosecution witnesses because this is what the lay client expects or in order to create an impression, for example, attacks on the integrity of police officers when giving evidence (see McConville *et al.*, 1994: 219–20).
8   For current English law on the particular issue of concealing the identity of a witness from the accused, see *Taylor* [1995] *Criminal Law Review*, 253.
9   Fuller exploration of the relevance of the ECHR might extend to a consideration of Articles 3, 5 and 8. Article 3 prohibits, *inter alia* the 'inhuman or degrading treatment' of individuals. The cases show that the treatment must be intended to humiliate – that is that the humiliation is not incidental to some other, legitimate goal, but there may still be room to argue that the state has a duty to ensure the protection of witnesses from such treatment (c.f. Harris *et al.*, 1995: 80–84). Article 5 might also be invoked

where there is evidence of threats to the witness which might infringe her right to liberty and security of person. And reliance might be placed on Article 8 to prevent intrusive questioning that unduly infringes a witness's right to a private life.

10 This principle, sometimes termed the subsidiarity principle, has been invoked by the European Court of Human Rights when making determinations on paragraph 2 of Articles 8, 9, 10 and 11, and requires that an exception to a Convention right be allowed only after all other means of securing the objective have been tried or are likely to be ineffective. It is, in effect, a way of insisting that exceptions should be made only as a last resort.

11 As in *Brown (Milton Anthony)*, [1998] 2 Cr. App. R. 354.

12 *Croissant* v. *Germany* (1993) 16 EHRR 135, and *Imbroscia* v. *Switzerland* (1993) 17 EHRR 441.

13 The importance of judicial attitudes is recognized in the JUSTICE report (1998: 54–55).

14 Helen Reeves, address to the 1998 Victim Support AGM, July 1998.

15 The article by Dignan and Cavadino (1996) presents a more elaborate (and helpful) typology, which cannot be examined in detail here.

16 For a different discussion of these themes, cf. Sebba (1996: ch. 7).

17 This point is argued more fully by von Hirsch (1993: ch. 3), and by Ashworth and von Hirsch (1998).

18 My chief concerns here are quantification and incarceration, accepting that restorativists prefer (where appropriate) measures that can be seen as restoration of the community, such as community service orders: see Zedner (1994) and Walgrave (1995).

19 This is the law in England and Wales: see Ashworth (1995: 256–61).

20 Dignan and Cavadino (1996: 173), make this point strongly, in criticizing the two models of restorative justice they describe as 'civilian' and 'reparative'. For a different approach see Cretney *et al.* (1994).

21 Other approaches might also be considered: for example, Victim Support has argued that a statement by the judge in open court, or a letter from the judge to the victim or victim's family, might be ways of helping reduce the effects of crime and 'thereby to restore the confidence of victims and their families' (Victim Support, 1995: 13). See also Sebba (1996: ch. 8).

22 Cf. Cavadino and Dignan (1997b: 236), who classify this as a combination of a 'conventional' model with a welfare model.

23 This chain of reasoning may be found in Cavadino and Dignan (1997b: 237).

24 The Crime (Sentences) Act 1997, s. 50, requires copies of any pre-sentence report on an offender (discussing the offence and the offender's background, and in some cases the victim's reaction) to be given to both prosecution and defence, so as to facilitate challenge to any doubtful assertions. Cf. Hoyle *et al.* (1998), who found that most victim statements in the English experiment tended to understate, rather than overstate, the impact of offences, to some extent because they were prepared soon after the crime and before some after-effects had become apparent.

24 For example, the facilitator may assume that discussions and negotiations should be based on the actual harms suffered by the victim, rather than on the harms intended or knowingly risked by the offender. The issue of principle this raises may not be confronted.

References

Albrecht, H-J. (1997), 'Sentencing and Punishment in Germany', in M. Tonry and K. Hatlestad (eds), *Sentencing Reform in Overcrowded Times: a Comparative Perspective*, New York: Oxford University Press, 177–87.

Ashworth, A. (1993), 'Victim Impact Statements and Sentencing', *Criminal Law Review*, 498–509.

Ashworth, A. (1995), *Sentencing and Criminal Justice*, (2nd edn), London: Butterworths.

Ashworth, A. (1997), 'Sentencing', in M. Maguire, R. Morgan and R. Reiner (eds), *The Oxford Handbook of Criminology*, (2nd edn), Oxford: Clarendon Press, 1095–135.

Ashworth, A. (1998), *The Criminal Process*, (2nd edn), Oxford: Oxford University Press.

Ashworth, A. and von Hirsch, A. (1998), 'Desert and the Three Rs', in A. von Hirsch and A. Ashworth (eds), *Principled Sentencing: Readings on Theory & Policy*, (2nd edn), Oxford: Hart Publishing, 331–35.

Baird, V. (1998), *Rape on Trial*, London: Society of Labour Lawyers.

Blake, M. and Ashworth, A. (1998), 'Some Ethical Issues in Prosecuting and Defending Criminal Cases', *Criminal Law Review*, 16–32.

Bottoms, A.E. (1995), 'The Philosophy and Politics of Punishment and Sentencing', in C. Clarkson and R. Morgan (eds), *The Politics of Sentencing Reform*, Oxford: Clarendon, 17–49.

Braithwaite, J. and Mugford, S. (1994), 'Conditions of Successful Reintegration Ceremonies: Dealing with Juvenile Offenders', *British Journal of Criminology*, **34**(2), 139–71.

Braithwaite, J. and Pettit, P. (1990), *Not Just Deserts: A Republican Theory of Criminal Justice*, Oxford: Oxford University Press.

Brereton, D. (1997), 'How Different are Rape Trials? A Comparison of the Cross-Examination of Complainants in Rape and Assault Trials', *British Journal of Criminology*, **37**(2), 242–61.

Cavadino, M. and Dignan, J. (1997a), *The Penal System*, (2nd edn), London: Sage.

Cavadino, M. and Dignan, J. (1997b), 'Reparation, Retribution and Rights', *International Review of Victimology*, **4**, 233–53.

Christie, N. (1977), 'Conflicts as Property', *British Journal of Criminology*, **17**(1), 1–14.

Crawford, A. (1997), *The Local Governance of Crime: Appeals to Community and Partnerships*, Oxford: Clarendon Press.

Cretney, A., Davis, G., Clarkson C. and Shepherd, J. (1994), 'Criminalizing Assault: the Failure of the "Offence against Society" Model', *British Journal of Criminology*, **34**(1), 15–29.

Dignan, J. (1999), 'The Crime and Disorder Act and the Prospects for Restorative Justice', *Criminal Law Review*, 48–60.

Dignan, J. and Cavadino, M. (1996), 'Towards a Framework for Conceptualising and Evaluating Models of Criminal Justice from a Victim's Perspective', *International Review of Victimology*, **4**, 153–82.

Ellison, L. (1998), 'Cross-Examination in Rape Trials', *Criminal Law Review*, 605–15.

Erez, E. (1994), 'Victim Participation in Sentencing: And the Debate Goes On...', *International Review of Victimology*, **3**(1/2), 17–32.

Erez, E. (1999), 'Who is Afraid of the Big Bad Victim? Victim Impact Statements as Victim Empowerment and Enhancement of Justice,' *Criminal Law Review*, 545–56.

Erez E., Roeger, L. and Morgan F. (1997), 'Victim Harm, Impact Statements and Victim Satisfaction with Justice: An Australian Experience', *International Review of Victimology*, **5**, 37–60.

Erez, E. and Tontodonato, P. (1992), 'Victim Participation in Sentencing and Satisfaction with Justice', *Justice Quarterly*, **9**, 394–415.

Fionda, J. (1999), 'New Labour, Old Hat: Youth Justice and the Crime and Disorder Act 1998', *Criminal Law Review*, 36–47.

Garland, D. (1996), 'The Limits of the Sovereign State: Strategies of Crime Control in Contemporary Society', *British Journal of Criminology*, **36**(4), 445–71.

Harris, D.J., O'Boyle M. and Warbrick, C. (1995), *The Law of the European Convention on Human Rights*, London: Butterworths.

Home Office (1975), *Report of the Advisory Group on the Law of Rape*, Cmnd 6352, London: HMSO.

Home Office (1997), *No More Excuses: A New Approach to Tackling Youth Offending in England and Wales*, Cm. 3809, London: Home Office.

Home Office (1998), *Speaking Up for Justice*, Report of the Interdepartmental Working Group on the Treatment of Vulnerable or Intimidated Witnesses in the Criminal Justice System, London: Home Office.

Hoyle, C., Cape, E., Morgan, R. and Sanders, A. (1998), *Evaluation of the 'One Stop Shop' and Victim Statement Pilot Projects*, A Report for the Home Office Research Development and Statistic Directorate, Bristol: Department of Law, University of Bristol.

Hudson, J., Morris, A., Maxwell, G. and Galaway, B. (1996) (eds), *Family Group Conferences: Perspectives on Policy and Practice*, Annadale, NSW: The Federation Criminal Justice Press.

JUSTICE (1998), *Victims in Criminal Justice*, Report of the Committee on the Role of the Victim in Criminal Justice, London: JUSTICE.

Kaiser, G., Kury, H. and Albrecht, H-J. (1991) (eds), *Victims and Criminal Justice*, Freiburg: Max-Planck Institute.

Lacey, N. (1988), *State Punishment*, London: Routledge.

Lees, S. (1997), *Carnal Knowledge: Rape on Trial*, Harmondsworth: Penguin.

Luban, D. (1993), 'Are Criminal Defenders Different?', *Michigan Law Review*, **91**, 1729–66.

McColgan, A. (1996), 'Common Law and the Relevance of Sexual History Evidence', *Oxford Journal of Legal Studies*, **16**, 275–307.

McConville, M., Hodgson, J., Bridges, L. and Pavlovic, A. (1994), *Standing Ac-*

cused, *The Organisation and Practices of Criminal Defence Lawyers in Britain*, Oxford: Clarendon Press.

Miers, D. (1992), 'The Responsibilities and Rights of Victims of Crime', *Modern Law Review*, **55**, 482–505.

Morris, A., Maxwell, G. and Robertson, J.P. (1993), 'Giving Victims a Voice: a New Zealand Experiment', *Howard Journal*, **32**(4), 304–21.

Mosteller, R.P. (1997), 'Victims' Rights and the United States Constitution: an Effort to Recast the Battle in Criminal Litigation', *Georgetown Law Journal*, **85**, 1691–1715.

Mosteller, R.P. (1998), 'Victims' Rights and the Constitution: Moving from Guaranteeing Participatory Rights to Benefiting the Prosecution', *St Mary's Law Journal*, **29**, 1053–65.

New Zealand Ministry of Justice (1995), *Restorative Justice: A Consultative Paper*, Ministry of Justice: Wellington.

Pettit, P. and Braithwaite, J. (1993), 'Not Just Deserts, Even in Sentencing', *Current Issues in Criminal Justice*, **4**, 222–39.

Rock, P. (1993), *The Social World of an English Crown Court*, Oxford: Oxford University Press.

Sebba, L. (1996), *Third Parties: Victims and the Criminal Justice System*, Columbus: Ohio State University Press.

Shapland, J. and Bell, E. (1998), 'Victims in the Magistrates' Courts and Crown Court', *Criminal Law Review*, 537–46.

Temkin, J. (1993), 'Sexual History Evidence – The Ravishment of Section 2', *Criminal Law Review*, 3–20.

Umbreit, M.S. (1994), 'The Effects of Victim-Offender Mediation', *Overcrowded Times*, **5**(1), 5–7.

Victim Support (1995), *The Rights of Victims of Crime: A Policy Paper*, London: Victim Support.

Victim Support (1996), *Women, Rape and the Criminal Justice System*, London: Victim Support.

von Hirsch, A. (1993), *Censure and Sanctions*, Oxford: Clarendon Press.

von Hirsch, A. (1998) 'Law and Order', in A. von Hirsch and A. Ashworth (eds), *Principled Sentencing: Readings on Policy and Theory* (2nd edn), Oxford: Hart Publishing, 410–23.

Walgrave, L. (1995), 'Restorative Justice for Juveniles: Just a Technique or a Fully Fledged Alternative?', *Howard Journal*, **34**(3), 228–49.

Wasik, M. and von Hirsch, A. (1988), 'Non-Custodial Penalties and the Principles of Desert', *Criminal Law Review*, 555–72.

Weigend, T. (1997), 'Germany Reduces Use of Prison Sentences', in M. Tonry and K. Hatlestad (eds), *Sentencing Reform in Overcrowded Times: a Comparative Perspective*, New York: Oxford University Press: New York, 177–87.

Zedner, L. (1994), 'Reparation and Retribution: Are they Reconcilable?', *Modern Law Review*, **57**, 228–50.

PART III
VICTIMS AND RESTORATIVE JUSTICE

10 The Practice of Family Group Conferences in New Zealand: Assessing the Place, Potential and Pitfalls of Restorative Justice

Allison Morris and Gabrielle Maxwell

Introduction

'Restorative justice' is a new way of describing practices which have been around for a long time. Daly and Immarigeon (1998) locate the concept's modern history in the development of victim/offender reconciliation programmes and victim/offender mediation in the 1970s, but acknowledge its early roots in the ways in which certain indigenous, cultural and religious groups resolved conflicts or disputes. Central to the ideas underlying restorative justice are the involvement of victims in processes that have the potential to repair the harm they have experienced, the involvement of offenders in making amends for that harm, and the restoration of some kind of balance between the two. However, in its modern revival, restorative justice has shown itself to be remarkably flexible: for example, restorative justice processes have been used pre-court as part of diversion, pre-sentence to inform sentencers, pre-release as part of a prison programme and so on; they have also been used to determine how to deal with offenders, the placement of abused and neglected children and the placement of the children of women in prison.

For us, restorative justice is a process which drastically reduces the role of courts, the judiciary and other criminal justice professionals by returning the offence to those most affected by it and by encouraging them to determine appropriate responses to it. Family group conferences were introduced into the youth justice system in New Zealand in November 1989 by the Children, Young Persons and Their Families Act 1989 (the 1989 Act). Although there is no specific reference to the term 'restorative justice' in the debates introducing family group conferences, their underlying philosophy shares these key features. To this extent, then, the practice of family group conferences in New Zealand can serve as a basis for discussions about the place, potential and pitfalls of restorative justice.

In discussing these, we will draw from research on and experience with the New Zealand youth justice system.[1] There are clearly now a number of different models of conferencing[2] in operation in different jurisdictions.[3] Not all are based on restorative principles. For example, the models of conferencing adopted in some parts of Australia (specifically in Wagga Wagga[4] and in the Reintegrative Sharing Experiment (RISE) in Canberra) and copied in some areas of the United States[5] are explicitly based on Braithwaite's (1989) notion of 'reintegrative shaming'[6] – a concept both difficult to operationalize and arguably at odds with restorative ideals. We will return to this point later.

Family Group Conferences in New Zealand

The Place of Family Group Conferences

The New Zealand model of conferencing was strongly influenced by traditional Maori concepts of conflict resolution,[7] is used for all medium-serious and serious offending (except murder and manslaughter) and operates both as a barrier to court processing (for young people who have not been arrested)[8] and as a mechanism for making recommendations to judges presentence (for young people who have been arrested).[9] This means that a young person cannot be prosecuted in the Youth Court[10] unless he or she has been arrested by the police or has been referred to a family group conference and the conference recommends a prosecution. In practice, most conferences reach an agreement which avoids prosecution. It also means that judges cannot dispose of a case without taking into account the recommendation of the family group conference. In practice, most judges accept its recommendations. In contrast, most other jurisdictions which have introduced conferences have used them only selectively for non-serious offending and solely as an alternative to court processing.

Key Features of Family Group Conferences

We already noted the similarity between the features of family group conferences and restorative justice. In summary, these are:

- involvement of those most affected by the offending – specifically the offender, the offender's family and the victim – in determining appropriate responses to it
- decision-making by agreement
- the use of a facilitator
- the acceptance of responsibility by offender for his or her actions
- making amends to the victim.

In addition, family group conferences are meant to be culturally appropriate and sensitive – attributes not necessarily required within a restorative justice process, although arguably consistent with it.

Describing Family Group Conferences

Conferences normally include the offender, members of his or her family and whoever the family invites, the victim(s), their support, a representative of the police and the facilitator or manager of the process (in New Zealand this is the youth justice coordinator). Sometimes a social worker[11] and/or a lawyer[12] is present.[13]

The main goal of a conference is to formulate a plan about how best to deal with the offending. There are three principal components to this process:

- ascertaining whether or not the young person admits the offence – conferences only proceed if the young person does this[14]
- information-sharing among all the parties at the conference about the nature of the offence, the effects of the offence on the victims, the reasons for the offending, any prior offending by the young person and so on
- deciding the outcome or making recommendations to the court.

The family group conference is a meeting between those entitled to attend held in a relatively informal setting. The room is usually arranged with comfortable chairs in a circle. When all are present, there may be a prayer or a blessing depending on the culture and customs of those involved. The facilitator then welcomes the participants, introduces them and describes the purposes of the meeting. What happens next can vary, but usually the police representative reads out a summary of the offence. The young person is asked if he or she agrees that this is what happened and any variation is noted. If he or she denies the offence, the meeting progresses no further and the police may consider referring the case to the Youth Court for a hearing. Assuming the young person agrees, the victim, or a spokesperson for the victim, is then usually asked to describe what the events meant for them. A general discussion of the offence and the circumstances underlying it then occurs. This would include what the offending has meant for everyone and the options for holding the offender accountable and for making good the damage. The professionals and the victim then leave the family and the young person to meet privately to discuss what plans and recommendations they wish to make. When the family is ready, the others return and the meeting is reconvened. The family or young person then outlines what they propose, and everyone discusses the proposal. Sometimes at this point the young person and the family apologize to the victim. Once there is agreement among all present, the details are formally recorded and the conference concludes, sometimes with the sharing of food.

Provided the plans and decisions have been agreed to by all those attending the family group conference and, for court referred cases, are accepted by the Youth Court judge, they are binding on all those involved. The plans are meant to take into account the views of the victims, the need to make the young person accountable for his or her offending and provision for any measures that might prevent future re-offending by enhancing the well-being of the offender or strengthening the family. The range of possible options here are limitless (as long as they are agreed to by the parties) and can include an apology, work in the community, reparation or involvement in some programme.[15] The most usual outcomes are apologies and community work. Few cases result in financial reparation to the victim because of the limited financial resources of the young offenders and their families.

Conferences take much longer than courts to reach resolutions. In our research (Maxwell and Morris, 1993) around 10 per cent of the conferences took more than two hours;[16] more than a quarter took between one and a half and two hours; almost a third took between an hour and an hour and a half; and just under a third took less than an hour. Family group conferences can take place wherever the offender and his or her family wish, provided (since 1994) the victim agrees. Most commonly they are held in rooms in the Department of Social Welfare or in community rooms and occasionally they are held in *marae* (meeting houses) or in the family's home.

Evaluating Family Group Conferences and Restorative Ideals

It is clear from the above that there are a number of ways in which the practice of family group conferences reflects restorative processes and practices. For example, both victims and offenders can participate in the decision about how best to deal with, and make amends for, the offending, victims may feel better about what has happened to them as a result of this participation, reconciliation between offenders and victims may take place, outcomes may be agreed to by both victims and offenders, offenders may acknowledge responsibility for their actions and may make amends (actual or symbolic) to their victims, and both victims and offenders may leave the meeting with a sense of reconnectedness with their communities. The following sections elaborate these points.

Involving Victims in Family Group Conferences

Victims are arguably the parties most affected by offending and are the parties most in need of healing for the damage caused by it, yet they have had little direct voice in the juvenile (or criminal) justice system and have received little from it to aid their healing. In contrast, victims can be involved in conferences. Although the research on New Zealand conferences (Maxwell and Morris, 1993) indicated that victims attended only around half the family group conferences,[17] the reasons for this were related primarily to poor practice: they were not invited, the time arranged was unsuitable for them or they were given inadequate notice. There will always be a minority of victims who choose not to participate in conferencing, but the New Zealand research found that, when asked, only 6 per cent of victims said that they did not wish to meet the offender. This is a clear indicator of most victims' willingness – indeed, desire – to be involved in these processes.

Meeting Victims' Needs

The New Zealand research also showed that, when victims were involved in conferencing, many found this a positive process. About 60 per cent of the victims interviewed described the family group conference they attended as helpful, positive and rewarding. Generally, they said that they were effectively involved in the process and felt better as a result of participating. Victims also commented on two other specific benefits for them. First, it provided them with a voice in determining appropriate outcomes. Second, they were able to meet the offender and the offender's family face-to-face so that they could assess their attitude, understand more why the offence had occurred and assess the likelihood of it recurring.[18]

About a quarter of the victims, however, said that they felt worse as a result of attending the family group conference. There were a variety of reasons for this. The most frequent, and perhaps the most important, was that the victim did not feel that the young person and/or his or her family were truly sorry. Other less common reasons included the inability of the family and young person to make reparation, the victims' inability to express themselves adequately, their difficulty of communicating cross-culturally, a lack of support offered to them, the perceived failure of the offender to show remorse to the victim for the offending, a feeling that their concerns had not been adequately listened to and a feeling that people were disinterested in, or unsympathetic to, them. In other words, victims' concerns were again primarily rooted in poor practice and were not fundamental objections to conferencing *per se*.

Victims' Satisfaction with Outcomes

A significant percentage of victims also tended to be satisfied with the outcomes from conferences. In the main, as noted previously, these took the form of apologies to victims and community work (either for the victim or for an organization nominated by the victim) rather than direct reparation to victims. Some victims, however, were dissatisfied because they saw the decision of the family group conference as too soft or too harsh. But, more frequently, victims were dissatisfied because the promised arrangements broke down afterwards or they were simply never informed about the eventual outcome of the family group conference. The responsibility for this lay more often with professional staff than with the young person and his or her family. Overall, victims were less satisfied than the professionals and families with the outcomes from conferences, but even this lower figure is probably higher than the levels of satisfaction that victims would express after court hearings and sentences by judges.

Involving Offenders in Conferences

There are good reasons why young offenders should be involved in decisions about how best to deal with their offending. First, Article 12 of the UN Convention on the Rights of the Child provides a basis for giving young people the opportunity to both express their views and to have them taken into account in all matters affecting them, but particularly in any judicial or administrative proceedings. Second, a sense of control and choice over what is happening is important in any commitment to change and hence in any decision to stop offending. And, third, effectively involving young offenders in processes is one way of holding them accountable for their actions.

However, conventional juvenile (and criminal) justice systems do not much encourage their involvement. Carlen (1976) catches the essence of this nicely in her analogy of defendants as the 'dummy player' in a game of bridge. In courts, the principal players are the professionals, and the legal representative's role is expressly to speak for his or her client. This is not so in conferencing where offenders are expected to actively participate in discussions about how best to deal with the offending.

Young offenders (and their families) participating in the New Zealand research on conferencing were asked a number of key questions: 'Did you feel that you made the decision?', 'How involved were you in reaching the decisions?' and 'In your view, who really decided?'. About a third of the young offenders said that they had felt involved in the process. If responses indicating that the offender felt 'partly' involved are added to this, then we can conclude that nearly half felt involved in some way: they were able to say what they wanted to and to speak openly without pressure. However, almost a half felt that they had not been involved in the family group conferences and that decisions had been made about them, not with them.[19] Technically, outcomes have to be agreed to by all the parties at the conference, but the young offender's voice seemed to have become subsumed within the family's.[20] It needs to be acknowledged, however, that even this relatively low rate of involvement in conferences is still considerably higher than offenders' involvement in conventional courts. This would certainly fit with the experience of one of the authors (Allison Morris) as a juvenile court magistrate in England for ten years (see also Asquith, 1983).[21]

Involving Families in Family Group Conferences

As families are both the primary socializers and the primary mechanism of social control for their children, it makes sense to give them responsibility, in partnership with the state, for dealing with their children's offending. In conventional juvenile justice contexts, however, the families of young offenders are often excluded from the process of decision-making. Courts are typically described by them as alien and remote, families' participation is typically described as rare and their communication is typically described as routine. Families in conventional juvenile justice systems tend also to be held responsible for their children's offending in an entirely negative way: they may be blamed or even penalised.[22]

On the other hand, in the most direct sense, families in New Zealand are involved in conferences. They can determine the process and procedures to be followed, who should be invited to participate in the conference and where the conference should be held. These responsibilities can be viewed as symbolically empowering. Families are also expected to come up with a plan to deal with the offending – arguably, real empowerment – and so it is important to know what happens in practice.

There is no doubt that families do participate in conferences in New Zealand. In our research by (Maxwell and Morris, 1993), almost all conferences were attended by family members and two-fifths were also attended by members of the young person's extended family (the figure for Maori was much higher – almost 60 per cent).[23] More than two-thirds of the families interviewed felt that they had been involved in what had happened at the family group conference and about the same proportion of families identified themselves as the decision-makers, at least in part.[24] Less than a fifth said that they had not felt involved. Eighty-five per cent of families also said that they were satisfied with the outcome of the conference. Conferencing, therefore, offers a participatory option that empowers families and allows them, without increasing stigma or blame, to play a pivotal role in arriving at decisions about their children. In this way, 'making parents responsible' can be given a constructive meaning.[25]

Criminal justice systems have traditionally separated victims and offenders. However, bringing victims and offenders together for a family group conference was, for most families, a constructive process. Few families found the presence of the victim to be at all unusual or inappropriate. Moreover, many commented that they viewed the victim's presence positively, because of the possibility of reconciling the victim and the young person, and because the victim's contribution could help teach the young person to accept responsibility and to be accountable for what he or she had done.

Restorative Justice and Reconviction

Arguably, restorative justice can be described as successful if victims and offenders feel involved in the process and in the decision, if victims feel better as a result of the process and if offenders make amends to victims. However, preventing re-offending is also a legitimate expectation. Indeed, although a lack of reconviction is conventionally seen as a measure of success for offenders, it could equally be described as a measure of success for victims. Preventing 'their' offender from re-offending is, after all, what most victims want, and if there was evidence that their involvement in restorative justice processes might minimize the harm to future or potential victims, then victims would probably have even greater reason to participate in them.

Our recent research in New Zealand (Morris and Maxwell, 1997) indicates that the probability of reconviction is *reduced* when certain of the potentially restorative aspects of family group conferences are achieved. Regression analysis suggested that those offenders who apologized to victims were three times less likely to be reconvicted than those who had not, and that those offenders who participated in conferences with victims were more than four times less likely to be reconvicted than those offenders whose conferences were not attended by victims. More recently, Maxwell and Morris (1999) found that young people who attended family group conferences and who felt that they had made amends to their victim were less likely to be reconvicted six years after the conference. In further work with this data, we have created a composite variable which we have called 'remorse' and which consists of the offender remembering the conference, completing the agreed tasks, feeling and demonstrating that he or she is sorry for the offence and feeling that they had repaired the damage to the victim; this variable also distinguished those not reconvicted from those persistently reconvicted.

Restorative Justice and Involving the Community

There is some debate about the involvement of the community in restorative justice and about the nature of any such involvement. In part, this is explained by the fact that different individuals have different 'constituencies' in mind when they refer to 'the community'. The meaning of 'community' is vexed, at least criminologically speaking, if not more broadly. For example, it can mean a geographic locality, community representatives (elected or self-appointed), the offender's family and family group, or the offender's social circle. In some jurisdictions, community representatives who have no direct connection with the young people appearing before them – for example, lay magistrates in England or members of children's hearings in Scotland – make the decisions about and for young people who have committed offences.

Members of the wider community do participate in certain types of conference in some jurisdictions – for example, in those conferences based fairly explicitly on notions of 'reintegrative shaming' (Braithwaite, 1989). In other jurisdictions members of the wider community may be invited to conferences to provide support or information by the family (as in New Zealand) or by the coordinator (as in South Australia). Community members are not involved in these conferences as of right. To be otherwise would be at odds with the principles underlying conferencing.

There is, however, a community which is involved in conferencing and this depends on a narrower, and perhaps more meaningful, definition of community, at least as far as offenders and victims are concerned. By this we have in mind notions of 'community of interest', 'community of care' or 'community of concern': the specific community which the offenders identify with – their family group, peers, friends, colleagues and so on. This 'community' can play a supportive role at conferences and can reinforce the offender's acceptance of the wrongness of his or her offending.[26] There is also a broader notion of 'community of interest' which comprises the offender and his or her support and the victim and his or her support. Returning the offence to this group for its resolution is not only the essence of conferencing, but also the essence of restorative justice. We advocate the involvement of the community in restorative processes only in this precise and narrow sense.

Shaming and Restorative Justice

Earlier we stated that it may be difficult to operationalize the notion of 'reintegrative shaming' and suggested that, in practice, shaming could be at odds with restorative ideals. In some jurisdictions (not in New Zealand as noted above), community participants are invited to conferences for offences where there is no 'direct' victim as such.[27] This raises questions about their role in the process and seems to indicate that their role – and presumably the role of victims more generally – is to shame.

Data from RISE (Sherman and Strang, 1997) indicate that offenders who had experienced conferences were more likely than offenders who had experienced courts to say that they felt ashamed of the offences they had committed. They were also more likely to say that they felt that they had repaid their debt to society and to the victim and that the conference had enabled them to make up for what they had done. We would wish to distinguish these two components – 'shaming' and 'making amends'. There is certainly no evidence that 'feeling ashamed' was the key ingredient in offenders feeling that they had made amends. Moreover, the researchers' observations that conferences were more likely than courts to produce the 'right' kind of shame (courts were likely to produce either 'no shame' or the 'wrong' type of shame) do not help us make that connection. It requires *the offenders themselves* to make this linkage. It seems unlikely that young offenders see shaming by the police (who were the facilitators in many of these conferences) or by members of a community to which they may have no connection as 'reintegrative' and hence as restorative. It also seems unlikely that the potential power of meetings between offenders and victims to move towards a reconciliation is realized where the primary role of the victim is scripted as 'shamer'.

There is some support for this view from recent research by Maxwell and Morris (1999). We found that young people who attended family group conferences and who felt that they had made amends to their victim were less likely to be reconvicted six years after the conference whereas those young people who felt that they had been shamed by the process were more likely to be persistently reconvicted six years later. This is a potentially important finding because it brings into question the role of shaming in restorative processes.

Restorative Justice through Family Group Conferences

The Potential

Victims, offenders and their communities of interest should be centrally involved in, rather than excluded from, decisions about how offending is responded to. This chapter has described one mechanism for doing so: family group conferences. In summary, research on family group conferences has shown that:

- victims, offenders and their communities of interest can be involved in the juvenile justice system
- agreements between all the parties involved are able to be reached
- a significant proportion of victims, offenders and their communities of interest feel positively towards conferencing and are satisfied with the outcomes.

The Possible Pitfalls

Research on family group conferences in New Zealand has also shown that:

- some offenders remained uninvolved in the decision-making process
- victims, offenders and their communities of interest were not always well briefed about the process
- families did not always have the information they needed to formulate plans
- professionals did not always keep a low profile during the conference
- some victims felt worse as a result of their attendance
- some victims were dissatisfied with the eventual outcomes.

The question which has to be asked here is whether or not these findings are related to some fundamental flaws in restorative justice processes. We argue that they are not (Maxwell and Morris, 1993). Rather, they point to poor practice, especially with respect to practice towards victims. For example, good practice suggests that victims should be consulted about the timing and venue of conferences and informed of them in good time, that they should be well briefed about what to expect at a conference, that they should be supported throughout the process and that their agreement should be sought for the proposed outcome. Thus, overall, most of the concerns expressed by the key parties could be addressed by training the process facilitators to be effective.

A number of pitfalls of a more theoretical nature have been raised about restorative justice. The New Zealand research does not directly address these, but nevertheless experience there does offer some response. A number of commentators (Warner, 1994; Polk, 1994) have raised concerns about the lack of attention to legal rights in a restorative process – for example, the offenders participating are not usually or always provided with legal advice or representation. Other commentators (for example, Warner, 1994) have expressed concerns that the sanctions agreed to may not be proportionate or consistent. Yet others (White, 1994) dismiss the process as a system of social control in disguise.

These various criticisms can be addressed at a number of different levels. First, they are accusations that can be levelled at informal processes generally and would rule out all pre-court diversion processes. Offenders, for example, are not given legal advice before agreeing to a police warning. In most jurisdictions now, this would affect the majority of young offenders, and warnings can be coupled with quite extensive and incursive sanctions. Second, these are criticisms which the traditional juvenile justice system has not successfully resolved. For example, a considerable body of research indicates wide disparities in sentencing practices and discrimination on the basis of such factors as race and region (Hood, 1992). Third, it is possible, in some degree, to develop strategies for overcoming these failings – if failings they are. As noted before, there are limits on the level of sanctions which can be imposed by conferences in South Australia. In South Australia, too, legal advice is available to the young person. And, fourth, the values underlying these criticisms stem from conventional juvenile (and criminal) justice processes and are fundamentally at variance with those underlying a restorative process. Thus, it can be argued that legal representation impedes the ability of victims and offenders to talk directly to one another, that consistency and proportionality are constructs which serve abstract notions of justice which stand in place of agreements that attempt to restore the social balance between victims and offenders within their communities and that, while social control remains an integral part of restorative justice processes, social control itself must assume a new meaning as power is relocated within the social group.

Extending Family Group Conferences to Adult Offenders

There is popular support in New Zealand for restorative justice – perhaps based in part on its experience of family group conferences. A Listener/Heylen poll in 1994 found that 55 per cent of respondents agreed or strongly agreed that offenders should meet with their victims and, where possible, try to put things right. Only a quarter disagreed with this. Furthermore, in 1998 the Ministry of Justice published its analysis of submissions in response to a 1995 discussion document on restorative justice (Ministry of Justice, 1995). Briefly, the majority of the 113 submissions made supported restorative justice, with only nine being strongly opposed to it. Consequently, as part of a subsequent budget process, the government considered proposals for putting in place restorative justice programmes for adults, although it decided against funding these, at that time, on the grounds that expenditure increases had to be focused 'on areas of highest priority' (Ministry of Justice, 1998: 6). Nevertheless, there already are in existence a number of programmes which operate pre-court (diversion)[28] or pre-sentence[29] and their number seems likely to increase.

Thus restorative justice for adults in New Zealand continues to grow in a piecemeal fashion. Although this may be appropriate for a process which requires, and survives on, community support, there are risks attached to the government employing a hands-off approach to restorative justice and a hands-on approach to conventional justice processes. The risk for restorative justice is that it will never form a central part of New Zealand's criminal justice system and, in practice, there are likely to be issues around a lack of standards, a lack of resources and inadequate monitoring. The risk for the criminal justice system is that New Zealand's penal population will continue to grow with no corresponding increase in community safety, at considerable cost and with little likelihood of reducing re-offending.

Conclusion

The family group conference is a mechanism for making decisions about how best to deal with an offender's criminal behaviour. To the extent that it involves the victim, the offender and their communities of interest in this decision, that process can be described as restorative. Thus research on conferencing has implications for the implementation and practice of restorative justice. This research shows that conferencing, and hence restorative justice, is more often and more effectively responsive to victims than conventional justice systems and demonstrates that restorative justice processes can 'work' for victims as well as offenders. It provides them with both a presence and a voice and, through the process, they may gain the opportunity for some healing, some understanding of what happened and why, and some closure.

Furthermore, outcomes may, and often do, include putting things right for victims. For example, the offender or his or her family may make reparation to the victim or the offender may perform some work either for the victim or for an organization or person nominated by the victim. To this extent, outcomes may also be restorative. But outcomes could also involve counselling or some other programme for the offender whilst the victims' needs remained unmet – and such outcomes could not be described as restorative. This need not, however, detract from the power and potential of the conferencing process as a restorative one.

In practice, although successful restorative justice processes put victims at the heart of what happens, most conferences will not be able to meet the direct financial, practical or emotional needs of victims through counselling or reparation. The majority of offenders who come into the criminal justice system, and hence who are likely to participate in any kind of restorative justice process, have limited financial resources. In practice, too, at least in New Zealand, holding offenders accountable for their actions has taken precedence over meeting victims' needs – or at least meeting those needs which require financial resources to be met. This means that the state must acknowledge its role and responsibilities in the partnership to make amends: specifically, its responsibility to adequately resource Victim Support and other community agencies to ensure that the full range of victims' needs are also met.

Notes

1   We carried out research in five areas of New Zealand during 1990–91, collecting data on 195 young offenders referred to a youth justice family group conference (70 were also dealt with in the Youth Court). We observed and recorded what happened during the family group conference, collected data from police and social welfare files and interviewed family members, young people, police officers and social welfare staff who were involved in the family group conference and victims (for more detail see Maxwell and Morris, 1993). Since then, we have continued to monitor New Zealand's youth justice system and its potential impact on re-offending. See, in particular, Maxwell and Morris (1996), Morris and Maxwell (1997) and Maxwell and Morris (1999).

2   A variety of names have been used – family group conferences, family conferences, effective cautioning conferences, community accountability conferences, diversionary conferencing, community youth conferencing. There are differences also in the ways in which these models have been translated into practice. For example, in some jurisdictions, conferencing is managed by the police, in some by the courts, in some by social welfare and in some by voluntary organizations. Furthermore, the offender is the central focus in some jurisdictions; in others, it is the victim. The proportion of young

offenders dealt with through conferences also differs. For example, conferences are used for around 20 per cent of young offenders in New Zealand and around 10 per cent in South Australia.

3   See Alder and Wundersitz (1994) and Bargen (1995) for a discussion of Australasian models; LaPrairie (1995) for a discussion of the contrasts between Australasian models and sentencing circles in Canada; Hardin (1996) and Immarigeon (1996) for a discussion of the relevance of conferencing for the United States; and Hudson *et al.* (1996) for examples of conferencing in a number of other jurisdictions.

4   The original form of conferencing developed in Wagga Wagga is no longer operative but the model has been very influential in parts of the United States.

5   An example is the Real Justice group originating in Philadelphia but now found in many parts of the USA and Canada.

6   Stigmatic shaming is a recognized part of the criminal justice system; many of its rituals serve to signify the separation and segregation of defendants. In 'reintegrative shaming', at least in theory, the offence rather than the offender is condemned and the offender is reintegrated with, rather than rejected by, society.

7   The victims' movement also emerged at this time in New Zealand as elsewhere. It culminated in the passing of the Victim of Offences Act 1987 which gave victims a number of 'rights' and resulted in the formation of the Victims Task Force. Neither of these touched the youth justice system directly but the time was ripe for victims' views to be taken into account in that part of the justice system undergoing radical overhaul.

8   The police cannot refer young offenders who have not been arrested to court without first referring them to a family group conference.

9   There are strict statutory criteria governing the arrest of young people. Only around 10 per cent of young offenders in New Zealand are arrested and subsequently appear in the Youth Court.

10   The Youth Court is a branch of the District Court and deals with youth justice issues only; it is closed to the public to preserve the confidentiality of its proceedings.

11   Social workers are not 'entitled' to be present at conferences within the terms of the 1989 Act unless they are already involved with the child – for example, where the child is in the care of the Social Welfare Department. In the early days of conferencing, a high proportion of social workers attended conferences. This is no longer the case.

12   Where young people have been arrested and subsequently appear in court, a youth advocate will be appointed to represent them. Recent research (Morris *et al.*, 1997) shows considerable regional variation in the extent to which the youth advocates appointed to represent the young person in the Youth Court also attended conferences. Some youth advocates felt that attending the conference was an important part of their role; others did not. As a result, only about half of the youth advocates surveyed said they routinely attended most conferences involving their clients. Interestingly, many of the other professionals who attend family group conferences did not see the attendance of the youth advocate at a conference as an important part of their role. Rather, they were seen as a hindrance.

13   In some other jurisdictions, members of the offenders' peer group are also encouraged to participate, and, in some other jurisdictions, members of the community are invited, depending on the type of offence. In Canberra, for example, in offences involving driving under the influence of alcohol, community participants are invited (because there is no 'direct' victim as such) and in conferences in Sparwood, British Columbia, women from the Women's Resource Centre participate in conferences about domestic violence and insurance adjusters, rescue personnel or ambulance attendants may participate in conferences dealing with driving offences.

14   In addition in New Zealand, conferences take place after an offence has been proved in the Youth Court where a young person has previously denied the offence.

15   In other jurisdictions, strict limits are placed on the sanctions to ensure that young persons are not worse off than they would have been had the case gone to a court. In South Australia, for example, there are limits on the sanctions which can be imposed. Thus a limit of three months for any diversionary sanction is set by statute (s. 8(6)(b) of the Young Offenders Acts 1993 (1993 Act); so too is the requirement to have regard to the sentences imposed for comparable offences by the Court (s. 8(4)(a) of the 1993 Act). There is a limit of 75 hours for any community work agreed to as part of diversion (s. 8(1)(b) of the 1993 Act). In South Australia, too, legal advice is available to the young person.

16   For young offenders participating in RISE in Canberra, the average conference lasted 71 minutes compared with an average of 13 minutes for court hearings (Sherman and Strang, 1997).

17   The proportion attending family group conferences is certainly now greater in some areas. Wundersitz and Hetzel (1996) present preliminary findings on conferencing in South Australia and report that 75–80 per cent of the conferences there had at least one victim present. This figure is not, however, supported by the *Annual Statistical Report of the Office of Crime Statistics* (1998) which stated that only 47 per cent of conferences in 1997 had at least one victim present.

18   These positive findings seem confirmed by the preliminary results from RISE which suggest (on the basis of interviews with 35 victims of offenders sent to conferences and 36 victims of offenders sent to court) that conferences make victims feel safer and more involved with the process (Strang and Sherman, 1997). Compared with those victims whose offenders appeared in court, victims who participated in conferences had more information, were more likely to attend the hearing, were more likely to receive an apology, were more likely to receive some kind of repair for the harm of the crime, were more likely to feel some sympathy towards the offender and were less likely, after the conference, to feel angry.

19   There are a number of reasons for young people's lack of involvement. First, young people's views have not generally been valued over the views of adults. Young people therefore need to be given the opportunity – the space – to speak. This right (and responsibility) places a corresponding duty on adults including professionals, victims and members of the young person's family to listen. Second, to elicit the young person's views and to involve them in decisions will take time and effort. Some young people may feel under attack from their family and from the victim, and they will certainly not become involved if the environment is one of hostility and blame, rather than encouragement and support. Thus involving young people requires a shift in focus and an acceptance by adults generally and professionals specifically that young people's voices should be heard. In South Australia the police and the young person are specifically named as having to agree to the outcome. This may make a difference to young people's perception of their involvement. Research on this matter has not yet been published.

20   Although about a quarter of the young people said they did not know who had decided the outcome, the group most frequently identified by them as the decision-makers was their family. This was stated by about a third.

21   More recent data from RISE confirms the potential benefits of conferencing for young people (Sherman and Strang, 1997; Sherman and Barnes, 1997). There, young people were randomly allocated to conferences or to courts, and young people were subsequently interviewed about their experience. In all, 111 young offenders had been

interviewed at the time of the above report. Key findings were that: 77 per cent of the young offenders who had experienced conferences said that they were able to express their views compared with 54 per cent of those who went to court; 95 per cent of the young offenders who had experienced conferences said that they had understood what was going on in the process compared with 80 per cent of those who went to court; 75 per cent of the young offenders who went to conferences felt they had been treated with respect compared with 62 per cent of those who experienced court. Clearly, attending a conference is experienced as being 'better' than attending a court on these measures, although the high proportion of young people reporting positive experiences at courts is somewhat puzzling and contradicts previous research on courts. However, crucial questions remain unanswered: did these young people actually feel involved in reaching the decision about the outcome? And, in the young people's view, who did make the decision? Without this information it is difficult to draw conclusions about the extent to which RISE conferences effectively involve young people in the conferencing system.

22   In England, parents can be fined for the offences of their children and mandatory parenting classes for the parents of offenders have recently been introduced.

23   This is primarily due to the fact that the *whanau* (extended family) plays a more important role in Maori society. Traditionally, *whanau* were involved in all key decision-making as well as in the rearing of children.

24   The professionals alone were identified as the decision-makers by 15 per cent of the families. These professionals seemed not to have accepted a redefined role for themselves as information providers and support givers rather than decision-makers. This could be resolved by better briefing of professionals about their roles and better training in the objectives of conferencing.

25   There was also little doubt that those families who had experienced both conferences and courts preferred the process of family group conferences to the process of courts. Their comments highlighted the participatory nature of the family group conference process and the greater degree of support available to them at the family group conference in contrast to the stress that accompanied a court appearance. As well as feeling more comfortable at the family group conference, families also understood more of what had happened and believed that it provided a more realistic forum for decision-making.

26   To the extent that the young person is part of a community which adheres to cultural ways of resolving offending, it would seem appropriate to try to accommodate these. Conferencing, unlike courts, has shown an ability to be responsive to different cultural practices. However, cultural processes should only be accommodated where they broadly correspond to the philosophy underpinning restorative processes and practices. There should be no place for forums which are punitive or retributive or which are hierarchical and patriarchal.

27   In RISE conferences in Canberra, for example, community participants are invited to conferences for offences involving driving under the influence of alcohol.

28   Three pilot projects were set up in 1996 through funding from the Crime Prevention Unit. For an evaluation see Tuhiwai Smith and Cram (1998). Two of these pilots are still running and have since been evaluated (Maxwell *et al.*, 1999). These pilots differ from family group conferences in that a community panel acts as the decision-maker.

29   Examples of these are Te Oritenga and Justice Alternatives. These are loosely based on family group conferences, and victims and offenders are the key decision-makers.

References

Alder, C. and Wundersitz, J. (1994) (eds), *Family Conferencing and Juvenile Justice*, Canberra: Australian Institute of Criminology.

Asquith, S. (1983), *Children and Justice: Decision-making in Children's Hearings and Juvenile Courts*, Edinburgh: University Press.

Bargen, J. (1995), 'A Critical View of Conferencing', *The Australian and New Zealand Journal of Criminology*, Special Supplementary Issue, 100–103.

Braithwaite, J. (1989), *Crime, Shame and Reintegration*, Cambridge: Cambridge University Press.

Carlen, P. (1976), *Magistrates' Justice*, London: Martin Robertson.

Daly, K. and Immarigeon, R. (1998), 'The Past, Present and Future of Restorative Justice', *Contemporary Justice Review*, **1**, 21–46.

Hardin, M. (1996), *Family Group Conferences in Child Abuse and Neglect: Learning from the Experience of New Zealand*, Washington, DC: ABA Center on Children and the Law.

Hood, R. (1992), *Race and Sentencing*, Oxford: Clarendon Press.

Hudson, J., Morris, A., Maxwell, G. and Galaway, B. (1996) (eds), *Family Group Conferences: Perspectives on Policy and Practice*, Annandale, NSW: Federation Press.

Immarigeon, R. (1996), 'Family Group Conferences in Canada and the United States: An Overview', in J. Hudson, A. Morris, G. Maxwell and B. Galaway (eds), *Family Group Conferences: Perspectives on Policy and Practice*, Annandale: Federation Press, 167–79.

LaPrairie, C. (1995), 'Altering Course: New Directions in Criminal Justice Sentencing Circles and Family Group Conferences', *The Australian and New Zealand Journal of Criminology*, Special Supplementary Issue, 78–99.

Maxwell, G.M. and Morris, A. (1993), *Families, Victims and Culture: Youth Justice in New Zealand*, Wellington: Social Policy Agency and Institute of Criminology, Victoria University of Wellington.

Maxwell, G.M. and Morris, A. (1996), 'Research on Family Group Conferences with Young Offenders in New Zealand', in J. Hudson, A. Morris, G. Maxwell and B. Galaway (eds), *Family Group Conferences: Perspectives on Policy and Practice*, Annandale: Federation Press, 88–110.

Maxwell, G.M. and Morris, A. (1999), *Understanding Reoffending*, Wellington: Institute of Criminology.

Maxwell, G.M., Morris, A. and Anderson, T. (1999), *Community Panel Adult Pre-Trial Diversion: Supplementary Evaluation*, Wellington: Crime Prevention Unit.

Ministry of Justice (1995), *Restorative Justice: A Discussion Paper*, Wellington: Ministry of Justice.

Ministry of Justice (1998), *Restorative Justice: The Public Submissions*, Wellington: Ministry of Justice.

Morris, A. and Maxwell, G.M. (1997), *Family Group Conferences and Convictions*, Occasional Papers in Criminology New Series: No. 5, Wellington: Institute of Criminology.

Morris, A., Maxwell, G.M. and Shepherd, P. (1997), *Being a Youth Advocate: An Analysis of their Roles and Responsibilities*, Wellington: Institute of Criminology.

Office of Crime Statistics (1998), *Crime and Justice in South Australia, 1997: Juvenile Justice A Statistical Report*, Adelaide: Office of Crime Statistics, Attorney General's Department.

Polk, K. (1994), 'Family Conferencing: Theoretical and Evaluative Questions', in C. Alder and J. Wundersitz (eds), *Family Group Conferencing and Juvenile Justice*, Canberra: Australian Institute of Criminology, 123–40.

Sherman, L. and Barnes, G. (1997), 'Restorative Justice and Offenders' Respect for the Law', Canberra: unpublished.

Sherman, L. and Strang, H. (1997), 'The Right Kind of Shame for Crime Prevention', Canberra: unpublished.

Strang, H. and Sherman, L. (1997), *The Victim's Perspective*, Canberra: unpublished.

Tuhiwai Smith, L. and Cram, F. (1998), *An Evaluation of the Community Panel Diversion Pilot Project*, Auckland: Auckland Uniservices Ltd.

Warner, K. (1994), 'The Rights of Young People in Family Group Conferences', in C. Alder and J. Wundersitz (eds), *Family Group Conferencing and Juvenile Justice*, Canberra: Australian Institute of Criminology, 141–52.

White, R. (1994), 'Shaming and Reintergrative Strategies: Individuals, State Power and Social Interests', in C. Alder and J. Wundersitz (eds), *Family Group Conferencing and Juvenile Justice*, Canberra: Australian Institute of Criminology, 181–96.

Wundersitz, J. and Hetzel, S. (1996), 'Family Conferencing for Young Offenders: The South Australian Experience', in J. Hudson, A. Morris, G. Maxwell and B. Galaway (eds), *Family Group Conferences*, Annadale, NSW: The Federation Press, 111–39.

11 Integrating a Multi-Victim Perspective into Criminal Justice Through Restorative Justice Conferences

Richard Young[1]

Introduction

Recent debates about how to integrate 'a victim perspective' within criminal justice have tended to portray crime as entailing a violation of one individual by another. It will be argued here that the image of the 'individual victim' is misleading and that it is more fruitful to theorize crime as typically affecting multiple victims in a range of ways. It will then be suggested that such a multi-victim perspective is, or at least should be, an integral part of 'restorative justice conferencing'.[2] A restorative conference is taken here to mean a meeting at which all those with a stake in the resolution of the issues surrounding a crime are brought together in the presence of a facilitator to discuss the harm the offence caused and how it might be repaired. Restorative conferences, also known as 'community conferences' and 'family group conferences', have been introduced within the context of criminal justice in a number of jurisdictions – most notably New Zealand, Australia and the United States (for the background to this development see Chapter 10 by Morris and Maxwell in this volume). One of the most important initiatives in the UK is that of the Thames Valley Police, a police service covering three English counties. Its officers have been trained to use conferencing techniques when finalizing criminal cases for which the public interest does not require a prosecution. This chapter will draw on a small-scale study of the Thames Valley initiative in illustrating how a multi-victim perspective is being integrated into these practices and in commenting on some of the wider issues raised by the use of such a perspective.

Theorizing the Victim Perspective in Criminal Justice

Why is there a need to develop theoretical concepts with which to approach the issue of how to integrate a victim perspective into criminal justice? Garland has written that:

> ... 'theory' is not some kind of flight from reality. Properly pursued, theoretical argument enables us to think about that real world of practice with a clarity and a breadth of perspective often unavailable to the hard-pressed practitioner. It allows us a chance to escape the well-worn thought routines and 'common-sense' perceptions which penality – like any other institution – builds up around itself like a protective shell. Theory enables us to develop analytical tools and ways of thinking which question these established habits of thoughts and action, and seek alternatives to them. (Garland, 1990: 277)

In other words, theory is an immensely practical tool, allowing us to see, for example, that what is taken for granted may be merely historically contingent, thus enabling us more easily to identify alternatives to current arrangements.

What are the well worn thought routines and common-sense perceptions that surround the place of the victim within criminal justice? If this question had been asked as recently as 30 years ago, the answer would have been clear and long established. The victim had no recognized role within the criminal justice system. Crime was conceptualized as primarily an infraction of society's laws, and the state controlled the processes of defining crime, prosecuting defendants and punishing offenders. If victims had suffered particular harm or loss, their remedy lay in the private law of tort, not the public law of crime. Thus William Blackstone, in his *Commentaries on the Laws of England*, published in 1778, asserted that:

> Public wrongs, or crimes and misdemeanours, are a breach and violation of the public rights and duties due to the whole community, in its social aggregate capacity ... since besides the wrong done the individual, they strike at the very being of society. (Book IV: 5)

This 'offence against society' model of criminal justice has come under increasing attack in recent years for a variety of reasons, of which three are particularly critical.[3] First, there has been a realization that this model is indeed historically contingent rather than inevitable. Various scholars have argued that the offence against society model supplanted a much older conception that the justice process should provide mechanisms for victims to use in seeking to recover compensation for the harm done to them.[4] A second reason has been the growing awareness of the vital role victims play in reporting crime to the police and in providing evidence in court (see Maguire, 1982; Shapland *et al.*, 1985). Greater recognition of victims' interests within the criminal process can thus be justified by the instrumental need to encourage victim cooperation with state prosecution processes.[5] The third reason is the resurgence of a philosophical belief that crime is fundamentally a matter directly concerning victims and that they therefore should have the right to be centrally involved in criminal justice (Christie, 1977; Barnett, 1977; Cavadino and Dignan, 1997).

A debate is thus now underway about the proper role of the victim within criminal justice and the various ways in which criminal justice might be remodelled in order to integrate a victim perspective (Dignan and Cavadino, 1996; Cavadino and Dignan, 1997; Ashworth, Chapter 9 in this volume). Of course the degree of 'integration' seen as desirable depends on one's preferred model of criminal justice (see the useful typology in Dignan and Cavadino, 1996). For example, those who adhere to the retributive, or just deserts, model of criminal justice are prepared to concede only a relatively minor (information-giving) role for victims in decisions concerning prosecution and sentence, whereas those who support restorative forms of justice argue that victims have the right to be an active participant in discussions about how the harm caused by an offence might be repaired. My interest here, however, is in the concept of 'the victim' that might be employed within *any* reshaping of the criminal justice system aimed at integrating a victim perspective. For whilst the *role* of the victim is no longer treated as something to be taken for granted, *the victim* is usually treated as an unproblematic concept. Indeed, the rise of concern for victims has, I would argue, generated a simplistic image of crime as something committed against an individual identifiable victim. For example, Wundersitz and Hetzel describe the restorative justice paradigm as holding that:

> ... criminal behaviour is primarily a violation of one individual by another. When a crime is committed, it is the victim who is harmed, not the state; instead of the offender owing a 'debt to society' which must be expunged by experiencing some form of state-imposed punishment, the offender owes a specific debt to the victim which can only be repaid by making good the damage caused. ... (Wundersitz and Hetzel, 1996: 113)

The concept of victim embodied in this statement – that of an individual violated by another individual – is commonly found in the restorative justice literature.[6] As this paradigm represents a reaction to the offence against society model of crime, it is understandable that it places such emphasis upon a 'flesh and blood' victim. Nonetheless, it is misleading to conceptualize crime and victimization in this way, as I will now seek to illustrate.

First, much crime is committed by, through, or on behalf of, organized groups, corporate entities or organs of the state (Box, 1983: ch. 2; Fattah, 1989a; Nelken, 1997; Lacey and Wells, 1998: 502–34). This is a point repeatedly made in the critical victimology literature (for example, Mawby and Walklate, 1994: ch. 2) and repeatedly overlooked in policy discussions about the role of the victim. The extent of such crime is difficult to gauge as its victims tend to be generalized and are often unaware of their victimization (as where they have been sold dangerous products or exposed to unsafe working conditions). One study which attempted to explore this issue through the use of a victim survey concluded that 'the victimization of individuals as consumers, tenants and workers ... can be considered to be more extensive than is true of street crimes' (Pearce, 1990: 49). Similarly, Levi (1993) has noted that the alleged loss in any one of the recent major fraud cases (for example, Maxwell, BCCI, Guinness) in England and Wales exceeds the annual figure recorded by the police for the total amount stolen in thefts and burglaries. Mawby and Walklate (1994: 32) comment that everyday conceptions of victimization have become broader in the light of well publicized cases of major corporate fraud, mis-selling and negligent or reckless manufacturing and work practices. Nonetheless, the dominant image of crime remains that of one individual preying on another.[7]

Less commented on by 'victimologists' is the point that much 'conventional' or 'street crime' does not conform to this dominant predatory image.[8] The offence of carrying an offensive weapon in a public place (Prevention of Crime Act 1953, s. 1) lacks an individual victim, as do many driving offences such as driving with excess alcohol, speeding and various other forms of unsafe driving. Someone outside their home who has with them items for the purpose of committing burglary, theft or deception commits an offence (Theft Act 1968, s. 25(1)), as does someone who has anything with them for the purpose of damaging property belonging to some other person (Criminal Damage Act 1971, s. 3). Yet such persons need not yet have violated any particular individual's interests, nor indeed have any particular victim in mind. This is true also of those who conspire to commit an offence (Criminal Law Act 1977, s. 1) or who incite others to commit an offence (see, for example, *Invicta Plastics* v. *Clare* [1976] RTR 251), or those who attempt an offence (Criminal Attempts Act 1981, s. 1). Conspiracy, incitement and attempt are all offences in their own right, but they do not always fit comfortably with the notion that crime involves one individual violating another.

The unifying rationale for these offences is 'crime prevention' in the sense that their existence enables state officials to interrupt behaviour (through stopping or arresting) which, if left unchecked, might well cause substantive harm to another individual. Much of the criminal law has this preventive focus, as might be expected of laws which for, well over a century, have been firmly based on an offence against society model.[9] However, this is not to say that such offences are merely reflective of such a model. Rather, they reflect the viewpoint that preventing harm is a more effective strategy of social control than responding to it after the event.

Paradoxically, offences with a preventive rationale may nonetheless involve the infliction of harm. Those preparing to commit offences or engaging in dangerous behaviour can be regarded as showing a lack of concern for the rights or interests of other citizens, and this may be damaging to such citizens' sense of security.[10] Such second-order harm is particularly obvious in cases where an offender's preparatory steps *are* aimed against particular individuals, as is often the case with attempts and conspiracies. It requires no straining of language to speak of someone having been the victim of an attempted murder, nor is it difficult to imagine the psychological harm that such a crime might cause the targeted individual. But, for our present purposes, the more important point is that second-order harm can be caused even where the offence in question was not aimed at anyone in particular. This harm might occur simultaneously at various levels of generality. At the level of a spatially defined community one might argue, for example, that those who habitually drive too fast through residential areas are blighting the lives of those who live there. Similarly, those going about equipped for theft or burglary in a particular locality may (if their activities become known) threaten the locals' sense of security. In some cases, such as speeding, a particular group of people who have been victimized in this sense may be identifiable. In other offences, such as being equipped, it may be harder to distinguish such a group (since it may be unclear within which locality the offender planned to steal or burgle). At the most general level of society one can, of course, conceptualize most offences as causing second-order harm to the interests of all *potential* victims.

Not all offences with a preventive rationale cause any obvious second-order harm as defined above, however. Indeed, at first sight, a considerable amount of criminal law seems to be aimed at preventing conduct that threatens only the person engaging in it. Examples are laws that insist on safety equipment being worn when driving a car or riding a motorcycle, or laws prohibiting the use of certain drugs. The rationale for such laws can extend well beyond mere paternalism, however. The helmetless motorcycle rider, for example, can be seen as exposing others to the risk of 'public ward' harm. The danger posed by the offence is that society will incur enormous medical expenses as a result of an accident in which a head injury is suffered, as well as the costs of caring for others to whom the rider owed responsibilities.[11] Where such costs would fall on private individuals we might term this 'private ward' harm. Similarly people who take drugs may be less capable of protecting themselves from harm (thus giving rise to the threat of 'public ward' and 'private ward' harms), and less able to regulate their own behaviour so that it poses no threat to others. Whilst such offences clearly do not fit the image of crime as a matter of one individual violating another, they nonetheless proscribe behaviour which can be constructed as threatening the interests of multiple (not always identifiable) individuals.

Those offences where it might be thought that the stereotypical image of the individual victim holds good include such staple fare of the courts as criminal damage, burglary, theft, deception and personal assaults. A vast number of such offences, however, is committed against corporate victims such as businesses, local authorities, government agencies and churches. 'Shoplifting' (Mirrlees-Black and Ross, 1996), theft by employees, (Ditton, 1977) and social security and tax fraud (Cook, 1989) are examples of crimes routinely committed against corporate victims. Difficulties often arise in deciding which individual within the corporation most aptly represents the victim for the purposes of criminal justice processes such as giving evidence in court, participating in mediation and reparation schemes, or submitting a victim impact statement.

Less obviously, similar difficulties arise in relation to such apparently individualized offences as theft of, or from, a privately owned car, burglary of a dwelling or assault against the person. Take the case of house burglary under English law. A person is guilty of burglary if he or she enters any building with intent to commit theft, criminal damage, serious bodily harm or rape (Theft Act 1968, ss. 9(1)(a) and 9(2)). It is not necessary to the offence that anything is stolen or damaged or that anyone's person is violated. It is also burglary if a person enters a building as a trespasser and then steals or inflicts serious bodily harm whilst in the building, or attempts to do either of these things (Theft Act 1968, s. 9(1)(b)). The definition of either type of burglary is silent on who is 'the victim' of this offence,[12] and a moment's reflection suggests that determining this may often be difficult. One possibility is to treat whoever owns the house as the victim. This would mean treating a landlord of burgled premises as the victim rather than the tenants, thus ignoring the criminal invasion of the latter's sense of security and privacy. But to focus on those who live in a house would be just as partial, ignoring a landlord's legitimate interest in the offence and its resolution. Moreover, there will often be people present or living in the burgled premises who lack any property interests in it, such as guests or children. It would be wrong to assume *a priori* that such categories of people suffer only an indirect or diluted form of victimization and that they should therefore be denied the 'victim' label. Thus in their study of child victims Morgan and Zedner (1992: 73) found that a significant minority of children whose homes had been burgled were 'deeply and lastingly affected' by the experience.

Nor do the difficulties of identifying 'the individual victim' disappear if one examines offences that *are* defined as involving the infliction of harm by one person on another – the various forms of assault. Two points are worth making here. One is that the application of the labels 'offender' and 'victim' is always a matter of 'social construction' – that is, 'the product of a complex interaction of personal and group perception of events and the contexts in which they take place' (Miers, 1978: 9). In the case of assaults (and many other offences) these labels demarcate dichotomous or idealized roles ('bad' offender, 'good' victim) in contexts which are often not conducive to such idealization. As Christie observes:

> When it comes to violence between men, a great amount of it takes place in public places, while both offender and victim are intoxicated, and in situations where it is rather unclear who initiated the violent action. Statistically, this is the typical pattern. (Christie, 1986: 25)

The Wundersitz and Hetzel (1996) formulation, that crime involves one individual violating another, thus giving rise to a duty to repair the violation, fails rather miserably to capture the murky morality of many offender–victim interactions.

The second point about the difficulties of defining the 'victim' of an assault concerns, to borrow a phrase from tort law, the 'remoteness' of consequences. It is typically not just the person physically injured who suffers as the result of an assault. For example, an assault that causes serious injury and hospitalization is likely to cause substantial indirect harm to the victim's family or friends in terms of distress and inconvenience. It may also damage the position of those who rely on the victim for various forms of support (as where an assault leads to depression or a loss of wages). Zedner (1997) observes that those who see assaults take place may experience profound shock or guilt for failing to intervene. She concludes that 'the impact of crime on those who are witnesses or obliged to live with its consequences may be such that they should properly be recognized as victims in their own right' (ibid.: 593). Rock (1998) has documented how this notion of indirect victimization receives little recognition within traditional criminal justice in cases of deadly assault, even though the harm caused (for example, to parents of murdered children) is so severe (Spungen, 1997). The indirect victimization present in non-fatal assaults (and other offences) receives even less attention. The adoption of an individual victim perspective increases the risk that this form of harm will be neglected altogether. Morgan and Zedner (1992) provide a good illustration of this point in their study of child victims. They sought to identify children who were 'indirect' victims of crimes committed against persons close to them but found that no reliable figures were kept by any agency: 'the possibility that children may be indirect victims was scarcely recognized by the majority of agencies interviewed' (ibid.: 38).

A further social aspect to the impact of crime is revealed through envisioning victims as living in communities of one sort or another. An offence that is apparently committed against just one person may, from another perspective, be seen as committed against the community from which that individual is drawn. The spraying of racist graffiti on a vehicle is a good example of this. Whether one sees the harm caused to an ethnic minority community in this case as direct and members of that community (other than the vehicle owner) as 'victims' might depend on whether the crime is constructed as one of criminal damage or one of harassment. What is incontrovertible is that to regard such offences as discrete incidents involving individual victims is to ignore the wider social processes, relationships and effects involved in racially motivated offences.[13] Moreover, offences of this kind often cause multiple forms of second-order harm, defined above in our discussion of 'preventive' offences as an undermining of the sense of security of those whose interests are threatened by such an offence. As Pearson *et al.* (1989: 135) observe, 'A black person need never have been the actual victim of a racist attack, but will remain acutely aware that she or he belongs to a group that is threatened in this manner'.

The term 'community' or 'group' may not always be the most helpful way of thinking about this aspect of victimization, however, as people are differentiated according to social cleavages such as age, sexuality and gender where a common identity (characteristic of the standard image of communities) may be lacking (on the contestable nature of 'community' see Crawford, 1997: ch. 5). A sharp increase in the number of sexual attacks on young women living in urban areas is likely to be regarded as particularly threatening by people who share such characteristics even though they would not normally think of themselves as forming a community or social group. Thus, the term 'community', like the term 'victim' is problematic, giving rise to difficult questions about how one can incorporate a 'community' perspective within criminal justice.

To summarize, the definitional problem facing those who depict crime as a matter of one individual violating another is that the criminal law is not structured in that way, nor is social life so simple. A crime typically involves a range of harms to multiple victims, affecting individuals, groups, communities and society as a whole. This means that the adoption of the concept of a multi-victim perspective may help bring the complexity of crime and victimization into better focus. It would, of course, be naive to believe that merely adopting a different theoretical image of victimization will result in the consensual resolution of all definitional difficulties or the correction of myopic tendencies. Rather, the fact that some forms of victimization suffer from a relative lack of recognition is primarily a reflection of the differential distribution, throughout society, of the economic, social and political power to claim, apply or deny the victim label.[14] Nonetheless, given that the conceptual tools brought to bear on an issue can make a difference to how that issue is perceived and addressed, it may be argued that the undermining of the 'individual victim' image attempted here has practical implications.

Applying the Multi-Victim Perspective in Police-Led Restorative Conferences

It is one thing to adopt a perspective, but quite another to determine the policy consequences that might flow from it. In particular, one might ask how the complexities highlighted by a multi-victim perspective could ever be integrated into a criminal process that has shown itself reluctant to accommodate even the stereotypical individual victim within its structures and procedures.[15] For the purposes of illustrating some of the possibilities and issues involved it will be useful to draw on a small-scale study of 'restorative cautioning' carried out in the Thames Valley Police area of Aylesbury in the summer of 1997.[16]

A caution may be defined as a formal disposal of a criminal case determined by the police without the involvement of the courts. At the time of the Aylesbury research its use was governed by guidelines.[17] The stated purposes of a police caution were: to deal quickly and simply with less serious offenders; to divert them from unnecessary appearance in the courts, and to reduce the chances of their re-offending.[18] A caution was administered in person by a police officer, usually at a police station. It was supposed to take the form of a warning that a caution could influence the decision whether or not to prosecute if the person should offend again, and that it might be cited if the person should subsequently be found guilty of an offence by a court.[19]

It is worth emphasizing that the practice of police cautioning pre-dates any official guidance concerning its use and that it has evolved with remarkably little statutory intervention or authority.[20] Its use has been shaped at least as much by shifting organizational, political and ideological pressures as by Home Office guidelines. Thus research has repeatedly demonstrated that police cautioning rates and practices vary greatly within and across police forces and areas.[21] Part of this variation in practices concerns the patchwork of 'caution-plus' schemes under which offenders in some parts of the country might experience some additional 'intervention', usually aimed at reducing the risk that they would re-offend (see Crawford, 1996). It was against this background that the Aylesbury process was developed.

Virtually all cautions in the Aylesbury police area are administered by the Restorative Cautioning Unit. This consists of two Thames Valley Police constables and one civilian support worker. After a quiet start in 1995, in the year beginning 1 April 1996 it administered 167 cautions, and in the year to 1 April 1998 some 430.[22] The most distinctive feature of the Aylesbury cautioning process, as observed in 1997, lay in its commitment to invite those most directly affected by an offence, including any 'primary' victim, to attend and take part in the cautioning session. Crucially, this commitment existed in relation to *all* cases disposed of by way of a caution, not just those where an identifiable primary victim was involved. The cautioning police officer sought to facilitate discussion of two major issues in turn: first, the range of harms caused by the offence, including any second-order and indirect harm; second, how any of the interests or relationships damaged might be restored by the offender. It follows that, although they would not have explicitly referred to it as such, the cautioning officers had adopted a multi-victim perspective in their work.

The reason for the adoption of this perspective lay in the theory which underpinned the cautioning process, that of 'reintegrative shaming' (Braithwaite, 1989). This argues that crime is most effectively controlled by making offenders ashamed of their behaviour in a way that promotes their reintegration into their community. This shame can most effectively be produced by exposing offenders to the disapproval of their actions by those whom they most care about (such as family and friends), and by making them aware of the consequences of their offending behaviour (by hearing victims and others talk about the harm caused by the offence).[23] Reintegration is achieved by avoiding any open-ended stigmatization and degradation of the person who has offended, by making them aware that others care about them, and by allowing offenders to gain self-esteem by making amends for their behaviour – this last point creating an obvious link with restorative justice theory. As we have seen, however, many offences lack 'primary' individual victims to whom amends can be made. Moreover, such primary victims may not wish to participate in a cautioning session.[24] To the extent that reintegrative shaming works best when offenders are exposed directly to people they have harmed, the adoption of an individual victim perspective could have created a major impediment to success. Only by adopting a multi-victim perspective embracing those indirectly harmed by an offence could the cautioning process aim to be restorative and reintegrative in all cases.

The Aylesbury process is inspired by the well known 'community conferencing' model associated with Australian practices, particularly in Wagga Wagga, and analytical accounts of schemes based on this model are provided elsewhere.[25] Here, the aim will be to examine the model from a multi-victim perspective, drawing on the Aylesbury process for illustrative material in discussing some of the difficult issues that such a perspective raises.

Which 'Victims' are Represented in the Conferences?

It was argued above that criminal offences typically cause a range of harms at various levels of abstraction. Only some of these levels were explicitly catered for by the Aylesbury process. Those invited to restorative conferences were the offenders and victims (as conventionally defined) and a limited number of those who stood in 'caring' or 'supporting' relationships to these people.[26] The part played by such 'communities of care' ensured that a criminal offence was not treated as something that was merely the private concern of the primary victim and the offender – a limitation of much victim–offender mediation work (Braithwaite and Daly, 1994; Dignan and Cavadino, 1996). Their presence enabled the cautioning police officer to highlight what Braithwaite and Mugford (1994:144–45) refer to as the 'collateral damage' caused by an offence – in other words, the multiple forms of indirect and second-order harm caused within these 'communities of care'.

Other forms of 'community' implicated by an offence were not directly represented by those invited to the conference, however, and neither were the interests of all potential victims (as embodied by the notion of the public interest). Yet it does not necessarily follow that these broader interests were unrepresented altogether. Braithwaite and Mugford argue that the conference facilitator has a duty to speak up 'on behalf of any public interest beyond the set of private interests assembled for the conference' (Braithwaite and Mugford, 1994: 147). Dignan and Cavadino, whilst agreeing that the facilitator might represent *the* public interest, suggest that another 'constituency [of community interests] – the local neighbourhood, in which both victim and offender may live – seems unrepresented in this model, at least in its empirical manifestations to date' (Dignan and Cavadino, 1996: 1978). We have already seen that thinking of 'community' in terms of spatial boundaries is problematic. A different formulation of Dignan and Cavadino's point might be that the model does not allow for the representation of people who, despite not standing in 'caring' relationships with the offender and primary victim, suffered second-order or indirect harm as a result of the offence. There seems no reason in principle, however, why facilitators of restorative conferences could not seek to identify and invite some such people, nor why facilitators could not act as the mouthpiece for such interests where this 'constituency' was not physically represented.[27] In Aylesbury the cautioning officers routinely identified second-order harm caused by apparently victimless offences and would summarize this harm when second-order victims declined to attend, as in the following example:

> PC: Now, you know, you've got you two guys standing waiting to be served and then a knife goes on the floor – makes people very very worried for their own safety. First of all because they didn't know if they were about to be robbed. And they were also concerned about the safety of their customers, because the cafe is busy, any time of day you know. And they were very concerned about that, people coming in with a knife. And they wanted me to put that over to you. (Case 9, possession of an offensive weapon)

Where an offence involved an identifiable victim, however, it seemed, in the cautions observed, that more indirect forms of victimization (other than within the offender and victim's 'community of care') were overlooked. This lends some support to Dignan and Cavadino's perception that broader 'community' interests are not particularly well represented in the actual practice of restorative conferencing. Nevertheless, there is nothing inevitable about this.

The Ranking of Victims' Claims for Repair

The integration of a multi-victim perspective into conferencing gives rise to the question of how the claims of the various categories of victim for restoration should be ranked, given that an offender's ability to make reparation may be limited. It can be argued that the primary victim or victims (if any) should take precedence over other claims, given that, as Watson *et al.* (1989: 219) point out, they will have suffered an actual infringement of their rights in ways not shared by others harmed by an offence. The symbolic importance of any primary victims was established in the Aylesbury process by the facilitator's practice (once the offenders had told their story) of drawing out their perspective before that of anyone else harmed by the offence. The facilitator also asked the main victim what outcome they desired before putting that question to anyone else. In practice, all participants seemed to work on the implicit assumption that, whilst those suffering second-order or indirect harm might have a *need* for symbolic reparation, only the primary victim (if any) had a *right* both to material and symbolic reparation. The symbolic reparation sought was similar for all types of victims: an apology, coupled with reassurance that the offender would stay out of trouble in future. There was thus no conflict evident between the claims of the various categories of victim represented in the Aylesbury cautioning sessions. Nonetheless, a multi-victim perspective must be acknowledged to carry a risk that the primary victim's special status will become somewhat submerged – something against which facilitators need to guard.

Just Deserts and the Multi-Victim Perspective

A separate issue is whether it is fair to encourage the offender to take responsibility within a state-sponsored forum for multiple forms of harm. There is a danger that offenders will be required to make good all the harms that their actions have caused whether or not these were foreseen or, indeed, were reasonably foreseeable. Thus the spectre of disproportionately harsh outcomes of cautioning sessions arises. But because cautioning outcomes are negotiated between all those present, and given that those present are usually there because they care about the offender or want reassurance that the offence will not be repeated, this difficulty seems rarely to arise in practice. Moreover, as Braithwaite and Mugford have noted, 'the closer people get to the complexities of particular cases, the less punitive they get' (Braithwaite and Mugford, 1994: 149). In Aylesbury, at any rate, it appears that, as noted above, symbolic reparation is regarded as sufficient amends for all those harmed by an offence, save for any primary or direct victim. There is a need for safeguards, however, both to ensure that the amount of reparation agreed is not so high as to be against the public interest (as where offenders agree to pay more than they can realistically afford) nor so low as to undermine the public interest in seeing that an offence is censured appropriately. This is not a problem that is specific to restorative conferences, nor is it one that is incapable of principled resolution as Cavadino and Dignan (1997) have shown.[28] It is therefore not further discussed here.

The Use of Indirect or Abstract Harm in the Production of Victim Empathy and Reintegrative Shame

Some have argued that it is unproductive to expect offenders, especially if they are young, to empathize with corporate victims (Blagg, 1985: 270–73), or with victims affected only indirectly or potential (second-order) victims (Retzinger and Scheff, 1996: 330). On the other hand, the restorative conference provides a suitable forum for making the more abstract consequences of offending 'come alive' for offenders. Coming face-to-face with potential victims who express a sense of insecurity as the result of an offence, or with those affected indirectly, is more likely to induce empathy than a lecture from a magistrate or police officer on the social ramifications of crime. Moreover, even if offenders remain unmoved by the sentiments expressed by such victims, those there 'in support' of the offender may be affected, and any display of this affect may be difficult for the offender to ignore.[29]

It is, of course, true that the greater the degree of non-conformity with the ideal individual victim stereotype, the more difficult it will be to achieve victim empathy and reintegrative shame. And as King (1997) notes, it is not just offenders that may lack victim empathy. In his view:

> A family which regarded shop-lifting as the fault of shopkeepers for putting temptation in the path of children or drink-induced brawls as youthful high spirits could not be expected to be designated as suitable for a family group conference as an alternative to court proceedings. (Ibid.: 152)

King's position, however, underestimates the dynamic potential of a conference to challenge everyone's preconceptions or constructions of what an offence meant. As Braithwaite and Mugford (1994) have observed, 'the reality of the meeting between victim, offender, and others tends to undermine stereotyping' (ibid.: 149). It is the communal nature of the conference which allows information to be exchanged and a richer understanding of the offence to emerge, thus allowing an appropriate amount of censure to be expressed.

One of the Aylesbury cases observed illustrates this well. A youth had been caught by an officer riding his bicycle on a pavement and told to get off and walk. When the youth thought the officer was no longer looking he got back on his bike and continued to ride on the pavement. The following day the same officer saw the youth riding on the pavement again, took his name and address from him, and reported the offence. Only the youth, his father and the police facilitator attended the subsequent cautioning session. The youth said that he rode on the pavement frequently because the roads were often dangerously busy. He explained that he had got back on his bike on the first occasion because he was in a rush and that he would not have done so if he had realized the officer was still watching him. The facilitator immediately acknowledged that most police officers would agree that the pavement was often safer to cycle on than the road and suggested that the real issue was that he had got back on the bicycle so soon after being told to dismount. On being asked by the facilitator how he thought this would make the officer feel the youth replied, 'Er, very peeved off. Because I'm not doing what I was told'. The facilitator, agreeing with this assessment, then articulated the reporting officer's point of view and, in so doing, added further contextual background to the offence:

PC: It wasn't so much that you were riding on the pavement, although from what I gather there were quite a lot of people around, it's that you got back on. The way they see it you're taking the mickey out of them, and obviously an officer in the town centre has got a very difficult job to do. And I think if you let people treat you like that then obviously you have no authority at all. This is a very minor thing compared with a lot of things they come up against, but obviously you've got to be in a position of control, and that is the nature of their job. And however petty it is to you that you are only cycling on the pavement … .

At this point the youth's father interjected: 'It starts off with cycling on the pavement and builds up to bigger things.' He said that he had not realized, prior to the cautioning session, that his son had got back on his bicycle on the first occasion and that this was bound to make the officers think that he 'was taking the rise out of them'. He explained that he had told his son to ride on the pavement if the road was dangerous 'but that he's got to use his loaf. If it's crowded, you get off. You've been told.'. The youth then immediately conceded that there had been numerous pedestrians using the pavement on both occasions, but contended that he had not been cycling 'much more dangerously than other people' only to be firmly told by his father that 'that was beside the point'. The youth also pointed out that the road adjacent to the pavement was a particularly busy and unsafe one. His father agreed but reiterated that the solution was to walk the cycle along the pavement until there were no pedestrians (or police officers!) about. The youth accepted this, and the facilitator reaffirmed this position. When asked by the facilitator if he wished to do anything 'to perhaps make amends to the officers concerned or anybody else' the youth suggested a letter of apology to the officer who stopped him. The facilitator drew the cautioning session to a conclusion by saying that the apology would be 'really appreciated … because working in the town centre, like I said before, it's not an easy job as you probably know, and to have people just blatantly take no notice of what you say, it's so depressing'.

It would be easy to characterize this case as exemplifying the way in which the police can use the law for their own ends, enforcing a minor offence only when a 'contempt of cop' has been committed. One might further argue that this was an illegitimate use of a sledgehammer to crack a peanut. But this is not the sense one gained from observing this 20-minute conference. Rather, a respectful exchange of views and information took place enabling all three participants to learn something more about the offence. The facilitator learnt that the youth had not got back on his bike as an act of deliberate defiance; the father that his son had been reported for having got back on his bike when it was unsafe to do so and in sight of the officer who had told him to get off; and the youth that it was a good idea to show continuing respect to police requests to dismount because (as he put it in interview afterwards) '... now I know that the police do have a lot of authority for minor things'. Thus a seemingly harmless and obviously relatively trivial offence had been invested with greater texture and meaning, whilst at the same time not been blown out of proportion. In interview, all three participants separately expressed their unreserved satisfaction with the process in this case.

A final point worth making briefly is that, contrary to the impression gained from some of the relevant literature (for example, Scheff, 1998), conferences can be effective in the sense of promoting a richer understanding of the multiple ramifications of crime even if victim empathy is not pronounced. Thus, in the cycling case discussed above, the offender expressed the main lesson he had learnt in cognitive not affective terms. Similarly, in a shoplifting case observed, the offenders remained emotionally unmoved by the store representative's account of the harm caused by such theft, but learnt that their assumption that the store had been able to sell the stolen food (a classic Sykes and Matza (1957) neutralization technique) was incorrect.

An important precondition to this type of cognitive learning appears to be that exchanges of information take place in a respectful way. As the examples discussed by Blagg (1985) suggest, where an abstract victim speaks to an offender in an authoritarian manner, any messages communicated will tend to be resisted, deflected or ignored. But if the victim can avoid 'talking down' to the offender then the messages communicated may be listened to and accepted, even though personal harm and empathy with the victim may be lacking. It was clear from interviewing offenders that the Aylesbury facilitators were remarkably successful in respectfully communicating the multiple ramifications of an offence. As one young offender put it:

> I think [the police officer] acted quite, er, not parental, but friendly. I thought it was going to be a bit more sterner from the police. Just talking very harshly and stuff like that. I thought I was going to be talked down to. But when I actually got in she was fine. (Interview 42)

Several of the offenders interviewed acknowledged, without prompting, that they had gained a better appreciation of the various forms of harm caused by their behaviour through the conference. As one put it, 'I hadn't thought about how it might affect other people until [the cautioning officer] explained it to me. I didn't realize that it would cause that much harm' (Interview 12). Offenders did not usually seem to be ashamed of having caused second-order or indirect harm but, given that such consequences were often unforeseen at the time of the offence, this is understandable. Nonetheless, their increased cognitive awareness might be an important factor in reducing the risk of them re-offending in future.

Do Offenders and their 'Communities of Care' have a Claim to Victim Status?

The emphasis in the restorative conferencing process on the range of harms caused by an offence clearly opens up the possibility that offenders and those who care about them will be treated, for some purposes, as if they were victims. Where parents of young offenders are concerned, it is not difficult to see why this might be the case. Parents often experience inconvenience and distress as a result of their child's arrest and frequently feel that their trust in their children has been betrayed. The same is often true of spouses or friends of adult offenders. Thus in one Aylesbury case the cautioning officer drew out of an offender's mother a range of harms caused by the apparently victimless crime of possessing cannabis:

PC: The journey to the police station, what was that like?
OS: We were just in shock, because we just didn't know that he was doing anything at all. You know, until a few weeks beforehand we didn't even know that he was smoking cigarettes. We certainly never thought he'd do any sort of drugs. He'd be drunk occasionally, but not drugs. So it was a shock. ...
PC: So you arrived at the police station ... . So what's it like for a mum to watch her son being fingerprinted and photographed and DNA tested?
OS: Horrible.
PC: Probably some sleepless nights?
OS: Yes ... . And I've just been watching him all the time. Because I don't know what he's going to do. Because he's done one thing you worry that he's going to do something else. ... He's always been fairly well behaved. I've always trusted him, up till now. I'm just still shocked about it really. And worried. He's only just 15 just a few weeks ago. He's pretty young, wanting to go to college. I don't want him jeopardizing that and spoiling his life. (Case 13)

As for those people being cautioned, these were never labelled in the cautioning process as either 'offenders' or 'victims'. Nonetheless, the questions put to them about the multiple forms of harm caused by the offence and its aftermath invariably drew out the harm caused to the offender as a result of being arrested (in terms of guilt, worry and the unpleasantness of the processes associated with detention). In addition, in bringing the cautioning session to a close, the cautioning officer emphasized that any future offence was likely to result in a court appearance – something that would cause great damage to the offender's social position, particularly as regards job prospects. The focus was on the need for the offender to be aware of this, so that such harm to self could be avoided.

This emphasis on self-harm, combined with the restorative emphasis of the conference, led the cautioning police officers to think seriously about how such harm to the offender (as well as to others) might be avoided in future. This welfarist ethos was also a product of the dynamic nature of the exchanges in the cautioning sessions, which often revealed the background, situational pressures and interactions that had contributed to the offence. Thus in one shoplifting case it emerged that the offenders (aged 16 and 17) had been homeless and hungry at the time they had stolen a few sweets. They acknowledged that they were not justified in stealing but argued that they 'had a reason' for what they did: '... when you've not eaten for days you don't think straight, that's why we stole sweets instead of some decent food.'

Sometimes the complex background to an offence called the very labels 'victim' and 'offender' into question. In an assault case in which only the offender and his wife (both in their early fifties) attended the caution, the offender explained that the victim was disliked by everyone on the estate where he lived. Apparently the victim had a violent disposition (he was known to have assaulted both his wife and his child) and was in the habit of driving dangerously fast on the narrow estate roads. Neighbours worried about the safety of their children had spoken to him about their concerns on numerous occasions, but to no avail. On the occasion of this assault the victim's driving had forced the offender's son's car off the road. The offender had gone up the victim's garden path to remonstrate with him and been punched three times on the chin before hitting back with a blow to the victim's head. After a brief struggle he walked away, saying the victim was not worth hitting. The offender's wife called out to the victim that the trouble had started because of his dangerous driving and the victim retorted that she should stand in the road next time 'so I can kill you'. This enraged the offender who chased after the victim, caught up with him and punched him two more times. The offender was then pulled away by his wife. The victim then punched her in the face. The offender (who did not realize that his wife had been assaulted until later) telephoned the police to explain that, as he put it, 'best you get up here, I've just slapped a neighbour'. The victim later lost consciousness for over an hour, necessitating hospital attendance. Nonetheless when the cautioning officer asked the offender to identify who he thought had been harmed by the offence he replied, 'Me! There's no harm been caused to him. None whatsoever, because that is his attitude. His attitude is "sod everybody else"'. Subsequently he accepted that his wife had been harmed too (as his arrest had caused her great distress) but he was evidently not prepared to accept that his neighbour deserved the 'victim' label. His wife verified his account and it also tallied with most, although not all, of the 'facts' contained in the police file available to the facilitator.[30]

The facilitator adopted an interesting tack for the remainder of the cautioning session, suggesting to the offender that 'perhaps you let yourself down by lowering yourself to his [the victim's] level' by punching him on the head. This was a suggestion that the offender, who had never been in trouble with the police before, eagerly accepted. This was not to say that the offence was condoned: the facilitator made it clear that the offender had committed a serious offence and had responded inappropriately when provoked. The offender accepted that he had done wrong and agreed with the facilitator that he should have telephoned the police when assaulted, rather than hitting back. He expressed a sense of injustice, however, that the victim had escaped all formal censure. In his view, the victim had initiated the interaction by his dangerous driving, the victim had thrown the first punch and the victim had assaulted his wife – not exactly the 'ideal victim' (Christie, 1986).

This is a classic example of the kind of messy case that can end up in the criminal process. It illustrates why Scheff's argument (1998: 105) that successful conferencing depends upon 'making sure that all of the shame connected with the crime is accepted by the offender ... acknowledging his or her complete responsibility for the crime ...' is misconceived. Far preferable is the view that 'a condition of successful reintegration ceremonies is that they leave open multiple interpretations of responsibility while refusing to allow the offender to deny personal responsibility entirely' (Braithwaite and Mugford, 1994: 146). This latter position was certainly that adopted by the Aylesbury officers observed, and their exposure to the tangled stories that lay behind some offences undoubtedly contributed to this.[31]

This finding bears on the debate as to whether conferencing represents a co-option by the state of 'families' and 'communities' (King, 1997: 158), and thus an extension of the net of formal social control. Braithwaite and Mugford (1994:160) acknowledge this possibility but argue that conferencing in practice strengthens or extends the net of *informal* social control with the help, or at the expense, of state control. To the extent that formal state control *is* increased through conferencing, it may nonetheless be a novel type of state control – one geared away from stereotypical constructions of crime and displaying a commitment to repair not punishment. The multi-victim perspective reminds us, however, that police-led conferencing initiatives, such as that in the Thames Valley, will not cater for all categories of offenders and victims. As Davies notes, it is personal and property crimes:

... that are the everyday business of our local police services. It is therefore the victims of these latter types of crimes that form the basis of the police's idea of what a victim looks like and we must remember that this is problematic. (Davies, 1996: 73)

By the same token, the police's idea of what an offender looks like will not be totally transformed through facilitating restorative conferences. That could only be achieved if local police services were invited by other policing agencies to run conferences for crimes which are not normally their province, such as corporate fraud, health and safety offences and crimes against the environment.

Conclusion

The restorative justice paradigm usefully reminds us that criminal offences often cause significant harm to the interests, bodies and feelings of individual victims. It would be a mistake, however, to replace the well worn thought routines of traditional criminal justice – with its blindness to victims generally – with a myopic concept of crime as something committed against an individual victim. I have thus argued that a multi-victim perspective has distinct advantages over an individualized victim perspective in that it more fully encompasses the gritty social reality of crime and its multiple effects. Ultimately, however, one might infer from the above discussion that the concept of 'victim' is of limited value, whether prefixed by 'multi' or not. As Christie (1986: 29) suggests, when 'offenders' and 'victims' are brought face-to-face, such labelling is usually revealed as unhelpful. Nonetheless, the adoption of a multi-victim perspective in restorative conferences may be a useful interim step towards the demolition of stereotyped images of crime.

Notes

1   Thanks are due to Andrew Ashworth, Adam Crawford, Kimmett Edgar, Stephen Farrall, Carolyn Hoyle and David Rose for their helpful comments on this chapter.
2   As noted by King (1997: 135–36), those supporting the concept of restorative justice conferences have turned '"conference" into a verb, so that it is now possible to talk of "conferencing" a child or a family, or of a case having been "conferenced"'.
3   For general surveys of the growth of victimology see Koffman (1996: ch. 2), Zedner (1997) and Croall (1998: ch. 5).
4   See the historical sketch by Davis (1992: 1–6). For a more critical historical and cross-cultural appraisal see Mawby and Walklate (1994: ch. 3).
5   Such instrumental thinking may result in the state recognition of victims' interests taking a predominantly symbolic form: Elias (1986: 303–34).
6   For other examples, see Barnett (1977: 288) and Zehr (1990: 182): 'Crime, then is at

its core a violation of a person by another person …' I acknowledge that much of the restorative justice literature recognizes at least some aspects of the broader social dimensions of crime (see, for example, ibid.), but I maintain that the 'core' image of crime generally to be found in this literature is misleading. It is worth adding that the offence against society model of criminal justice also tends to operate with simplistic notions of individual victims.

7 The term 'multi-victim perspective' perhaps has some special value in challenging this image, echoing the message that some of the most serious forms of crime are committed by multinational companies against a multitude of victims.

8 The examples given in the text which follows are drawn from English criminal law but have their counterparts in jurisdictions throughout the world.

9 It should be added that many criminal laws with a preventive focus have a much longer history than this (for example, conspiracy).

10 See Clarkson and Keating (1998: 466–67 and 530–31). For a discussion of this theme in the context of reparative-based theories of punishment see Watson et al. (1989).

11 See Kaplan (1971) for a fuller discussion of the justifications discussed in this paragraph, as well as the criticisms to which they can be subjected.

12 This silence is typical of criminal laws. Thus the point made by Elias (1986: 301) that, 'what we regard as criminal also defines whom we consider crime victims' is true only in a very general sense. This is not to deny that crime is defined, as he puts it, 'selectively and politically' with the result that those who suffer certain forms of harm are effectively precluded from claiming the 'victim of crime' status.

13 See Bowling (1998: 157–162 and ch. 7). Similar points can be made in relation to abusive and violent behaviour against women (for example, see Genn, 1988) and children, both in and out of the home.

14 See, for example, Rock (1986) and also the various contributions on the theme of neglected types of victimization in the collection edited by Fattah (1989b).

15 See, for example, Shapland (1988) and Shapland and Cohen (1987). A full discussion of the reasons for this institutional inertia and the mechanisms needed to overcome it is to be found in the report of the JUSTICE Committee on the role of the victim in criminal justice (JUSTICE, 1998).

16 This study, more fully reported in Young and Goold (1999), paved the way for a three-year project on the Thames Valley Police initiative in restorative cautioning funded by the Joseph Rowntree Foundation (beginning 1 April 1998) conducted by myself and Dr Carolyn Hoyle. The latter project is not drawn on here except for background material.

17 Home Office Circular 18/1994 'The Cautioning of Offenders' and the *National Standards for Cautioning* (Revised), issued as an attachment to that Circular. Under the Crime and Disorder Act 1998, the system of cautioning for young offenders (but not for adults) is to be replaced by the introduction of 'reprimands' (essentially for first offences) and 'final warnings' (for second offences). A third offence will nearly always result in prosecution. See, further, Fionda (1999) and Dignan (1999).

18 Three conditions had to be satisfied before a caution could be administered: there had to be evidence of the offender's guilt sufficient to give a realistic prospect of conviction; the offence had to be admitted, and the offender (or in the case of a juvenile, his or her parents or guardian) must have given informed consent to being cautioned. In addition, the police were supposed to take account of the public interest principles contained in the Code for Crown Prosecutors, regarding which see Ashworth and Fionda (1994).

19 See *National Standards for Cautioning* (Revised), Note 2D. For a discussion of the forms that the delivery of a caution may take in practice see Young and Goold (1999).

20 The trend in recent legislation, however, has been for records of cautions to take on

much of the same significance as those of convictions: see Soothill *et al.* (1997) and Uglow (1998).

21   The issues and the relevant research are discussed in Sanders and Young (1994: 227–29). For more recent research findings see Evans and Ellis (1997).

22   Only brief details of the main elements of the Aylesbury study need be given for the purposes of this chapter. Fifteen cautioning sessions were observed and tape-recorded, and the participants were interviewed after the session was complete. A total of 15 offenders, six victims and ten other participants (usually the parent or partner of the offender) were interviewed in this way. In addition, the cautioning police officer was interviewed in detail about each caution administered, and police case files relating to these cautions were examined.

23   Whilst exposure to victims' feelings was not a strong theme in Braithwaite's original formulation of his theory, in subsequent work he has acknowledged the importance of this to reintegrative shaming: see, for example, Braithwaite and Mugford (1994) and Braithwaite and Daly (1994).

24   'Victims' (whether individuals or corporate representatives) attend less than half of the Aylesbury cautioning sessions. Five of the 15 observed sessions involved victims, in three more the victim chose not to attend and in the remaining seven the offence lacked an obvious identifiable victim.

25   For Wagga Wagga, see Moore with Forsythe (1995); for South Australia see Wundersitz and Hetzel (1996); and for Aylesbury see Young and Goold (1999).

26   Of the 15 cautions observed, the average number of persons attending was 3.3 (including the facilitator). Whilst conferencing techniques were always employed, the small number of attendees undoubtedly limited the potential for exploring the multiple implications of offending behaviour.

27   It may be difficult to find such 'representatives' when the 'community' in question is disorganized and/or riven with internal schisms and hierarchies but that is not a justification for not looking: Crawford (1997: 168–72).

28   In June 1998 the Thames Valley Police issued guidelines for the facilitation of restorative conferences by its officers. These require facilitators to avoid suggesting or prescribing reparative outcomes whilst at the same time ensuring that any reparation agreed is not contrary to public interest considerations and does not exceed that which would have been imposed by a court. The guidelines thus incorporate the notion of 'state veto' advocated by Cavadino and Dignan (1997).

29   Braithwaite and Mugford (1994: 144) make this point in relation to primary individual victims but there is no reason why it should not apply also to other forms of victim.

30   This inconsistency is not surprising given that police files are often constructed so as to sharply differentiate the roles of victim and offender and thus render the case as something that can be dealt with effectively within the traditional criminal process: McConville *et al.* (1991).

31   As Christie puts it: 'Knowledge makes for realistic and multi-dimensional evaluation – and sanctions directed against those deserving sanctions' (Christie, 1986: 29).

References

Ashworth, A. and Fionda, J. (1994), 'The New Code for Crown Prosecutors: (1) Prosecution, Accountability and the Public Interest', *Criminal Law Review*, 894–903.

Barnett, R. (1977), 'Restitution: a New Paradigm of Criminal Justice', *Ethics*, **87**(4), 279.

Blagg, H. (1985), 'Reparation and Justice for Juveniles', *British Journal of Criminology*, **25**(3), 267–79.

Bowling, B. (1998), *Violent Racism*, Oxford: Clarendon Press.

Box, S. (1983), *Power, Crime and Mystification*, London: Tavistock.

Braithwaite, J. (1989), *Crime, Shame and Reintegration*, Cambridge: Cambridge University Press.

Braithwaite, J. and Daly, K. (1994), 'Masculinities, Violence and Communitarian Control', in T. Newburn and E. Stanko (eds), *Just Boys Doing Business?*, London: Routledge, 189–213.

Braithwaite, J. and Mugford, S. (1994), 'Conditions of Successful Reintegration Ceremonies: Dealing with Juvenile Offenders', *British Journal of Criminology*, **34**(2), 139–71.

Cavadino, M. and Dignan, J. (1997), 'Reparation, Retribution and Rights', *International Review of Victimology*, **4**, 233–53.

Christie, N. (1977), 'Conflicts as Property', *British Journal of Criminology*, **17**(1), 1–15.

Christie, N. (1986), 'The Ideal Victim', in E. Fattah (ed.), *From Crime Policy to Victim Policy*, Houndmills, Basingstoke: Macmillan, 1–17.

Clarkson, C. and Keating, H. (1998), *Cases and Materials on Criminal Law*, (4th edn), London: Sweet & Maxwell.

Cook, D. (1989), *Rich Law, Poor Law: Different Responses to Tax and Supplementary Benefit Fraud*, Milton Keynes: Open University Press.

Crawford, A. (1996), 'Alternatives to Prosecution: Access to, or Exits from, Criminal Justice?', in R. Young and D. Wall (eds), *Access to Criminal Justice: Legal Aid, Lawyers and the Defence of Liberty*, London: Blackstone Press, 313–44.

Crawford, A. (1997), *The Local Governance of Crime: Appeals to Community and Partnerships*, Oxford: Clarendon Press.

Croall, H. (1998), *Crime and Society in Britain*, London: Longman.

Davies, P. (1996), 'Crime, Victims and Criminal Justice Policy', in P. Davies, P. Francis and V. Jupp (eds), *Understanding Victimisation*, Newcastle: Northumbria Social Science Press, 71–89.

Davis, G. (1992), *Making Amends*, London: Routledge.

Dignan, J. (1999), 'The Crime and Disorder Act and the Prospects for Restorative Justice', *Criminal Law Review*, 48–60.

Dignan, J. and Cavadino, M. (1996), 'Towards a Framework for Conceptualising and Evaluating Models of Criminal Justice from a Victim's Perspective', *International Review of Victimology*, **4**, 153–82.

Ditton, J. (1977), *Part-time Crime*, London: Macmillan.

Elias, R. (1986), 'Community Control, Criminal Justice and Victim Services', in E. Fattah (ed.), *From Crime Policy to Victim Policy*, Houndmills, Basingstoke: Macmillan, 290–316.

Evans, R. and Ellis, R. (1997), 'Police Cautioning in the 1990s', *Home Office Research and Statistics Directorate, Research Findings No. 52*, London: Home Office.

Fattah, E. (1989a), 'Victims of Abuse of Power: the David/Goliath Syndrome', in E. Fattah (ed.), *The Plight of Crime Victims in Modern Society*, Houndmills, Basingstoke: Macmillan, 29–73.

Fattah, E. (1989b) (ed.), *The Plight of Crime Victims in Modern Society*, Houndmills, Basingstoke: Macmillan.

Fionda, J. (1999), 'New Labour, Old Hat: Youth Justice and the Crime and Disorder Act 1998', *Criminal Law Review*, 36–47.

Garland, D. (1990), *Punishment and Modern Society*, Oxford: Clarendon Press.

Genn, H. (1988), 'Multiple Victimisation', in M. Maguire and J. Pointing (eds), *Victims of Crime: A New Deal?*, Milton Keynes: Open University Press, 90–100.

JUSTICE (1998), *Victims in Criminal Justice*, Report of the Committee on the Role of the Victim in Criminal Justice, London: JUSTICE.

Kaplan, J. (1971), 'The Role of the Law in Drug Control', *Duke Law Journal*, 1065.

King, M. (1997), *A Better World for Children? Explorations in Morality and Authority*, London: Routledge.

Koffman, L. (1996), *Crime Surveys and Victims of Crime*, Cardiff: University of Wales Press.

Lacey, N. and Wells, C. (1998), *Reconstructing Criminal Law*, London: Butterworths.

Levi, M. (1993), *The Investigation, Prosecution and Trial of Serious Fraud*, Royal Commission on Criminal Justice Research Report No. 14, London: HMSO.

McConville, M., Sanders, A. and Leng, R. (1991), *The Case for the Prosecution*, London: Routledge.

Maguire, M. (1982), *Burglary in a Dwelling*, London: Heinemann.

Mawby, R.I. and Walklate, S. (1994), *Critical Victimology*, London: Sage.

Miers, D. (1978), *Responding to Victimisation*, Abingdon: Professional Books.

Mirlees-Black, C. and Ross, A. (1996), *Crime Against Retail Premises in 1993*, Home Office Research Findings No. 26, London: Home Office.

Moore, D. with Forsyth, L. (1995), *A New Approach to Juvenile Justice: An Evaluation of Family Conferencing in Wagga Wagga*, Report to the Criminology Research Council, Wagga Wagga: Centre for Rural Social Research, Charles Stuart University.

Morgan, J. and Zedner, L. (1992), *Child Victims*, Oxford: Clarendon Press.

Nelken, D. (1997), 'White-Collar Crime', in M. Maguire, R. Morgan and R. Reiner (eds), *Oxford Handbook of Criminology*, (2nd edn), Oxford: Clarendon Press, 891–924.

Pearce, F. (1990), *Second Islington Crime Survey: Commercial and Conventional Crime in Islington*, Middlesex Polytechnic: Centre for Criminology.

Pearson, G., Sampson, A., Blagg, H., Stubbs, P. and Smith, D.J. (1989), 'Policing Racism', in R. Morgan and D.J. Smith (eds), *Coming to Terms with Policing*, London: Routledge, 118–37.

Retzinger, S. and Scheff, T. (1996), 'Strategy for Community Conferences: Emotions and Social Bonds', in B. Galway and J. Hudson (eds), *Restorative Justice: International Perspectives*, Amsterdam: Kluger Publications, 315–36.

Rock, P. (1986), 'Society's Attitude to the Victim', in E. Fattah (ed.), *From Crime Policy to Victim Policy*, Houndmills, Basingstoke: Macmillan, 31–49.

Rock, P. (1998), 'Murderers, Victims and Survivors', *British Journal of Criminology*, **38**(2), 185–200.

Sanders, A. and Young, R. (1994), *Criminal Justice*, London: Butterworths.

Scheff, T. (1998), 'Community Conferences: Shame and Anger in Therapeutic Jurisprudence', *Revista Juridica Universidad de Puerto Rico*, **67**(1), 97.

Shapland, J. (1988), 'Fiefs and Peasants: Accomplishing Change for Victims in the Criminal Justice System', in M. Maguire and J. Pointing (eds), *Victims of Crime: A New Deal?*, Milton Keynes: Open University Press, 187–94.

Shapland, J. and Cohen, D. (1987), 'Facilities for Victims: the Role of the Police and the Courts', *Criminal Law Review*, 28–38.

Shapland, J., Willmore, J. and Duff, P. (1985), *Victims in the Criminal Justice System*, Aldershot: Gower.

Soothill, K., Francis, B. and Sanderson, B. (1997), 'A Cautionary Tale: the Sex Offenders Act 1997, the Police and Cautions', *Criminal Law Review*, 482–90.

Spungen, D. (1997), *Homicide: The Hidden Victims*, London: Sage.

Sykes, G. and Matza, D. (1957), 'Techniques of Neutralization: A Theory of Delinquency', *American Sociological Review*, **22**, 664–70.

Uglow, S. (1998), 'Criminal Records Under the Police Act 1997', *Criminal Law Review*, 235–45.

Watson, D., Boucherat, J. and Davis, G. (1989), 'Reparation for Retributivists', in M. Wright and B. Galaway (eds), *Mediation and Criminal Justice: Victims, Offenders and Community*, London: Sage, 212–28.

Wundersitz, J. and Hetzel, S. (1996), 'Family Conferencing for Young Offenders: The South Australian Experience', in J. Hudson, A. Morris, G. Maxwell and B. Galaway (eds), *Family Group Conferences*, Annadale, NSW: The Federation Press, 111–39.

Young, R. and Goold, B. (1999), 'Restorative Police Cautioning in Aylesbury – From Degrading to Reintegrative Shaming Ceremonies?', *Criminal Law Review*, 126–38.

Zedner, L. (1997), 'Victims', in M. Maguire, R. Morgan and R. Reiner (eds), *The Oxford Handbook of Criminology*, (2nd edn), Oxford: Clarendon Press, 577–612.

Zehr, H. (1990), *Changing Lenses*, Scottdale, PA: Herald Press.

12 Extending the Victim Perspective Towards a Systemic Restorative Justice Alternative

Lode Walgrave

Risks in Isolating the Victim Perspective from Restorative Justice

The victim movement has gained much ground in recent years. Whereas it was initially narrowly focused on promoting the victim's rights in his or her conflict with the offender, most of its advocates are now oriented towards a much broader goal of improving the whole social, personal and, indeed, juridical position of those who have been victimized by a crime.

From a Victim Movement to Restorative Justice

The reasons for this shift are easy to understand. First, it has increasingly been perceived that while more severe punishment for the offender may, in some cases, satisfy the immediate emotions of outrage and revenge, in the longer term, it does not contribute to the restoration or healing of victims. As a consequence, their non-satisfaction may provoke an escalating culture of retribution that is disastrous for social life in general. Second, the victims may seem to be the losers in their coalition with the criminal justice system. The system may hear them, but only to the extent that what they say is useful as a witness. Many victims who once had confidence in the criminal justice system later came to feel betrayed by it. Finally and most importantly, practice has demonstrated that many victims are more satisfied if they succeed in a constructive interaction with the offender.

The latter observation has led to a steady growth of various different practices wherein the victim and the offender are brought together in a guided interaction – direct or indirect, face-to-face or supported by family members or other intimates – in order to proceed together through a process aimed at constructively settling the aftermath of the crime (Umbreit, 1994). Although these practices constitute much more than just a variation on the same theme, I shall provisionally refer to them collectively by the term 'mediation'. Such practices and the accompanying reflection on mediation have contributed considerably to the emergence of a broader concept, called 'restorative justice', to the extent that both terms are often used as synonyms (Marshall, 1996; Galaway and Hudson, 1996).

However, the roots of restorative justice are multiple, and not only victim-based (Faget, 1997; Van Ness and Strong, 1997). Critical criminology has convincingly described the negative effects of criminal justice and its inability to assure peace in social life, to the extent that some came to argue for abolishing the criminal justice system. Many adherents of restorative justice are inheritors of this tendency and consider this vision as an alternative for criminal justice as a whole (van Swaaningen, 1997). Another root of restorative justice is communitarianism. As a reaction to the fragmentation of our postmodern Western societies, some advocate the revival of community as the organic resource of informal mutual support and control. Communities are, at the same time, a means and an end for restorative justice. They are a means in that they are needed as the 'niches' wherein reintegrative shaming and restorative processes can take place (Braithwaite, 1989); they are an end because it is believed that achieving restorative processes in a community helps revive community life (McCold, 1996). Still other movements and tendencies have 'spin-offs' in restorative justice, such as the feminist movement (Harris, 1991), the indigenous emancipation movements (Corrado and Griffiths, 1999), religious movements (Zehr, 1990) or the juvenile justice critics (Walgrave, 1995; Bazemore and Walgrave, 1999a).

It is, in fact, only recently that practitioners and scientific researchers have become aware that there seems to be an important fundamental commonality. Increasingly, the victim perspective is being fused with other streams of thought to form an emerging broader paradigm in the approach of justice, based on an 'emancipatory' view on communities and society and called restorative justice.

Why we Should not Integrate an Isolated Victim Perspective into the Criminal Justice System

Should the victim perspective be more integrated into the criminal justice system? This question seems to suggest that the victim perspective should be detached from the restorative justice tendency and follow its own path towards integration into the criminal justice system, or towards at least a privileged partnership with it. I take the view that victims have much to lose if their perspective becomes isolated from the broader restorative justice approach.

Integrating the victim perspective into the criminal justice system can mean different things and can happen in different degrees. Many experiments of this nature are currently taking place, some of which are reported in this book. At the lowest level, integration might mean that criminal justice agents are made more respectful towards victims. Currently, victims are often used, or even misused, as witnesses in the criminal investigation, and then left alone with their grievances and losses. Many victims undergo a secondary victimization by the criminal justice system (Shapland, 1985). This has become very clear from the feminist critique of the way in which the judiciary deals with victims of sexual offences, but it is too often true in general. At present, efforts are being made to improve the reception of victims, at many levels and in many places, and such efforts should be continued and enforced. But this is far from being enough. After all, this is basically a question of respect. Many police officers should be better educated and better prepared for the human context in which they operate.

In addition, integrating the victim perspective into the criminal justice system could mean that the criminal justice system would leave more space for people to work with victims (and with offenders, if that work includes mediation). However, this is not integration into the criminal justice system; rather, it is providing exits from the justice system towards a 'victim-circuit'. This leads to several problems. First, it is unclear whether this is seen as a form of diversion or simply as an additional offer to victims. If it is an additional offer, the problems revolve around the way in which the victim-circuit and the criminal justice system run parallel to each other, especially if the victim agency includes mediation in its offer. If it is meant as diversion, the main problem is to find a procedure and criteria for selecting the cases.

Finally, integrating the victim perspective into the criminal justice system could also mean that criminal procedures themselves include more opportunities for victims to be heard and gain satisfaction. The central focus of the criminal procedure on assessing the criminal act and the culpability, and defining the penalty, would then be completed by another focus on victims' experiences, rights and needs.

Such options have been demonstrated through the Belgian law on 'the Regulation of a Procedure for Mediation in Penal Matters' (1994). According to this law, the public prosecutor may dismiss a case with a possible maximum penalty lower than two years' imprisonment, if the offender agrees to cooperate in reparation, treatment, training or community service or a combination of these.[1] To put that disposition into operation, a mediation magistrate has been appointed in each of the 27 Belgian courts of first instance (to select the cases, supervise the work and chair the final mediation session), together with one or more mediation assistants, to carry out the fieldwork with the offenders and (possibly) the victims. Here, the system has really opened up possibilities for working with victims, and the mediation workers are fully integrated into the system. After two years and more than 10 000 referrals, it seems that reparation (as the single condition or in combination with others) has been imposed most often – in 51 per cent of all cases (Dewulf, 1996 and Davreux, 1997, cited in Aertsen and Peters, 1998). Nevertheless, evaluation of this initiative has highlighted significant problems, such as: the mediators' dependence on getting appropriate referrals; the marginal position of victims in most, so-called, 'mediations', despite the explicit purpose of the law to restore to victims their rights; the punitive undertone of the procedures, especially in the final session which is often a kind of 'mini-trial'; and the obvious tendency of net-widening (Dewulf, 1996 and Davreux, 1997, cited in Aertsen and Peters, 1998). Although some may consider this to be a bad example, it is one of the only formal integrations about which we know, and it may be an exemplar of what a victim perspective risks if it agrees too easily to be integrated within criminal justice.

In my opinion, integrating an isolated victim perspective into the criminal justice system would be detrimental for work with victims:

> The justice system is not an administration like another. It fulfils symbolic functions which requires it to respond to other imperatives than rapidity and efficiency. It is composed of actors with technical monopoly and high ideological weight … . (Faget, 1997: 77, translated from the French)

A victim perspective, included into such a system, does not have enough technical, professional or ideological countervailing power to survive undamaged. On its own, it is not strong enough to resist the tendency of the existing justice system to incorporate new ideas into its own rationale. There also is a great danger that victim work would degrade into some kind of a 'sub-justice' ('*sous-justice*', Faget, 1997: 158). It would not be 'soft justice' (Bonafé-Schmitt, 1992), but would simply not be justice at all.

Second, the diversionist model appears less diversional than that opted for by its proponents. In fact, the first diversionist experiments in juvenile justice seemed to be net-widening (Lemert, 1981), which increasingly also seems to be the case with a diversionist option in victim work. Of course, widening the net that offers victim support is a good thing, *per se*, but if it is designed as only a diversionist opportunity it would be restricted to victims of non-serious crimes, thereby excluding the most victimized persons.

Finally, integrating an isolated victim perspective into the criminal justice system, or enhancing its complementariness, would leave the core of the criminal justice system itself out of the discussion. The need for legislation 'to define when it is legitimate to apply force and how much force, due process to protect citizens from abuse of authority, etcetera' (Marshall, 1996: 37), does not necessarily mean that we have to accept the existing punitive justice system. This is a crucial point on which, I will elaborate further.

The Retributive Emotion and the Instrumentalist Illusion of Penal Law

Basically, the penal law system inflicts harm on an offender in accordance with strict legalistic and procedural rules. Two types of rationale underpin this system (Tulkens, 1993).

First, the concept of retribution considers penal law simply as the upholder of principles and values laid down by the state, intervening when those principles have been violated in order to redress the balance. Its function is retributive (von Hirsch, 1976). From this perspective, the effectiveness of the punishment is of no more than secondary importance. The essential factor is proportionality: the harm inflicted by criminal law must be proportional to the harm caused by the offence. However, this retributive basis is the subject of many contentions (Braithwaite and Pettit, 1990):

1   It is based on a naive view of humankind, supposing people to be possessed of completely free will to choose whether to integrate into society or not. This simply is not true.[2]
2   If the point of retribution is to restore the moral balance, it must be asked what morality we are dealing with (is it geared to public order, personal security, property and not, for example, solidarity or social and economic equity?) and wherein lies the balance to be preserved (given the imbalance in property and power).
3   There can be no intervention on the grounds of principles which do not examine the effect of that intervention on the social system. The contention that the action of penal law is formal confirmation of the state's attachment to certain rules or values is a hollow claim unless it is controlled in practice.

The second rationale, therefore, is based on an instrumentalist view of criminal law. Penal justice must serve a purpose, particularly since 'in the entire course of its operation, it can only be a series of harms' (Bentham, cited in Tulkens, 1993: 482). This approach sees the criminal justice system not as the only favoured means of upholding society's fundamental values, but simply as one instrument among others for the governance of society. The instrumentalist approach is open to empirical control.

1   An extensive body of research shows that punitive prevention (or deterrence) is far less general than may be thought. It is effective only in certain conditions, for certain offences and certain types of offender (Piliavin *et al.*, 1986).
2   It is apparently more the exception than the rule for an offender to be reformed by application of the conventional penalties of criminal law. On the contrary, in fact: various studies suggest that they have a marginalizing and labelling effect (Lipton *et al.*, 1975).[3]
3   As already stated, the preservation of the victim's rights is certainly not central to existing penal justice procedures. Other existing systems are far more effective in addressing the rights and needs of victims (Wright, 1996).

Criminal law has been given still other functions (Trépanier, 1989), but it appears that most, if not all, arguments in favour of the instrumentality of penal law are more cosmetic than based on established facts.

As Tulkens (1993) also notes, the two tendencies in penal justice are not always clearly differentiated. Instrumentalist illusion is in fact grafted on to retributive emotion. The instrumentalist conception would seem admissible only insofar as it assimilates into the conviction that the existing societal rules are absolute and non-negotiable and can be enforced only by societal action through penal law.

These criticisms of the penal justice system must not lead us to reject any justice system. Any democratic society needs a judicial system to channel and control the use of force, which is often inevitable in the settling of the aftermath of a crime (van Swaaningen, 1997). However, the penal justice system is so deeply dysfunctional and socially destructive that a fundamental rethinking of the way in which society and communities deal with crime is badly needed. In fact, the quest is not 'to replace penal law with better penal law, but with something better' (Radbruch, cited in Tulkens, 1993: 493). A victim perspective, on its own, cannot contribute to a better penal law, but it can ground the quest for 'something better'. For a growing number of scholars and practitioners, this is to be sought in the direction of restorative justice.

A Programme for Restorative Justice

At present, the concept of restorative justice has different definitions and interpretations (McCold, 1998). Some emphasize restorative justice as a process (Marshall, 1996), while others accept whatever process or procedure may lead to restorative outcomes (Walgrave, 1995). Restorative justice is promoted as a potentially systemic alternative (Bazemore and Walgrave, 1999b), or is confined as an opportunity for diversion (Dünkel, 1996). Some absolutely exclude any use of coercion, whereas others accept that coercively imposed sanctions may be restorative. Restorative justice is often used as synonym for victim–offender mediation (Hudson and Galaway, 1996), whereas other publications include community as an essential party involved (McCold, 1996). Adding to this confusion are the variety of new 'appellations' which have emerged, such as 'positive justice', 'social justice', 'relational justice', 'community justice' and the like. I shall stick to the most common denomination which, to my mind, also expresses the core of what is meant – namely, 'restorative justice'.

This diversity is not surprising, given the earlier mentioned variety of influences and philosophical contexts. The concept of restorative justice is even necessarily still flexible, because its development needs controversies and openness for new reflections and reformulations. But if the words 'restorative' and 'justice' have a meaning, it must be possible to find some principles which should be common to all interpretations and experiments which define themselves as 'restorative justice' (Walgrave and Bazemore, 1999).

A Tentative Definition of Restorative Justice

For the purpose of making our own vision clear, Bazemore and I (1999b) compared our perspective with that of a recently much referenced definition. Tony Marshall defined restorative justice as a 'process whereby the parties with a stake in a particular offence come together to resolve collectively how to deal with the aftermath of the offence and its implications for the future' (Marshall, 1996: 37). However, although this definition undoubtedly says much about the constructive and human richness which a restorative justice approach can include, we found it too narrow. First, we believe that the core of restorative justice is more than just a process: as I shall argue, some kinds of sanction can be parts of restorative justice. Second, many restorative justice actions can be undertaken without the 'coming together' of 'the parties with a stake in the particular offence'. We include, for example, several services provided for victims, whether or not an offender is involved. Finally, Marshall's definition does not at all refer to restoration, which is, in our view, essential in restorative justice. Even if the stakeholders in a crime collaborate in a process to a conclusion, that conclusion should be restorative and not, for example, purely treatment-oriented or blaming.

Instead, Bazemore and I see restorative justice as 'every action that is primarily oriented towards doing justice by restoring the harm that has been caused by a crime' (Bazemore and Walgrave, 1999b: 48). In our opinion, this definition provokes the key questions and principal discussion lines concerning restorative justice – namely:

● What is the 'harm caused by a crime'?
● Who (and what) shall we consider as suffering that harm?
● How can that harm be restored?
● What is justice and how can it be done?

The answers to these questions are interrelated.

The harm   A focus on the harm provoked by the offence is the key to understanding restorative justice and to distinguishing it from both the traditional retributive and rehabilitative justice models. This is why we call restorative justice another paradigm.[4] According to the restorative justice paradigm, the problem posed by a crime is to be considered through the harm it has caused, and the primary function of the reaction against it is not to punish, nor to rehabilitate, but to repair or compensate for that harm. According to this paradigm, restorative justice can function in the absence of a known offender: the main goal is to restore the harm, so that persons or agencies can provide support, assistance and compensation to victims, without an offender involved. However, if the offender is known, his or her accountability must be taken seriously and his or her contribution to the restorative action will make it much more restorative.

In principle all kinds of harm are considered, including material losses, physical injuries, psychological consequences, relational troubles and social dysfunctions, in so far as they have been caused by the occurrence of an offence. Retributionists primarily consider the harm to an abstract juridico-moral order, which should be balanced by an equal harm to the offender. Rehabilitationists do not focus on harm but on the offender's needs.

The victim   Who we should consider as suffering the harm is a matter for discussion among proponents of restorative justice. All agree that the injuries and losses inflicted to the actual victim and his or her intimates are at the centre of the restorative action. Most authors also include community into their options, but it is difficult then to define such community and to make the kind of harm that it has suffered more concrete.

Considerable disagreement exists about the question as to whether society should also be considered as a victim. Some fear that recognizing society as a victim will cause a shift back to the retributive situation in which the state has set itself up as the main victim, pushing the actual victim into a subordinate position. Our view is, however, that organized society inevitably has a role to play in the settlement of a crime and it is therefore better to specify that role accurately in order to avoid the feared dominance of the state. One of the most delicate challenges in the restorative justice undertaking is to conceive the role of the state (or government) in such a way that it does not impede the real restorative process, while playing its norm-enforcing role (Van Ness and Strong, 1997).

The restoration   The issue of how restoration can be achieved, poses two sub-questions relating to process and the outcome of that process.

First, the possible reparative outcomes include a wide range of actions of restitution, compensation, reparation, reconciliation and apologies. They may be direct or indirect, concrete or symbolic. Depending on the nature of the victimization under consideration, they may be addressed to the actual victim, his or her intimates, at a community or even at society. Several types of victim restitution or community service seem to be some kind of archetypes of such actions, but creative practitioners are still inventing new forms of restoration of which we cannot think yet.

Second, different processes exist to aim at such restorative outcomes. The most important distinction between them is based on voluntariness. Generally accepted as restorative are the processes of voluntary negotiation and concertation, direct or indirect, between the offender and his or her victim, as individuals or backed by their intimates (victim–offender mediation, restorative group conferences and the like). But a divergence of views exists on the question whether (juridical) procedures and coercion may also lead to restorative sanctions. Some proponents hold a strong view about the voluntariness of restorative justice processes, excluding therefore all reference to pressure and coercion. Later in this chapter, I shall develop arguments to include some coercive juridical procedures under the restorative justice umbrella.

Doing justice   Restorative justice is not only about restoration, it is also about justice. 'Justice' has two meanings here. On the one hand, it refers to a feeling of equity, of being dealt with in a just way, according to a subjective balance of rights and wrongs. Restorative justice then means that it aims at optimal satisfaction of all parties with a stake in the offence. Victims should feel that their victimization has been taken seriously and that the compensation and community support were reasonably in balance with their sufferings and losses. Offenders should feel that they have transgressed the limits of social tolerance and that they are being given the opportunity to make amends for their mistake in a constructive way.

But justice also refers to legality. Restorative justice then means that the restorative process and its outcomes respect the legal safeguards to which all citizens are entitled. Even in the voluntary settlements of the aftermath of an offence, victims and offenders have legal rights to which mediation, for example, is bound. Participation may in no way be imposed, agreements must be accepted and reasonable in relation to the seriousness of the harm and to the accountability and the capacities of the parties. When a coercive procedure is entered, all legal guarantees such as legality, due process and a proportionate maximum of the sanction must be observed. This aspect of justice provokes a debate on the role of the state and its justice system in the restorative justice process, to which I shall return later.

For a Maximalist Option on Restorative Justice

The aforementioned points of debate among restorative justice advocates and researchers is based on a fundamental divergence. Many have turned to restorative justice because of their dissatisfaction with the functioning of the formal criminal justice system, and they rule out any state intervention in what they regard as a purely communitarian process. They observe the enormous benefits of the informal, voluntary settlements in practice and are anxious to preserve these by excluding, as far as possible, any intrusion by formalization and state ruling (Fattah, 1993). Prominent scholars therefore prefer to keep restorative justice as a form of diversion from the criminal justice system, rather than running the risk of losing the benefits of the informal settlement (Marshall, 1996; Dünkel, 1996). Others, however, believe that restorative justice could point to a badly needed, fully-fledged alternative to both the retributive and rehabilitative approaches to crime (Walgrave, 1994; 1995; Bazemore and Umbreit, 1995; Wright, 1996; Van Ness and Strong, 1997; Bazemore and Walgrave 1999a). This option is promoted especially with regard to juvenile justice where restorative justice could help avoid the shift downwards to a renewed 'just deserts' approach.

Those who promote restorative justice as a form of diversion try to withdraw as many cases as possible from the criminal justice system. They develop ways to resolve crime conflicts outside the system by empowering communities to resolve their own crime conflicts in constructive ways and by engaging in convincing experiments that expand the range of restorative justice approaches. They improve methodical skills for achieving these kinds of solutions, train professionals and volunteers in these skills, inform the public about the knowledge and attitudes which are favourable to these kinds of voluntary restorative response to crime and plead for more reserve by the judiciary in using its interventionist power. However, they exclude the justice system as such from their reflections and experiments, on the basis of their lack of belief in the criminal justice system's potential for achieving real justice and peace in the community. In so doing, they leave the cornerstone of the social response to crime with the traditional punitive or rehabilitative approaches.

For many, and I am among those, the diversionist option is not sufficient. The reasons have already been mentioned: first, it would probably select the less serious cases for restorative solutions, whereas it is the victims of the most serious crimes who are most in need of reparation and restoration; and, second, it would leave the existing criminal justice system out of the discussion and fail to offer any alternative to both the retributive and purely rehabilitative systems of reacting to crime. There is a need for a fully-fledged alternative that, in the longer term, should come to replace, rather than complement, existing dominant processes and logics (Walgrave, 1995; Van Ness and Strong, 1997; Bazemore and Walgrave, 1999a).

So long as restorative justice is presented as being only a model of voluntary settlement between victims, offenders and communities, based on free agreements between the parties concerned, it will be condemned to remain some kind of a 'soft ornament' at the margin of the 'hard core' of criminal justice. Successful settlements with serious cases will continue to be interesting curiosities and anecdotal exceptions, without real impact on the fundamental options with regard to criminal justice. Therefore, what is needed is an 'ambitious' or 'maximalist' version of restorative justice theory instead of a restricted one which confines itself to a marginal position within the existing systems of retributive or rehabilitative justice.

Most of the literature on restorative justice is concerned with variations on the mediation theme. In mediation, the restorative aspect speaks for itself. The encounter in the mediating process is often felt as being restorative or, as some say, healing[5] (Van Ness and Strong, 1997: ch. 5). It can lead to apologies, restitution, reparation, compensation, forgiveness, reconciliation and/or reintegration. When the proximate community is involved, the anger, fear and other emotions caused by the offence can directly be observed and sensed. All these phenomena and processes can be observed and controlled.[6]

While the development of such solutions are undoubtedly immensely valuable in the search for constructive responses to offences, it is not correct to consider mediation (in whatever form) as a synonym for restorative justice, as is often done (Hudson and Galaway, 1996; Marshall, 1996; Fattah, 1993), especially not in its maximalist option.

Theoretically, the maximalist restorative justice option should provide a restorative response to all types of crime, and this response should satisfy, as far as possible, all kinds of problem and need caused by the occurrence of the crime. Mediation has two shortcomings here. First, it basically reduces the settlement of a crime to an interaction between the victim and the offender (and their intimates), neglecting the unrest and other needs within the broader collectivity.[7] Second, it excludes the use of force, leaving all offences that cannot be voluntarily settled outside the restorative approach.

This highlights two basic questions for the maximalist approach to restorative justice. First, does the settlement of the consequences of a crime involve a third, more collective party, besides the individual victim and the offender (and their immediate social environments) and how can this third party be put into operation? Second, can restorative justice be applied in cases where voluntary participation is reached insufficiently and how can this be done?

In Search of the Third Party: Its Definition and Function

Not all proponents of restorative justice are convinced that the response to an offence should involve also a third, collective party. Some believe that the victims and their intimates are in the best position to speak for the community as well (Fattah, 1993). Reintroducing the third party separately, it is argued, would be detrimental to the actual victim (Harland and Rosen, 1990).

The Need to Consider a Collective Third Party

The third party is nevertheless unavoidable in a fully-fledged restorative justice system, since confining restorative justice to victim–offender-centred exchanges would reduce the offence to a conflict between just two parties, excluding the community or society, as a separate party, from the conflict settlement. In juridical terms, restorative justice would turn into a reformulation of the civil law of torts (Barnett and Hagel, 1977). Civil law aims at settling a conflict between two (groups of) citizens. It is reactive, acting only in response to a complaint. If no complaint is made, civil justice will not be activated.

Restorative justice, on the contrary, is based on a reformulation of offences now falling under criminal law. Criminal law is in principle proactive: it can initiate proceedings itself, even in the absence of a complaining victim. In practice, criminal justice acts proactively only to a small degree, but this difference in principle shows that other problems are implicated here. It is not just the victim and offender, but also the broader social or societal group who are concerned by the wrongdoing (Bussman, 1992). This means that there are therefore at least three parties involved and that a fully-fledged restorative response to offending should in principle include all three.

How is this third, collective party then involved in a restorative justice approach? In the traditional retributive system, the involvement is evident, inasmuch as it is argued that public law and order are violated by a transgression and should be rebalanced by a proportionate public reaction against the perpetrator. But restorative justice speaks in terms of harm and suffering. What is the harm suffered by the collectivity that does not coincide with the injuries to the actual victim? The literature is not very certain. Some quote 'the impact of the offence on the rights of citizens or on society in general' (Thorvaldson, 1990: 27); others point to the 'loss of public safety, damage to community values and the disruption, caused by crime'(Van Ness, 1990: 9) or 'physical, emotional or economic harm' (Gehm, 1992: 548). Most public losses are indirect and abstract. Despite the obviousness that the 'collectivity' suffers harm by the occurrence of crime, it is difficult to render this concrete.

Maybe the problem can partly be resolved by reversing the question: what would happen if the community and/or society did not intervene after the occurrence of an offence? Besides the possible material damages, the community would probably suffer from a loss of peace in its midst. The victim and his or her supporters (family and peers) would not accept what had been done to them and they might try to 'make things even'. Acts of revenge would risk escalating into a kind of vendetta, dragging down the community as a whole. The community would lose peace and be dominated by fear of crime which in turn would affect the general quality of life through a loss of solidarity and mutual respect. Common values might fade away. What is at stake here is more than just the individual victim's losses. An offence is a threat to the peace and quality of life in a community, which it will lose if nothing happens.

But the state has much to lose too. If institutionalized society does not intervene adequately against crime, the public will lose its belief in public rules and in the authorities' power to preserve order and justice in social life. People would not feel assured of their 'dominion', would see each other as rivals and the government as a threat. Society would collapse or would deteriorate into a tyranny. Such societies 'would lose their freedom' (Braithwaite, 1989: 186). What is at stake for all citizens in a crime is their dominion as a set of rights and freedoms, which is guaranteed by the state and its institutions.

Consequently, public losses as a result of a crime threaten the peace and general quality of social life and the dominion of all citizens. They have to be considered separately from the injuries to the individual victim, but they may not compete with them.[8] This is clearly demonstrated by the public unrest caused by some crimes, because of their seriousness or their repetition. The general public is shocked by, or indignant about, some crimes, and social life in general is disturbed by the repetitive occurrence of street crime, proving that the impact of crime transcends the concrete victimization and indicating that more needs to be done than merely responding to the concrete victims' needs.

A pragmatic argument is that reducing the social response to a victim–offender settlement would in fact turn much crime into a sort of gamble. Stealing, for example, would be a very interesting undertaking: 'If I steal a car, and I am caught, I can mediate with the victim and compensate him or her for the car. Tomorrow, I can try again; if I am lucky enough not to be caught, I'll have a car.'

Clearly, the harm caused by many offences goes beyond the actual victims' suffering and losses and the social reaction after the occurrence of an offence cannot be limited to caring for the victims (even if this is crucial). It should also include the collectivity as a third, separate party.

How to Define this Third Party?

Restorative justice commentators often include the 'community', and not the state, as a party in the restorative settlement of an offence. However, its definition is very vague and often contradictory in the various theories and practices. As long as restorative justice practice is confined to local and provisional experiments, one can accept that some creative *flou artistique* persists. But the ambition to develop restorative justice into the predominant way in which official dealings with crime are structured, provokes the need for formalization and rule setting. We shall have to come to grips with relations between the parties, agencies and processes of restorative justice, on the one hand, and the formal society and its institutions, on the other.

Building on communities for finding constructive responses to crime presupposes that a community really exists, and this is not self-evident (Crawford, 1995). In modern Western societies, the community as a set of 'dense networks of individual interdependencies with strong cultural commitments to mutuality of obligations' (Braithwaite, 1989: 85), hardly remains, especially in cities (Braithwaite, 1993; Crawford, 1996). 'How can we then thrust towards neighbourhoods a task that presupposes they are highly alive?' (Christie, 1977: 12). Christie himself admitted in 1977 that he only had weak arguments against this sceptical question, and there is no reason to believe that things have changed positively since then.

Instead, the victim and the offender are mostly involved in several networks of interdependencies, of which some surpass territorial boundaries – families, school, work, peer groups, sports clubs, political associations, internet lists (Braithwaite, 1993; McCold, 1996). An employee who is temporarily incapable of work as a consequence of a violent assault possibly entails many secondary victims. His family suffers emotional troubles and financial consequences, his employer sustains economic losses, the insurance company has to make disbursement, his snooker partners have to find someone else, and his neighbours suffer feelings of insecurity. It is unclear how a generic concept such as 'the community' can cover all this.[9]

The all-too-easy reference to 'the community' sometimes seems to be based on a kind of *fata morgana*, a mirage of what may exist somewhere deep in our memories, but which we cannot really make concrete: 'Community ... has become ... the antidote to the fin de siècle crisis of modernity' (Crawford, 1997: 148).

A second problem here is that of representation. Even if the concept of community(ies) is defined satisfactorily in some contexts, it will have to be decided who should represent that community and how their suitability is to be determined. In most cases the disorganized or morally not 'right-minded' people will not be considered as acceptable for community representation in a restorative settlement of a crime (Crawford, 1997). For example, suppose the local gang were to set itself up as the representative of the community of young people to deal with locally committed offences? Thus there is a need to indicate a power that will decide which persons and/or groups are acceptable to represent the community or communities concerned. Criteria and sound procedures need to be designed. Will the mediator be the representative of the 'healing community', as is mostly the case in victim–offender mediation (Umbreit, 1994)? Will the family and other intimates of the victim and the offender play the role of the 'reintegrative shaming' community (Braithwaite and Mugford, 1994)? Will a board of citizens represent the 'reparative sanctioning' community (Silkinson and Broderick, 1998)? Will that depend on the nature of the conflict (McCold, 1996)? Which characteristics of the conflict will then decide on the kind of community to be involved in the restorative process?

All this scepticism is not to reject communitarianism. Communitarianism is first of all a programme, not an existing situation. Striving for the revival of supportive communities does not mean that we can now already build on them to develop a generalized systemic alternative in dealing with the aftermath of an offence. The serious criticisms of the judicial systems and their abolitionist consequences of the 1970s have sometimes tended to turn the concept of the community into a mythical belief, without sufficient attention to the possible political, conservationist, moralizing lapses of its use (van Swaaningen, 1997; Crawford, 1997).

Communities cannot merely be constructed in opposition to formal societies. Also in restorative justice, one has to look for a constructive relation between the community, or communities, as the 'life-world' – the 'living social body' with its ample resources of relationships, shared emotions, commitments, bonds and supports – on the one hand, and the society, the system(s), as the formal organization with its institutions, rules and powers, on the other. The state and its systems are not just the Leviathan. They are also protectors of rights and legally defined guarantees (van Swaaningen, 1997), or dominions (Braithwaite and Pettit, 1990).

In a constitutional democracy the state and its government should be nothing other than the formalized institutionalization of the community or the community of communities. As Braithwaite and Pettit (1990) advance, the 'good' state and its government should safeguard the 'dominion' of the citizens, by which they mean the whole range of societally guaranteed rights and freedom that all citizens enjoy. Governments have to set and enforce the rules which ground peoples' 'dominion' and which should form the frame for developing prosperous communities. Both the community and government have complementary missions in dealing with the aftermath of an offence (Van Ness, 1996; Van Ness and Strong, 1997). The community, aiming at peace in its midst, can offer healing to the victim and rehabilitation to the offender. The government, oriented towards order in society, brings support to redress the victim and guarantees fairness to the offender. Together, community's peace and society's order result in safety.

Of course, this is theory. The power of the state and its institutions has overruled communities. Through its socioeconomic, urbanization and criminal policies the state has contributed to their decline. In criminal policies the role of communities has been neglected, so that attention to making or keeping the peace has diminished dramatically. Instead, governments have focused only on preserving public order, and have done so in a way that has enhanced conflict within communities or has even threatened community life itself.

However, excluding the formal state from dealing with crime, would lead us to a kind of local justice, which constitutes 'a dangerous path' (Crawford, 1997: 291). Rather, 'decentralised local autonomy which encourages bottom-up approaches to policy-making needs to be bounded by principled and normative constraints of social, rather than local, justice' (Crawford, 1997: 289). We have to rethink and reformulate the relationship between the formal state and the communities, instead of rejecting it. In the Declaration of Leuven (1997), the role of the state has been delimited as follows:

The role of public authorities in the reaction to an offence needs to be limited to:
– contributing to the conditions for restorative responses to crime;

- safeguarding the correctness of procedures and the respect for individual legal rights;
- imposing judicial coercion, in situations where voluntary restorative actions do not succeed and a response to the crime is considered to be necessary;
- organising judicial procedures in situations where the crime and the public reactions to it are of such a nature that a purely informal voluntary regulation appears insufficient. (Ibid.: Proposition 3)

This proposition, first of all, argues that government should leave space to communities and empower them to solve constructively the aftermath of offences. The criminal justice system should accept a subsidiary role, secondary to the responses given in the community. Communal initiatives to respond to local crime should be supported, if they meet certain conditions, but the authorities should guarantee respect for the individual legal rights of the victim and the suspect or offender as well. Communities have to be submitted to a certain degree of control which would be strictly concentrated on ensuring that nobody is forced to cooperate in a restorative process at the communal level, that the process leaves space for free discussion and that its outcome does not exceed a proportionate maximum.

If voluntary restorative actions within a community do not succeed and a response to the crime is nevertheless considered to be necessary, coercion may be necessary. In a constitutional state public coercive intervention is acceptable only if it is carried out by a judicial authority, which is itself subject to legal and procedural rules. As the local communities are, in many cases, rather weak, there will often be a prominent need to call upon the judicial system.

The impact of some crimes can transcend the local community in which they have been committed, in which case, an informal voluntary regulation within the local community would be insufficient. Here also, judicial coercion and procedures are needed to keep the peace in communities and order in society.

A crucial question now is whether public authorities' reactions to an offence in coercive and non-voluntary circumstances, as identified in the third and fourth situations outlined in Proposition 3 of the Declaration of Leuven (cited above), constitute the end of the restorative responses to crime.

Restoring Public Losses: Community Service

Public action in itself may contribute to the restoration of public losses since, by this action, citizens are assured that their dominion is taken seriously, which can partly restore feelings of safety and order.

If the offender is arrested, he or she should also primarily act to reduce or remove the threat to peace in the community and to the dominion of all citizens. The offender should engage in acts of restoration, or can show repentance and express his or her willingness to respect the rules and peace in the community. The offender can also make the restoration more concrete and agree to make restitution to the actual victim or undertake community service.

Community service is commonly defined as 'unpaid work done by the offender for the benefit of a community or its institutions meant as a compensation for the harm caused by an offence to that community'. The community has been victimized by the loss of peace and of the quality of life, citizens are threatened in their dominion and this may be compensated by community service. The compensation may only have a symbolic aspect, but it is no less important for that. The community is restored through the material results of the service rendered and through the peace restoring gesture of the offender. Dominions are restored because the response to the intrusion into the dominion has been supported, and possibly even organized, by government. Government has taken the dominions seriously, which is reassuring for citizens.

The option for including community service in the restorative justice responses to an offence is not without problems.

First, accepting community service as a restorative response towards community, or even society, could again entail too much attention to the restorative claims from societal institutions to the detriment of the actual victim's needs (Harland and Rosen, 1990). This has to be avoided by searching for a balanced restorative approach, with balanced attention to the needs of the victim, the community and the offender as well (Bazemore and Maloney, 1994). What has to be done here is to clarify accurately 'the nature and extent of the harm done to society at large, as well as the most appropriate means for the offender to repair that harm' (Van Ness and Strong, 1997: 55).

Much of the resistance against including community service in the restorative frame is based on its use in non-restorative contexts, as illustrated in the Table 12.1.

Some practices use community service as a punishment. The objective is not to restore a harm by fulfilling a compensating service, but to inflict a suffering by imposing an unpleasant, and even degrading, task. The offender must feel pain, it is argued, in order to be deterred from re-offending and to satisfy the victim's feelings of revenge (Higgins and Snyder, 1996). Rather than a restorative response, this is a form of retributive forced labour. In most countries where rehabilitation is predominant in juvenile justice systems, community service is mostly used as a method of re-education

Table 12.1   Community service in different judicial settings

	Punitive	Rehabilitative	Restorative
Objective	Deterrence	Adequate treatment	Reasonable restoration
Content	Painful for offenders	Adapted to the needs of offenders	Symbolic for harm to community
Duration depends on ...	Seriousness of crime	Treatment needs	Seriousness of harm
Evaluation according to ...	Just desert	Conforming behaviour	Peace in community

(Geudens, 1996) and is primarily intended to influence the offender's attitudes, competencies and social networks. This does, in fact, make it a form of treatment, but it is not focused on restoring harm to victims or to community or society. On the contrary, the victims' or community's losses are often used as tools in the re-education programme. Quite understandably, many restorative justice advocates are hesitant, or even reluctant, to accept the incorporation of such responses into the restorative concept.

However, community service can also be used restoratively, if it is meant to compensate for harm, restore peace in the community and contribute to feelings of safety in society. The explicit motivation for the service, the content and duration of the service and the way in which it is coached will now turn around the harm and its restoration, including the reintegration of the offender, as this is important for restoring peace in the community.

Therefore, the necessary inclusion of community service in the restorative justice approach needs to be guided by an accurate description of how restorative community service could, and should, be carried out, a strict setting of the conditions for restorative community service in practice and by a great sensitivity to possible non-restorative implementations of community service. After all, the potential for restorative justice to become a fully-fledged systemic alternative depends on the possible inclusion of ways to restore the harm to community and society (Walgrave and Geudens, 1996).

In a fully-fledged restorative paradigm for responding to crime, community service is the necessary counterpart, with regard to the community, of what restitution is, with regard to the actual victim. Both have in common:

1 a definition of crime as an injury to victims (concrete and societal). This is quite a different definition from the retributive definition of crime, which considers it as a transgression of a general juridical–ethical rule;
2 an intervention primarily oriented towards restoration of that injury, which is unlike the 'constitutionalized revenge' to which the retributive response is oriented and also different from the treatment aims of the rehabilitative approach;
3 the acceptance of the offender's accountability and his or her active and direct involvement in the restorative action. The retributive or rehabilitative responses reduce the offender to a passive object of retribution or treatment; and
4 the judicial framework, common to both intervention models. This may be surprising in reference to the principle of subsidiarity, which gives priority to voluntary settlements of crime in the community, without judicial intervention. But even in cases of victim–offender mediation, the judicial background is necessary. It offers the framework for designing and guaranteeing the legal rights of the victim and the offender. Moreover, the very fact that there is an exit into judicial processing of the crime leads to a greater certainty that the non-judicial agreements are based on genuinely voluntary commitments by the parties involved. If this judicial warrant is not available, the restorative responses may go off the rails towards outcomes that are not 'just' at all.

Restorative Coercion

Most of the literature on restorative justice is on voluntary deliberations, reintegrative shaming, exchanging gestures of re-acceptance, respect and willingness to re-enter the community in a constructive way, leading to reparation, reconciliation, and/or reintegration. However, even if the voluntary restorative response to crime broadens its range of applicability, it will continue to have its limits. In many cases, force will have to be used, and that raises the need for a system that can use coercion, according to due process, to protect citizens from offenders and from abuse of authority as well (Marshall, 1996). That is why 'diversionists' maintain the criminal justice system in their vision, whereas maximalists explore the possibilities for developing a restorative coercive justice system.

Can Restorative Actions be Enforced?

The apparent non-feasibility of a restorative process does not mean that it is impossible to impose restorative sanctions, as is illustrated in the following examples:

1   The victim and/or the local community are not prepared to conclude a reasonable restorative settlement, while the offender himself is willing to do so. In such cases, it would not be unfair to subject the offender to the traditional retributive system. The offender should be offered the opportunity to accomplish a restorative action. Because the victim or the community are absent from the negotiation, a settlement should be made with a judicial authority. As mediation cannot be forced, the restorative action can consist of making formal restitution, doing work for the benefit of a victims' fund or in doing community service.

2   The offender himself may refuse to accomplish a reasonable restorative action. As the victim and the community are not able to intervene coercively, it is up to the judicial institution to impose, possibly, a sanction. The sanction can be of a restorative kind: the offender can be forced to make restitution, to work for the benefit of a victims' fund or to do community service.

3   Some offences are so serious that they transcend the impact on local communities. Here, a coercive public intervention and sanction by the formal justice system may be considered necessary, possibly even on top of the settlement with the actual victims and the community. In this case, the restorative aspect of public judicial intervention is not entirely lost. First, space can be left for initiatives for voluntary restorative settlements, parallel with the judicial intervention. Second, the content of the imposed sanction can be restorative. As with the earlier two previous examples, the sanction can be to make restitution, to do work for the benefit of a victims' fund and/or to do a community service. If concerns for security necessitate it, the offender could be incapacitated through a forced stay in a closed facility, but restorative actions should be attempted from within that facility.

Of course, such coercive interventions do not involve the complete potentials of the restorative paradigm, nor does it achieve its most constructive purposes. In coercive restorative sanctions there is no encounter, participation is considerably reduced, reintegration is unsure and reparation is only elementary (Van Ness and Strong, 1997). There are, however, several reasons for favouring coercive restorative sanctions over the forced retributive or rehabilitative interventions.

First, the mere fact that something is actually done for the victims and for the community is more beneficial than the retributive response, criticized by Martin Wright as 'balancing the harm done by the offender with further harm inflicted on the offender. That only adds to the total amount of harm in the world' (Wright, 1992: 525).

Second, there is a reintegrative advantage. Even if the offender does not freely accept carrying out a restorative action, he or she may, in the longer term, understand the sanction in a constructive way, and the chances of him or her being re-accepted by the community are greater than after a retributive action. This also seems to be true in regard to rehabilitative measures, as demonstrated by the results of research on the impact of restorative sanctions on the offender (Walgrave and Geudens, 1997; Schiff, 1999). Moreover, conducting restorative sanctions within the community is also educational for the community itself in that the community has the opportunity to observe young offenders doing constructive services, which may contribute to the deconstruction of stereotyped images and enhance the chances for reintegration.

Finally, it gives more coherence in principles. The option of restorative justice consequentially is extended. Even if individual persons (victims or offenders) or communities do not adhere to the constructive character of the restorative response, the state should have the mission to stick to the principle and to act, as far as possible, with it.

Coercive Restorative Sanctions and Legal Rules

The acceptance of force in the imposition of restorative actions entails the necessity for legal safeguards. There is no longer any question of an agreed compensation arrangement as the result of mediation or another form of deliberation. Since imposed restitution or community service involve a restriction of freedom, the accountability for the offence and the extent of the restriction of freedom must be determined. This can only be done according to legal safeguards: formal rules must be established and their observation must be controlled carefully. This is especially true in relation to community service, where direct reparation has been removed, hence making the link between the offence and the sanctions more tenuous and more difficult to perceive. In general, the literature concerning restorative experiments in a judicial context pays little attention to this issue.[10]

According to the republican theory of criminal justice (Braithwaite and Pettit, 1990), the fundamental function of criminal justice is to protect and promote the 'dominion' (meaning the whole range of societally guaranteed rights and freedoms for all citizens) of all the parties involved (victims, offenders and other citizens). The restorative orientation appears to fit into this

conception. The recognition and restoration of victims' and citizens' dominion are expressed in the material reparation and psychological restoration
aimed at through apologies, restitution or compensation to the victim and
through the symbolic or (partly) material reparation through community service. Braithwaite and Pettit also prefer 'punishments' which include a restorative option (ibid.: 127).[11] If society plays a role in this process, this
simultaneously reaffirms society as an ordered community, secure in its rights.

In the republican theory of criminal justice no restriction of freedom is
self-evident, but must be positively justified by the demonstrable gains in
terms of dominion for those involved. This leads to the principle of 'parsimony in punishment':

> The state should use those legislative, enforcement and sentencing options which
> are minimally interventionist until the evidence is clear that more intrusive
> practices are required to increase dominion. More than that, the state should
> actively search for alternative ways of promoting dominion to such intervention-
> ist policies as criminal punishment. (Ibid.: 79–80)

Accordingly, restorative justice gives priority to extrajudicial solutions to
crime conflicts and seeks 'alternative ways of promoting dominion' into the
community. But parsimony does not mean exclusion. The theory, therefore,
also accepts that sanctions can be imposed.

The coercion that is exercised constitutes an infringement of the citizen's
dominion and that must only take place under strict and controllable conditions. The judicial authorities are bound by 'the recognition of uncontroversial criminal justice rights' and must demonstrate that they 'take the rights
seriously' (ibid.: 75). The formalization of proceedings is most important
for achieving this. 'Denunciation is a central justification for the criminal
justice system' and this must be done publicly so that it can send 'an
important reprobative message to the community' (ibid.: 177). Public response to the infringement of a norm demonstrates that the defence of
dominion is taken seriously, which may promote feelings of security and the
belief that the authorities will uphold this. Moreover, the public character of
the judicial proceedings offers opportunities for controlling the procedure
itself, submitting the social controllers themselves to public control, which
is necessary for counterbalancing power relations.

Essential for a good criminal justice system is that it is 'satiable'. This
requirement is met by the principle of proportionality, which places emphasis on the relationship between the seriousness of the crime and the upper
limit of permissible state intervention. In mediation the very existence of an
agreement suggests that the parties involved feel that the contents of the
agreement to be reasonably proportional.

However, this is no longer the case when a restitution or a community service are imposed. There is no question here of a negotiated outcome, and the link between the offence and the demanded compensation is often less direct. This is one of the most delicate issues in the maximalist restorative justice undertaking. Theoretically, proportionality can be constructed into the restorative justice frame, but restorative proportionality deviates significantly from traditional criminal proportionality (Walgrave and Geudens, 1996). There is no point in determining a 'just desert' on the basis of a retributive link between the moral–juridical severity of the offence and the degree of punishment that would restore the moral balance (von Hirsch, 1993). Instead, a 'correct restoration' is required here, to be determined on the basis of a link between the seriousness of the material, relational and social harm caused by the offence and the degree of restorative effort imposed on the offender. Currently, there is a lack of experience, tradition, comparison and reflection that could produce, in the longer term, a general framework in which the gravity of public losses can be estimated and reasonable forms and amounts of compensation could be indicated.

Concluding Remarks

As yet, restorative justice is far from being a fully completed set of practices based on a well defined theory of justice. Rather, it is a movement, as well as a field, of experimentation and research, based on an intuitive ideal of justice in an ideal society. It is a programme that orients theoretical and ethical reflection, experimentation and empirical research (Walgrave and Bazemore, 1999).

The Research Agenda

The concept and theory of restorative justice need to be explored further. The search is for a commonly acceptable 'core' of a normative theory about restorative justice that would offer a broad framework with which to pull together, encircle and compare existing practices. It would also offer a framework for resistance against all-too-easy misuses of originally restorative schedules into the retributive or rehabilitative contexts, wherein experiments now have to take place.

The juridical status of the restorative justice practice has to be investigated. The ambition, to develop restorative justice into a systemic alternative, needs reflection on the juridical and societal status of its implementation. Restorative justice, including its communitarian fundamentals, has to be prepared to take its place in the societal organization and to include the basic principles of a constitutional democratic state. Restorative justice practitioners and researchers have to cope with the tension between human emotional and relational processes and the formal rules which hold essential guarantees against misuses of power. They must not repress this tension but work within it, in order to prevent the restorative justice practices from deteriorating into being highly unjust.

Empirical research must further check whether restorative justice practices meet their expectations for victims, communities and offenders. According to the literature, victims should be better off psychologically and they enjoy better reparation than in a traditional procedure. Restorative processes should lead to more constructive conflict resolution and peace in neighbourhoods and other communities. Offenders are expected to accept more easily restorative sanctions and to reintegrate better after such sanctions. The general public should be willing to accept restorative interventions more readily than is usually assumed. Whether all these promises are kept in practice remains to be proved. Much empirical data exists, but there is still a great deal to do. Despite many methodological problems, linked with evaluative research, high-quality research should be conducted to gather empirical data on the processes and outcomes of restorative interventions.

The limits of restorative justice are to be explored. Propagating it as the dominant model in reacting against crime does not mean that it will be the only one. This is, in fact, also the case for the retributive and the rehabilitative responses. At present, the retributive model is clearly dominant, but most societies do accept that simple retribution cannot be applied to juveniles or the insane. The rehabilitative approach is dominant in juvenile justice, but this system is limited by the demands for correct legal safeguards and by security reasons. Accordingly, we have to find the limits of a restorative approach. At first glance, one can think of four possible limits – crime seriousness, public security, coercivity and need for rehabilitation – but none of these seems to be decisive in excluding possible restorative justice responses (Walgrave, 1994).

The applicability of restorative justice is also limited, of course, by the skills of those who implement it in the field. As practice with mediation and community service is relatively recent, methodologies are still developing (see Umbreit, 1994). It can be expected that as methodological skills increase, fieldworkers will be able to deal with more difficult cases, which could extend the limits of restorative justice.

The restorative justice movement aims at social change, and this necessitates a strategy for enhancing its acceptability (see also Van Ness and Strong, 1997).

Victim Perspective, Restorative Justice and the Criminal Justice System

The question of whether a victim perspective should be integrated into the criminal justice system must be answered from a strategic point of view. There is a paradox here: on the one hand, there is a need for concrete experiments with victim work in contact with the criminal justice system, but, on the other hand, too close cooperation could become a major threat to the restorative justice paradigm that underpins this work.

Crucial experiences have been built up thanks to the creativity of practitioners and the open minds of many criminal justice officers. Exemplary local partnerships, built on personal relations and mutual trust between social workers and criminal justice officers, have given rise to initiatives which have been directional in the development of victim work specifically, and of restorative justice ideas in general. This should be continued and extended as much as possible.

A good example is the 'Mediation for redress' experiment in Leuven (Peters and Aertsen, 1995). This experiment is not about diversion, because it deals with cases which are being prosecuted. Based on a close cooperation with the local public prosecutor, as a result of which the mediation team has significant influence on the selection process, it succeeds in attracting serious cases and successfully mediating in most of them (Aertsen and Peters, 1998). Thanks to its strong basis in restorative justice theory, the experiment is less vulnerable to incorporation into the system as merely a technique. Positive results, amongst others, are: the growing confidence of local criminal justice officers in a restorative approach; the level of interest of external justice and political authorities in the experiment; further development of adequate methodologies for guiding mediation processes; and the deeper and more balanced scientific understanding of the restorative potentials and risks. However, the basic purpose of the experiment is to reorientate the criminal justice system itself towards a restorative direction, and it is very questionable whether this is realistic. Experiments such as this may serve as a leverage in the strategy for changing the criminal justice system, but only if it is supported and oriented by a platform outside the criminal justice system where the broader theoretical basis of restorative justice is continually being developed.

If not, it would simply be integrated as a part of the criminal justice system itself, and then a major threat arises. The system is highly hierarchic, with many levels between the top and the fieldworkers, strict role definitions and internal sanctions. The distance from the living field is great, so that changes in real needs, problems, possibilities and approaches only reach the top in a filtered way. Hierarchy principally functions as the guard of conservative ideology within the organization. It controls the compliance with rules and seeks to confirm its internal power.

The closer the cooperation, the greater the loss of autonomy. In cooperation, part of the autonomous decision-making power is handed over to a consultative body, composed of the partners (Meijlaers, 1992). To give up a part of its autonomy and power is formally impossible for the criminal justice system, which is why whatever close partnerships exist with the criminal justice system, they will always operate to the detriment of the cooperating agency (the restorative justice agency, the welfare agency or others).

When the restorative model seems to be really successful, the system tries to incorporate it. Restorative justice then runs the risk of being 'domesticated' into a simple technique. In rehabilitative juvenile justice systems, processes of mediation and outcomes such as restitution or community service are used in a rehabilitative perspective, adapting these schemes uniquely to the re-educative needs of the offender, while neglecting victims' justified claims for restoration and possible opportunities for reconciliation (Dongier and Van Doosselaere, 1992; Geudens, 1996). But restitution and community service are also often misused as additional punishments (Dünkel, 1990). Community services are selected because of their painfulness and/or humiliating character (Higgins and Snyder, 1996). Obligation for restitution is maximized and added to a punishment. Such actions are to be understood fully in the retributive tradition, trying to respond to the wrongdoing by inflicting harm on the wrongdoer. In other practices, mediation is preserved for mild offences that would, in any case, not have given rise to judicial consequences. This net-widening is not bad *per se* – as it offers more victims the opportunity of restoration – but it has no impact on the system. On the contrary, it unburdens the traditional system and thus contributes to the comfort of that system.

In fact, one of the most serious problems for the future of restorative justice is the enthusiasm with which police officers, magistrates and judicial social workers insert mediation and community service as simple techniques into their daily practices of punitive or rehabilitative work. A victim perspective should not be integrated, as such, into the criminal justice system. It needs the support of the broader restorative justice paradigm and theory to be able to preserve its renewing appeal. It has to mature within the restorative justice context in order to form, in the longer term, a fully-fledged alternative to the criminal justice system, instead of being absorbed immediately by that very system.

Notes

1   There is a much justified criticism on the denomination of that law, as it is clear that some of the conditions to be dismissed have nothing to do with mediation.

2   Even the rational choice perspective in aetiologic criminology has to refer to non-rational backgrounds and determinants to explain the differences among people in the choice for committing an offence or not, given the same opportunities to do so (Cornish and Clarke, 1986).

3   Exaggerated though the celebrated 'nothing works' claim may be, it is clear that reform of the offender cannot be the primary purpose of criminal law.

4   Kuhn's definition of a paradigm is about scientific problems (Kuhn, 1962), but we think that we can transpose the concept here to problems in policy and practice, because restorative justice offers another basic approach to the definition of the problems posed by a crime and to the way in which they have to be resolved.

5   The word 'healing' is increasingly being used to indicate what the ideal outcome of a restorative justice process would be (see, for example, Van Ness and Strong, 1997). In my opinion, this is going too far. Healing refers to a medical concept of treating illness. It would easily lead to some kind of therapeutic sessions, which have, in my mind, no place in a justice process. That is not to say that therapeutic interventions for victims (and offenders) should be excluded, but they have to take place in another circuit.

6   Historically, in fact, this kind of regulation dominated the dealing with the aftermath of the offence. It is only later that the state gradually assumed the role of primary victim, pushing aside the interests of the individual victims (Schafer, 1977; Weitekamp, 1999).

7   One could speak of community, or network, or society, or other groupings. I provisionally use the more neutral word 'collectivity' to indicate that the conflict caused by a crime may transcend the two directly involved parties, the indicated victim and the known offender.

8   The damage to society caused by certain currently criminalized behaviour is open to doubt. From the restorative point of view, this would be a reason to withdraw them from the criminal justice system and to possibly have them settled under civil law.

9   Referral to the concept of 'communities of care' (Braithwaite and Daly, 1994) is no solution to the problem of formalizing the community as the 'third party'. This would leave it to the victim and the offender themselves to 'compose' their community of care for the mediation process, as is mostly the case in the family group conferences (Braithwaite and Mugford, 1994). Such 'communities of care' are primarily extensions of the interests of the victim and the offender. They are not the 'third party' we are considering here.

10   In a review of 28 published and analysed experiments in ten different countries in the USA, Europe and New Zealand, only very little comment explicitly on the subject of legal safeguards was identified (Walgrave and Geudens, 1996).

11   There are some problems with the term 'punishment'. A punishment strictly means a wilful infliction of suffering as a reaction to an undesirable behaviour. In an imposed restorative action the painfulness is not deliberately inflicted, but may be a consequence of the restriction of freedom (Wright, 1992). Therefore, an imposed restorative action is not 'punishment' in the strict sense of the word. In using the term 'punishment', Braithwaite and Pettit (1990) probably mean 'restriction of freedom as a response to an offence', which mostly will be unpleasant.

References

Aertsen, I. and Peters, T. (1998), 'Mediation and Restorative Justice in Belgium', *European Journal on Criminal Policy and Research*, **6**(4), 507–25.

Barnett, R. and Hagel, J. (1977), *Assessing the Criminal: Restitution, Retribution and the Legal Process*, Cambridge, MA: Ballinger.

Bazemore, G. and Maloney, D. (1994), 'Rehabilitating Community Service: Toward Restorative Service Sanctions in a Balanced Justice System', *Federal Probation*, **58**(1), 24–35.

Bazemore, G. and Umbreit, M. (1995), 'Rethinking the Sanctioning Function in Juvenile Court: Retributive or Restorative Responses to Youth Crime', *Crime and Delinquency*, **41**, 296–316.

Bazemore, G. and Walgrave, L. (1999a) (eds), *Restorative Juvenile Justice: Repairing the Harm of Youth Crime*, Monsey, Criminal Justice Press.

Bazemore, G. and Walgrave L. (1999b), 'In Search of Fundamentals and an Outline for Systemic Reform', in G. Bazemore and L. Walgrave (eds), *Restorative Juvenile Justice: Repairing the Harm of Youth Crime*, Monsey: Criminal Justice Press, 45–74.

Bonafé-Schmitt, J.P. (1992), *La Médiation: Une Justice Douce*, Paris: Syros-Alternatives.

Braithwaite, J. (1989), *Crime, Shame and Reintegration*, Cambridge: Cambridge University Press.

Braithwaite, J. (1993), 'Shame and Modernity', *British Journal of Criminology*, **33**(1), 1–18.

Braithwaite, J. and Daly, K. (1994), 'Masculinities, Violence and Communitarian Control', in T. Newburn and E. Stanko (eds), *Just Boys Doing Business? Men, Masculinities and Crime*, London: Routledge, 189–213.

Braithwaite, J. and Mugford, S. (1994), 'Conditions of Successful Reintegration Ceremonies: Dealing with Juvenile Offenders', *British Journal of Criminology*, **34**(2), 139–71.

Braithwaite, J. and Pettit, P. (1990), *Not Just Deserts: A Republican Theory of Criminal Justice*, Oxford: Oxford University Press.

Bussman, K. (1992), 'Morality, Symbolism and Criminal Law: Chances and Limits of Mediation Programs', in H. Messmer and H.U. Otto (eds), *Restorative Justice on Trial: Pitfalls and Potentials of Victim-Offender Mediation. International Research Perspectives*, Dordrecht: Kluwer Academic Publishers, 317–26.

Christie, N. (1977), 'Conflicts as Property', *British Journal of Criminology*, **17**(1), 1–15.

Cornish, D. and Clarke, R. (1986), 'Introduction', in D. Cornish and R. Clarke (eds), *The Reasoning Criminal. Rational Choice Perspectives on Offending*, New York: Springer, 1–16.

Corrado, R. and Griffiths, K.T. (1999), 'Implementing Restorative Youth Justice: A Case Study in Community Justice and the Dynamics of Reform', in G. Bazemore and L. Walgrave (eds), *Restorative Juvenile Justice: Repairing the Harm of Youth Crime*, Monsey: Criminal Justice Press, 237–61.

Crawford, A. (1995), 'Appeals to Community and Crime Prevention', *Crime, Law and Social Change*, **22**, 97–126.

Crawford, A. (1996), 'The Spirit of Community: Rights, Responsibilities and the Communitarian Agenda', *Journal of Law and Society*, **23**(2), 247–62.

Crawford, A. (1997), *The Local Governance of Crime: Appeals to Community and Partnerships*, Oxford: Clarendon Press.

Declaration of Leuven (1997), 'On the Advisability of Promoting the Restorative Approach to Juvenile Crime', *European Journal of Criminal Policy and Research* **5**(4), 118–22 and *European Journal of Crime, Criminal Law and Criminal Justice* **6**(1), 421–25.

Dongier, S. and Van Doosselaere, D. (1992), 'Approaching Mediation in Juvenile Court: Rationale and Methodological Aspects', in H. Messmer and H.U. Otto (eds), *Restorative Justice on Trial: Pitfalls and Potentials of Victim–Offender Mediation. International Research Perspectives*, Dordrecht: Kluwer Academic Publishers, 501–11.

Dünkel, F. (1990), 'Médiation Délinquant–Victime et Réparation de Dommages. Nouvelle Evolution du Droit Pénal et de la Pratique Judiciaire dans une Comparaison Internationale', in F. Dünkel and J. Zermatten (eds), *Nouvelles Tendances dans le Droit Pénal des Mineurs*, Freiburg: Max-Planck Institute, 2–81.

Dünkel, F. (1996), 'Täter-Opfer Ausgleich. German Experiences with Mediation in a European Perspective', *European Journal of Criminal Policy and Research*, **4**(4), 44–66.

Faget, J. (1997), *La Médiation: Essai de Politique Pénale*, Ramonville Saint-Agne: Erès.

Fattah, E. (1993), 'From a Guilt Orientation to a Consequence Orientation. A Proposed New Paradigm for the Criminal Law in the 21st Century', in W. Küper and J. Welp (eds), *Beiträge zur Rechtswissenschaft*, Heidelberg: Müller Juristische Verlag, 771–92.

Galaway, B. and Hudson, J. (1996) (eds), *Restorative Justice: International Perspectives*, Monsey: Criminal Justice Press.

Gehm, J. (1992), 'The Function of Forgiveness in the Criminal Justice System', in H. Messmer, and H.U. Otto (eds), *Restorative Justice on Trial. Pitfalls and Potentials of Victim–Offender Mediation. International Research Perspectives*, Dordrecht: Kluwer Academic Publishers.

Geudens, H. (1996), 'De Toepassing van de Gemeenschapsdienst door de Belgische Jeugdrechtbanken (implementation of community service in the Belgian juvenile courts)', *Panopticon*, **17**, 499–520.

Harland, A. and Rosen, C. (1990), 'Impediments to the Recovery of Restitution by Crime Victims', *Violence and Victims*, Special Issue on Social Science and Victim Policy, **5**(2), 127–32.

Harris, M. (1991), 'Moving into the new Millennium: Toward a Feminist Vision of Justice', in H. Pepinsky and R. Quinney (eds), *Criminology as Peacemaking*, Bloomington: Indiana University Press, 83–97.

Higgins, D. and Snyder, R. (1996), 'North Carolinians Want Alternative Sentences for Nonviolent Offenders', *Overcrowded Times*, **7**(4), 12–15.

Hudson, J. and Galaway, B. (1996), 'Introduction', in B. Galaway and J. Hudson (eds), *Restorative Justice: International Perspectives*, Monsey, Criminal Justice Press, 1–14.

Kuhn, T. (1962), *The Structure of Scientific Revolutions*, Chicago: University of Chicago Press.

Lemert, E. (1981), 'Diversion in Juvenile Justice: What Went Wrong?', *Journal of Research in Crime and Delinquency*, **22**, 34–46.

Lipton, D., Martinson, R. and Wilks, J. (1975), *The Effectiveness of Correctional Treatment: A Survey of Treatment Evaluation Studies*, New York: Praeger.

Marshall, T. (1996), 'The Evolution of Restorative Justice in Britain', *European Journal of Criminal Policy and Research*, **4**(4), 21–43.

McCold, P. (1996), 'Restorative Justice and the Role of Community', in B. Galaway and J. Hudson (eds), *Restorative Justice: International Perspectives*, Monsey: Criminal Justice Press, 85–101.

McCold, P. (1998), 'Restorative Justice: Variations on a Theme', in L. Walgrave (ed.), *Restorative Justice for Juveniles. Potentials, Risks and Problems for Research,* Leuven: Leuven University Press, 19–53.

Meijlaers, S. (1992), *Samen Werken aan een Preventief Beleid* (Working Together for a Preventative Policy), 2 vols, KU Leuven: Onderzoeksgroep Jeugdcriminologie.

Peters T. and Aertsen, I. (1995), 'Restorative Justice: in Search of New Avenues in Dealing with Crime', in C. Fijnaut, J. Goethals, T. Peters and L. Walgrave (eds), *Changes in Society, Crime and Criminal Justice in Europe, Vol. 1*, Den Haag: Kluwer Law International, 311–42.

Piliavin, I., Gartner, R., Thornton, C. and Matsueda, R. (1986), 'Crime, Deterrence and Rational Choice', *American Sociological Review*, **51**, 101–19.

Schafer, S. (1977), *Victimology. The Victim and his Offender*, Reston: Prentice Hall.

Schiff, M. (1999), 'The Impact of Restorative Sanctions on Juvenile Offenders', in G. Bazemore and L. Walgrave (eds), *Restorative Juvenile Justice: Repairing the Harm of Youth Crime*, Monsey: Criminal Justice Press, 327–56.

Shapland, J. (1985), 'The Criminal Justice System and the Victim', *Victimology*, 585–99.

Silkinson, H. and Broderick, J. (1998), 'A Case Study of Restorative Justice: the Vermont Reparative Probation Program', in L. Walgrave (ed.), *Restorative Justice for Juveniles. Potentials, Risks and Problems for Research*, Leuven: Leuven University Press, 301–15.

Thorvaldson, S. (1990), 'Restitution and Victim Participation in Sentencing', in B. Galaway and J. Hudson (eds), *Criminal Justice, Restitution and Reconciliation*, Monsey: Willow Tree Press, 23–36.

Trépanier, J. (1989), 'Principes et Objectifs Guidant le Choix des Mesures Prises en Vertu de la Loi sur les Jeunes Contrevenants', *Revue du Barreau*, **4**, 559–605.

Tulkens, F. (1993), 'Les Transformations du Droit Pénal aux Etats Unis: Pour un Autre Modèle de Justice', in *Nouveaux Itinéraires en Droit. Hommage à François Rigaux*, Brussels: Bruylandt, 461–93.

Umbreit, M. (1994), *Victim Meets Offender. The Impact of Restorative Justice and Mediation*, Monsey: Criminal Justice Press.

Van Ness, D. (1990), 'Restorative Justice', in B. Galaway and J. Hudson (eds), *Criminal Justice, Restitution and Reconciliation*, Monsey: Willow Tree Press, 7–14.

Van Ness, D. (1996), 'Restorative Justice and International Human Rights', in B. Galaway and J. Hudson (eds), *Restorative Justice: International Perspectives*, Monsey: Criminal Justice Press, 17–35.

Van Ness, D. and Strong, K.H. (1997), *Restoring Justice*, Cincinnati: Anderson.

van Swaaningen, R. (1997), *Critical Criminology. Visions from Europe*, London: Sage.

von Hirsch, A. (1976), *Doing Justice: The Choice of Punishments*, New York: Hill and Wang.

von Hirsch, A. (1993), *Censure and Sanctions*, Oxford: Clarendon Press.

Walgrave, L. (1994), 'Beyond Rehabilitation: In Search of a Constructive Alternative in the Judicial Response to Juvenile Crime', *European Journal on Criminal Policy and Research*, **2**(2), 57–75.

Walgrave, L. (1995), 'Restorative Justice for Juveniles: Just a Technique or a Fully Fledged Alternative?', *Howard Journal*, **34**(3), 228–49.

Walgrave, L. and Bazemore, G. (1999), 'Reflections on the Future of Restorative Justice for Juveniles', in G. Bazemore and L. Walgrave (eds), *Restorative Juvenile Justice: Repairing the Harm of Youth Crime*, Monsey: Criminal Justice Press, 359–99.

Walgrave, L. and Geudens, H. (1996), 'The Restorative Proportionality of Community Service for Juveniles', *European Journal of Crime, Criminal Law and Criminal Justice*, **4**(4), 361–80.

Walgrave, L. and Geudens H. (1997), 'Restorative Community Service in Belgium', *Overcrowded Times*, **8**(5), 3 and 12–15.

Weitekamp, E. (1999), 'History of Restorative Justice', in G. Bazemore and L. Walgrave (eds), *Restorative Juvenile Justice: Repairing the Harm of Youth Crime*, Monsey: Criminal Justice Press, 75–102.

Wright, M. (1992), 'Victim–Offender Mediation as a Step Towards a Restorative System of Justice', in H. Messmer and H.U. Otto (eds), *Restorative Justice on Trial. Pitfalls and Potentials of Victim-Offender Mediation. International Research Perspectives*, Dordrecht, Kluwer Academic Publishers, 525–39.

Wright, M. (1996), *Justice for Victims and Offenders*, Winchester: Waterside Press.

Zehr, H. (1990), *Changing Lenses: A New Focus for Crime and Justice*, Scottsdale: Herald Press.

13   Salient Themes Towards a Victim Perspective and the Limitations of Restorative Justice: Some Concluding Comments

Adam Crawford

In this concluding chapter I intend to pick up on a few of the themes raised by various contributors, and on some of their points of convergence and divergence. I will then go on to highlight a number of critical issues with regard to restorative justice and the place of the victim within it. In particular, I will focus on questions of legitimacy and responsibilities within a restorative justice paradigm and explore some of the limitations of restoration as a principle of justice. In so doing, I will take a deliberately critical view of the restorative justice literature in order to identify some of the challenges which the integration of a 'victim perspective' present for restorative justice and our theorization of its potential as a transformative force within and around the criminal justice complex.

Some Converging Themes

As contributors to Part I of this volume note, the concept and status of 'victim' is itself highly problematic. The proliferation of victim surveys and victimological research since the 1980s disclosing, recording and classifying forms of harm and the scale of pain engendered by acts of crime has unknowingly catapulted victimhood to the forefront of contemporary debate. However, there is a danger that, in the appropriation and ascription of the term 'victim', it may become increasingly drained of its significance to the extent that 'we are all victims now!'. Our knowledge about the complex relationships between victimization and offending, and victims and offenders which David Miers explores in Chapter 4, remains very much in its infancy. Nevertheless, what is increasingly apparent is a distinct area or spatial dimension to these relationships which is often ignored in debates concerning restorative justice and the integration of a victim perspective within criminal justice, as currently conceived.

Research into the distribution of victims reminds us that the prevalence of victimization differs significantly between areas. Victim surveys have demonstrated that the distribution of victimization is anything but random. This is vividly illustrated by Jan van Dijk's analysis of the international data from the International Crime Victim Surveys in Chapter 5. Furthermore, the British Crime Surveys have shown that a substantial minority of victims of crime, living in a minority of residential communities, suffer a significant disproportion of victimization (Trickett *et al.*, 1992). As Tim Hope notes: 'More than one-half of all property crime – and more than one-third of all property crime-victims – are likely to be found in just one-fifth of the communities of England and Wales' (Hope, 1997: 148). Hence, crime has a distinct spatial dimension, one which is interwoven with inequality and the distribution of poverty. In this sense, crime may well be conceived as a 'regressive tax on the poor' (Downes, 1983). If so, the tax burden appears increasingly to be falling more heavily on those most economically and socially vulnerable. According to analysis of the British Crime Surveys, the distribution of victimization in England and Wales has become more spatially concentrated since the 1970s (Trickett *et al.*, 1995). Moreover, high crime areas seem to suffer a 'double concentration effect', whereby not only are they afflicted by higher levels of crime but also they are marked by a greater concentration of multiple and repeat victimization, such that victims are victimized at a greater frequency rate in high crime areas than in low crime areas.

The phenomenon of repeat victimization and the way in which public policy responds to it has significant implications, as Jan van Dijk reiterates in Chapter 5. However, it remains unclear whether high crime areas are the consequence of higher numbers of repeat victims (namely individual characteristics) or whether repeat victimization is largely the product of a high crime area which sustains victim concentration (namely community or area characteristics). In other words, repeat victimization may reflect, and be an expression of, a high crime area rather than a high crime area being a product of high numbers of repeat victims. In answering the question, 'Do certain areas have high crime rates because more people are victimized or because there is more revictimization of the same people?', criminological commentators, in their exploration of repeat victimization, may have been looking at the phenomenon through the wrong end of the telescope. Nevertheless, repeat victimization research has highlighted the importance of connecting victim-centred services to the wider tasks of crime prevention and community safety (Farrell and Pease, 1993). As Forrester *et al*. notes: 'To acknowledge that the best predictor of the next victimisation is the last victimisation is to acknowledge that victim support and crime prevention are two sides of the same coin' (Forrester *et al*., 1990: 45). Importantly, these observations require responses to victimization which address the area or community dimension to crime and its relationship to inequality. In short, it challenges any theory of appropriate responses to crime – such as restorative justice – to tackle issues of area difference and inequality or, in other words, to have a theory of political economy.

Moreover, as noted by a number of contributors, we need to ask whether it is appropriate to conceive of victimization as a single event affecting an individual, as victim. Questioning this dominant conceptualization has three implications. The first is to problematize the 'events-orientation' of official statistical and legal categorization as well as dominant victimological research methods, in the form of victim surveys. More qualitative research, particularly with regard to multiple or repeat victims, by contrast, suggests that violence and abuse, rather than constituting 'events' are better conceptualized as processes involving complex ongoing relationships. Hazel Genn, for example, has highlighted 'the difficulties which may be involved in isolating those events which are to be counted as "crimes" for survey purposes from the normal course of day-to-day existence of these multiple victims' (Genn, 1988: 99). Hence, there is a need to understand victimization more clearly in terms of the relational context in which it is grounded.

The second implication concerns the manner in which policy discourse has appropriated the victim as an ideal construct against the background of the 'individualization of the victim', which informs both Leslie Sebba's and Edna Erez's chapters. Here, categories of victim, or even individual victim, attributes and personality, have increasingly come to influence criminal justice. The victim has not only become 'individualized' but also reified and abstracted from his or her social context.

The third implication relates to the existence of extended, 'significant others' who are correspondingly affected by victimization and associated harms. To this extent, Richard Young in Chapter 11, prefers the notion of 'multiple victims' to capture these 'significant others', be they family, peers, neighbours, associates or wider 'community members'. As he suggests, this expanded notion of victim feeds into restorative justice models of harm and the appropriate parties with a stake in, and responsibility for, responses to victimization.

And yet, this expansion of the notion of who qualifies as a victim raises the question: where to stop? How far can we stretch the label of 'victim' before it becomes redundant or emptied of any symbolic or social significance that it carries? However, this may be precisely the legitimate aim of such an endeavour; by stretching and opening up the term 'victim' we may simultaneously rid it of its idealized imagery. In this context, is 'victim' a descriptive term subject to empirical specification or an emotive, and hence subjective, one? And, to paraphrase Nils Christie, to what extent can the phenomenon of victimization be investigated both at the personality level and at the social system level (Christie, 1986: 18)? Or, as David Miers investigates in Chapter 4, what are the social processes through which the label 'victim' is claimed, ascribed and denied? It is worth noting that these processes are not passively experienced but are also, in part, actively shaped by those caught up by them. Hence, how do victims as individuals and groups construct, and to what extent are they constructed by, 'the processes in which they are anchored' (Rock, 1998: 186)?

Normative and Empirical Arguments

In debates concerning victims and criminal justice, as with other fields of criminology and socio-legal regulation, there is a running tension between what *is* and what *ought to be*. This has tended to produce a bifurcation of focus between, on the one hand, philosophers and jurists who have been concerned with issues of justice and allied normative debates and, on the other hand, criminologists and victimologists who have concentrated on empirical findings and evaluation research. The former have often left themselves open to accusations of utopianism and idealism, while the latter have tended to immerse themselves in highly specified empirical arguments, often with scant regard for normative and philosophical issues. As a result, there has been insufficient criminological and victimological engagement with public debates on issues of the normative foundation and direction of public policy. Attempts to answer the highly problematic and contingent questions, 'Does the latest policy initiative work?' or 'Do its outcomes meet its explicit objectives?' , whilst not irrelevant in themselves, tend to obscure the questions 'What ought to be our standards of behaviour as a society?', 'What social institutions should we be building?' and, in this context, 'What should be the place, status and role of victims within criminal justice?'. In this criminological light, crime and victimization are too often seen as a technical problem requiring administrative solutions. By contrast, there is a pressing need for criminology and victimology to reconnect empirical with normative debates, such that the one informs the other.

One example of the differing emphasis upon empirical and normative issues within this volume is reflected in the points of departure in the positions taken by Edna Erez and Andrew Ashworth with regard to victim impact statements. In Chapter 8 Edna Erez's primary concern is with the empirical description of the manner in which these forms of victim input have been implemented and their consequent impact and effect. To this end, and on the basis of empirical research findings, she articulates the failure of victim impact statements, where introduced, to realize either the 'high hopes of the victim rights advocates' or the 'misgivings of the opponents of victim participation' (Erez and Rogers, 1999: 216). She demonstrates that the reform has had little or no effect on the processing or outcomes of criminal cases and has failed to transform court practices in ways prophesied by both its critics and supporters, primarily because the legal profession has circumvented the reform's spirit.

In Chapter 9 Ashworth, by contrast, focuses on normative concerns and debates about the appropriateness of victim impact statements. He suggests that victim impact statements are an inappropriate intrusion into criminal justice procedures and sentencing. They are 'wrong', to his mind, because they contravene certain cherished principles – namely, that sentencing should be a matter of public interest 'on which the victim has no particular claim to be heard' and it would be unfair if offenders' sentences varied according to the particular victim whether he or she is vengeful or not, or even chooses to be involved in the process. From this perspective, victim impact statements appear to offend principles of proportionality, equality of treatment for offenders and the notion of the public interest within criminal justice.

Where Ashworth presents a normative argument premised upon principled legal grounds, by contrast, Erez presents an empirical account which commences from the measured effects of victim impact statements on the court processes, outcomes and wider social and legal provision. Erez notes the manner in which legal occupational cultures and organizational factors, such as managerialist concerns within the courts, produce in-built forces of moderation and normalization which have limited the effect of victim input reforms and undermined the expected benefits of providing a voice to victims. The reality, she suggests, is that reason has not been supplanted by passion, that legal occupational cultures and organizational practices have resisted and deflected such an outcome. In this context, victims can derive a certain benefit from victim impact statements, even though the reality of their impact may fall far short of victims' expectations and, more importantly, their desires.

However, for me, this leaves an awkwardness and uncertainty in the fact that, even on the basis of the empirical evidence, so lucidly reviewed by Erez, the argument for inclusion of victim impact statements rests on a form of 'implementation failure' rather than the realization of the reform's spirit or intended aims. In this sense, the 'voice' accorded to the victim through a victim impact statement is a mixed one which simultaneously satisfies and disappoints. However, the question that this begs is how these inherent tensions will, or may, be resolved in the future. Neither organizational nor legal culture, nor indeed the social effects of victim impact statements, are static phenomena but are subject to the processes of change influenced by wider social and political concerns. This reminds us that culture is temporally bounded: it is continually undergoing a process of challenge, change and adaptation. Thus, as Nelken suggests, we need 'to treat culture as a process of becoming and a point of departure as much as a functioning whole' (Nelken, 1995: 444). Consequently, we need to ask 'How and to what extent the empirical here-and-now (which is not static) may be influenced by and, in turn, influence wider normative debates?'.

Where there have been genuine attempts to engage in such a reconnection of empirical and normative arguments – for example, in some of the literature on 'restorative justice' – there remains, nevertheless, an ever-present danger that these become confused. This is particularly evident, for example, with regard to debates about the role of 'community' within crime, responses to victimization and restoration. Community occupies a pivotal place within restorative justice. The ultimate aim of restorative justice is the revival of communal bonds of informal control, the reintegration of the offender and the victim within the moral community and the restoration of communal order. Within restorative justice literature the decline of 'community' is associated with both increased victimization and the theft of disputes by the modern state (Christie, 1977). Restorative justice becomes both a vehicle for the revival of community and is premised upon the existence of community as a pre-eminent site of social control. In this virtuous cycle 'community' is a means to an end, as our moral voices are nourished by communities and our moral values are attainable because of the social pressures, such as 'reintegrative shaming' (Braithwaite and Mugford, 1994) which communities bring to bear on their members. But it is also an end in itself, in that the restoration of 'community' is evidence of a moral order which acts to prevent crime. In this context, both means and ends can, and often do, collide and become confused.

Here, as I have argued elsewhere (Crawford, 1997), there exists, all too often, a slippage between a sociological and ideological understanding of 'community': between what 'community' *is* and what it *ought* to be – the empirical authenticity of 'community' as distinct from its normative appeal. Much of the recent communitarian literature, which has significantly influenced restorative justice debates, is marked by exactly such a rhetorically powerful slippage. The normative appeal of community is confused with empirical reality, such that many communitarians and some proponents of restorative justice seem to want it both ways. The present weakness of 'community' is simultaneously seen as 'the problem' – the cause of most contemporary social ills – and 'the solution' in that within weak or 'light communities' (Young, 1999) people are assumed to be able, and potentially prefer, to switch and move freely between communities if they disagree with their practices or values, and/or remain within a 'community', whilst dissenting from the dominant moral voices therein. Yet, it is precisely the ability of a 'community' to bring social pressures to bear upon its members, its persuasive capacity, which has ambiguous consequences. In reconnecting the empirical with the normative, the ideal of community should be forced to confront empirical reality, which reminds us that communities are often marked (and sustained) by social exclusion, forms of coercion and the differential distribution of power relations (Crawford, 1997).

Victims in the Service of Other Ends

One of the themes that resonates throughout this volume concerns the ends served by the integration of victims within criminal justice. The notion of 'a victim perspective' is by no means politically neutral but rather is infused with different ideological perspectives. The voice of the victim has been tossed around in the turbulent seas of political debate. The diversity of new initiatives within and across different jurisdictions which have sought to improve the plight of victims in the criminal justice system – some of which are outlined in the various contributions to this volume – is testimony to the rise of a vocal victims movement. This movement has diverse origins and has spoken with many different voices, articulating a variety of demands. One of the more established and reasoned voices has been that of Victim Support in England and Wales, whose contribution is outlined by Helen Reeves and Kate Mulley in Chapter 6. Victim Support's view has tended to reiterate the point that the responsibility for decision-making should not lie with the victim but with the state. This right for victims not to have to make decisions regarding the offender, spelt out in Victim Support's *The Rights of Victims of Crime* (1995), has led it to oppose the introduction of victim impact statements along the lines of the US and Australian models. It has preferred to offer services outside of, and around, the criminal justice process, whilst simultaneously calling for greater informational rights of victims with regard to the processing of their cases.

And yet, despite its status as a non-governmental organization, Victim Support has increasingly come to constitute an adjunct to the formal criminal justice apparatus, casting other victims' groups, such as rape crisis centres, into the shadows and on to the margins while, at the same time, securing itself a place at the centre of governmental policy. Victim Support both occupies a seat on the government's interdepartmental Victims Steering Group and is the subject of charter standards of service delivery, under the Victim's Charter (Home Office, 1996), almost as if it were like any other public organization (Rock, 1999). As such, it represents and reflects an increasing blurring of the boundaries between the state and civil society, as it has become incorporated in the task of delivering criminal justice.

However, in contrast to Victim Support there have also been impassioned calls advocating that victims be given a central role in key processes and decision-making with regard to criminal justice. Like others, Andrew Ashworth correctly warns of the dangers of victims being used 'in the service of severity'. It is not by chance that the rise of the victim movement and the growth of victims' rights have coincided with a brand of 'populist punitiveness' (Bottoms, 1995: 39–41) and the return of vengeance (Sarat, 1997). Not only is there the danger of the political manipulation of crime victims (Elias, 1993) but it may also be accompanied by the triumph of passion over reason, which strikes at the heart of modern legality and common morality. Ashworth also notes the dual – but some might say opposing – danger of 'victims in the service of offenders'. It was, for example, with some justification that mediation and reparation schemes set up in the UK in the mid-1980s were criticized for becoming a 'new deal for offenders' or at least the subordination of a 'good idea' in the service of offender diversion (Davis *et al.*, 1988; see also Young, 1989; Davis, 1992) rather than the 'new deal for victims' which the Home Office had proclaimed.

Managerialist Reforms in Criminal Justice and the Place of Victims Therein

However, to Ashworth's two explicit dangers we can add a third – namely that of 'victims in the service of system efficiency'. Here, the concern is that victims may be appropriated by, or at least been caught up within, a managerialist inspired challenge to the normative assumptions of criminal justice. This managerialism – influenced as it is by a neoliberal ideology – seeks to inspire a fundamental transformation in the scope and internal working of the public sector. 'Reinventing government' according to its high priests, Osborne and Gaebler (1992), is described as little less than a political and management 'revolution'. In recent years, and somewhat belatedly compared to other public services, criminal justice has become embroiled in this new logic. As a result, organizations have increasingly become the subject of new 'system objectives': criteria against which the success or failure of the criminal justice system is, or should be, evaluated. These new system objectives are largely concerned with 'smooth management', 'efficiency' and 'economy'. Moreover, these reforms claim to speak on behalf of 'consumers' and taxpayers, feeding off critiques of self-serving professional élites – such as those whom Shapland (1988) rightly castigated some time ago with regard to victims of crime. As such, recent reforms have claimed to represent a challenge to the 'cosy cultures of professional self-regulation' (Power, 1997: 44). Concerns about the place of victims within criminal justice, notably in the UK, have been swept along by these dynamics.

Where once victims were treated as if they were peripheral to criminal justice processes they have now been accorded a greater degree of prominence. In part, the refashioning of victims as rational choice customers, albeit often only tentatively as in the Victim's Charter (notably in its first incarnation), has given victims a new standing as consumers of a public service. To some extent, recent 'new public management' reforms, requiring performance measurement and the response to 'customers' for whom services are delivered, have disrupted Shapland's fiefdom image through new forms of accountability (notably financial and managerial). However, as Joanna Shapland notes in Chapter 7, these have served, perversely, to increase the isolation and introspection of many criminal justice agencies. They have done so, first, because they accord little attention to negotiating shared purposes and collaboration, particularly where there is no hierarchy of control and, second, because they focus attention on narrowly construed service delivery and 'customers' of a particular segment of criminal justice at a given time and place within the process, rather than upon cross-cutting, horizontal accountabilities and responsibilities.

Hence, victims are only considered relevant in so far as they relate to narrow core responsibilities, with little regard to the relation between the victim and criminal justice as a 'systemic' whole. As a consequence, victim services lack coherence, coordination and synergy. Instead, they tend to manifest a lack of clarity, confused and often conflicting aims and overlapping priorities. Services for victims of crime seem to suffer from a similar malady to that noted by the Social Exclusion Unit (SEU) in a report into services for socially deprived neighbourhoods in the UK – that of 'initiative-itis' (SEU, 1998: 38), which seek only to address parts of the problem, are contradictory and limited in scope.[1] Moreover, as Renée Zauberman argues in Chapter 2, it is questionable to what extent victims who turn to the criminal justice system can be conceptualized in the same ways as consumers of other public services.

Moreover, there are elements within the managerialist 'revolution' which run counter to the relational and human dynamic which advocates of a victim perspective and restorative justice hold dear. Managerialist reforms – under the three Es of efficiency, effectiveness and economy – have seen the construction and institutionalization across different criminal justice agencies of 'auditable performance', whereby complex tasks are reduced to easily comparable – albeit largely arbitrary – numeric codes of 'administrative objectivity'. As a consequence, 'justice is increasingly understood not as a rational system but through the rationality of the system' (Feeley and Simon, 1994: 178). The resultant 'new penology' (Feeley and Simon, 1992) is informed by a neoclassical understanding of human behaviour and connects with neoliberal notions of individual responsibility and choice. Here the public is manipulated 'as a demographic mass or aggregate, bypassing the res cognitans of individuals altogether … the new practices radically reframe the issues, and target something very different, that is, the crime rate, understood as the distribution of behaviours in the population as a whole' (Feeley and Simon, 1994: 175–78). Victims, like offenders, are increasingly caught up in this logic and construed as the abstract and universal 'abiographical individual' (O'Malley, 1992): whereby victims and offenders – as rational choice actors, abstracted from their social context – come to represent the *homo economicus* of classical economics translated into neoconservative thinking about crime.[2] As a consequence, there is little space for interpersonal dynamics, relational justice or notions of 'human proximity'.

The concern with regard to integrating a victim perspective within criminal justice, here, is that under such pressures victims' interests can become subverted by organizational requirements or the needs of the system as a whole, to the extent that victims are 'consumed by' rather than the 'consumers of' criminal justice. Moreover, managerialist pressures introduce a somewhat contradictory dynamic within the traditional tensions between rehabilitative and retributive justice. This is largely because they represent a 'demoralization of justice', whereby non-normative, administrative concerns take precedence over moral, 'human' or normative issues. For example, Edna Erez, in Chapter 8, notes the manner in which managerialist concerns within the courts have served to limit the effect of victim input reforms and undermined the expected benefits of providing a voice to victims. She shows how they have subverted at least some of the intentions of the reforms. Here, we have an apparent paradox which sees the coexistence of, on the one hand, the rise of passion and vengeance (over reason) and, on the other hand, the administrative, normalizing and rationalizing urge of managerialist reforms.

At first sight, the dangers of 'victims in the service of severity' and of 'victims in the service of system efficiency', appear contradictory. However, this very ambiguity lies at the heart of current criminal justice. In this vein,

David Garland has identified the importance of 'two contrasting visions' at work:

> ... the passionate, morally toned desire to punish and the administrative, ration-
> alistic, normalising concern to manage. These visions clash in many important
> respects, but both are deeply embedded within the social process of punishing. It
> is in the conflict and tension between them that we find one of the key determi-
> nants of contemporary penal [and criminal justice] practice. (Garland, 1990:
> 180)

These normative and managerialist concerns are to be found in diverse aspects of criminal justice. It is this tension which we see expressed in some of the more contradictory elements of criminal justice policy rhetoric and mood swings in political populism, as well as in some of the institutions to which they give rise.[3] Consequently, official criminology has become in-creasingly dualistic and polarized. Garland (1996) calls these two voices within official criminology: a 'criminology of the self' and a 'criminology of the other'. Punitive populism and the concern with managerialist solu-tions are both rooted in 'political ambivalence' concerning uncertainties as to the role and capacity of the modern state. It is almost as if they are 'actually twinned, antithetical phenomena' in which one provokes the other. And yet, at the heart of the populist tendency, which has pulled victim advocacy in its wake, is a process of denial:

> A show of punitive force against individuals is used to repress any acknowledge-
> ment of the state's inability to control crime to acceptable levels. A willingness
> to deliver harsh punishments to convicted offenders magically compensates a
> failure to deliver security to the population at large. (Garland 1996: 460)

On this account, punitive rhetoric and policy are as much a product of problems of state sovereignty and legitimisation as they are a rational response to the problems of crime. Consequently, as Garland argues, state sovereignty over crime is simultaneously denied – as being 'beyond the state' – and symbolically reasserted – through periodic episodes of hys-terical and populist denials of the state's limitations (ibid.: 462). Limita-tions of traditional criminal justice – police and punishment – are recognized in certain instances only to be discounted or ignored in others. This dual-istic denial and recognition produces volatile shifts in the state's presenta-tion of its own capacity for effective action in crime control. It is therefore not surprising that concerns about the treatment of victims should become caught up in this paradox. For, as Renée Zauberman clearly argues in Chapter 2, the historic treatment of victims, and their place within crimi-nal justice in particular, is intrinsically bound up with the modern state's presentation of itself, its sovereignty, capacity for action and claims to legitimacy.

Restorative Justice and Victims of Crime

As Lode Walgrave notes in Chapter 12, the concept of restorative justice and the place of victims within it, remains an open-textured subject of competing definitions. This leaves initiatives implemented in its name especially vulnerable to the dangers already discussed. This vulnerability has increased as 'restorative justice' has moved increasingly centre-stage in contemporary policy debates. In the 1980s and early 1990s restorative justice principles and programmes tended to be small-scale, with marginal impact upon criminal justice systems. Apart from New Zealand's juvenile justice system and the reforms heralded by the 1989 Children, Young Persons and Their Families Act (reviewed by Morris and Maxwell in Chapter 10), they occupied peripheral positions. More recently, this picture has begun to change, at least at the level of policy rhetoric.

In England and Wales, for example, the Crime and Disorder Act 1998 claims to have the promotion of restorative justice and the interest of victims at its very heart, particularly with regard to changes in juvenile justice. The British government's White Paper, provocatively entitled *No More Excuses*, which set out the intention behind the legislative proposals, proclaimed to 'build on principles underlying the concept of restorative justice' (Home Office, 1997: para. 9.21). It spoke of the 3 Rs of 'restorative justice': 'Restoration, Reintegration and Responsibility'. The policy defines these as follows: 'restoration' is where young offenders apologize to their victims and make amends for the harm they have done; 'reintegration' is where young offenders, as a consequence of paying their debt to society, put their crime behind them and rejoin the law-abiding community; and 'responsibility' is where young offenders – and their parents – face the consequences of their offending behaviour and take responsibility for preventing further offending. As a consequence, reparation constitutes a key theoretical and practical base for interventions undertaken under the auspices of 'reprimands', 'final warnings' and 'reparation orders', the introduction of 'action plan' orders and the work of 'youth offending teams' (YOTs), as well as the most recent proposals for Youth Offender Panels as outlined in the Youth Justice and Criminal Evidence Act 1999. The victim is to be accorded a more central role in the process involved either through direct or indirect mediation (see Dignan, 1999). In addition, this legislative package is heavily infused by the logic of the Audit Commission's *Misspent Youth* (1996) report with its considerable managerialist agenda (see Newburn, 1998;

Crawford, 1998). Together, the proposals appear to represent a significant development in the incorporation of restorative justice in the UK, such that they should ensure that restorative justice is 'no longer a marginal, irregular and highly localised activity' (Dignan, 1999: 53). However, it remains to be seen whether this represents the incorporation of restorative justice and mediation as elements within an essentially retributive system or the building blocks of, what Walgrave describes as, 'a fully-fledged systemic alternative'.

Continental Europe has seen parallel, but different, developments. In France, for example, the elaboration of restorative justice has been associated with a wider policy of *justice de proximité* (proximal justice) which, as well as embodying elements of 'territorial proximity' through processes of decentralization and a 'temporal proximity' which affirms the need to develop faster procedures to deal with case overload and to bring cases to a speedier resolution, also holds out for a greater 'human proximity' which asserts the belief that the parties to a dispute should be the subjects, and not objects, of justice (Wyvekens, 1996; 1997). Instead of exacerbating conflicts it seeks party-centred processes which are relational. This has been institutionalized through the rapid spread of the *Maisons de Justice et du Droit* (MJDs) which provide mediation of cases under the supervision of local prosecutors, as well as victim–offender mediation provided by victim and probation-related services (Faget, 1997; Crawford, 2000). A key element of the MJD is the 'mediation' of disputes that it offers, whereby victims and offenders are given the opportunity to resolve their disputes, through forms of reparation, in the presence of a third party. As such, the MJDs have been an instrumental institution in the elaboration of restorative justice in France.

More recently, the *Maisons de Justice* model has been appropriated and adapted by the Dutch under their policy of 'Neighbourhood Justice' (*Justitie in de buurt*) (Boutellier, 1997).[4] Even in the USA, where the criminal justice system is highly retributive and such experimentation as mediation and restorative justice has tended to generate considerable research interest but remain a peripheral concern of mainstream criminal justice, recent developments in the name of restorative justice have been considerable. For example, with regard to adult community corrections in Vermont and elements of the correctional system in Minnesota, policies have been restructured to conform with restorative principles.

Nevertheless, this blossoming of interest and furious activity presents new dilemmas. Thus, we need to consider the congruence between 'restorative justice' and other prevailing, favoured policies and wider political programmes. Moreover, we need to ask the question 'Why now?'. Is restorative justice merely the (re)discovery of a 'good idea' or is it more fundamentally connected to wider change? If so, what broader social and political shifts have fuelled or influenced the appeal of restorative justice? Is it, as Sebba contemplates, representative of a postmodern age or a return to a premodern age? Or does it reflect a growing civilianization, humanization or privatization of criminal justice?

Moreover, we need to consider the diverse interests with often conflicting motivations from which 'restorative justice' draws support, or that proponents claim for it. Forms of restorative justice have met with enthusiasm from divergent quarters, across the political spectrum and within professional and community groups. The divergent nature of the interests and groups promoting 'restorative justice' has resulted in initiatives meaning different things to different people. On one level, this has allowed the 'restorative justice movement' to gain support from diverse sources and to fit into the prevailing political rhetoric at given moments. However, it also means that specific initiatives can be, and have been, pulled in different, and often competing, directions as they try to meet the multiple aims and objectives and to satisfy the divergent demands of the different constituencies. In attempting (or claiming) to 'do too much', the danger is that 'restorative justice' initiatives can end up falling short on a number of fronts. As noted, the appeals which infuse 'restorative justice' need to be evaluated in relation to both their *normative* and *managerialist* claims. This reminds us of the need to connect developments in 'restorative justice' to simultaneous wider punitive developments. The important point here is that 'restorative justice' initiatives cannot be understood in isolation; they are not necessarily alternatives but related parts of a wider, dualistic and ambivalent criminal justice complex.

For example, there is a fundamental tension between the expectation, or hope, that restorative justice will result in economies to the public purse – be it by reducing imprisonment rates, reducing offending rates, encouraging desistance from crime and, hence, reducing the cost of criminal justice more broadly or by re-energizing civil society's own mechanisms of social control and conflict managing resources – and the notion that restorative justice initiatives will simultaneously address the hitherto unmet needs of victims and offenders. The former aspiration is clearly articulated in the British government's restorative justice proposals in the Crime and Disorder Act 1998. The British government's White Paper, *No More Excuses*, declared that the restorative proposals would yield 'significant savings to the criminal justice system' and went on to add that 'further savings may arise from the less direct impact of these proposals on a wide range of services' (Home Office, 1997: para. 10.7). And yet, one of the lessons of Victim Support, as well as a panoply of other public services (including the National Health Service), in the UK is that services such as these tend to reveal and expose a multitude of unmet needs. As David Downes has noted, the proposals in the

Act display a 'poverty of resource thinking' as they build on the assumption that restorative justice '*is* very cheap' (Downes, 1998: 196), coinciding with cuts in probation and local authority social services – exactly the kind of services which are likely to have extra demands placed on them as a result of the restorative elements in proposals such as the youth offending teams. Earlier and more extensive intervention through the apparatus of criminal justice, as restorative justice often implies, exhibits the well documented dangers of 'net-widening' (Cohen, 1979). But even if one concedes that not all net-widening is inherently negative – that social control can be benign as well as malign (Matthews, 1987; Cohen, 1989) – one must surely accept that, to do so, carries with it significant resource implications.

Lode Walgrave, in Chapter 12, calls for an 'ambitious' or 'maximalist' version of restorative justice theory. Yet while his vision is maximalist in its impact upon criminal justice, arguing for a central, rather than a restricted or marginal, position, it is also – appropriately I would argue – a limited vision with regard to the feasibility of restoration, its transformative potential beyond criminal justice and the role of the state. The danger for the restorative justice movement and for victims of crime may lie in proponents of restorative justice promising and claiming too much, which may only serve to disappoint in the face of falsely raised expectations.

Restorative Justice and Coercion

For some proponents of restorative justice, and victim–offender mediation before it, the 'sacred cow' has been that of 'voluntariness' – namely, that the parties should volunteer for restorative options, that they should have a choice. It has often been as a result of the attempt to keep to this principle that many restorative justice schemes and proponents remain 'minimalist', in Walgrave's terms (in that they remain small-scale and peripheral to criminal justice). And yet 'voluntariness', in this sense, is conceived as an all-or-nothing concept, whereby the parties either accept the process that they subsequently undergo or reject it, as if choice was unconditional. In reality, 'voluntariness' is much more contingent than this, particularly when located with what is essentially a coercive process – that of criminal justice. Restorative processes in and around the criminal justice system embody considerable 'incentives' and subtle 'inducements' (Silbey and Merry, 1986), as well as 'coercive sticks' which undermine such an absolutist notion of 'voluntariness'. As Walgrave maintains, restorative justice must confront, acknowledge and negotiate the reality of coercive power which structures and frames criminal justice and state power therein.

There is the danger that, where restorative justice remains a 'voluntary' appendage to an otherwise coercive criminal justice system, those offenders who volunteer into restorative justice initiatives are likely to be those who least need them – those already the most integrated into the (local) community. By contrast, those with the most tenuous relations of 'care' and who, for whatever reason, do not have networks of dense relations of trust and mutuality are less likely to 'volunteer'. Those who exist at the periphery of, or are most marginalized by, the dominant moral community are less likely to have a stake in restorative justice processes. As a consequence, they are also less likely to accord significant legitimacy to such processes.

Nevertheless, there remains the central paradox of trying to impose civility through coercion which lies at the heart of restorative justice (particularly as informed by its wider communitarian ideals of 'community regeneration'). 'Enforced reparation' is likely to be perceived as punishment by offenders and as lacking in genuineness from the victim's perspective. As such, Davis's research into victim–offender mediation noted that 'non-material reparation delivered in the shadow of a pending court appearance will generally fail to convince' (Davis, 1992: 213).

Legitimacy and Restorative Justice

Restorative justice immediately raises questions about legitimacy: it reconfigures the notion of the 'public interest' by, as Richard Young notes in Chapter 11, appealing to a much wider notion of stakeholders, who should be brought into the process of dispute processing and resolution. Restorative justice recognizes that crime is more than an offence against the state: it looks at the impact on victims and others involved (family and kinship) and how communities can help. As such, it appeals to more localized normative orderings and explicitly seeks to accommodate cultural diversity and difference. Ideally, the normative order should emerge from the extended parties themselves, rather than being imposed from above. However, this presupposes an unproblematic consensus, without addressing the question of what the moral community *is*. The restorative justice response tends to assume an organic wholeness of a given fixed collectivity – one which accords little space for, or acknowledgement of, intracommunity conflict and diversity of value systems. And yet, will victims and offenders belong to the same moral community? Some restorative justice initiatives explicitly attempt to recognize and accommodate the cultural needs of specific parties, or even cultural differences between victims and offenders. This may extend to the selection criteria of the third party or other parties to the dispute and/or its location and format. However, this recognition of multicultural heterogeneity raises a number of normative, as well as practical, dilemmas. For example, which cultural identities (ascriptions of difference) are sufficiently appropriate or worthy of acknowledgement and accommodation within the process of 'representation' or structure of negotiation? How inclusive can such a 'moral community' be before it loses any persuasive capacity it may have? And, consequently, how many different interests can be accommodated within the restorative process without fragmenting the unity of the third-party process and thus the notion and possibility of a 'moral community'?

Importantly, restorative justice extends beyond spatial or geographic communities to communities of interest – 'communities of care' – the networks of obligation and respect between the individual and everyone who cares about him or her the most – which are not bounded by geography (Braithwaite and Daly, 1995: 195). This marks a significant development in the understanding of contemporary communities. These 'communities of care', it is argued, are more relevant to contemporary modern living in urban societies. They encompass an expanded notion of 'community' which, in part, is a subjective one, in that the ascription to community membership or social identity is personal and not necessarily one which carries any fixed or external attributes of membership. In other words, 'communities of care' do not carry connotations of coerced or constrained membership. This is one of their appeals.

Community conferences and family group conferences, it is argued, go beyond some of the limitations of traditional victim–offender mediation through their involvement of wider community participants with whom the parties have a 'relationship of genuine care'. First, it opens up what can otherwise be a private process (Braithwaite and Daly, 1994: 206–7). Second, in so doing, it can limit the power which mediation accords to professional mediators so that both the power of mediators is curbed and the process is open to greater public scrutiny. Third, it confirms accountability on those citizens who have concern for victims and offenders. 'In contrast to mediation, conferences are designed to encourage community dialogue' (Braithwaite and Daly, 1994: 207). Finally, by incorporating extended members, it addresses the potential unequal bargaining power of the parties.

Community, in this sense, begins to look more like bilateral relations of trust than 'semi-autonomous social fields' which have rule-making capacities, and the means to induce compliance, but which are simultaneously set in a larger social matrix which can, and often does, affect and invade it (Moore, 1973: 720). Moreover, if 'community' is a free-floating social identity, internally ascribed and easily escaped, as Braithwaite and communitarians more generally imply, then, like dominant rhetoric, it fails to accord to 'community' any significant structural or institutional characteristics around which the persuasive capacity of communities are constructed and maintained. In addition, as already noted, the ideal of unrestricted entry to, and exit from, communities needs to confront the empirical reality of exclusion, differential power relations and coercion within communities.

Restorative justice holds out the promise that communities can give redress to victims for what has been taken from them. And yet, not all communities share the same access to resources, nor can they feasibly restore victims in the same ways or to the same extent. Communities are marked by different capacities to mobilize internally on the basis of mutual trust combined with a willingness to intervene on behalf of the common good – what Sampson *et al.* (1997) refer to as 'collective efficacy' – as well as differential relations that connect local institutions to sources of power and resources in the wider civil society in which it is located – what Hope refers to as 'vertical power relations' (Hope, 1995: 24). This reminds us that restorative justice, in its appeals to community involvement, must not disconnect a concern for community (dis)approval from a concern with political and economic inequality. Restorative justice should not become a byword for geographic (in)justice!

The allied questions of 'who restores what, to whom and why?' all raise issues directly concerning obligation and legitimacy. The legitimacy of restoration must rest on the legitimacy of the community itself. Why would someone want to be restored to, or reintegrated within, a moral community which had abused them, marginalized them or merely not valued them? Many offenders live peripatetic lives on the margins of communities. They experience community, not in its benign form, but often as one of alienation and, sometimes, hostility: for them 'the community' may suffer from significant and important empathy deficits. If we accept the point made by David Miers, in Chapter 4, of the thin and frayed lines between offending and victimization, offenders may themselves have been the victims of crimes against which the community has failed to act or respond (particularly given the high levels of non-reporting and non-recording revealed by victim surveys). This has particular implications for legitimacy in restorative justice which calls out for mutuality of respect. Young people who have been the victims of powerful adult abuse, may have good reasons not to accept, as legitimate, the dominant moral voice of a community which fails to recognize their suffering as worthy of sufficient attention or to address their marginalization. Communities have obligations and responsibilities to offenders and victims if they are to be seen as legitimate moral communities. Responsibilities cut both ways. This raises questions about the feasibility of community integration and hence about the feasibility of 'reintegrative shaming' (Braithwaite, 1989). Moreover, this raises questions about the feasibility of timescale and the feasibility of community integration. Can a limited intervention – such as that envisaged by family group and community conferences – really turn around people's lives? This is particularly problematic if these interventions are unable to tackle the structural problems that individuals confront or the causes of their criminality in a long-term and sustained manner.

From the victim's perspective there are also concerns as to the feasibility of restoration. Victims need recompense for their harm. This is a goal to which restorative justice appeals. However, most young people who have offended will not necessarily be able to make sufficient reparation. In this context, the public interest lies in public restoration to victims of crime – through schemes of compensation, for example. Under the benevolent veil of restorative justice the state must not be allowed to abandon its responsibility to compensation.

Making amends and restoring troubled relations in an unequal society may mean restoring unequal relations and thereby reaffirming inequality. If restorative justice is to be an element within a much wider policy concerned with constructing the conditions under which civility and mutuality breed, then it is limited by its reactive nature, since it requires harms to be inflicted before restorative interventions can begin to be put in place. As a consequence, its reactive essence, in responding to acts of victimization, confines its potential as a transformative ideology. Social policy (including employment, education, health and housing) rather than criminal justice policy, regardless of whether this is restorative or not, must be the primary vehicle for the construction of a just and equal social order. The danger is that restorative justice accords to reactions to crime a centrality which even Durkheim (1893) would not have accorded to it. Yes, responses to crime are fundamentally social and cultural events which seek to reaffirm a collective consciousness and social cohesion, but they are not the mainstay out of which the collective consciousness springs. In claiming a centrality in the construction of a just social order, restorative justice proponents accord to reactions to crime an overriding position which they may not deserve. A potential consequence is that fundamental public issues may become marginalized except in so far as they are defined in terms of their crimogenic qualities. This would represent the ultimate 'criminalization of social policy'. Here, two related lessons from the past 20 years of research warrant reiteration. First, reactions to crime alone do not constitute sufficient grounds for sustaining community interest and enthusiasm over time, even in locations where initial levels of awareness and participation were high (Rosenbaum, 1988; Palumbo *et al.*, 1997). Second, given the anxieties and emotions that crime evokes and its capacity to bifurcate through deep-seated fears of 'otherness', crime may be an inappropriate vehicle around which to construct open and tolerant communities, as opposed to those which solidify around 'defensive exclusivity' (Crawford, 1997).

Questions of Responsibilities

Implicit in restorative justice is a re-evaluation of the responsibilities of government, communities and individuals for responding to victimization and the harms of crime. Where traditional notions of justice treated the public as the recipient of an 'expert service' provided by criminal justice professionals, restorative justice calls upon 'public participation' and 'active citizenry',[5] as individuals and groups become reconfigured as partners in the process and co-producers of the outcome. The pluralization of responsibility that restorative justice heralds acknowledges the limits of the sovereign state in respect of crime control and security. It begins a long overdue recognition that the levers and causes of crime lie far from the traditional reach of the criminal justice system. As such, it acknowledges the need for social responses to crime which reflect the nature of the phenomenon itself and its multiple aetiology, as well as the importance of mechanisms of informal social control in the prevention of crime. This responsibilization allows the potential for a more participatory civil society which fractures the state's monopolistic and paternalistic hold. However, it also presents a danger of a conflation of responsibilities of the state and those of individuals – victims and offenders – as well as communities and other networks of 'care'. Such strategies of 'responsibilization' should seek to clarify, rather than blur, the distribution of responsibilities and simultaneously ensure the appropriate conditions under which the exercise of those responsibilities can be fulfilled and maximized. As the JUSTICE Committee declared, 'The criminal justice system must not place further duties on citizens without meeting its own responsibilities for the consequences of introducing those duties' (JUSTICE, 1998: 110). Unfortunately, much of the restorative justice literature and current policy, as Walgrave notes in Chapter 12, tend to obfuscate the role of the state and third parties, replacing these with a particularly ambiguous appeal to 'community' ordering and individual choice.

One concern here, which Victim Support in the UK has voiced, and is reiterated in Chapter 6 by Reeves and Mulley, is that in this 'corporatist' approach (see Crawford, 1994), victims become incorporated and implicated within decision-making processes, whether they like it or not. This can be a particularly heavy burden to impose on victims. Of particular concern is the possibility that they become a lone or isolated voice. Moreover, the pluralization of responsibility presents problems for accountability – responsibility being a core concept in traditional criminal legal philosophy with regard to blameworthiness and retribution. Joint and negotiated decisions, as the outcomes of restorative processes, tie the parties into 'corporate' decisions, but often fail to identify lines of responsibility thereafter and how these should be monitored, such that it becomes difficult to know who is accountable to whom, and for what. Moreover, there remains a bifurcation between the structural causes of crime and of individual responsibility in the commission of criminal acts. Conversely, lines of accountability are much clearer in retributive justice, which may serve to pull restorative initiatives in such a direction, particularly against a background of managerialist concerns for accounting.

Finally, it is worth noting that public participation and active citizenry in reactions to crime are paradoxical. The dangers of 'participatory pluralism' turning into 'populism' are ever-present, particularly in times of social fragmentation and mistrust (Jordan and Arnold, 1995: 171–72). The lessons from crime prevention research are that active citizenship once extolled can become difficult to control, rather like the contents of Pandora's box.

Conclusions

The aim of this deliberately sceptical chapter has been to raise some critical questions for consideration during a period of considerable and significant policy activity and intellectual thought with regard to the integration of a victim perspective within criminal justice and a broader restorative justice paradigm. It has sought to connect these developments to wider sociopolitical change and to highlight their possible contradictory implications. As the modern state seems to be coming to terms with its own inability to guarantee order, albeit hesitantly and ambivalently, we need to ask whether the shifts and developments outlined in the various contributions to this volume represent and reflect a growing civilianization, humanization or privatization of criminal justice. The latter raises the concern that governments should not be allowed to use 'restorative justice' as a means of unduly shifting the burden of justice on to individuals and communities. Restorative justice should not result in the state washing its hands of the matter by 'privatizing disputes'. Moreover, there is a danger of a confusion of aims within restorative justice, in part driven and reaffirmed by the diverse support which restorative justice has across the political spectrum and within professional and community groups. Are all the aims equally feasible or desirable? Or should proponents prioritize realizable objectives for practice. 'Restorative justice' initiatives risk eventually falling short on a number of fronts: in claiming too much, in seeing restorative justice as a wholly transformative logic, it may ultimately disappoint.

Nevertheless, the quest to give victims greater agency and voice within the process of responding to their victimization remains a central challenge for public, and criminal justice, policy. The manner in which restorative justice seeks to locate the victim within a wider reconfiguration of responsibilities, roles and expectations affords the potential to address such a challenge. Moreover, a 'limited' (in the sense that I have used it) notion of restorative justice offers an opportunity to encourage a stronger, more participatory civil society and challenge many of the modernist assumptions about professional expertise, specialization, state paternalism and monopoly. Consequently, restorative justice may allow victims to be treated more humanely and with due respect to their interests and needs. Simultaneously, it may also offer a more fertile soil from which a more progressive criminal justice policy could begin to establish itself and flourish – one which turns away from the 'punitive populism' of recent years. However, restorative justice should not be held out as the means through which civil society is to be (re)constructed. As far as possible victims' needs should be met outside the orbit of criminal justice. While crime may be a 'regressive tax on the poor', it does not follow that reactions to crime – in their criminal justice form – should, or even can, be the appropriate site of redistributive justice. Criminal justice, after all, is intrinsically reactive, bound up with state coercion and limited in its scope. As such, it is not the cradle of a society's civility. It should, however, reflect and express that civility, particularly with regard to the treatment of all those who turn to, or are caught up in, its machinations – not least of all the victims of crime.

Notes

1   A recent example of this in England and Wales has been the uncertain and ambivalent introduction of 'victim contact work' in the probation service, whereby, as a consequence of the Victim's Charter and subsequent Home Office circulars, the probation service has been given a responsibility to contact victims of 'serious violent or sexual offences' within two months of the sentence of the offender and prior to his or her release from custody in order to 'provide information to the victim about the custodial process, and to obtain information from the victim about any concerns he or she may wish to be taken into account when the conditions (but not the date) of release are being considered' (Probation Circular 61/1995). Recent research has highlighted the lack of clarity as to the policy's intention, its uncertain and ill-considered implications, its contradictory logics, its duplication of other initiatives and its hesitant and differential implementation (see Crawford and Enterkin, 1999).

2   This connects with Wolfgang's (1982) use of the term 'individualization' to invoke and focus upon *categories* of victims, as discussed by Sebba in Chapter 3 of this volume.

3   Moreover, it is this ambivalence which is reflected in the dichotomy between 'individualization of the victim' in the two senses to which Sebba refers in Chapter 3: between individualization in the narrow sense and categorization.

4   In 1997 there were five operating offices located in 'difficult neighbourhoods' in Amsterdam, Arnhem, Maastricht, Rotterdam and Velsen. In 1998 this was set to increase to eight. And the new government is committed to increase this to about 25 offices by the end of 2002. Each experiment has its own special features.

5 This is explicit in Braithwaite's (1995) 'republican theory' which sees 'restorative justices' as part of much wider changes in participatory democracy.

References

Audit Commission (1996), *Misspent Youth: Young People and Crime*, London: Audit Commission.

Bottoms, A.E. (1995), 'The Philosophy and Politics of Punishment and Sentencing', in C. Clarkson and R. Morgan (eds), *The Politics of Sentencing Reform*, Oxford: Clarendon Press, 17–49.

Boutellier, H. (1997), 'Right to the Community', *European Journal on Criminal Policy and Research*, **5**(4), 43–52.

Braithwaite, J. (1989), *Crime, Shame and Reintegration,* Cambridge: Cambridge University Press.

Braithwaite, J. (1995), 'Inequality and Republican Criminology', in J. Hagan and R.D. Peterson (eds), *Crime and Inequality*, Stanford: Stanford University Press, 277–305.

Braithwaite, J. and Daly, K. (1994), 'Masculinities, Violence and Communitarian Control', in T. Newburn, and E.A. Stanko (eds), *Just Boys Doing Business? Men, Masculinities and Crime*, London: Routledge, 189–213.

Braithwaite, J. and Mugford, S. (1994), 'Conditions of Successful Reintegration Ceremonies: Dealing with Juvenile Offenders', *British Journal of Criminology*, **34**(2), 139–71.

Christie, N. (1977), 'Conflicts as Property', *British Journal of Criminology*, **17**(1), 1–15.

Christie, N. (1986), 'The Ideal Victim', in E. Fattah (ed.), *From Crime Policy to Victim Policy*, London: Macmillan, 1–17.

Cohen, S. (1979), 'The Punitive City: Notes on the Dispersal of Social Control', *Contemporary Crises*, **3**, 339–63.

Cohen, S. (1989), 'The Critical Discourse on "Social Control": Notes on the Concept as a Hammer', *International Journal of the Sociology of Law*, **17**, 347–57.

Crawford, A. (1994), 'The Partnership Approach: Corporatism at the Local Level?', *Social and Legal Studies*, **3**(4), 497–519.

Crawford, A. (1997), *The Local Governance of Crime: Appeals to Community and Partnerships*, Oxford: Clarendon Press.

Crawford, A. (1998), 'Community Safety and the Quest for Security: Holding Back the Dynamics of Social Exclusion', *Policy Studies*, **19**(3/4), 237–53.

Crawford, A. (2000), 'Justice de Proximité – The Growth of "Houses of Justice" and Victim/Offender Mediation in France: A Very UnFrench Legal Response?', *Social and Legal Studies*, **9**(1), 29–53.

Crawford, A. and Enterkin, J. (1999), *Victim Contact Work and the Probation Service: A Study of Service Delivery and Impact*, Leeds: CCJS Press.

Davis, G. (1992), *Making Amends*, London: Routledge.

Davis, G., Boucherat, J. and Watson, D. (1988), 'Reparation in the Service of Diversion: the Subordination of a Good Idea', *Howard Journal*, **27**(2), 127–34.

Dignan, J. (1999), 'The Crime and Disorder Act and the Prospects for Restorative Justice', *Criminal Law Review*, 48–60.

Downes, D. (1983), *Law and Order: Theft of an Issue*, Fabian Tract 490, London: Blackrose Press.

Downes, D. (1998), 'Toughing it Out: From Labour Opposition to Labour Government', *Policy Studies*, **19**(3/4), 191–98.

Durkheim, E. (1893), *The Division of Labour in Society*, New York: Free Press.

Elias, R. (1993), *Victims Still*, Newbury Park: Sage.

Erez, E. and Rogers, L. (1999), 'Victim Impact Statements and Sentencing Outcomes and Processes: The Perspectives of Legal Professionals', *British Journal of Criminology*, **39**(2), 216–39.

Faget, J. (1997), *La Médiation: Essai de Politique Pénale*, Ramonville Saint-Ange: Edition Erès.

Farrell, G. and Pease, K. (1993), *Once Bitten, Twice Bitten: Repeat Victimisation and Its Implications for Crime Prevention*, CPU Paper 46, London: Home Office Crime Prevention Unit.

Feeley, M. and Simon, J. (1992), 'The New Penology: Notes on the Emerging Strategy of Corrections and Its Implications', *Criminology*, **30**(4), 449–74.

Feeley, M. and Simon, J. (1994), 'Actuarial Justice: the Emerging New Criminal Law', in D. Nelken (ed.), *The Futures of Criminology*, London: Sage, 173–201.

Forrester, D., Frenz, S., O'Connell, M. and Pease, K. (1990), *The Kirkholt Burglary Project: Phase II*, CPU Paper 23, London: Home Office.

Garland, D. (1990), *Punishment and Modern Society*, Oxford: Clarendon Press.

Garland, D. (1996), 'The Limits of the Sovereign State: Strategies of Crime Control in Contemporary Society', *British Journal of Criminology*, **36**(4), 445–71.

Genn, H. (1988), 'Multiple Victimization', in M. Maguire and J. Pointing (eds), *Victims of Crime: A New Deal?*, Milton Keynes: Open University Press, 90–100.

Home Office (1996), *The Victim's Charter: A Statement of Service Standards for the Victims of Crime*, London: Home Office.

Home Office (1997), *No More Excuses: A New Approach to Tackling Youth Offending*, CM. 3809, London: Home Office.

Hope, T. (1995), 'Community Crime Prevention', in M. Tonry and D. Farrington (eds), *Building a Safer Society: Crime and Justice a Review of Research, vol. 19*, Chicago: University of Chicago Press, 21–89.

Hope, T. (1997), 'Inequality and the Future of Community Crime Prevention', in S.P. Lab (ed.), *Crime Prevention at a Crossroads*, Cincinnati: Anderson Publishing, 143–58.

Jordan, B. and Arnold, J. (1995), 'Democracy and Criminal Justice', *Critical Social Policy*, **15**(2), 170–82.

JUSTICE (1998), *Victims in Criminal Justice*, Report of the Committee on the Role of the Victim in Criminal Justice, London: JUSTICE.

Matthews, R. (1987), 'Decarceration and Social Control: Fantasies and Realities', *International Journal of the Sociology of Law*, **15**, 39–60.

Moore, S.F. (1973), 'Law and Social Change: The Semi-Autonomous Social Field as an Appropriate Subject of Study', *Law and Society Review*, **7**, 719–46.

Nelken, D. (1995), 'Disclosing/Invoking Legal Culture: An Introduction', *Social and Legal Studies*, **4**(4), 435–52.

Newburn, T. (1998), 'Tackling Youth Crime and Reforming Youth Justice: The Origins and Nature of "New Labour" Policy', *Policy Studies*, **19**(3/4), 199–212.

Osborne, D. and Gaebler, T. (1992), *Reinventing Government: How the Entrepreneurial Spirit is Transforming the Public Sector*, Reading, Massachusetts: Addison-Wesley.

O'Malley, P. (1992), 'Risk, Power and Crime Prevention', *Economy and Society*, **21**(3), 252–75.

Palumbo, D., Ferguson, J.L. and Stein, J. (1997), 'The Conditions Needed for Successful Community Crime Prevention', in S.P. Lab (ed.), *Crime Prevention at a Crossroads*, Cincinnati: Anderson Publishing, 79–98.

Power, M. (1997), *The Audit Society*, Oxford: Oxford University Press.

Rock, P. (1998), 'Murderers, Victims and Survivors', *British Journal of Criminology*, **38**(2), 185–200.

Rock, P. (1999), 'Acknowledging Victims Needs and Rights', *Criminal Justice Matters*, **35**, 4–5.

Rosenbaum, D.P. (1988), 'Community Crime Prevention: A Review and Synthesis of the Literature', *Justice Quarterly*, **5**(3), 323–93.

Sampson, R.J., Raudenbush, S.W. and Earls, F. (1997), 'Neighborhoods and Violent Crime: A Multi-Level Study of Collective Efficacy', *Science*, **277**, 918–23.

Sarat, A. (1997), 'Vengeance, Victims and the Identities of Law', *Social and Legal Studies*, **6**(2), 163–89.

SEU (Social Exclusion Unit) (1998), *Bringing Britain Together: A National Strategy for Neighbourhood Renewal*, London: Cabinet Office.

Shapland, J. (1988), 'Fiefs and Peasants: Accomplishing Change for Victims in the Criminal Justice System', in M. Maguire and J. Pointing (eds), *Victims of Crime: A New Deal?*, Milton Keynes: Open University Press, 187–94.

Silbey, S. and Merry, S. (1986), 'Mediator Settlement Strategies', *Law and Policy*, **8**, 7–32.

Trickett, A., Osborn, D.K., Seymour, J. and Pease, K. (1992), 'What is Different About High Crime Areas?', *British Journal of Criminology*, **32**(1), 81–89.

Trickett, A., Ellingworth, D., Farrell, G., and Pease, K. (1995), 'Crime Victimisation in the Eighties: Changes in Area and Regional Inequality', *British Journal of Criminology*, **35**(3), 343–59.

Victim Support (1995), *The Rights of Victims of Crime: A Policy Paper*, London: Victim Support.

Wolfgang, M.E. (1982), 'Basic Concepts in Victimology Theory: Individualisation of the Victim', in H-J. Schneider (ed.), *The Victim in International Perspective*, Berlin: de Gruyter, 47–58.

Wyvekens, A. (1996), 'Justice de Proximité et Proximité de la Justice: Les Maisons de Justice et du Droit', *Droit et Société*, **33**, 363–88.

Wyvekens, A. (1997), 'Mediation and Proximity', *European Journal on Criminal Policy and Research*, **5**(4), 27–42.

Young, J. (1999), *The Exclusive Society: Social Exclusion, Crime and Difference in Late Modernity*, London: Sage.
Young, R. (1989), 'Reparation as Mitigation', *Criminal Law Review*, 463–72.

Index